A dictionary of education

Edited by P J Hills

Director, Primary Communications Research Centre,
University of Leicester

Routledge & Kegan Paul
London, Boston, Melbourne and Henley

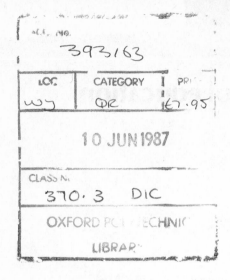
First published in 1982
Reprinted and first published
as a paperback in 1984
Reprinted in 1985
by Routledge & Kegan Paul plc
14 Leicester Square,
London WC2H 7PH, England,·
9 Park Street, Boston, Mass., 02108, USA,
464 St Kilda Road, Melbourne, Victoria 3004, Australia and
Broadway House, Newtown Road,
Henley-on-Thames, Oxon RG9 1EN, England
Set in Linotron Times
by Input Typesetting Ltd, London and printed
in Great Britain by St Edmundsbury Press,
Bury St Edmunds, Suffolk

Library of Congress Cataloging in Publication Data

Main entry under title:
   A Dictionary of education.
   (Routledge education books)
   Includes bibliographies.
   1. Education—Dictionaries.
   I. Hills, P. J. (Philip James)
   II. Series
LB15.D48   370'.3'21   81-22718
ISBN 0-7102-0388-8   AACR2

Contents

Introduction

We are apt to think that when we have consulted a dictionary and found out what a word means, we should then know how to use it. However, it is mainly through the use of a word that the meaning is shown. The challenge in compiling this dictionary was to create an awareness of the main areas of education and to provide conceptual accounts which show the reader how appropriate terms are employed within the context.

A standard dictionary contains an alphabetical list of terms with short, neutral definitions of each one. Definitions have to be brief, since there must be a large number of terms in order to give a comprehensive coverage, often in one volume. On the other hand, an encyclopedia develops these short definitions into larger accounts and therefore often runs into several volumes.

This dictionary allows the reader to explore the subject of education in one volume by conceptual accounts of the main areas of education, by interlinked entries, and, most important, by key references to further reading. It does not set out to be totally comprehensive in its coverage, nor does it adopt a neutral view of a subject. It is intended to give the reader an entry into the subject so that by subsequent exploration he can come to his own conclusions about the shades of meaning within the subject.

Although this dictionary is intended mainly for students, teachers and administrators in a wide variety of educational settings, we have tried to keep a much wider general readership in mind so that:

1 The areas of education chosen provide the reader with accounts that do not assume too much background knowledge.

1

2 Each area provides an exploration of the main terms in current usage.
3 Further reading is provided where appropriate, so that the reader can explore an area in more depth if he or she so wishes.

The areas of education

Fifteen areas of education have been chosen; these both overlap and complement each other. These areas fit into three broader concepts: firstly, settings for the process of education; secondly, the process itself; and thirdly, the methods and techniques that can be applied. Before we begin let us examine these in a little more detail.

1 Settings

The settings for the process of formal full-time education are dealt with in four areas:

Comparative education This area is concerned with a study of various educational systems taken largely in an historical perspective.

Administration of education This area focuses on the structure of the education system in England and Wales.

Educational organisations Here the concern is with the large number of organisations which play a part in the educational system.

Economics of education The economics of education is concerned with the inter-relationships between the economy and the educational system.

Education in the business/industrial sector is dealt with in the following three areas:

Industrial education and training This deals with educational activities connected with the making, supply and distribution of goods and services.

Business education and training Fifteen per cent of the working population is wholly or partly involved in administration, clerical, secretarial or data-processing information duties. This area deals with educational activities in this field and in the professions.

Management education and training This area is concerned with educational activities designed to help a manager improve his performance in his current job.

2 Process

The process of education is dealt with in four areas which constitute the four main traditional educational topics: namely, the history of education, the philosophy of education, the psychology of education and the sociology of education.

3 Methods and techniques

Here there are four areas:

Curriculum development This is concerned with the planning, implementation and evaluation of educational programmes, of courses of study, offered by educational institutions.

Educational technology This area is concerned with the application of a systematic approach to education involving the establishment of objectives and the determination of suitable methods and techniques for teaching and learning.

Educational research Educational research is concerned with the evaluation of education in terms of new curricula, systems and styles of education, etc.

Educational measurement Educational measurement is part of educational research in the same way that algebra is part of mathematics; here, although we relate it to the broader area, it is mainly problem-oriented and concerned with the principles of measurement.

The arrangement of the dictionary

The dictionary consists of two main sections, Part 1 containing short accounts of the main areas of education as defined above, and Part 2 consisting of the main body of entries.

Part 1 Areas of education

This consists of short accounts of each of the fifteen areas of education defined above. Within each one the main terms of the area have been *italicised* to indicate that an entry for the term will be found in Part 2. At the end of most of these accounts references to further reading have been given. There is also a list of terms at the end of each account, giving details of the entries to be found in Part 2.

Part 2 The entries

This section contains both entries for terms referred to in the accounts in Part 1 and subsidiary entries which are cross-referenced to other entries. This cross-referencing has been achieved either by *italicising* the terms in an entry which refer to another term, or by including a term at the end under a 'see also' heading. Where appropriate, reference to further reading has been given. At the end of each entry the area or areas which generated the terms have been identified in brackets.

How to use the dictionary

There are three main ways in which it can be used.
1   It can be used as one would any other dictionary, looking up terms either in Part 1, or, mainly, in Part 2.
2   It can be used to explore each of the fifteen main areas, first by reading the account in Part 1 and then by following the main terms through by means of Part 2 and cross-linking with the subsidiary entries.
3   By turning to the end of each account in Part 1 the scope of terms in each area can be seen, and specific terms dealt with in the area can be looked up in Part 2.

The compilation of the dictionary

In order to achieve the objectives stated above, a group of specialists in the various fields of education were brought together, each taking one of the areas in Part 1. Details of the specialists are as follows:

Administration of education
James Owain Jones, Assistant Director of Education, Clwyd County Council, Mold.

Business education and training
Brian Lusher, Training Manager, Carreras Rothmans Ltd, Aylesbury. Sue Ward, Head of Information Services, British Association for Commercial and Industrial Education, London.

Comparative education
Dr Raymond Jackson, Senior Lecturer in Education, St Mary's College, Twickenham.

Curriculum development
John B. Reynolds, Lecturer in Educational Studies, Department of Educational Research, University of Lancaster.
David Halpin, Research Officer, Northwestern Centre for Educational Management, Padgate.

Economics of education
Maureen Woodhall, Research Associate, University of London Institute of Education.

Educational measurement
Roy Childs, National Foundation for Educational Research, Windsor.

Educational organisations
Richard N. Tucker, Senior Assistant Director, Scottish Council for Educational Technology, Glasgow.

Educational research
Dr Duncan Harris, Director, Science and Technology Education Centre, University of Bath.

Educational technology
Dr Philip Hills, Director, Primary Communications Research Centre, University of Leicester.

History of education
Dr John S. Hurt, Department of History and Philosophy of Education, Faculty of Education, University of Birmingham.

Industrial education and training
Brian Lusher, Training Manager, Carreras Rothmans Ltd, Aylesbury. Sue Ward, Head of Information Services, British Association for Commercial and Industrial Education, London.

Management education and training
Brian Lusher, Training Manager, Carreras Rothmans Ltd, Aylesbury. Sue Ward, Head of Information Services, British Association for Commercial and Industrial Education, London.

Philosophy of education
Dr Pat Smart, Department of Philosophy, University of Surrey, Guildford.

Psychology of education
Bernard Lovell, Department of Psychology, Garnet College, London.

Sociology of education
Dr Keith Fleming, Senior Lecturer in Sociology, Middlesex Polytechnic, London.

My thanks are due to all these for their help and patience throughout the whole exercise.

My especial thanks are due to Frances Mercer for her help in the final editing and the vast task of compiling the entries. She was ably assisted in her task by Sue Telfer, Hilija Saxby and John Lord. My thanks to them all.

Thanks are also due to the many people who commented on the original entries and who suggested modifications and additions. The final responsibility for balance and coverage must of course rest with me.

P. J. Hills
Leicester

Part one

Areas of education

Chapter 1

Administration of education

The structure of the education system in England and Wales is set out in the Education Act 1944, as amended. Administratively it is a partnership between central government, local government and teachers, with powers and duties pertaining to each.

The Act charged the Secretary of State with the duty to promote 'The education of the people of England and Wales . . . and to secure the effective execution by Local Authorities, under his control and direction, of national policy'. This gave the Secretary of State a strategic role in education planning which had not existed before.

The authority of central government is exercised both directly and indirectly. The Secretary of State, who is the political head of the *Department of Education and Science* (DES), can use legislation and regulations to lay down objectives, impose standards, and to confer powers. He has the power, albeit used sparingly, to give directions to a Local Education Authority (LEA) he believes is acting unreasonably. Moreover, certain decisions of the LEA are subject to his consent. The Secretary of State's regulations have the force of law and they can deal with such variety of subjects as the qualifications of teachers, awards to students, and standards of school premises.

The increasing share of public expenditure taken by education has meant the close involvement of central government, which exercises control by means of the rate support grant and the system of loan sanction for capital expenditure (see *education finance*). For example, there was a period when no loan sanction was forthcoming for a secondary school building project which did not conform with a plan for reorganisation on comprehensive lines.

The influence of the DES is exercised in a variety of ways. It

9

directs thinking into various aspects of the education service by commissioning research and publications of various kinds. These range from the very detailed reports of the *Central Advisory Councils* or *Committees of Enquiry* to Green Papers (which are discussion papers intended to test public reactions) and to White Papers, which are official statements of policy. Moreover the Department publishes surveys and bulletins of various kinds where the influence of *Her Majesty's Inspectors* is discernible. They, through their contact with LEAs and schools and colleges and their involvement with the *Schools Council* bring their influence to bear on the policy of the Department.

The circulars issued by the DES do not have the force of law. They deal with a variety of matters ranging from, for example, the education of mentally handicapped children in hospital, in-service courses for teachers, provision of dual-user sports facilities, to the introduction of comprehensive education. These circulars have a persuasive effect on Authorities. They have been used to influence LEAs in cases of policy where no statutory powers exist. Circular 10/65 on comprehensive education (1965) was the trigger for the widespread change towards comprehensive education of the following decade. Some Authorities ignored it, and this led to legislation in 1976, since repealed, to compel the introduction of comprehensive education.

The Act also created the category of *direct grant schools*, which were part financed from central government; and it also gave the Secretary of State regulatory powers over *independent schools*.

If central government defines national objectives, the task of implementing them falls on the 104 Authorities in England and Wales, which consist of the *Inner London Education Authority* and the councils of 47 counties, 36 metropolitan districts and 20 outer London boroughs. It is incumbent on each Authority to establish an Education Committee, to which non-elected members (normally representing bodies with an interest in education) are co-opted, and to appoint a *Chief Education Officer* (sometimes known as a Director of Education), who will have a staff of professional educationalists to assist him.

The Act imposes on LEAs the duty of providing an education service. They employ teachers (whose salary scales are determined nationally by the *Burnham Committee*), they furnish and equip the schools, they build new county schools, maintain existing ones, and contribute to the maintenance of *voluntary schools*. The staffing level, expressed as the pupil/teacher ratio, and the *capitation allowance* for schools may vary according to each Authority's financial resources and its determined priorities.

10

The ages of *compulsory school attendance* are laid down by law, but within this age range an LEA can determine its own pattern of school provision, subject to the Secretary of State's direction on *nursery schools*. For example, the *Leicestershire plan* of secondary education developed in the 1950s was unique to that county. The traditional and still predominant system involves a change from primary to secondary schools at the age of 11. But there has developed in recent years the intermediate stage of the middle school, which pupils attend from the age of 8 or 9 until 13 or 14. Another development has been the *sixth form college* and *tertiary college* for 16–18-year-olds. Until the trend for *comprehensive secondary schools* gathered momentum after the publication of circular 10/65 in 1965, most LEAs provided secondary education in grammar schools and secondary modern schools on the basis of selection at the age of 11. Although selection at this age still prevails in some areas, well over 80 per cent of secondary pupils in the public sector now attend comprehensive schools.

LEAs have a duty to make provision for children who suffer any disability of mind or body by educating them by methods appropriate to their handicap. They may set up their own special schools or classes or, if they have no school appropriate to a particular handicap, pay to have pupils educated at a school run by another LEA or independently. A new development, following the 1978 Warnock Report into the educational needs of handicapped children, is the proposed integration as far as possible of handicapped children into ordinary schools. (See *special education*.)

The Act also imposed the duty of providing further education, i.e. education either full or part time for students over the school-leaving age at institutions other than schools. This includes *adult education*: LEAs maintain colleges of technology, of further education, of art, of commerce, of agriculture. Some have now developed into colleges of advanced technology with university status or polytechnics. Others have amalgamated into institutes of higher education and have diversified to provide courses in social work, management studies, etc. These continue to be administered by the LEAs. The training of teachers at colleges of education has been a function of LEAs, either individually or jointly, the cost being shared by all LEAs. (See *further education and technical colleges; college of higher education*.)

Other duties undertaken by LEAs include the provision in accordance with regulations of school *transport, milk and meals, grants to students,* a *youth service,* and a *careers service.* Another important requirement is that LEAs appoint Boards of Managers

11

for primary schools and *Boards of Governors* for all. LEAs ceased to have direct responsibility for the *school health service* in 1974.

It will be seen that in this education system there is no one mainspring of power. Authority is in fact dispersed. The responsibility to ensure that children are educated is the parents'; it is the LEA which has to provide the schools to enable parents to do their duty; the education of the children themselves rests with the professional teachers who have considerable freedom to decide what is taught and how. Only where *religious education* is concerned are certain matters prescribed by law. Where the organisation and internal management of a school are concerned, the power and the responsibility rests with the headteacher, as the Rules and Articles of Government usually make clear, though much would depend upon the head and his style of management as to how he exercises his authority. (See *headteacher*.)

The system in Wales is as described above except that the Secretary of State's responsibility is exercised, with but few exceptions, by the Secretary of State for Wales. In addition there has existed since 1948 a *Welsh Joint Education Committee*.

Entries to be found in Part 2

Adult education. Assisted places scheme. Banding. Board of Governors. Burnham Committee. Capitation allowance. Careers education. Careers service. Central Advisory Council. Chief Education Officer. College of higher education. Committee of Enquiry. Community school. Comprehensive secondary school. Compulsory school attendance. Department of Education and Science. Direct grant school. Education finance. Education social worker. Eleven-plus examination. Establishment or discontinuance of schools. Further education and technical colleges. Grants to students. Headteachers. Her Majesty's Inspectors. Independent school. Inner London Education Authority. Leicestershire plan. Milk and meals. Mixed-ability grouping. Nursery school. Pastoral care. Playgroup. Public examinations. Religious education. School health service. School psychological service. Schools Council. Secretary of State for Wales. Setting. Sixth form college. Special education. Streaming by ability. Team teaching. Tertiary college. Transport. Vertical (or 'family') grouping. Voluntary schools. Welsh Joint Education Committee. Youth Service.

Chapter 2

Business education and training

The 1971 UK census indicated that some 15 per cent of the working population was wholly or partially involved in *administrative* or *clerical work, secretarial* or *data-processing information* duties.

Until fairly recently it was unusual for most staff in business to receive any systematic training other than that provided on the job. The professions (*accountancy*, for example) have always, of course, had their own regulated entry, often requiring examination success. Most people entering office work learned their jobs from their seniors. The major reason for this was the existence of a large number of unemployed, relatively well-educated people. This was certainly true up to the Second World War, and so-called white-collar work attracted the reputation of being suitable only for those with a reasonable level of education. This enabled employers to over-recruit, knowing that people would acquire the necessary job skills and knowledge quickly. Where specific skills and knowledge were demanded by the job, people were expected to acquire them by their own efforts and at their own expense. This led to the development of the *evening class* (or night school) system which remains to this day. Now, good employers allow employees paid time off to acquire qualifications. This has led to *day-release* and other part-time systems. Schools and colleges have developed to meet demands for education and training.

A number of factors have led to developments in this sector. First, the number of people in administration has increased. Second, the range of work has become much wider, from semi-skilled because of the introduction of machinery, to very highly skilled because of the advent of computers. Third, we have been a full-employment society until very recently, and most educated people

13

have had a much wider choice of employment than hitherto. Fourth, attitudes to office work have changed.

Often demand has exceeded supply, and this together with the erosion of differentials between blue and white-collar workers has led to high job mobility, high levels of absenteeism and unionisation. Improving the productivity, therefore, of white-collar staff has become vital to most organisations. Laissez-faire is no longer enough.

Two of the mentioned changes have produced marked effects on business education and training and deserve some further attention. First, the range of equipment now available to help office efficiency has grown astoundingly in recent years. Addressing machines, automatic frankers, duplicators, photocopiers and so on have enabled employers to compensate for the lack of pre-war calibre staff, by de-skilling jobs. This has led to the creation of a large number of semi-skilled jobs where the needs are for people trained to operate repetitively at speed for relatively long periods to a high degree of accuracy. Training for these jobs has a great deal in common with that for factory operatives. The widespread use of computers has also produced a large number of semi-skilled jobs (punch operators and so on). In-company training and further education have expanded to meet these training demands. Second, the development of management services (such as *personnel and training*, information systems, *accountancy*) has created demands for highly trained (and often highly educated) specialists to support the appropriate functional manager or executive. The impact of this development has been large. Taken together with the creation of the *Industry Training Boards*, the last few years have seen the creation of a range of business-orientated education and training programmes. The *Council for National Academic Awards* has approved many degree-level courses in *business studies* and universities as well as *polytechnics* offer courses of study specifically related to jobs in business. Examples include not only business studies but also subjects like computing science, management services and so on.

Bodies like the *Business Education Council* have been formed to control *national diplomas* and *national certificates* in business-related subjects. Many of the professional institutions have tightened their standards, revised or rewritten their syllabuses, raised the quality of their examinations, and generally sought to improve both their status and their control of entry. It is probably true to say that most institutions would like to control entry to their professions as tightly as doctors or lawyers.

Many professional bodies utilise the further education sector to provide courses. Organisations such as the *British Association for Commercial and Industrial Education* have contributed by providing specialised training programmes. The *Manpower Services Commission* through schemes like the Training Opportunities Scheme have provided substantial funds to help people to qualify for careers in business, at all levels. The national and *regional examining bodies* and organisations like the *City and Guilds of London Institute* have been heavily involved in the development of business education and training. New qualifications have been introduced, as the needs of organisations have changed.

A significant feature of recent years has been the emergence of business as a subject worthy of academic study, together with the gradual formation of a body of knowledge. This draws heavily on other disciplines, such as economics. Courses of study are often wide-ranging and many include specialised options, by means of which successful candidates may gain exemption from some of the requirements of professional institutions. The demand for highly qualified staff has also led to the growth of specialised systems of learning (such as correspondence schools), while the need for sound, job-related training has given rise to extensive in-company departments providing courses, as well as growth in the private supply sector, such as *management consultants*.

As always in British systems, all the various elements manage to co-exist in a kind of compromise, so that the range and choice of education and training available astonish by their multiplicity.

Further reading

The Central Training Council Report, 'Training for Commerce and the Office', HMSO, 1966, is still useful but must be read with care because of the enormous advances in office equipment since it was written. Most Industry Training Boards have produced recommendations on training for the business sector. Annual reports of the various bodies provide useful information. The prospectuses of polytechnics and other educational institutions provide useful information on the context of courses and can therefore help with the development of in-company programmes by suggesting subject areas.

One general point about business and industry, which applies to some extent to other areas in the dictionary: in the case of organisations, details of courses offered, etc. can change quite rapidly. It is always advisable to check with the original source for absolutely up-to-date information.

Entries to be found in Part 2

Accountancy. Administrative. Banking. Block release. British Association for Commercial and Industrial Education. British Correspondence Colleges, Association of. Business Education Council, Scottish Business Education Council. Business studies. Certificate in Office Studies. Certified Diploma in Accounting and Finance. City and Guilds of London Institute. Clerical work. Consultants and private organisations. Council for National Academic Awards. Courses. Courses: entry requirements. Data-processing/information services. Day release. Directed private study. Distance learning. Education. Educational academic courses: applications. Entry requirements for professional institutions and associations. Evening class. Full-time study. Funding for education/training. Further education: major establishments. Industrial Society. Industry Training Board. Insurance. Libraries. Management consultants. Manpower Services Commission. Membership gradings. National certificate. National Colleges. National diploma. National Training Index. Personnel and training. Polytechnic. Professional associations. Qualifications. Regional examining bodies. Secretarial courses. Training.

Chapter 3

Comparative education

Comparative education is concerned with the study of various educational systems. Recent interest in the topic has been enhanced by:

(a)   the attention given to the newly independent states who desire to improve their educational systems;
(b)   the activities of international organisations such as UNESCO;
(c)   the increased interest shown in the study of foreign languages;
(d)   the attraction of countries overseas, which has been stimulated by the reduced cost and ease of foreign travel;
(e)   the perennial concern that administrators show in improving their educational systems.

Comparative education has a distinguished history and has long been of interest to the major educational theorists. Plato, for example, studied the nearby Spartan educational system so that he might devise a more suitable one for the Athenian state. The findings were enshrined in his classic work 'The Republic'. Cicero compared Greek and Roman education in 'De Republica', Comenius visited England in 1641 to advise on the school system, and Rousseau, in his 'Considerations on the Government of Poland' (1763) included among his recommendations the establishment of a secular system of education.

The development of comparative education may be divided into three major stages:

(a)   the descriptive and borrowing phase, coming to an end late in the nineteenth century;

(b) the era of prediction, corresponding with the first half of the twentieth century;

(c) the phase of rigorous analysis which developed during the early 1960s.

The descriptive and borrowing stage included the works of the eminent philosophers mentioned above, the accounts of travellers and the writings of educational administrators whose investigation of foreign school systems was specifically designed to help them to improve their own. Xenophon (410–350 BC) gave details of Persian education (in 'Cyrophaedia'), Julius Caesar (102–42 BC) provided accounts of the education of the Belgians and the Celts (in the 'Gallic Wars'), Marco Polo wrote about Chinese schools (in 'The Discovery of the World'), Sir William Petty (1623–87) advised on schools in Pennsylvania (in 'The Method of Inquiring into the State of any Country'), La Chalotais commented on science education in Russia (in 'Essay on National Education', 1763), while Condorcet (1743–94) compared education in England, Italy and Germany (in 'Report of Public Instruction'). Very important was the contribution by Jullien in 1817; he devised the first comprehensive scheme of education systems.

During the first half of the twentieth century the prediction stage developed. Comparativists of this school, such as Kandel and Hans, were interested in anticipating or predicting the likely effects of the adoption of particular educational policies based on careful and expert observation of similar policies operating in other countries. The phase following on from this was that of analysis, which had had its roots in earlier developments. Exponents of this approach, such as Bereday and Holmes, sought to produce more rigorous studies by using techniques already being applied in the social sciences. These studies are considered to be scientific, objective and non-melioristic, and therefore more appropriate to comparative education.

The *type of study* being used includes *area studies*, cross-cultural studies of various types, case studies and cross-temporal studies. Comparativists have some general agreement on the *purpose of comparative education*; these have been said to be (a) to promote knowledge, (b) to assist reform and development, (c) to improve knowledge about one's own educational system, and (d) to promote international goodwill.

Comparative education is *cross-disciplinary*, that is, comparativists use the methodologies of a number of the social sciences. In particular sociologists, economists and political scientists have made contributions to more rigorous comparative studies; their efforts have been supplemented by the work of psychologists and, more recently, by anthropologists.

The early comparative studies were made mainly by travellers who wrote of many things, including educational practices, they saw on their journeys abroad. The accounts were descriptive, selective and unsystematic. The end of this era is thought to have been marked by the publication in 1817 of Jullien's plan, which advocated a more rigorous study of foreign educational systems. After that time administrators interested in improving their own educational systems travelled abroad specifically to assess what their colleagues were doing. They tried to emulate the 'best' practices, and this was known as *educational borrowing*. By the twentieth century, scholars, mainly historians, founded what may be termed the *historical-humanistic school*. *Kandel's approach* was characteristic of their methodology, which sought to describe the educational system and explain the 'immanent and permanent forces' which shaped school and college practices. In establishing generalisations it was hoped that predictions and procedures by which the educational system might be improved would be forthcoming.

By the 1960s dissatisfaction with these studies prompted comparativists to adopt a *social science approach* which involved using the methodologies of sociologists, psychologists and others. This social science school included empiricists and those who showed preferences for the *problem approach*. These comparativists claimed that their work was more scientific than previous approaches and that it gave more valuable perspectives and provided more viable recommendations for policy makers. All researchers in comparative education, however, have to face a number of *methodological difficulties* which include: (a) identifying, collecting and interpreting relevant data; (b) problem identification; (c) issues of comparability; and, (d) difficulties concerning terminology.

Interest in comparative education was stimulated by universities such as the Teachers College, Columbia University, New York and the University of London Institute of Education. Increasingly, would-be teachers have first contact with comparative education in their initial training. However, courses in comparative education are becoming available now in universities and colleges in many parts of the world; these also sponsor research and initiate published works. Many international agencies are also engaged in arranging conferences, commissioning publications, arranging meetings of experts and promoting research in colleges in many countries. These agencies include *UNESCO*, the *Organisation for*

European Co-operation and Development, the *Council of Europe*,
the *Commonwealth Secretariat*, the *International Bureau of Education*, the *International Association of Universities*, the *International Institute of Educational Planning*, and the *International Association for the Evaluation of Educational Achievement (IEA)*.
Comparative education societies have also initiated conferences,
supported journals and co-operated with other societies in order
to further the purpose of comparativists. Societies have been organised at global (World Council of Comparative Education Societies), at regional and at national levels.

A survey of publishing and *research trends* indicates that area
studies are popular and that researchers tend to write about countries which are characterised by being among the wealthy, the
most powerful or the most populous. The topics covered by these
researches include the improvement of educational systems, on
methodological and, to a lesser extent, on historical premises.

The *future of comparative education* is likely to be characterised
by an even greater emphasis than at present on the use of social
science and empirical techniques. It is likely that anthropologists
will continue to challenge traditional approaches to comparative
education, but they will have to produce more convincing evidence
of the viability of their techniques than they have at present.

Further reading

Bereday, G. Z. F., 'Comparative Method in Education', Holt,
Rinehart & Winston, 1964.
Hans, N. A., 'Comparative Education', Routledge & Kegan Paul,
1958.
Holmes, B., 'Problems in Education: A Comparative Approach',
Routledge & Kegan Paul, 1965.
Holmes, B., 'Diversity and Unity in Education', Allen & Unwin,
1980.
Kandel, I. L., 'Comparative Education' Houghton Mifflin, 1933.
King, E. J., 'Other Schools and Ours', Holt, Rinehart & Winston,
1973.

Entries to be found in Part 2

*Agricultural extension. Area study. Chinese experience. Commonwealth Secretariat. Comparative education societies. Council of
Europe. Cross-disciplinary approach. Cross-disciplinary nature of*

comparative education. Ecological approach. Economist's contribution. Educational borrowing. Empirical approach. Factor approach. Future of comparative education. Harmonisation. Historical approach. Historical-humanistic school. Interest in comparative education. International Association for the Evaluation of Educational Achievement (IEA). International Association of Universities (IAU). International Bureau of Education (IBE). International Institute of Educational Planning (IIEP). Intra-regional studies. Jullien's plan. Kandel's approach. Localisation. Methodological difficulties. National character. Organisation for European Co-operation and Development (OECD). Philosophical approach. Political scientists' contribution. Problem approach. Purposes of comparative education. Research trends in comparative education. Social lag. Social sciences. Social sciences approach. Sociological approach. Sociologists' contribution. Type of study. UNESCO.

Chapter 4

Curriculum development

Curriculum development could be summarised as the planning, implementation and evaluation of the educational programmes, or courses of study, offered by schools and colleges. Notwithstanding the technical flavour of the summary, the process is characterised rather by the practical, judgmental nature of the decisions which run through it. Basically they are decisions about what is to be taught and how learning is to be organised; they are practical and judgmental in the sense that they entail the integration within teachers' practices of several different considerations: the form of the knowledge or skills to be imparted; the mental growth of the learners in question; the context of the learning, including the human and material resources and constraints; and the values and interests of those involved. Such decisions are often evident only as piecemeal adjustments to syllabuses, timetables, etc., but social pressures and educational diversity increase the need for explicit principles to guide, co-ordinate, monitor and justify the substance of teaching programmes. Curriculum development has attempted so far to provide an appropriate vocabulary by drawing mainly upon an end-means or 'engineering' viewpoint; but, as many of the dictionary entries will indicate, that viewpoint needs sensitive application and major adaptation to accommodate the circumstantiality of classrooms and distinctive character of teachers' practices.

Thus most teachers espouse broad definitions of the *curriculum*, such as 'all the learning experience planned and guided by the school'. The point of this conception is twofold: to signal concern with the total learning environment, inasmuch as the pupil's all-round development depends upon more than the knowledge transmitted at him; and to place component 'subjects' in the context of the design of the *whole curriculum*. Hence it helps to recognise the way in which the whole curriculum represents a 'selection from *culture*', assumptions about what knowledge and skills merit formal transmission in society (Lawton, 1973). Interpreted from this perspective, we may question and clarify the contribution of particular patterns of *curriculum organisation*, subject-based by tradition, towards the longer-term purposes of schooling. What assumptions are made about which pupils should study particular areas of knowledge? Should there be a *core curriculum* for all pupils?

Views on such issues may gain support because they serve the interests of particular social or professional groups. Thus there is a sense in which ideology plays a central role in curriculum discussion, and in which curriculum development is a form of socio-political action (The Open University, 1976). However, this may be only intermittently recognised since both pupil and teacher expectations are channelled by the social milieu of the school, its *hidden curriculum*, and by the pervasive *classroom system* and assessment procedures.

What is sometimes called curriculum theory provides analysis of the main elements which can be attributed to any curriculum: its subject-matter, objectives, learning activities, outcomes and their evaluation. Analysis of the first element, for example, leads to consideration of the *structure* of knowledge to be communicated, and its relationship to the basic curriculum resource provided by major *disciplines of knowledge*. But it is equally significant to understand how such elements are combined into working programmes through *curriculum design*. A course need not be 'subject-centred'. Learning can be organised around interests, themes or problems. Forms of curriculum *integration*, if knowledgeably planned, may well make the pupils' use of knowledge more active and critical.

Thus the appeal of the *Tyler rationale* or 'objectives' approach to curriculum design is to offer a methodology by which conventional content or vague 'educational purposes' can be translated into effective 'educational experiences' via definition of behavioural *objectives*. Using a *taxonomy of objectives* the course designer can make more perceptive connections between teaching material and appropriate forms of pupil assessment. In open-ended learning activities, educational purposes may be formulated as *expressive objectives*. But teachers' actual curriculum practice may be better interpreted via the alternative *process model of curriculum design*, which articulates the way in which teaching may be guided by procedural principles and criteria intrinsic to worthwhile subject matter (Stenhouse, 1975).

Differing conceptions of means-end relationships also influence *curriculum evaluation*. If the merits of a course can be appraised in terms of its contribution to the achievement of specified objectives, the emphasis may be upon *summative evaluation* and tests of final pupil performance. Similar assumptions make the demand for teacher *accountability* a major issue. However, 'new' approaches to evaluation, such as *illuminative evaluation*, emphasise what is intrinsic to a particular educational situation, and the ideal of understanding rather than passing judgment on what happens. Similarly, *democratic evaluation* aims to reflect and inform the whole spectrum of interest involved, avoiding the narrower regulative intent of much evaluation.

The implications of these concepts for rationality in curriculum judgment arise mainly from considerations of the 'what?' of curriculum development, the curriculum itself. The 'how?' of curriculum development, the development process itself and its social context, entails comparable problems. Though often initiated by individual teachers, curriculum change impinges upon others' practices, thus requiring a balancing of interests and institutional support. Indeed, curriculum development can be seen as mediation between the world of the classroom and its changing social environment (The Open University, 1976). Curriculum design is in fact only part of the more complex social process of curriculum planning. In turn, curriculum planning needs to be seen in the context of *curriculum control*: administrative mechanisms and tacit conventions which limit teacher discretion and regulate key processes like assessment. The exercise of influence and actualities of decision making are often invisible but embedded in social practices. It helps analysis, therefore, to try to distinguish the *curriculum planning models* which steer or legitimate such practices and the *strategies of curriculum change* which can modify them. Although there has been the same tendency as with curriculum design to rationalise decisions within end-means or 'engineering' assumptions, alternative orientations to the wider development process, such as the rational-interactive or situational model, are possible. Because it emphasises that teachers' 'real' curriculum objectives arise within their particular classroom/school situations, it helps to justify and guide an emphasis on *school-based curriculum development*.

Different educational systems exhibit different *styles of curriculum development*. They reflect the ways in which development agencies have to work within sedimented curriculum traditions while drawing upon *diffusion of curriculum innovation* and *support systems*. In England and Wales, for example, the development strategy of the Schools Council was until recently strongly influenced by subject interests and the idea of teachers' (curriculum) autonomy. National curriculum projects, based mainly on the research/development model of *knowledge utilisation*, were set up to meet the needs of subjects rather than whole curriculum priorities. Curriculum change was piecemeal, depending upon local subject-centred initiatives and informal dissemination. But it is now apparent how curriculum development reflects changes in the social climate. Economic stringency has brought into the open the previously hidden politics of the curriculum.

The ideas outlined in this overview indicate the extent to which thinking about curriculum development has been engendered by a planning perspective. It may be evident, however, that if planning is formally and narrowly conceived, that perspective may fail to register how implicit constraints and informal adaptations to them affect curriculum realities. There is particular need to recognise the 'situated' nature of teachers' practices; for example, the way in which teachers, in response to competing demands made upon their self-esteem and management ability by classroom circumstances and outside expectations, adopt a sceptical stance or *practicality ethic* towards proposals for change. This cautious view has been reinforced by fuller analyses of the process of curriculum *implementation*, especially the mutual adaptation necessary between curriculum innovators and teachers who have to incorporate their ideas in day-to-day practices. Clearly, therefore, curriculum development is bound up with teacher professionality, notably teachers' collaborative planning, *self-monitoring*, negotiation, etc. Recent writing may distinguish *curriculum-in-transaction* from curriculum as intention. Thus it may stress skills of deliberation or the practical wisdom to find common ground between different perceptions of curriculum tasks and reach defensible decisions.

Further reading

Lawton, D. 'Social Change, Educational Theory and Curriculum Planning', University of London Press, 1973.

Stenhouse, L. 'An Introduction to Curriculum Research and Development', Heinemann, 1975.

Open University, 'Culture, Ideology and Knowledge', Units 3 and 4 of course E 203 (M. Skilbeck), Open University Press, 1976.

Schools Council, 'The Practical Curriculum', Methuen Educational, 1981.

Curriculum development

Entries to be found in Part 2

Accountability. Core curriculum. Classroom system. Culture. Curriculum. Curriculum control. Curriculum deliberation. Curriculum design. Curriculum evaluation. Curriculum-in-transaction. Curriculum organisation. Curriculum planning model. Democratic evaluation. Diffusion of curriculum innovation. Disciplines of knowledge. Expressive objectives. Hidden curriculum. Illuminative evaluation. Implementation. Integration (integrated studies). Knowledge utilisation. Objectives. Practicality ethic. Process model of curriculum design. Professionality. School-based curriculum development. Self-monitoring. Strategies of curriculum change. Structure. Styles of curriculum development. Summative evaluation. Support system. Taxonomy of objectives. Tyler rationale. Whole curriculum.

Chapter 5

Economics of education

The economics of education is a branch of economic analysis which is concerned with the inter-relationships between the economy and the education system. Economists have begun to apply their analytical techniques to two sets of relationships. On the one hand, the education system exerts a powerful impact on the economy. Modern industrialised economies require skilled manpower, and schools and colleges transmit much of the knowledge and the skills which young people will need when they join the labour force. Thus the relationships between education, training and employment are of vital importance to the economist.

Equally important are the ways in which the economy affects education. The amount of money available for education, the methods by which the government, employers and individuals finance education or training, and the way in which resources are allocated between different types of education are all partly dependent upon economic policies. All these topics therefore form part of the subject matter of the economics of education.

Only fairly recently has the economics of education been recognised as a distinct branch of economic analysis, but the subject has a long history. Two hundred years ago, Adam Smith discussed the way in which education makes a worker more productive, and in the nineteenth century Alfred Marshall wrote 'There are few practical problems in which the economist has a more direct interest than those relating to the principles on which the expense of the education of children should be divided between the state and the parents.' In spite of this, education did not seriously attract the attention of economists until about twenty years ago. A number of American economists at that time began to explore the idea that expenditure on education represents an important form of investment. They reasoned that investment in *human capital* could be analysed in the same way as investment in physical capital had been traditionally analysed by economists. This had considerable implications for *educational planning*. Throughout the world in both industrialised and developing economies, governments began to examine more carefully the links between the development of their education systems and their economic policies and targets.

At first, it was hoped that it might be possible to measure the *contribution of education to economic growth*. When it proved to be impossible to measure this in a precise way, many other economic techniques and methods of analysis were applied, in the hope that governments would be able to allocate resources more effectively, to achieve faster economic growth. The underlying assumption, or belief, was that education is a profitable form of investment; increased expenditure on education therefore would yield economic and social returns in the form of higher national income in the future.

Several countries attempted to use *manpower forecasting* as a basis for educational planning. The central assumption of this approach is that the growth and development of the economy generates a certain demand for qualified manpower and that the education system should be developed in accordance with these forecasts of manpower requirements. The objective of educational planning therefore is to gear the growth of secondary and higher education to satisfy future demand for educated manpower and thus to avoid the twin problems of shortages or surpluses of manpower. Such a simplistic idea of the relationship between education and employment had less influence in Britain than in many other countries, although there have been several attempts in this country to predict demand for teachers and doctors, and also scientists and engineers. Unfortunately most attempts at manpower forecasting have failed because of the difficulties of predicting technological change, and because the forecasts have assumed a rigid relationship between the educational system and the labour market, which is not found in the real world.

An alternative approach, advocated by some economists, is to apply *cost-benefit analysis* to education. This consists of measuring all the direct and indirect economic benefits of education, comparing the benefits with the total *costs of education*, so that resources can be allocated to those types of education which appear to be the most profitable forms of investment. Measurement of the economic benefits of education – both from the point of view of the individual and society as a whole – has proved to be so difficult that this also remains a highly controversial approach to the problem of planning the future growth of educational expenditure.

In Britain, at least, most attempts at planning the scale of higher education, including both the Robbins Report and the more recent attempts to consider higher education in the 1990s, have tried to forecast the level of private (sometimes rather confusingly called social) *demand for education*, in other words the number of qualified secondary school-leavers who wish to enter higher education. Economists have contributed to this debate by trying to analyse the influence of such factors as the life-time earnings of graduates, and the costs of university education on the demand for higher education.

This has focused attention on the *finance of education*, and the way in which money is provided, from central and local government funds and from individuals. Two distinct questions have dominated research in this area. The first is how different methods of financing education affect the *efficiency* of resource allocation. As we have already seen, the question of efficient allocation of resources has been one of the central pre-occupations of much of the research on methods of educational planning. Equally important in studies of educational finance is the question of the fairness of alternative methods of distributing resources, and in particular the implications of alternative ways of financing education.

Two particular proposals for changing the way of financing education in the UK have attracted attention: one is that the present system of means-tested grants for students in higher education should be replaced by a system of *student loans*, such as exists in several European countries and the USA; the other is that primary and secondary education should be financed by means of a system of *education vouchers*. Both proposals have been advocated by economists on grounds of both efficiency and equity.

Most of the issues discussed so far have been concerned with the macro-economics of education – the relationship between the economy and the education system as a whole. Micro-economics, which deals with individual institutions, has been applied on a small scale to schools and colleges. For example, there have been a few attempts to examine the inputs and outputs of different educational institutions in order to compare their *productivity*. This is an example of what is often called *cost-effectiveness analysis*, but because of the problem of defining and measuring the output of education, many educationalists and also some econo-

29

mists believe that it is inappropriate to try to apply such techniques to education.

However, increasing constraints on the growth of public expenditure in both developed and developing economies have focused more attention on the costs of education, despite the difficulties of measuring the 'output' or economic benefits produced by education. Questions such as whether there are *economies of scale* in education are relevant, whether or not one believes that the techniques of cost-benefit or cost-effectiveness can provide guidance about the allocation of resources in education.

Further reading

Blaug, M., 'An Introduction to the Economics of Education', Penguin, 1962.

Woodhall, M. and Ward, V., 'Economic Aspects of Education', National Foundation for Educational Research, Slough, 1972.

O'Donoghue, M., 'Economic Dimensions in Education', Gill & Macmillan, 1971.

Blaug, M., 'The Economics of Education: a Selected Annotated Bibliography', Pergamon Press, 1978.

Entries to be found in Part 2

Age-earnings profiles. Alpha-coefficient. Average cost. Contribution of education to economic growth. Cost-benefit analysis. Cost-effective analysis. Costs of education. Demand for education. Demand function. Economies of scale. Educational planning. Education voucher. Efficiency. Finance of education. Forgone earnings. Graduate tax. Human capital. Income-contingent loan. Investment. Labour market. Manpower forecasting. Marginal cost. Opportunity cost. Production function. Productivity. Rate of return. Screening hypothesis. Student loans. Substitutability.

Chapter 6

Educational measurement

'Whatever exists at all exists in some amount. To know it thoroughly involves knowing its quantity as well as its quality.' So said Thorndike in 1918 and this remains true today. 'Knowing its quantity' is another way of saying 'measuring it' and what does it mean to measure something? Fundamentally we can say that measurement entails certain rules and procedures for assigning numbers to attributes in such a way that the numbers represent the quantity of the attribute. It is necessary to be clear that it is not the object, organism or event itself which is being measured. For example, we don't measure 'a piece of wood' but we measure one of its attributes such as its length or weight.

The physical sciences have some well-developed measurement systems: a good example of this is length. It is not necessary to develop complex rules for using a ruler since what is to be done is obvious. We obtain a numerical value by seeing how many times we can fit the ruler into the object to be measured. This system can be sophisticated by taking one 'stick' as a standard against which other instruments are calibrated, thus allowing different people to measure length and to discuss results in terms which are directly related and interchangeable.

In educational measurement we are faced with attributes that do not lend themselves to such intuitive procedures. This is often true in the physical sciences as well, since, for example, we cannot readily observe how much copper or how much tin there is in a piece of bronze. We therefore develop complex procedures for arriving at the quantities of each. Similarly we cannot see how much 'intelligence' a child has. However, measurement of human attributes causes problems beyond those of establishing procedures, and these are the problems of defining what we are measuring. At least there is little controversy about the composition of bronze, which is made from two well defined elements. Intelligence, on the other hand, may be a mixture of a large number of attributes which are not only badly defined but may not even have been postulated. Defining attributes is therefore a major problem for educational measurement since loose definitions allow scope for individuals to make different interpretations of the numerical results of any measurement procedure.

Another major problem is that there are no fundamental standards to act as the units of measurement. In measuring length a choice of any 'stick' of any length could serve as the standard around which a system of measurement can be built. In measuring, say, intelligence, there is no obvious 'stick' to choose. The kinds of 'stick' most commonly used are the *items* which make up *tests*, but no single item and no single test would be acceptable as the standard for the attribute it purports to measure.

Both the problems of definition and of standards have to be overcome to some extent before there can be a useful measurement system. How this has been tackled is described briefly below.

In considering the first problem of defining educationally meaningful attributes we can identify two main sources, both of which apply to measurement science as a whole. One source is the inability to measure the attribute directly which means that we must rely on measuring its effect. Temperature is a clear example, where we measure the effect it has on the expansion of mercury in a tube. Similarly mathematical computation is measured by the outcome of responding to a sample of items which have been designed to represent the *domain* called 'computation'. We cannot measure computation without looking at the outcome to a number of specified tests. The other source of the problem of definition is that there are numerous variables which will alter the effect of our attribute. Gravity has an effect on the height of mercury in a way which is independent from the effect of temperature. Likewise fatigue will alter the results of a maths test in a way which is unrelated to a person's ability to do the test. The reason that the definition problem is more acute in educational measurement is not that the difference is one of kind but one of degree. A maths test result can be affected by lighting, emotional trauma, motivation and many other factors, most of which have not been properly defined themselves. This makes them difficult to control. Such confounding variables do influence results in the physical sciences but they have generally been more easily identified. This may no longer be as true for present-day resarch in the physical sciences, which means that there will be a convergence between the methodologies used in the physical and social sciences to overcome the problems.

The attempts to overcome the definitions problem can be divided into two approaches, although neither is used entirely alone. One approach is to analyse logically a domain of interest in terms of strictly behavioural outcomes such as 'addition of all single figure integers'. Tasks (or items) can be devised which represent this domain, and success in part or all of this domain demonstrates that the person has some of the attribute in question. This approach dominates the *attainment* area of educational measurement where attributes are highly dependent on conscious teaching. The other approach to definitions relies far more heavily on statistical techniques. This is primarily because logical analyses have not been able to define clear domains. An example is attempting to define intelligence where the attribute has a hypothesised effect in a large number of situations. Some of these situations will, by definition, be new situations which have not yet occurred. How then can the boundaries be drawn up using a pure logical approach? It is true that in the area of *psychological measurement* attributes have a greater generalised effect on behaviour, and this increases the number of situations in which they can be measured. This generalised effect gives much greater scope for *data* collection; and it is the vast quantities of data available that have made it necessary for educationalists and psychometricians to use techniques for investigating and ordering these data with the aim of gaining a clearer picture of the attributes which are likely to underlie the outcomes. Until the present the most common techniques have involved *correlational* methods, the most advanced of which are grouped under the name *factor analysis*. It is likely, however, that new methods, such as those based on *item characteristic curve theory* will provide alternative methods for investigating data in order to suggest and define underlying attributes.

The second major problem of finding standard units in which to express the quantities of our attributes has been overcome in a rather crude but nonetheless an effective manner. It is crude because a similar method for determining length would provide a less adequate measurement system than the one already available. It is best to illustrate this by using the analogy that every test item requires a different amount of the attribute before it can be tackled successfully, but we do not know how much of the attribute is required. It is like measuring length using a bundle of sticks all of unspecified lengths and asking whether our object is longer than the stick (i.e. passes) or shorter than the stick (i.e. fails). The score of passes and failures will give a measure of length. Obviously, a short stick will be passed by more objects than a longer one. This illustrates what happens when we obtain a test score. In order to improve the interpretations made from this basic procedure we take a fixed bundle of sticks (cf. items in a test) and see how various people score on them. The process involved for doing this is called *standardisation* and involves administering our test to a carefully selected and defined *population*. Our interpretations can then be made in relation to the *distribution* of scores, usually with reference to a *measure of central tendency* such as the mean and a *measure of dispersion* such as the standard deviation. To illustrate the kinds of statement that can then be made consider expressing a person's height as 'taller than 95 per cent of the people of Britain'. This may be unsatisfactory when we already have a good measurement system for length but it is extremely useful when no such system exists. Other forms of interpretation rely on the domain model where results are expressed in terms of percentage success for that domain. Such tests fall within the category of *criterion-referenced* or *domain-referenced tests*. The process of test construction, however, is more sophsticated than merely combining items which seem to the constructor to be appropriate. This is because there are problems of obtaining consistency in our measures and so an item's *discrimination* is calculated to help to ensure that the final test will have a high *reliability*, and reduce the *errors of measurement* associated with any test. It is also important that the items are of an appropriate *difficulty* for the population it is intended to test. Such procedure is called an *item analysis*.

The tests that are finally constructed provide numerical values for attributes. These form *scales* of measurement, and the properties of these scales vary according to the attribute concerned and the procedures involved. The success of such a scale rests on establishing empirically the relation between it and those outcomes which should be affected by the attribute. Thus there is a well-established relation between thermal dynamics and the height of mercury in a tube or vaporisation of water. The establishing of a relationship between the attribute and its effects demonstrates the usefulness of the scale which is called *validity*. Validation is the final stage in developing a measurement system for an attribute, and it is at this stage that many attributes and their associated scales are dropped in favour of other more successful ones.

Further reading

Thorndike, R. L. (ed.), 'Educational Measurement', 2nd ed., American Council on Education, 1971.
Bloom, B. S. et al. (eds), 'Handbook of Formative and Summative Evaluation of Student Learning', McGraw-Hill, 1971.
Guildford, J. P. and Fruchter, B., 'Fundamental Statistics in Psychology and Education', 6th ed., McGraw-Hill, 1978.

Entries to be found in Part 2

Aptitude. Attainment. Attitude. Bank. Battery. Calibration. Correlation. Criterion-referenced test. Data. Diagnosis. Difficulty. Discrimination. Distractor. Distribution. Domain. Errors of measurement. Evaluation. Facility. Factor. Factor analysis. Free answer. Grade. Histogram. Individual differences. Intelligence. Ipsative. Item. Item analysis. Item characteristic curve theory. Kurtosis. Measure of central tendency. Measure of dispersion. Multiple-choice. Normal distribution. Objective. Percentile rank. Population. Psychological measurement. Psychometrics. Quotient. Reliability. Sample. Scale. Score. Significance. Skew. Standardisation. Standard scores. Test. Trait. Validity. Variance.

Chapter 7

Educational organisations

Since education covers such a vast range of interests, ages and subjects; and since the processes of education are dependent upon the interchanges of information and opinion between people, it is perhaps inevitable that a great many organisations should be formed which play a part within the educational system, for people find support in organised groups and often development can only spring from co-ordinated effort. Directories and yearbooks provide lists of bodies, connected in one way or another with education, which run into thousands. The degree to which a nation's educational system is controlled by government does not appear to alter substantially the sort of sub-structure of organisations that develops.

One can distinguish several types of organisation: administrative, professional, research and supportive. Such classifications can be used to suggest broad groupings of organisations but should not be considered as exclusive categories. A body that has an administrative function may also provide controls to a profession, it may carry out research and it may be supportive of education through the provision of resources or information. Whilst the examples quoted in this section are British (and some European) it is interesting to apply the same sort of model of organisational structure to other countries. Differences of a minor nature may emerge: some systems will have a greater involvement of private enterprise interests, others will have more parts of the overall structure dependent upon the government through its Ministry of Education.

Whatever the balance, there appears to be a pattern in which administration of the statutory provision of education is carried out through a government department. This will be in accordance with extant statutes and the policy of the ruling government. Since this is also linked to the government system of financial control, it is the main force of change (or stasis) within the system, and the policy carried out by this government department will shape the forms and relationships of the majority of the other organisations. Educational administration is thence carried out through a tiered structure of regional and local organisations dealing with all the necessary aspects of finance, buildings, staffing, material provision and educational policy and practice. Parallel to this structure is another organisational pattern which controls and administers the examinations and setting of standards which are required of the recipients of education.

Professional organisations interlock easily with the administrative structures in that they give groups of professionals within education loci for exchanges of views, the maintenance of professional standards and the advancement of specialised interests. Such groups may be concerned directly with administration or, as in the case of professional unions or associations, with the protection of conditions of service; others may be solely concerned with a specific subject within the curriculum. However, all have a contribution to make to education and support the unofficial organisational structure that surrounds and assists the official structure. The extent to which this is true can be seen by the degree of representation from governmental bodies, both national and local, on professional associations.

Research organisations, some of which also have a developmental role, are often established by the official educational structure but are given an autonomous identity. Thus, although they are here grouped separately, the input of research that they give to the established system will be evident.

The remainder of this 'unofficial' structure is made up of a wide variety of groups and organisations which provide support and information. Almost all of these are based on a special interest, a specific subject or sector. Though some may be founded by 'official' monies, most arise out of the independent efforts of people sharing a particular professional interest. The resulting organisations serve to feed into the educational system resources, advice and information. This latter group, the supportive organisations, act as a balancing mechanism to the whole system in that they fill gaps and satisfy needs as they are perceived to arise. Whilst one may find the occasional example of two or more organisations with the same objectives, resulting perhaps from differences in the personalities involved, the majority are the sole representative of a particular educational interest. As with the evolution of species, organisations grow up because of current conditions; and those that survive have adapted successfully to the changes within the world of education. Therefore, though this is a somewhat simplistic view of the structure one can conceive of educational organisations in the pattern shown in Figure 1.

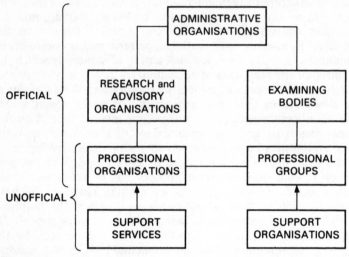

Figure 1

Entries to be found in Part 2, listed under headings in Figure 1

Administrative organisations

Academic Liaison Offices. Assessment of Performance Unit. Association of Northern Ireland Education and Library Boards. Commission of the European Communities. Convention of Scottish Local Authorities. Council of Europe. Council of Local Education Authorities. Department of Education and Science. Department of Education for Northern Ireland. Educational Disadvantage Unit. European Cultural Foundation. Scottish Education Department. Welsh Joint Education Committee. Welsh Education Office.

Examining bodies

Consultative Committee on the Curriculum. Examining bodies. Schools Council.

Research and advisory organisations

This is given as an entry itself.

Professional organisations

Advisory Council for Adult and Continuing Education. Association of Chief Officers of Area Boards for Education and Libraries. Association of Directors of Education in Scotland. Association of Education Officers. Careers organisations in education. Council for National Academic Awards. Further Education Staff College. General Teaching Council for Scotland. Industrial Training Board. National Federation of Community Associations. National Institute of Adult Education. Open University. Professional organisations. Scottish Institute of Adult Education. Society of Education Officers. Teachers' unions and professional associations. Training and Further Education Consultative Group. Training Services Division. Universities Central Council on Admissions. University Grants Committee. Workers Educational Association.

Professional groups

Health Education Council. Parents' organisations. Scottish Health Education Group. Trades Union Congress.

Support services

Within the range of organisations which are here termed 'support services' are those that are part of the governmental system, those that receive government or local authority support but remain autonomous, and those that provide support as independent companies. The element which they have in common is that as part or whole of their function they provide support to education.

British Broadcasting Corporation. Broadcast organisations. Central Bureau for Educational Visits and Exchanges. Independent television. Local radio. Museums Education Services. Sports Council of Great Britain.

Support organisations

Amongst those organisations which service education or stimulate innovation and development are a number of organisations whose declared function is to develop audio-visual resources and to promote educational development through the principles of educational technology. Any short selection such as this does an injustice to those organisations left out. There are many more related to specific subjects.

Association for Educational and Training Technology. British Film Institute. Council for Educational Technology for the United Kingdom. Educational Foundation for Visual Aids. Educational Television Association. International Council for Educational Media. Scottish Council for Educational Technology. Society for Academic Gaming and Simulation in Education and Training.

Chapter 8

Educational research

Although some educational research is aimed at extending the boundaries of knowledge, the bulk of educational research in recent years has been aimed at providing information, tools and instruments for decision making. A better title for some of this research may be *educational evaluation*. The evaluation may be of new curricula, systems and styles of education. There are four styles that are used:

1 Controlled enquiry, which is based on the classic concept of the scientific experiment. This style of enquiry assumes that it is possible to have a disinterested unbiased approach based on classical logic. It often makes assumptions that there are clear standards for judgment based on a *null hypothesis* as a foundation for statistical calculations. The researcher maintains distance between himself and what is to be studied. The ultimate aim is to produce precise unambiguous statements often for the sake of extending empirical knowledge. This style of carrying out research usually involves large numbers of learners, often comparing different backgrounds and/or methods of teaching. The tests are developed as instruments to enable the collection of data about individuals, such as *intelligence tests* and *examinations, attitude scales, personality assessment*, tests of *creativity* and *questionnaires*. Associated with this style are the *standardised scores* on tests. The reporting of this style of enquiry is usually statistical, often involving complex *analysis of data*. An excellent paper by Campbell and Stanley (1963) outlines the designs for educational research using this style and the following one of conceptual inquiry. The advantages are that a large quantity of data is collected which may form a basis for generalising from the sample to the population. The disadvantage is the impersonal style, making it difficult for the reader or teacher to identify with the conclusions. In addition, detailed data are sacrificed for the sake of general conclusions. Critics of the approach suggest that it is impersonal, based upon the questions the researcher wants to ask, and smacks of fertilising seeds (learners) and comparing growth. Advocates of the approach point to objectivity, precise thinking and logical development leading to generalisable conclusions. It is an analytical piece-by-piece collection of information.

2 *Conceptual enquiry*, which is based also upon the idea of science being value-free and not biased politically. However, this approach not only acknowledges that other bases than the scientific approach exist, but consciously attempts to use these other approaches. This style acknowledges that the norm is an opinion based on theoretical perspective and not an axiom. The basic assumption of the style is that there are ever-expanding research programmes. These programmes derived from the continual attempt to develop new conceptual frameworks, to try out innovations and to view these innovations from a variety of perspectives. There is no specified and preferred logic. Associated with this style are *curriculum development, educational technology, innovation strategies*, and the use of techniques from other disciplines. A model of the approach is one of conflict between existing and new strategies (for example *criterion-referenced measurement, norm-referenced measurement*).

The reporting of this style of research can take a variety of formats. It usually involves persuasion based on a preferred basis (e.g., discovery learning), use of examples showing the effectiveness of the new idea, and often psychological or other evidence. The examples seldom have a statistical basis. Such an enquiry may be a decision to carry out a *cost analysis* or cost-benefit analysis. In this case data on the use of resources, facilities and staff would be the basis of the analysis. Certain *observation schedules* would also come into this category; in these an attempt is made to quantify data. Each is an analytical piece-by-piece collection of information with some attempt to bring together the pieces to form a whole.

3 *Active general enquiry*, which is based on the assumption that it is not possible to have a disinterested unbiased approach, but that any researcher has a preconceived and interested value base for his work. The other main assumption is that education is a human activity and that educational research is to promote human development on the widest possible scale. The researcher deli-

berately makes contact with and interacts personally with the learning environment. A continual contact is made to enable the researcher and those with whom he is working to get to know themselves and one another better. The basis of such work may include observation, interviews and informal discussions in order to get a picture of the environment. The development of *illuminative evaluation* is in this category. The researcher may choose co-operation or conflict as his basis for collecting data. The reporting style is still that of an outsider judging. However, the researcher usually admits openly his bias. The report is a result of subjective filtering by the researcher based on his bias or by using an advocate and an adversary approach, leaving the reader to make a decision. The report usually includes case studies and direct quotations. Such reports are very readable (almost in the style of a novel), but are not quantitative and provide problems for generalisations. The emphasis is on detailed information rather than generalisations, but the approach attempts to look at the whole rather than collect specific bits of information.

4 *Active specific enquiry*, which is a relative newcomer in the field of educational research, has a more general modus operandi. Its origins are more in the area of literature, poetry, music and art rather than science. The ultimate aim is to enable a specific individual to know himself better. In the context of educational research the researcher acts as an enabler to the teacher or teacher-learner situation so that the participants may improve understanding. The basic assumption is different from the other three styles because the researcher is not intending to report to other people what he finds. His report will be mainly about the methods of enabling. He is committed to action-oriented research. This particular style presents problems to the teacher. If he is a teacher involved in such an activity he can identify clearly with what is taking place. Anyone outside the action has difficulty comprehending what is taking place. The most satisfactory reports are those of the teacher involved in the action. Some styles of research in this area lend themselves better to reporting than others. One such style has been developed from psychiatry, the *personal construct*. The approach is very much a holistic one.

Obviously there are overlaps between these paradigms, and no one method is 'better' than another. Much published work, until recent years, used exclusively the first or second paradigm. It is now more common to mix paradigms to give a range of hard data and illuminating case studies.

The reporting of educational research is through a wide range of journals, reports, theses and dissertations. Access to the range of reports is through one of the *educational abstracting systems*.

Further reading

Nisbet, J. D. and Entwistle, N. J., 'Educational Research in Action', Hodder & Stoughton, 1972.

Ebel, R. L. (ed.), 'Encyclopaedia of Educational Research', 4th ed., Collier Macmillan, 1969.

Gage, N. L. (ed.), 'Handbook of Research on Teaching' (particularly D. T. Campbell and J. C. Stanley, 'Experimental and Quasi-Experimental Designs for Research in Teaching' pp. 171–246), Rand McNally, 1963.

Travers, R. M. W. (ed.), 'Second Handbook of Research on Teaching', Rand McNally, 1973.

Entries to be found in Part 2

Aims. Analysis of data. Aptitude. Attitude scale. Cluster analysis. Correlation. Cost analysis. Creativity. Criterion-referenced measurement. Curriculum analysis. Divergent thinking. Domain referenced measurement. Educational abstracting systems. Educational evaluation. Examinations. Factor analysis. Goal. Illuminative evaluation. Individual differences. Innovation strategies. Intelligence tests. Interaction analysis. Likert scale. Mean. Nonparametric statistics. Norm-referenced measurement. Null hypothesis. Objectives. Objective test. Observation schedules. Parametric statistics. Personal construct. Personality assessment. Population. Programmed learning. Questionnaire. Reliability. Sample. Scaling. Self-rating. Semantic differential. Skills analysis. Standard deviation. Standardised score. Systematic. Task analysis. Thurstone scale.

Chapter 9

Educational technology

The term educational technology is an unfortunate one in that to some it indicates an exaggerated concern with the mechanisms of education like *audio-visual media* and *computers*.

In November 1964 Skinner gave a lecture to the Royal Society entitled 'The Technology of Teaching' (Skinner, 1968). This was perhaps the forerunner of the term 'educational technology'; Skinner used it not essentially in a mechanistic sense, but rather to emphasise that because of the nature of the emerging principles of *programmed learning* education was no longer only an art.

These principles underlined the importance of the learner as central to the teaching/learning process, pointing to the change from a largely teacher-oriented process to one where a student can take responsibility for his own progress. It was this change in emphasis that led to the emergence of the discipline of educational technology.

Educational technology is basically the application of a systematic or *systems approach* to education. Such an approach is often seen in terms of three main aspects: (1) the specification of the educational *objectives* of a course; (2) the determination of the *teaching/learning methods* to be used; and (3) the *evaluation* of course material in terms of the objectives set for it.

Such a systematic approach to education accepts the student as central to the learning process and is concerned with the variety of methods that can be used, such as *self-teaching techniques, individualised instruction*, etc. It is also concerned with the need for the student to explore and develop a variety of *study skills*.

With the development of *information technology*, teaching/learning methods are likely in the future to be influenced by the new technology and developments in micro-electronics.

To date *educational communication* has largely been an interaction between students, teachers and *books*. In the future a variety of resources are increasingly likely to be made available to students, often in specially designed *resource centres* which will not only have a variety of audio-visual media, *games and simulations*, etc., but will also house computer terminals with quick, easy access to information databanks.

Educational technology should be seen not as the machine taking over the teacher's role, but rather in terms of a developing science of education which uses a host of methods, techniques and resources to assist the teacher and support the student in the learning task.

Further reading

Hills, P. J., 'Teaching and Learning as a Communication Process', Croom Helm, 1979.

Howe, A. and Romiszowski, A. J., 'International Yearbook of Educational and Instructional Technology, 1978–79', Kogan Page, 1978.

Skinner, B. F., 'The Technology of Teaching', Appleton-Century Crofts, 1968.

Entries to be found in Part 2

Audio tape recorder. Audio-tutorial. Audio-visual media. Books. Computer. Data bank. Educational communication. Evaluation. Feedback. Film. Games and simulations. Group method. Individualised instruction. Individually prescribed instruction. Information technology. Keller plan. Linear programme. Multiple-choice programme. Pressey. Prestel. Programmed learning. Resource centre. Self-teaching techniques. Skinner. Slide. Study skills. Systems approach. Tape/slide. Teaching/learning methods. Television. Terminal. Videotape recorder.

Chapter 10

History of education

The *Charity schools* established at the end of the eighteenth century under the aegis of the Society for Promoting Christian Knowledge constitute, for all practical purposes, the first organised attempt at producing institutionalised education for the masses. Although initial enthusiasm had waned by about 1730 it was not until fifty years later that another venture, the *Sunday school* movement, began. The social and political upheavals engendered by population growth, increasing urbanisation, the war with France, 1793–1815, and the industrial and agricultural 'revolutions' brought increasing concern for the social training and instruction of the poor. Day schools were sponsored by various *religious societies* in the early nineteenth century. These became increasingly dependent on public money provided by the *Committee of the Privy Council on Education*, which by 1861, the year of the publication of the Newcastle Report, was providing nearly £1,000,000 a year. In an attempt to contain, if not reduce, expenditure the Education Department introduced the *Revised Code*.

During the 1860s a series of privately sponsored surveys made in the great cities suggested that half the children of England were receiving little or no formal education. However, as a study of *literacy rates* suggests, this does not mean that they did not learn to read and write in some other way. At the end of the decade the Liberal government, possessing a substantial majority, was able to pass the contentious *Elementary Education Act 1870* which at last ended the religious societies' monopoly of state-provided funds. During the next half-century a series of acts gradually made *school attendance* compulsory until the age of 14 years.

Completely divorced from the schools for the children of the poor were those for the offspring of the burgeoning middle classes and the landed aristocracy. Whereas the latter had relied heavily

47

on private tutors and the Grand Tour to complete the education of their sons, they now began to send them in increasing numbers to non-local boarding schools giving a predominantly classical education, the *Public Schools*. Socially ambitious middle-class parents, whose wealth came from industry and commerce, provided a new clientele for these schools and the *universities of Oxford and Cambridge*. Valuing the competitive entrepreneurial ideal, they wanted the reform of those institutions that had failed to move with the times. Hence the Public Schools, the *endowed schools*, and the universities of Oxford and Cambridge became the objects of scrutiny by Royal Commissions. The new device of *school examinations*, a product of Benthamite reform, the contemporary competitive ethic, and the growing professionalisation of middle-class occupations gave parents a yardstick by which to judge the schools. It also enabled the pioneers of *girls' education* to argue that girls were as educable as boys. The increasing challenge to Britain's industrial leadership in the 1860s prompted a group centred around Lyon Playfair to demand improvements in *technical and scientific instruction*. By the end of the century higher-grade schools, the new civic universities, the *City and Guilds of London Institute*, technical colleges and polytechnics, and the Science and Art Department were responding to this need.

The multiplicity of institutions involved in secondary and technical education, the many ways in which they were financed, and the problems facing working-class children in transferring from the elementary to the secondary school were highlighted in the Bryce Report of 1895. The *Education Act 1902* at last brought elementary and secondary schools under the same administrative umbrella, although they continued to run under separate regulations and methods of *teacher training* remained divorced from each other. The new opportunities now available to working-class children raised the problem of their *selection for secondary education*, an issue that was not resolved until the *comprehensive school* provided a viable alternative to the *tripartite system*.

The Second World War, as did the earlier ones of 1899 and 1914, prompted public concern about the physical and intellectual well-being of the country's human resources. The provision of *school meals and the school health service* and the education of the *handicapped child* became the concern of the state. The Education Act 1944 abolished all fees in maintained secondary schools – those in elementary schools had lingered on until 1918 – theoretically making a grammar school education available to the poorest child. During the next twenty years doubts about the reliability of the selection procedure for secondary education increased, and the success of novels such as E. Blishen's 'Roaring Boys' (1955) reflected public concern about the state of the secondary modern school. At the same time these schools began to enter their abler pupils for the same examinations that children were sitting from the grammar schools. The publication of Circular 10/65 requesting Local Authorities to prepare plans for the reorganisation of their schools on comprehensive lines was the first step towards the abolition of a selective system of education in the public sector, an objective yet to be attained.

Meanwhile, the growing material prosperity of the 1950s and 1960s nurtured the belief that higher education offered not only a passport to a better job but was also a 'right' and a 'good' in itself. Economic pressures for an increase in the size of the trained scientific labour force reinforced these expansionist tendencies. The Crowther Report, '15 to 18' (1959) and the Robbins Report on Higher Education (1963) and the Newson Report, 'Half Our Future' (1963) drew attention to the reserves of ability still untapped by the education system at various levels. In tertiary education reforms in teacher education, the expansion of the universities, and the creation of thirty *polytechnics* were amongst the major achievements of an era that ended with the public expenditure cuts of 1974.

Further reading

Archer, R. L., 'Secondary Education in the Nineteenth Century', Cambridge University Press, 1921; reprinted Frank Cass, 1966.

Armytage, W. H. G., 'Four Hundred Years of English Education', Cambridge University Press, 1970.

Curtis, S. J., 'History of Education in Great Britain', University Tutorial Press, 1967.

Digby, A. and Searby, P. 'Children, School and Society in Nineteenth Century England', Macmillan, 1981.

Gosden, P. H. J. H., 'Education in the Second World War', Methuen, 1976.

Harrison, J. F. C., 'Learning and Living 1790–1960', Routledge & Kegan Paul, 1961.

Hurt, J., 'Education in Evolution', Hart-Davis, 1971; Paladin, 1972.

Hurt, J. S., 'Elementary Schooling and the Working Classes, 1860–1918', Routledge & Kegan Paul, 1979.

Lowndes, G. A. N., 'The Silent Social Revolution', Oxford University Press, 1969.

Simon, B., 'Studies in the History of Education, 1780–1870' (1960); 'Education and the Labour Movement, 1870–1918' (1965); 'The Politics of Educational Reform, 1920–1940' (1974); Lawrence & Wishart; available in paperback, 1974.

Sturt, M., 'The Education of the People', Routledge & Kegan Paul, 1967.

Whitbread, N., 'The Evolution of the Nursery-Infant School', Routledge & Kegan Paul, 1972.

Entries to be found in Part 2

Arnold, Thomas (1795–1842). Beloe Report. Certificate of Secondary Education. Charity school. City and Guilds of London Institute. Cole, Sir Henry (1808–82). College of Preceptors. Committee of the Privy Council on Education. Comprehensive secondary school. Education Act 1902. Elementary Education Act 1870. Endowed school. Factory children. Forster, W. E. (1818–86). Girls education. Girls' Public Day School Trust. Handicapped child. Kay-Shuttleworth, Sir James Phillip, first baronet (1804–77). Literacy rate. London polytechnics. Lowe, Robert, first Viscount Sherbrooke (1811–92). Monitorial system. Multilateral school. Playfair, Sir Lyon, first Baron Playfair (1816–98). Polytechnic. Public School. Ragged school. Religious societies. Revised Code. Royal Society of Arts. School attendance. School examinations. School meals and the school health service. Science and Art Department. Selection for secondary education. Standards of the Revised Code 1862. Sunday School. Teacher training. Technical and scientific instruction. Tripartite system. Universities of Oxford and Cambridge. Whisky money.

Chapter 11

Industrial education and training

The term 'industry' is generally and loosely used to describe all those activities involved in the making, supply and distribution of goods and services. Reference to the education industry in the same textbooks as analyses of manufacturing tend to blur some of the distinctions that perhaps we should be careful to make. Terms like *Industry Training Boards* (ITB), which cover something like half the working population of the UK and are referred to by everyone except themselves as Industrial Training Boards, further the confusion.

In this section, we shall use the word 'industrial' to indicate two things. First, we are concerned by and large with manufacturing, the production of goods and their subsequent servicing and maintenance. Essentially, this kind of activity in an economy like that of the UK is concerned with the creation of wealth and its distribution through profits. These profits can be attributed to private shareholders or to the state. We therefore cover all manufacturing industry, from the nationalised state corporations like gas and electricity to the smallest owner-manager enterprise. Second, we tend to favour using the word 'industrial' to indicate those jobs involved in direct work upon the products of manufacturing. We thus include shop-floor staff, technical and engineering specialists, and the skilled crafts. Occasionally, we shall step outside these boundaries because some terms (like the *Industrial Training Act* and the *Employment and Training Act)* cover wide references.

The characteristics of *operative* training are such that it has produced a number of specifically aimed techniques, such as *systematic training* based on skills and task analysis. Although many jobs described as operative are not in the classical sense skilled, we shall see that many demand a high level of expertise. Craft *apprenticeship* is one of the very few career openings available to the 16-year-old school-leaver. For boys it remains a major opportunity, and as many as 40 per cent of 16-year-old boys leaving school in any one year enter apprenticeships. Under the influence of the ITBs apprenticeships have improved considerably in quality over the last few years.

Of all the categories of industrial employment the most difficult to define with precision is *technician*, and therefore technician training. It has been estimated that there are as many as 4,000,000 people in technician jobs in the UK. The idea of a technician occupational group with special education and training needs is relatively recent and an adequate definition of the term is not easy. Generally, technician jobs lie between the qualified engineer or technologist and the skilled craftsman. Technicians understand general principles affecting their work but probably do not have a detailed theoretical grasp.

Technologists are of increasing important in the UK industrial sector, largely because of the acceleration in the speed of change in technologies. Their education and training are usually at the level of a university degree and they need an understanding of the fundamental principles of their subject. Their skills lie in the application of the scientific method to industrial problems.

Provision for craft, technician and technologist education is made within the UK formal education system. The *Technician Education Council* is steadily expanding its range of activities including the transfer of courses formerly run by the *City and Guilds of London Institute* to qualify successful people for membership of institutions. There are also the graduate engineers to consider; see the *Council of Engineering Institutions*.

Most training is carried out in organisations. There has been a sharp increase in recent years in the quantity and quality of industrial training in response to legislation. The role of the *Manpower Services Commission* has been significant, especially through such systems as the Training Opportunities Scheme.

The aim of all these activities remain the provision of an adequate number of trained skilled people to run a modern industrial economy effectively. There is room to doubt whether this is as successful as government, industry, educationalists and trainers might wish. The government has recently brought forward proposals for a radical re-organisation of industrial training including the abolition of all but six of the statutory Industry Training Boards.

Entries to be found in Part 2

Apprenticeship. Attitude/knowledge/skills. Audio aids. Audio-visual aids. Automated programmed instruction. Character-building industry. Council of Engineering Institutions. Council of Technical Examining Bodies (TEB). Cumulative-part method. Diagnostic branching. Direct training services. Exemption (levy). Group Training Scheme. Human resources. Industrial Training Act 1964, and Employment and Training Act 1973. Industry Training Board (ITB). Industrial Training Service (ITS). Instructional specification. Instruction schedule. Job analysis. Job enrichment/enlargement. Key results. Key training grants. Learning curve. Link course. Manpower planning. Manpower Services Commission (MSC). Mobile instructor service. Module (modular) training. Multiple-skilling. Occupational analysis. Operative. Part-method. Preparatory courses. Re-training. Skill centre. Skills analysis. Technical Education and Training Organisation for Overseas Countries (TETOC). Technician. Technician Education Council (TEC), Scottish Technician Education Council (SCOTEC). Technologist. Training needs analysis. Training Services Division (TSD). Training within industry (TWI). Unified vocational preparation (UVP).

Chapter 12

Management education and training

Management is a difficult term to define and managers' jobs are difficult to identify with precision. There have been a large number of theories advanced together with a great deal of description based on observation. Because we have these difficulties the boundaries of management education are not clear. Here we use the term management to mean all those people who are responsible for achieving the organisation's objectives, either by being responsible for other people's work or for their own as specialists at the same level. Included in this are supervisors, who are usually responsible for a relatively narrow area of work. Management training is concerned with those activities designed to help a manager improve his performance in his current job.

In the last few years there has been an enormous expansion in activities described as management training and education, ranging from the formation of the *business schools*, to the emergence of the *Regional Management Centres* and to the development of a wide range of *education and training techniques*. Professional bodies like the *British Institute of Management* and institutions like the Institute of *Works Managers* have experienced substantial growth, both in membership and influence. *Degree courses* have come into being, at universities and polytechnics through the *Council for National Academic Awards*, both at first and at advanced levels. *Management development* has emerged as a separate discipline, with techniques like *management by objectives* and *organisation development*. Most organisations now use *appraisal* system as part of their management systems. A large number of *independent management education and training institutions* have sprung up, many based on particular theories like *Coverdale training, Kepner-Tregoe* and the *managerial grid*.

Management training tries to prepare a manager for a future

job and expanded responsibilities. Education deals with the theoretical foundations of management although, as we shall see, there is no defined body of knowledge called management but rather a collection of parts of other subjects like economics. Thus, qualifications like the *Diploma in Management Studies* cover a very wide range of topics from accounting to work study. A substantial part of most management education and training today is devoted to the *behavioural studies/sciences* and the use of techniques like *sensitivity training* derived from them. Since management is often deeply concerned with producing work through other people this emphasis is not surprising.

It is clear that managers learn best by doing. Through *coaching* and *counselling* the boss is critical in this kind of learning. *Self-assessment* and *self-development* through active learning methods (or *learner-controlled training*) fits this concept well. However extensive the knowledge, however clever the training techniques and however advanced the skills the manager has, in the end the manager is responsible for his own performance. Therefore, he has to manage his own learning and growth.

Approaches to management education and training that recognise this kind of self-responsibility are likely to be more successful than any others. In addition, such approaches recognise that all managerial jobs are unique. There are many influences that produce this uniqueness, from the size of the organisation to the individual's managerial style. This uniqueness forces training specialists to use skills and techniques different from those they would adopt for, say, training operatives. Managers need individualised education and training programmes. There will be some common elements which can be dealt with in a general way. But most parts of the manager's job are particular to that manager doing that job and therefore any education or training needs to reflect that.

It is impossible to cover fully the wide variety of management education and training, and this section therefore tries to deal with the most important parts and those that have most recently developed and which appear to contribute in the UK.

Entries to be found in Part 2

Action-centred leadership. Activity learning. Appraisal. Appreciation training. Assessment centre. Behavioural studies/sciences. British Institute of Management (BIM). Business school. Career development and planning. Coaching. Computer-aided learning

(CAL), computer-assisted learning, and computer-assisted training (CAT). Computer-managed learning (CML). Counselling. Coverdale training. Criterion-referenced instruction (CRI). Degrees: advanced: post-graduate and post-experience. Degrees in business and management, etc. Diploma in Management Studies (DMS). Discovery learning (discovery method). Education and training techniques. European Research Group on Management (ERGOM). Evaluation of management training. Incident method (process). Independent management education and training institutions. Interactive skills. Intervention. Learner-controlled training. Management. Management by objectives (MBO). Management centres. Management development. Management development adviser. Management game (exercise). Managerial grid. National Examinations Board in Supervisory Studies (NEBSS). Open University. Organisation development (OD). Professional management association. Regional Management Centre (RMC). Role-playing. Self-assessment/self-development. Sensitivity training. Simulation. Supervisory management. Systematic training. T-group. Works manager.

Chapter 13

Philosophy of education

Education presents an area of multi-disciplinary study deriving mainly from the *empirical* sciences of psychology and sociology. Some of the problems which seem to defy solution belong not to these empirical sciences but to philosophy. It is therefore important that the educationalist should have some notion of the way in which both sets of problems can be dealt with. Thus, he will need to know something of the research methods necessary for work in sociology or psychology, but he should also have some acquaintance with the kinds of technique appropriate for dealing with philosophical questions.

The philosopher is concerned with two related activities: (a) ascertaining the *meaning* of a proposition or concept, and (2) considering the nature of the evidence which is offered in support of a particular proposition. Briefly he is asking 'what do you mean?' and 'how do you know?' These questions are frequently connected, because it may only be possible to offer justification for a proposition when one has ascertained its meaning. But equally the way in which we must verify or justify a proposition may throw further light on meaning.

The studies of philosophy and education seem to interact in three main areas:

1 Many of the recurring problems in educational discussion are philosophical problems belonging to well-defined areas of philosophy. Discussions arise concerning *equality*, such as equality of opportunity or the justification of *positive discrimination*. Many questions regarding the construction of the curriculum make appeals to value-judgments which belong to *ethics* and *aesthetics*, and choices are made by reference to the notions of *intrinsic* good or *utilitarianism*. Thus the philosopher is not concerned with the

causes of our adoption of certain moral or aesthetic preferences but with our attempts to justify them.

2 Education involves the use of concepts which are highly abstract and ambiguous. It is important that such concepts should be scrutinised. Thus enthusiasts advocate 'child-centred' or 'progressive education', but what is it that is being advocated? It is part of the philosopher's task to differentiate persuasive definitions from purely descriptive statements. Similarly, concepts such as *education, indoctrination* or *autonomy* need analysis. Many of the terms abstracted from the sciences of psychology or sociology are in need of similar examination. Recent controversy over intelligence and intelligence testing is sufficient to warn the student that *intelligence* is not the same kind of entity as, say, white or red blood corpuscles, which can be located, counted and measured. Similarly, we need to ensure that words used by educationalists mean the same within educational discourse as they do within science or within philosophy. Terms such as *theory, knowledge* and *socialisation* tend to be words of this type.

3 Most of the work done by philosophers interested in educational problems has tended to lie within these two areas. However, a third area should not be overlooked. Many movements in education are initiated from an adherence to particular philosophical and metaphysical assumptions and beliefs. It is therefore important to be able to have some method of evaluating such beliefs. It is equally important that one should be able to distinguish the metaphysical reasons adduced for certain types of education, from the empirical evidence which is often intermingled with it. *Plato* and Froebel present systems of this kind.

It is important when consulting works of reference on the meaning of philosophical terms that one should not think of meanings in the sense of 'what a word stands for'. One should ask how a word is being used and what task it has within a particular context of *language game*. The important thing to grasp is why particular words such as *necessary, a priori, analytic contingent*, etc., are part of the philosopher's vocabulary, and what task he is able to fulfil by employing terms of this nature at all.

Further reading

O'Connor, D. J., 'An Introduction to the Philosophy of Education' (especially Ch. 1), Routledge & Kegan Paul, 1957.
Langford, G., 'Philosophy and Education', Macmillan, 1968.

Lucas, C. J., 'What is Philosophy of Education?' Collier-Macmillan, 1969.

Entries to be found in Part 2

Achievement/task analysis. Aesthetics. Aims. Analytic statement. A posteriori judgments. A priori knowledge. Autonomy. Contingent statement. Deductive reasoning. Deschooling. Determinism. Education. Emotive. Empirical and empiricism. Equality. Ethics. Falsification. Growth. Indoctrination. Inductive reasoning. Intrinsic. Knowledge. Language game. Logical geography. Logical positivism. Meaning. Necessary statement. Objectivity. Paradigm. Phenomenology. Plato. Positive discrimination. Positivism. Prescriptive. Relativism. Sociology of knowledge. Theory. Utilitarianism. Valid. Verification.

Chapter 14

Psychology of education

Psychology is concerned with the systematic study of all forms of behaviour both human and animal, using methods which have been derived from the natural sciences. A number of specialised branches of psychology have developed, including general psychology, physiological psychology, developmental psychology, social psychology and psychometrics, which is concerned with *mental testing*. A number of applied fields of psychology have also come into being that draw upon relevant findings in the various branches as well as carrying out research in their own area. Educational psychology is one of these applied fields, and it is concerned with the study of the many factors which influence the processes of human learning, particularly learning that takes place in educational settings. It studies the acquisition of intellectual, emotional, physical and social behaviour in both children and adults and tries to identify the environmental and other influences upon such behaviour. The field of educational psychology is of interest to teachers, community and youth workers and to others concerned with influences upon learning, especially learning in the young. Some educational psychologists work within the child guidance service, whilst others are involved with teacher training.

Not all psychologists have been in agreement about how the complexities of behaviour should be conceptualised; and during the brief history of the discipline, over the last hundred years or so, several *schools of psychology* have emerged; some are still influential. A number of different *theories of learning* have also been put forward. Educational psychology has drawn freely from these different approaches. As a result there are differences in emphasis between educational psychologists in the way that they study the field, dependent upon whether they take an eclectic approach or favour the orientation of one school or another.

Man's behaviour has its origins in physiological mechanisms, and a study of these mechanisms offers the educational psychologist some understanding of the internal influences upon the individual's mental, physical and emotional behaviour. There is a direct relationship between *brain and behaviour* which is becoming better understood. Man's physiological structure is genetically determined, but his potential has to be developed in a specific environment which may or may not facilitate the fullest development of the genetic inheritance. The inter-relationship between *heredity and environment* raises difficult issues for the educational psychologist, not least in his study of the factors which can influence the development of *intelligence*.

Each child goes through a number of broadly similar stages in its physical, intellectual, social and emotional growth. These aspects of *child development* must be taken into account in any systematic attempt to understand learning. Amongst the most significant work in this area has been the identification of an invariable sequence in the development of the growing child's intellectual functioning: the so-called *Piagetian stages of development*.

Piaget's work is concerned with cognitive development; with the effect of early learning upon later learning. A closely related area of educational psychology is concerned with the acquisition of cognitive strategies and with other aspects of human symbolic behaviour. Numerous studies have been made of *concept formation and attainment*; and the fast-growing field of psycholinguistics, which is concerned with the study of the relationship between *language and thought*, has provided important insights into the child's ability, unique in the animal kingdom, to acquire and use language.

The language skills which the child has acquired come to form the basis for much of his *learning, retention and recall* of new ideas. *Attention and perception* are both important in any consideration of learning and they are both influenced by the conceptual framework that the child has available. This framework of interconnected ideas determines what it is that he attends to in a new learning task, determines how the new learning is coded for storage in the *long-term memory* and determines how accurate the recall of the learning will be at some later date. No learning will take place unless some *motivation* to learn exists, and educational psychology has an extensive literature available that it can draw upon in this area.

There are useful generalisations that can be made about the learning and the stages of development of all individuals, but there are other influences upon the behaviour of the individual which can be understood only by acknowledging that each individual is in some ways unique. There exists a complex interaction between each person's mental, emotional, physical and social behaviour which results in his unique and more or less stable way of approaching his environment that manifests itself as his *personality*. Some aspects of personality seem to lead learners to approach cognitive learning tasks in a number of different ways, and there is an expanding literature concerned with the origins and consequences for learning of differences in *cognitive style*.

Almost all learning takes place in a social context. Educational psychology is concerned with all the *social aspects of learning*. For example, the well-adjusted child must acquire a whole range of social skills. The groups the child belongs to will have a major influence upon the attitudes he holds and upon his self-image, and the organisational contexts within which his education takes place will have significant bearings upon his educational progress.

Some educational psychologists are especially concerned to alleviate the effects of *handicap: intellectual, social, emotional and physical*. Work in this area often overlaps with that of others such as specialist teachers, psychiatrists, clinical psychologists, doctors, probation officers and social, youth and community workers. Although much of educational psychology is concerned with the education of the school child, the child's educational experiences make a significant contribution to his eventual occupational choice; educational psychology also includes the study of *vocational development and guidance*.

It is clear that there are far more influences upon the individual's learning than merely the formal lessons that he attends in school. Educational psychology has recently taken an increasing interest in the total *curriculum process*: all the experiences provided by an educational institution that contribute to the learning of its students. The importance of clarity in the expression of aims and objectives has been stressed. No *educational objectives* are of much use unless it is possible to assess in some fashion whether they have been achieved by the teaching programme that has been adopted. *Educational assessment* is a skilled task which needs to be undertaken with great care if it is to be both reliable and valid.

Further reading

Ausubel, D. P., Novak, J. D. and Hanesian, H., 'Educational Psychology: A Cognitive View', 2nd ed., Holt, Rinehart & Winston, 1978.
Child, D., 'Psychology and the Teacher', 2nd ed., Holt, Rinehart & Winston 1977.
Lovell, R. B., 'Adult Learning', Croom Helm, 1980.

Entries to be found in Part 2

Achievement motivation. Attention and perception. Autism. Behaviourism. Bloom's taxonomy. Brain and behaviour. Bruner's strategies in concept formation. Child development. Classical conditioning. Cognitive approaches to learning. Cognitive style. Concept formation and attainment. Convergent and divergent thinking. Curriculum process. Delinquency. Educational assessment. Educational objectives. Elaborated and restricted codes. Gagné's conditions of learning. Handicap: intellectual, emotional, social and physical. Heredity and environment. Humanistic psychology. Intelligence. Intelligence A, B and C. Intelligence quotient. Introversion-extraversion. Language acquisition device (LAD). Language and thought. Learning, retention and recall. Long-term memory. Maturation. Mental testing. Motivation. Objective test. Operant conditioning. Personality. Piagetian stages of development. Psychoanalytic psychology. Schools of psychology. Self-concept. Sensory memory. Seven-point plan. Short-term memory. Social aspects of learning. Sociometry. Streaming. Sylbs and sylfs. Theories of learning. Validity and reliability. Vocational development and guidance.

Chapter 15

Sociology of education

Anyone who wishes to become at home with the key concepts used in the sociology of education needs to gain some understanding of the different traditions of sociological theory upon which this specialisation has drawn in the course of its development. Sociology does not have a unified theory, with a unified set of concepts. Rather, each of a number of schools of sociological thought has given rise to its own distinct set of concepts, none of which can be detached from the theory in which it is embedded without undergoing a shift in meaning. It is therefore important, wherever such concepts enter into the sociology of education, to be able to recognise the nature of the sociological theory in terms of which they are being presented.

An account of the stages through which the sociology of education has passed in Britain since the 1950s can help to show to which particular theoretical perspectives its various key concepts belong. However, a point to make about some of the research in the early part of this period is that it started with certain basic concepts that owed little directly to any theory at all.

This is to some extent the case with the initial work of Jean Floud and A. H. Halsey, who together laid the foundations of the post-war sociology of education – as distinct from a still earlier tradition. One of the main topics of their own studies, and of some of those which they helped to bring together in 'Education, Economy and Society' in 1961, was the selection process within schooling. Floud and Halsey specifically investigated the part played by *social class* in determining which children had access to the secondary grammar schools of the day, this access being seen as a means to upward *social mobility* for the lower classes. The concept of social class they employed, however, was only loosely related to any sociological theory; and it was on the cogency of this concept that the cogency of their concept of social mobility also depended.

The importance of 'Education, Economy and Society' was as a seminal text. Among its readings, for example, was an early study of linguistic development by Basil Bernstein, whose subsequent work on *linguistic codes* ranks as a major contribution to the sociology of education. Another reading was an essay by the American sociologist, Talcott Parsons, on 'The School Class as a Social System'. The development of the sociological theory of *structural-functionalism* under Parsons's leadership had been a main feature of American sociology in the previous two decades; and Floud and Halsey, in their introduction to 'Education, Economy and Society', drew specific attention to the relevance of Parsonian theory for a consideration of education in relation to *social control*.

Much of the work in the sociology of education in the 1960s followed the trail of structural-functionalism, focusing on the process of *socialisation* in schools and on the kinds of *role* which individuals were called upon to adopt in their positions as pupils or as teachers. Neither the term 'socialisation' nor the term 'role' was the invention of structural-functionalism. Nevertheless, it was the concept of each as structural-functionalism expounded it that tended to be taken into the sociology of education and to shape its research.

Some researchers in the 1960s, though, turned to certain concepts elaborated early in the century by the German sociologist, Max Weber, particularly those of *authority* and of *bureaucracy*. Since one of the claims of structural-functionalism was that it incorporated elements of both *Durkheimian sociology* and of *Weberian sociology*, it was not inconsistent for researchers to think of drawing on structural-functionalism and more directly on Weber at the same time, and this was quite a common practice.

However, there were elements of Weberian sociology less easy to reconcile with the emphasis upon an analysis of social systems that developed within structural-functionalism, notably Weber's stress on the meaningfulness of social action. The difference of perspective here was highlighted by attacks upon structural-functionalism from other quarters, particularly from *symbolic interactionism*. Symbolic interactionism, as a school of thought in America, had its roots in the much earlier thinking of American social scientists like C. H. Cooley and G. H. Mead; but some of its protagonists gave it a new form by taking up a stance against what they saw as the structural-functionalist reduction of human beings to puppets. They were given added incentive to do this after Dennis Wrong, in a celebrated paper appearing in the 'American Sociological Review' in 1961, stringently criticised Parsons's approach, or what he called 'The Oversocialised Conception of Man in Modern Sociology', for its disregard of *conflict* within society.

The form of symbolic interactionism that developed in opposition to structural-functionalism professed to do justice to man as an active shaper of his own life, and demanded a transformation of the concept of role which would free it from its alleged structural-functionalist connotations of passivity. The theory attracted a number of sociologists of education. Some, however, were led in the further direction of *phenomenological sociology*, and towards the sociology of Alfred Schutz in particular.

Schutz's thinking was in tune with symbolic interactionism in many ways, one of these being the kind of significance he attached to Weber's concept of the meaningfulness of social action. However, there was a further orientation fundamental to his thinking; namely, that he grounded his theory in the philosophical phenomenology of Edmund Husserl and was centrally concerned to investigate the way in which human beings actually constructed their social world. It was this last aspect of his thought that was especially to affect one line of development of the sociology of education.

It achieved its effect, though, through a particular medium, the medium of Peter Berger and Thomas Luckmann's profoundly influential book, 'The Social Construction of Reality', first published in America in 1966. This treatise in the *sociology of knowledge* – as it was sub-titled – attempted to achieve a synthesis of various perspectives in sociology, but, above all, it argued for a re-definition of the sociology of knowledge that made the thinking of Schutz and of Karl Marx twin pillars of it.

This focus in mainstream sociology upon the sociology of knowledge fuelled an attempt to achieve a corresponding shift of focus in the sociology of education in Britain, marked by the publication in 1971 of 'Knowledge and Control', a collection of papers edited by Michael Young explicitly setting out to provide the sociology of education with new directions.

The *'new' sociology of education* – as it came to be called – turned its attention to the school or college curriculum, and insisted that what the curriculum presented as 'knowledge' should be regarded as problematic and made the subject of a critique. Both a Schutzian and a Marxian sociology of knowledge were invoked for the elaboration of such a critique. Lately, this new movement has swung towards a more purely Marxian perspective. Its key concept has become that of the *class struggle*, in association with which it has employed the secondary concepts of *ideology* and of *alienation* to further an analysis of the dehumanisation of knowledge.

The new movement succeeded in establishing sociological enquiry into the curriculum as a relevant concern of the sociology of education alongside those other concerns with which research was already associated. Its theoretical perspectives, moreover, offered still further alternatives to those already in existence, with the result that the sociology of education has now come to contain an extremely wide range of different perspectives.

It has been possible here only to indicate the main lines of difference between these perspectives. What needs to be further recognised is that each perspective includes its own additional alternatives within itself: each harbours its own theoretical controversies and internal conceptual disagreements. It is, in fact, this abundance of theoretical positions within the sociology of education that is likely to constitute the chief difficulty for any newcomer wishing to become familiar with the specialisation over its entire span.

Further reading

Halsey, A. H., Floud, J. and Anderson, C. (eds), 'Education, Economy and Society', Free Press, 1961.
Ashley, B., Cohen, S. and Slatter, R., 'An Introduction to the Sociology of Education', Macmillan, 1970.
Banks, O., 'The Sociology of Education', Batsford, 3rd ed., 1976.
Bernstein, B., 'The Sociology of Education: A Brief Account', in 'Class, Codes and Control', vol. 3, Routledge & Kegan Paul, revised ed., 1977.
Bernbaum, G., 'Knowledge and Ideology in the Sociology of Education', Macmillan, 1977.
Robinson, P., 'Perspectives on the Sociology of Education', Routledge & Kegan Paul, 1981.

Entries to be found in Part 2

Alienation. Authority. Bureaucracy. Classification and framing. Class struggle. Conflict. Consensus. Cultural capital. Cultural deprivation. Deschooling. Durkheimian sociology. Ethnomethodology. Ideology. Linguistic code. Mechanical and organic soli-

darity. *'New' sociology of education. Norm, normative. Organisation. Phenomenological sociology. Positivistic sociology. Reflexive sociology. Role. Social class. Social control. Socialisation. Social mobility. Social stratification. Sociological relativism. Sociology of knowledge. Status. Structural-functionalism. Symbolic interactionism. Weberian sociology.*

Part two

List of terms

The following is a list of the terms used in the areas of education discussed in Part 1, and is designed to be most profitably read in conjunction with the chapters to which cross-reference is given

Academic Liaison Officers Academic Liaison Officers (ALOs) are a group of people established in a wide range of government offices within Great Britain whose objectives are to keep those departments in touch with research being carried out in universities and other higher education institutions, and to assist the flow of information in the other direction by helping researchers to get appropriate information from government departments. (See Part 1, ch. 7).

Accountability Accountability has only recently become a significant idea in *curriculum* development. This reflects a general reaction, much more intense in the United States than in this country, against the apparent scale of curriculum change from the 1960s to the mid-1970s. We normally associate accountability with quasi-legal practices, for example, audits to check whether resources have been used for specified purposes. But it is clearly arguable how far this general conception can or should be applied to judge the extent to which individual schools or teachers have achieved curriculum specifications. So many factors impinge upon the practicality of an intended curriculum and the effectiveness of what teachers do. They need sufficient discretion to plan and implement curricula with initiative and flexibility. The restrictive influence and side-effects of assessing schools by testing children's performance of selected abilities is well documented. Thus a particular challenge of the concept of accountability is to meet the legitimate concerns of parents, employers, tax-payers, etc. without impairing teachers' longer-term, less easily testable curriculum aims. Recent discussions suggest that an equitable but constructive system of curriculum accountability would meet two main criteria: (1) maintain a balance between assessment of curriculum products, that is, how far the outcomes of a course of study match the standards which could be reasonably expected, and consideration of curricular processes, what actually happens in particular contexts; (2) be conducted in a way that ensures that the results are meaningful to a lay audience but defensible by professional interests against tendencies to oversimplification. In short, pressures to monitor the curriculum serve to reinforce the need for sensitive mediation between interest groups which results in useful diagnoses rather than narrow prescription. See also: *curriculum control, evaluation, implementation.*

Further reading

Becher, T., Erant, M. and Knight, J., 'Policies for Educational Accountability', Heinemann, 1981.

Sockett, H., 'Accountability in the English Educational System', Hodder & Stoughton, 1980.

Harlen, W. (ed.), 'Evaluation and the Teacher's Role', Macmillan, 1978. (See Part 1, ch. 4)

Accountancy This section describes the major professional institutions and associations.

Institute of Chartered Accountants in England and Wales: Fellowship is awarded only on the basis of educational requirements to the satisfaction of the Council. Associate status is granted to people who have successfully completed their training and who have passed the Institute's professional examinations. All entrants must have a training contract with a practising Chartered Accountant who is authorised to train. Graduates follow a 3-year programme and non-graduates, after a 9-month foundation course, a 4-year programme. The Council approves various colleges for the foundation course. Successful completion gives exemption from the foundation examination. Non-graduates need to be educated to degree entry level. Location: Chartered Accountants' Hall, Moorgate Place, London EC2P 2BJ; 01–628 7060.

The Institute of Chartered Accountants of Scotland, 27 Queen Street, Edinburgh EH2 1LA, 031–225 3687, has similar requirements.

The Association of Certified Accountants is incorporated by Royal Charter. Entry is based upon a combination of professional examinations and practical experience. Generally, candidates must be educated to at least two A–levels (or equivalent). Successful completion leads to Associate, and re-grading to Fellow depends upon service as an accountant, either with this body or another approved body. Location: 22 Bedford Square, London WC1B 3HS; 01–636 2103/9.

The Institute of Cost and Management Accountants has a structure of qualifications requiring examination success and experience. Only registered students may submit and registration requires five GCE passes including two at A–level (or equivalent). Associates must have passed examinations, be at least 21 years old and have had three years' practical experience. Fellowship is granted to those who have passed the examinations, are at least 26 years old and have had at least three years' practical experience. Location: 63 Portland Place, London W1N 4AB; 01–637 4716.

Other accountancy bodies include:

The Chartered Institute of Public Finance and Accountancy, 1 Buckingham Place, London SW1E 6HS; 01–828 7661.

The British Association of Accountants and Auditors Limited, Stamford House, 2/4 Chiswick High Road, London W4 1SE; 01–994 3477.

Institute of Accounting Staff, 29 Bedford Square, London WC1B 3HS; 01–636 2103/9. (For accounting technicians. Under auspices of the Association of Certified Accountants.) (See Part 1, ch. 2)

Achievement motivation Some individuals have a high level of motivation to achieve. They have a preference for moderately difficult tasks, prefer to take moderate risks in tasks involving skill and ability, have a high level of self-confidence and are prepared to defer their gratifications. The origins of a high level of achievement motivation are to be found in early independence training.

Further reading

McClelland, D. C. et al., 'The Achievement Motive', 2nd ed., Harvester Press, 1976. (See Part 1, ch. 14)

Achievement/task analysis Ryle pointed out that some processes use different words to point to their task and achievement aspects. Thus 'treat' points to the task, and 'cure' to the achievement. Some words, however, have only one word to cover both task and achievement aspects of the process; e.g. 'teach', 'educator'.

Further reading

Ryle, G., 'The Concept of Mind', Hutchinson, 1949.

Scheffler, I., 'The Language of Education', Blackwell (US edition, 1960). (See Part 1, ch. 13)

Action-centred leadership An approach to leadership training developed by John Adair, based on identifying and managing the needs the leader must satisfy if he is to lead others successfully. The three needs are: the task, or the need to achieve; the group, or the need to co-operate with others to achieve the task; and the individual, or the satisfaction of individual physical and psychological needs. (See Part 1, ch. 12)

Activity learning This is a general term used to describe those learning methods that use active participation. It includes field studies, *incident method, case studies, simulations, role-playing*, and group projects. All these are essentially parts of *learner-controlled training* methods. (See Part 1, ch. 12)

Administration This is usually taken to mean those functions in organisations that deal with the collecting, editing, storing and retrieval of information. Most managerial and supervisory jobs include administrative duties. Education and training in administration is a part or whole of many business and management courses. (See Part 1, ch. 2)

Admission to schools The 1944 Act enunciated the general principle that children were to be educated in accordance with the wishes of their parents, where this was compatible with efficiency and the avoidance of unreasonable public expenditure.

The 1980 Act supplemented this by giving parents the right to express a preference for a particular school (excluding *nursery* and *special* schools). LEAs and Governors must meet this preference unless it would prejudice the provision of efficient education or the efficient use of resources, be incompatible with the arrangements for admission made between the LEA and the Governors of a voluntary aided school, or unless in a selective school the child has not met the requirements as to ability and aptitude. LEAs and Governors of aided schools are required to publish rules governing admission to schools, information about the schools themselves, and arrangements for expressing a preference and for appealing. The LEA (or governing body of an aided school) is required to set up an appeals committee with an independent chairman. No person who was a party to the original decision may serve on an appeals committee. This procedure does not preclude either the right of general appeal to the Secretary of State, or to the Ombudsman where maladministration is alleged. (See Part 1, ch. 1)

Adult education This is a term which refers largely to non-vocational courses offered by LEAs, the *Workers Educational Association* and the extra-mural departments of certain universities. The courses are usually recreational in nature, but some examination and skills courses are also included. They are normally held in LEA premises such as schools, but there are some residential colleges and purpose-built centres. (See Part 1, ch. 1)

Advisory Council for Adult and Continuing Education Following the recommendations of the Russell Report on Adult Education 1973 and the Venables Report on Continuing Education 1976, the Council was established by the Secretary of State for Education and Science in 1977. The Council's function and terms of reference are to advise generally on matters relevant to the provision of education for adults in England and Wales, and in particular (a) to promote co-operation between the various bodies engaged in adult education and review current practice, organisation and priorities, with a view to the most effective deployment of the available resources; and (b) to promote the development of future policies and priorities, with full regard to the concept of education as a process continuing throughout life. (See Part 1, ch. 7)

Aesthetics Choices within *education* rest upon a series of value-judgments. Many choices are made on the grounds of 'usefulness'. Many other choices are made upon the assumption that certain types of art, music or literature are 'better' than others. Books of literary criticism, art theory and music describe and explain how these choices are made. The philosopher might want to ask a further question; that is, how can these canons of criticism themselves be justified? Nothing changes more rapidly than fashions in art and literature, and what is regarded as 'good' in one period is considered to be of 'bad taste' in another.

Providing one subscribes to ideals such as those of *Plato*, that there was a 'form' of beauty, that beauty itself existed, then art might be said to be those works which contained this form. But in many ways, the criticism made by David Hume has proved to be unassailable. He suggested that there is no beauty within objects. It is merely that particular objects give rise to feelings of pleasure. When we experience this feeling we say the object is 'beautiful'. But, he insisted, it is not that a feeling of pleasure accompanies the apprehension of beauty. The pleasure is the beauty. The consequences of this line of thought is 'subjectivism', in the assumption that when we are speaking of 'beauty' or 'good taste' we are talking about our own feelings. If this were really the case, it is difficult to see how criticism could attain the standards of *objectivity* it has attained.

In 'Language, Truth and Logic', Ayer suggests that terms such as 'beautiful' or 'good' are *prescriptive* and are not descriptive. That is, we are commending certain books or works of art. But, of course, the central problem remains: on what grounds are these being prescribed or commended? See also: *ethics, positivism, verification.*

Further reading

Hospers, J., 'Introduction to Philosophical Analysis', 2nd ed., Routledge & Kegan Paul, 1967.

Saw, Ruth, L., 'Aesthetics', Macmillan, 1972. (See Part 1, ch. 13)

Scruton, Roger, 'Aesthetics of Architecture', Methuen, 1979.

Age-earnings profiles Age-earnings profiles show the relationship between age and average earnings of workers throughout their working life. If the age-earnings profiles of highly-educated workers are compared with the age-earnings profiles of workers with less education, it is seen that the highly-educated earn more throughout their working lives. The additional lifetime earnings of educated workers are used in *cost-benefit analysis*, as a measure of the direct economic benefits of education. (See Part 1, ch. 5)

Agricultural extension Refers to those projects which anticipate the development of all community services, including education, through the promotion of agricultural development. (See Part 1, ch. 3)

Aims A general statement of intent, used as a basis for the development of a national school system or for an individual school's curriculum. The statement is too general to enable measurements of effectiveness to take place. Aims are often associated with more specific statements which enable clearer focusing. See also: *objectives.* (See Part 1, ch. 8)

Discussion concerning the aims of *education* was the traditional occupation of educationalists. Education was thought of as a process geared to a particular end or process. Thus a religious institute would think that the purpose of its educational endeavours was to 'bring men to God'. Thomas *Arnold* believed that its purpose was to 'produce Christian gentlemen'. *Plato* constructed his educational system in order to produce the 'just state'. In a recent book, O'Connor suggests five educational aims:

1 to provide children with the minimum skills necessary to take their place in society;
2 to give them some degree of vocational training;
3 to awaken a taste for knowledge;
4 to develop their critical powers; and

5 to enable them to appreciate their cultural and moral heritage.

The implication of O'Connor's list is clear; should any of these aims be rejected, then the educational system would be defective. The very fact that the system is concerned with 'education' lays certain demands upon it.

Peters has argued that the aims of education are not extrinsic but *intrinsic*; that being concerned with 'education' and not with 'training' or 'instructing' lays certain demands on the educator. The notion of education has certain aims and requirements written into it. If these processes are not carried out, then 'education' is not carried out either. Nonetheless, rapprochement between the intrinsic and extrinsic can be made. It is important that the demands of education should be met in order to fulfil the requirements of society, etc.

Further reading

Hirst, P. H., 'Knowledge and the Curriculum', Routledge & Kegan Paul, 1974.

Peters, R. S., 'Ethics and Education', Allen & Unwin, 1966.

O'Connor, D. J., 'An Introduction to the Philosophy of Education', Routledge & Kegan Paul, 1957. (See Part 1, ch. 13)

Alienation Alienation is a term that has been employed by many dissimilar thinkers in different fields, but its dominant use in the sociology of education is as a Marxian concept. Some Marxian theorists, it is true, reject the concept as one with no place in Marx's mature thought, but in the *'new' sociology of education* it is defended, and linked closely with the dehumanisation of knowledge.

A condition of alienation is one in which human self-fulfilment is not achievable, a condition in which human beings are actually dehumanised. Marx associates this condition with relations of material production which are orientated to something other than the satisfaction of human needs. His claim is that the *class struggle* is the ultimate source of alienation, and that the achievement of a classless society – and that alone – will bring an end to it. What has to be realised is that there is something basically wrong with the human condition because there is something wrong with the underlying structure of society.

One of the criticisms of the initial stance taken in the *'new' sociology of education* that has been voiced by those of its proponents calling for a reconceptualisation of it is that its attempt to link a phenomenological and a Marxian perspective led it at times to view alienation as a condition that could be remedied simply through a change of consciousness on the part of teachers and pupils. In 'Marxism and Education' (1978), Madan Sarup discusses alienation and schooling in the context of an extensive analysis of the 'new' sociology of education's position with regard to the relationship between *phenomenological sociology* and Marxian theory.

Further reading

Ollman, B., 'Alienation', Cambridge University Press, 1971.

Sarup, M., 'Marxism and Education', Routledge & Kegan Paul, 1978. (See Part 1, ch. 15)

Alpha-coefficient A term used to describe the proportion of the extra lifetime earnings of educated workers which is directly attributable to their education. In *cost-benefit analysis* it is necessary to multiply the earnings differentials of highly-educated workers by this coefficient, to allow for the fact that the higher earnings of the educated reflect factors such as ability or social class, as well as their higher levels of education. Most cost-benefit studies assume values of the alpha-coefficient that vary between 0.5 and 0.8. This means that 50 to 80 per cent of the extra earnings of graduates, compared with school-leavers, are assumed to be the result of higher education, and the remainder are assumed to be due to ability and other factors. (See Part 1, ch. 5)

Analysis of data The data to be analysed may have been collected using, for example, *aptitude* or *attainment* tests, or other instruments which give quantitative *data*. Data from different instruments may be compared in a variety of ways. Comparisons between scores on different instruments can be done by *correlation*. When a large number of factors are taken into account a more complex comparison is carried out; this is called *factor analysis*. Other useful information may be about small groups of the sample who exhibit similar grouped characteristics (e.g., high on ability, low on creativity, convergent personality, hard-working). In order to investigate this cluster a method called *cluster analysis* is used.

Researchers wishing to use statistical analytical techniques will find these available on computers at regional centres (e.g., universities in the UK) as standard programmes.

Different kinds of data require different techniques. For example, the result from an intelligence test which may have been derived by using a *normal distribution* and a set of equally weighted questions would require the use of *parametric statistics*, whilst a series of statements which are given numbers to identify them would require *non-parametric statistics*.

Data are usually collected from a *sample* of the total *population*. An example might be a sample of 16-year-olds: this sample should represent, as far as possible, the population of 16-year-olds. The selection of the sample would include relevant data for the study (for example, sex, socio-economic group, ability, etc.).

Further reading
Seigel, S., 'Non-Parametric Statistics for the Behavioural Sciences', McGraw-Hill, 1956.
Popham, W. J. and Sirotnik, K. A., 'Educational Statistics', Harper & Row, 1973. (See Part 1, ch. 8)

Analytic statement Analytic statements are true or false by virtue of their *meaning* and not by reference to states of affairs. In such statements the predicate restates, implicitly or explicitly, what has been stated in the subject. The classic example is 'bachelors are unmarried men'. The whole notion of analyticity has been criticised by Quine.

Further reading
Hamlyn, D. W., 'Theory of Knowledge', Macmillan, 1971.
Hospers, J., 'Introduction to Philosophical Analysis', 2nd ed., Routledge & Kegan Paul, 1967.
Quine, W. V. O., 'From a Logical Point of View', Harvard University Press, 1953.
Strawson, P. F. (ed.), 'Philosophical Logic', Oxford University Press, 1967. (See Part 1, ch. 13)

A posteriori judgment A proposition which can be known only by an appeal to experience. Such statements are therefore contrasted with the *analytic* and the *a priori*. The predicate of the statement provides further information about the subject, but this is obtained only by experience. An a posteriori proposition would also be *contingent*.

Further reading

Hamlyn, D. W., 'Theory of Knowledge', Macmillan, 1971.

Hospers, J., 'Introduction to Philosophical Analysis', Routledge & Kegan Paul, 1976. (See Part 1, ch. 13)

Appraisal There can be few major organisations in the UK today that do not use some method of appraising managers. The three main purposes are usually seen as: assessing potential; assessing past performance; and assessing training needs. In most organisations, appraisal is regarded as part of the total management development process.

Most appraisal systems are increasingly job results-oriented, although there has been a movement away from the form-ridden *management by objectives (MbO)*, approach of the late 1960s. *Personality* rating schemes are much less common. In most organisations managers are asked to assess past performance, usually by replying to set questions with a narrative. Emphasis is placed on analysing performance achievements against targets. Some schemes are for an assessment of strengths and weaknesses in such things as job knowledge, leadership and so on, but the realisation that this is generally unhelpful has meant much less of this kind of analysis.

There is some move to self-appraisal or *self-assessment*, and it is likely that this will accelerate as part of the general trend towards *self-development*. It has been reported by J. D. Mitchell that an individual's self-assessment of his potential was the most accurate as judged by later events. M. R. Williams in 'Performance Appraisal in Management' reported that the traditional boss-subordinate appraisal, on his analysis, had the following: 56 per cent made no reference to performance failures, shortfalls or weaknesses; 49 per cent mentioned positive personal qualities (as, 'gets on well with people', for example) but no statements of specific achievements; only 7 per cent contained concise statements of strengths and work behaviour contributing to achievement and effective performance. Research into *counselling* interviews, allegedly an integral part of most appraisal schemes, suggests an equally depressing picture.

Organisations need therefore, through their specialists, to ask two key questions. If managers seem as reluctant to carry out appraisals effectively, why bother at all? If there are good reasons for having appraisals, what are the most effective ways of having them carried out?

Further reading

Farnsworth, T., 'Management Development – developing a policy', in 'Industrial and Commercial Training', November 1970.

Lusher, B. T., 'Training the Experience Manager', in 'Industrial and Commercial Training', December 1972.

Randell, G., 'Staff Appraisal', British Institute of Management, 1974. (See Part 1, ch. 12)

Appreciation training This refers to short courses designed to give a generalised understanding of a topic or a subject area sufficient to enable the trainee to manage the activities of specialists. For example, senior managers often need an appreciation of finance and accounting but not specialised practitioner-level knowledge. (See Part 1, ch. 12)

Apprenticeship Most skilled craftsmen in industry have been trained under apprenticeship schemes. A craftsman has been defined in 'Glossary of Training Terms' (HMSO, 1967) as a 'skilled worker in a particular occupation, trade or craft who is able to apply a wide range of skills and a high degree of knowledge to basically non-repetitive work with a minimum of direction and supervision'. In industry, the word craft has no particular meaning. Skilled craftsman is the more usual description of a time-served trained worker.

Formal apprenticeships were first regulated and recognised by the 1563 Statute of Artificers. The traditional learning pattern was a master-pupil relationship; and it remained largely unaltered until the 1960s, an indication either of its effectiveness or of the reluctance of craft guilds and later skilled trade unions to change. Some apprenticeship schemes, particularly in enlightened firms, were first class; the majority were not. Largely as a result of the Industrial Training Act 1964 (itself a product of dissatisfaction in the main with skilled-worker training) there have been major changes in apprenticeships. The revolution has not been as great as many hoped and possibly more than some trade unions wished, but nevertheless most apprentices do now receive a thorough, systematic training in their chosen craft. Too many are still unskilled, and there are still considerable inflexibilities.

The government has announced its intention of seeking further reforms in apprenticeship arrangements through the 'New Training Initiative'. Most apprenticeships now comply with eight principles. Training tries to be flexible so as to inculcate good attitudes to technical change. The length of training is adjusted to the subject to be taught and to individual learning speed. Standards are recognised and certified. Assessment is by tests, training records and individual logbooks. Apprentices have opportunities for development beyond their initial acquisition of skills. Instructors are trained. Release on full pay for further education is standard, together with *further education* after the end of apprenticeship. The status of qualified people is ensured by these principles.

By and large, this is so. No doubt many apprentices still have experience of periods of under-employment and boredom, but most now receive a thorough and sound grounding upon which they can build a career. (See Part 1, ch. 11).

A priori knowledge *Knowledge* can be known prior to or without appeal to experience. An empiricist would maintain that such knowledge was derived solely from an understanding of the concepts involved and was therefore analytic. Mathematical knowledge would be considered knowledge of this kind.

Further reading

Hamlyn, D. W., 'Theory of Knowledge', Macmillan, 1971.

Hospers, J., 'Introduction to Philosophical Analysis', 2nd ed., Routledge & Kegan Paul, 1967.

Quine, W. V. O., 'From a Logical Point of View', Harvard University Press, 1953. (See Part 1, ch. 13)

Aptitude Aptitude is used to refer to potential rather than *attainment*. Special abilities such as, say, mathematical or sporting prowess are often referred to as aptitudes. Specialised areas of performance may also be referred to as aptitude. Measurement of aptitude is attractive because it enables identification of people with special abilities. (See Part 1, ch. 8)

An aptitude is a potential for acquiring certain skills or knowledge. As such it is used in a far more specific way than *intelligence*. It also covers areas not included under the umbrella called 'intelligence'. Thus we can have a mechanical aptitude *test* which attempts to measure the potential for learning skills in mechanics. (See Part 1, ch. 6)

Area studies Since area studies are generally national studies, it has been argued that they are not strictly comparative. Noah and Eckstein, for example, wrote that comparative study is one which utilises the social sciences, education and the cross-national study. The area study is one often employed by comparativists, and a number of points may be made in its favour:

(a) The researcher can practise economy of study since he has to focus only on one culture, one country and one set of documents.

(b) It may be as academically rigorous as any other type of comparative study since considerable skill is needed in determining the bases and sources of relevant data, in selecting and ordering those data and in interpreting the information gathered.

(c) It serves as an introductory topic on comparative education courses.

Students are given an opportunity to become familiar with the processes and principles of an educational system other than their own despite the claim that no true understanding of foreign educational systems is really possible without a knowledge of the language of the country concerned, and allowance made for cultural bias.

A variation of the area study is the *intra-regional study*.

Further reading

Bereday, G. Z. F., 'Comparative Method in Education', ch. 1, Holt, Rinehart & Winston, 1964.

Bristow, T. and Holmes, B., 'Comparative Education through the Literature', ch. 1, Butterworth 1966. (See Part 1, ch. 3)

Arnold, Thomas (1795–1842) As headmaster of Rugby School, 1828–42, he widened the school's curriculum by introducing mathematics and French. His reputation as a great reforming headmaster owes something to such fortuitous events as the publication of the somewhat adulatory 'The Life and Correspondence of Thomas Arnold' (1845) by Dean Stanley, the popularity of T. Hughes, 'Tom Brown's Schooldays', first published in 1856, the loyalty of a group of distinguished Old Boys at Oxford, and the development of Rugby football at his school.

Further reading

Bamford, T. W., 'Thomas Arnold', Cresset Press, 1960. (See Part 1, ch. 10)

Assessment centre In an assessment centre, individuals are assessed by a group of trained assessors using a variety of methods, such as *management games, simulations*, group discussions, and so on. This is an attempt to avoid or minimise the effects of subjectivity in individual appraisal systems. Face validity is high and it is suggested that it achieves better results than other methods. However, such centres are so expensive to organise and operate that few organisations are using them. (See Part 1, ch. 12)

Assessment of Performance Unit (APU) As a result of the government, professional, and public concern for the improvement of education, a unit has been set up by the DES with the objective of promoting the development of methods of assessing and monitoring the achievement of children at school. In addition to the unit's own work, a number of subject steering groups have been established as monitoring groups. Through this organisation it is hoped to identify the incidence of under-achievement of pupils in schools. (See Part 1, ch. 7.)

Assisted places scheme This is a scheme started in 1981 to assist parents of academically able children to pay for an *independent school* education for their children. Some 5,000 or more places were made available at certain independent schools and central Government provided financial assistance with the tuition fees in scale with parental means. Arrangements for admission, normally at the age of 11 or 13, are the responsibility of the schools themselves, but admission to a sixth form place on transfer from a maintained school normally needs the approval of the Local Education Authority. (See Part 1, ch. 1)

Association for Educational and Training Technology (AETT) Formerly the Association for Programmed Learning and Educational Technology, AETT is a voluntary body which brings together educational technologists. Each year the Association publishes 'Aspects of Educational Technology', the proceedings of the annual international conference. The journal of the association 'Programmed Learning and Educational Technology' appears four times a year. A world-wide directory of educational technology information, the 'International Yearbook of Educational and Instructional Technology' is also published. (see Part 1, ch. 7)

Association of Chief Officers of Area Boards for Education and Libraries, Association of Directors of Education in Scotland These provide for senior professionals in the respective countries that locus of contact and exchange that is essential for the professional standing and development that is essential for this level of staff. (See Part 1, ch. 7)

Association of Education Officers Also representing the interests of education officers, this association shares members in common with the *Society of Education Officers* and receives representatives from both the County Education Authorities and the Metropolitan Authorities. (See Part 1, ch. 7)

Association of Northern Ireland Education and Library Boards The boards responsible to the Department of Education for Northern Ireland maintain professional contact between their officers through the Association, thus providing for Northern Ireland an organisation similar to that of the *Council of Local Education Authorities*. (See Part 1, ch. 7)

Attainment Attainment has a meaning in everyday language which includes the concepts of both complete and irreversible attainment. Thus one can completely attain one's goal of sailing the Atlantic single-handed and, once carried out, there is no way that this attainment can be taken away. In education the word lacks both these concepts. Even a professor in mathematics has not completely attained mastery of the 'four rules', since even he would not be surprised if he made an occasional mistake. Likewise, someone's attainment in an area such as computation may decline on successive occasions.

This may help to clarify the difference between general usage and educational usage. The educational usage is based on describing a level on a *scale* for a certain attribute. The scale itself, however, has no true zero and no definable top level. The concept of such a scale can be implied in everyday usage but, as in the example above concerning sailing the Atlantic, it can also be dispensed with altogether.

There is also a difference between attainment measures and *psychological measurements*. This distinction hinges on the difference between attributes which claim to have explanatory value and those which have descriptive value. Psychological measures claim to explain behaviour because they measure attributes which underlie the behaviours themselves. Thus extraversion or *intelligence* are underlying attributes which are expressed in a variety of situations. Attainment measures on the other hand describe what behaviours a person has learned to perform. No underlying attribute is implied. Thus although 'intelligence' is supposed to have an important influence on attainment levels it is quite possible for an intelligent and an unintelligent person to have the same attainment. The attainment measure merely describes what skills or behaviours the person being measured has learned. The emphasis in attainment is on the level of skill a person has achieved through learning rather than his potential for achieving certain levels.

Further reading

Stodola, Q. and Stordahl, K., 'Basic Educational Tests and Measurement', Science Research Associates, 1967. (See Part 1, ch. 6)

Attention and perception At any one moment the number of sensations produced by environmental stimuli upon the numerous sense receptors of the body is vast. Attention is the term used to describe the ability to select, either on a voluntary or involuntary basis, some incoming stimuli to process, whilst ignoring others. Once a stimulus has been received in the sensory memory and has passed through to attention in the *short-term memory* it will then be processed in the *long-term memory*. Here it will be analysed using the framework of concepts which are the result of previous learning. This internal analysis of the sensations which have come from the environment is the process known as perception.

A number of factors both external and internal have been shown to influence the likelihood of stimuli going forward into attention. Amongst the external factors intense, novel and variable stimuli are more likely, other things being equal, to go forward into attention. Regular stimuli, such as the ticking of a clock, will come to be ignored. Some colours and sounds are more likely to get into attention than others. For example, a red and white design will receive greater attention than the same design in black and white, and high notes get into attention more easily than low notes. An individual may have a predisposition to attend to certain stimuli such as his own name. Internal factors which may affect attention, and hence what is subsequently perceived, include the individual's level of interest, his *motivation*, his level of physiological arousal and aspects of his *personality*. See also *language and thought; brain and behaviour; learning, retention and recall; cognitive style; sensory memory.*

Further reading

Broadbent, D. E., 'Perception and Communication', Pergamon, 1958.

Gregory, R. L., 'Eye and Brain: the Psychology of Seeing,' Weidenfeld & Nicolson, 3rd ed., 1977.

Vernon, M. D., 'The Psychology of Perception', Penguin, 1962. (See Part 1, ch. 14)

Attitude Attitudes are habitual ways of reacting to situations. In education they are considered very important since they affect the learning process. Attempts to measure attitudes usually involve *questionnaires*, where the person indicates his or her strength of feeling towards or against a number of statements. (See Part 1, ch. 6)

Attitude/knowledge/skills The attitude to perform (to want to perform), the knowledge upon which that attitude is based (to know what is required to want to perform) and the skills necessary to perform are essential for the achievement of competence in any job. Trainers need to understand how to identify them and how to inculcate them. (See Part 1, ch. 11)

Attitude scale Attitude scales attempt to measure learners' attitudes to key areas of the learning environment (for example, attitude to science, interest in school work, conforming, non-conforming). The difference between attitude scales and personality scales is that the former tend to be more specific rather than general. For attitude scales it is easier to define what is to be measured, which in turn limits their range of usefulness. Some general attitude scales are available (e.g., on attitudes to teachers, test anxiety), but usually a special scale has to be developed.

A variety of strategies is available for the development of attitude scales. The strategies include statistical procedures. The construction consists of writing a series of statements relating to the selected area which has been defined. The person who is responding to the statements is required to agree or disagree. Sometimes a scale of agreement and disagreement is used as in the *Likert scale*, or a set of about 25 statements is selected from a larger bank on the basis of their performance with a *sample* of the population as in the *Thurstone scale*. When scales have been developed and used, national agencies (for example, the National Foundation for Educational Research in the United Kingdom) quite often make them more widely available.

Not all scales are of the two types mentioned. Some use simple check lists (a list of statements on which students tick items that apply). From the student's selection deductions can be made about his attitudes. Another method is to use *semantic differentials*.

Further reading

Vernon, P.E., 'Intelligence and Attainment Tests', University of London Press (in particular ch. 9), (London) 1960.

Buros, O.K., 'Mental Measurement Yearbook' (7th Issue), Gryphon Press 1972. (This Yearbook appears at intervals, the first being published in 1938.) (See Part 1, ch. 8)

Audio aids These are those aids to effective training that use technology to communicate through the sense of hearing. The main instruments are record players, tape recorders/players, cassette recorders/players, and radios, but good use can be made of telephones, walkie-talkies, sound signal generators, and so on. The technology available is advancing rapidly. (See Part 1, ch. 11)

Audio tape recorder Audio tape or audio cassette recorders can be used to record and play back speech, sounds and music. Cassette recorders in particular can be obtained very cheaply and constitute a most flexible tool for education. They can be used simply to replay recorded lectures, or can be used in conjunction with printed materials or 35mm slides (*tape/slide*) to form carefully planned and integrated sequences of instruction which can be used by the individual pupil. (See Part 1, ch. 9)

Audio-tutorial The Postlethwait audio-tutorial method began in 1961 at Purdue University as an attempt to make some adjustment for the diversity of background of students in a first-year botany course. Taped material was related to textbook material, practical work and a laboratory manual. There were three main types of session:

1 A General Assembly Session (1 hour/week) for administration, visiting lecturers and personal contact with the instructor.
2 Independent Study Sessions where the taped material, practical work, etc. were used individually by the student (4 hours/week).
3 An Integrated Quiz Session (1 hour/week), small group sessions with an instructor.

Further reading
Postlethwait, S. N., Novak, J. and Murray, H., 'An Audio-Tutorial Approach to Learning', Burgess 1971, (See Part 1, ch. 9)

Audio-visual aids These are those aids which use the senses of both sight and hearing. It has been shown that training with these two sensory inputs achieves high effectiveness. There is a large variety of means available, including sound film, film-strip, tape/slides, broadcast television, closed-circuit television (CCTV), video recording, and so on. A recent development with enormous potential is the microprocessor, used in computer-assisted learning/training. (See Part 1, ch. 11)

Audio-visual media Whatever we learn, think about, or tell others must have originally come to us via one of our senses: sight, hearing, touch, smell or taste. Although it is possible to expose a student to real educational experiences, to show him actual objects, it is often more convenient to expose him to a representation of reality. A variety of such representations exists, including models and pictures of the real thing, descriptions both written and spoken. These representations make use mainly of the senses of sight and sound.

There is a variety of different visual, audio, and audio-visual media which can be used in education. These include simple display devices like blackboards and posters, overhead projectors, *slide* projectors and combinations like *tape/slide* equipment, sound *film* and *television* and video recordings.

Three types are often particularly used in education: the overhead projector, the 35mm slide projector and the audio cassette recorder. The overhead projector permits pre-prepared transparencies to be shown on a large screen but also offers the flexibility of the blackboard in enabling diagrams, etc. to be built up on the spot using a variety of coloured overhead projector pens or wax pencils. The 35mm slide projector can project large clear coloured representations of material prepared beforehand. The audio-cassette recorder can be used either to make audio recordings on the spot for immediate playback or to play pre-recorded material.

Radio programmes have been produced for schools for a long time; but an increasing use in schools, universities and colleges is being made of the *videotape recorder* which, when used in conjunction with a television receiver, can be used to record and play back 'off-air' *television* broadcast material, or when used in conjunction with a television camera can be used for the recording and immediate playback of local material. (See Part 1, ch. 9)

Authority Although Durkheim elaborates a concept of authority that is of obvious relevance for the educationist (see *Durkheimian sociology*), it is Weber's concept of authority that has been the more influential in the sociology of education.

Weber is concerned with the conditions under which rules become accepted as legitimate by those who are called upon to obey them. He views as sociologically significant the fact that it is only where a legitimate right to issue commands is seen to exist that there is any form of authority as distinct from sheer domination. Weber distinguishes three kinds of authority: legal, traditional and charismatic. Legal or, as it is often called, legal-rational authority rests on the acceptance of commands as legitimate in so far as they accord with explicit rules formally acknowledged to apply in the circumstances. Traditional authority rests on a belief in the sanctity of tradition.

Charismatic authority rests on the ability of an individual person to inspire devotion and allegiance by virtue of his exceptional qualities.

Various mixtures of these kinds of authority can be found, but modern society, Weber maintains, has come more and more to be organised on the basis of legal authority. Associated with this development has been the development of *bureaucracy*. For an extensive analysis of schooling in which the concepts of authority and of bureaucracy are central, see Frank Musgrove, 'Patterns of Power and Authority in English Education' (1971).

Further reading

Weber, M., 'The Theory of Social and Economic Organisation', Oxford University Press, 1947.

Musgrove, F., 'Patterns of Power and Authority in English Education', Methuen, 1971. (See Part 1, ch. 15)

Autism The autistic child appears to have a disability in interpreting sensory information, especially auditory and visual, that reaches him from the environment. He lacks the ability to symbolise and has great difficulty in acquiring language. Contact between the child and others is lacking. Excessive and persistent movement is typical.

Further reading

Furneaux, B., 'The Special Child', Penguin, 1969. (See Part 1, ch. 14)

Automated programmed instruction This is usually taken to mean *programmed instruction* by means of a teaching machine or, more latterly, an interactive computer (as in *computer-aided learning*) with minimal or no human intervention. The learning is carefully structured. A further development is integrated programme instruction which uses a variety of methods including automatic programme instruction. (See Part 1, ch. 11)

Autonomy Autonomy has some appeal as an aim of *education* because it emphasises the importance placed upon the development of the individual. A suitable end of this 'development' is the attainment of autonomy. However, it is not at all easy to ascertain what is meant by 'autonomy'.

Dearden suggests that 'a person is autonomous to the degree that what he thinks and does, at least in important areas of life, is determined by himself'. Decisions and actions come about in accordance with his 'own activity of mind'. But Dearden, aware of the inadequacy of this, warns that 'without morality . . . the more autonomous a person is, the worse he is likely to be'.

The term 'autonomy' has echoes of Kant; but for Kant the significant point of autonomy lay in the ability to act in accordance with a moral law which one had oneself formulated. The more recent versions lay emphasis upon 'acting independently'. It is this aspect which raises doubts about the desirability or adequacy of the *aim*. The notion suggests and fosters an erroneous view of the way in which an individual makes decisions within society. Most individuals act as members of committees or groups and have to learn to behave not autonomously but in a spirit of compromise and consensus.

Further reading

Dearden, R. F., 'The Philosophy of Primary Education', Routledge & Kegan Paul, 1968.

White, J., 'Towards a Compulsory Curriculum', Routledge & Kegan Paul, 1973. (See Part 1, ch. 13)

Average cost The average or unit cost of education is the total expenditure or cost divided by the number of students or pupils. In some cases it is more appropriate to calculate the cost per pupil-hour, or the cost per graduate, but in every case, the unit cost is derived from the total cost by dividing it by the total number of units. The average cost is not necessarily the same as the *marginal cost*. (See Part 1, ch. 5)

Banding This is the grouping together of a number of classes which follow a similar curriculum in a secondary school. Pupils can be 'setted' for various subjects within the band. (See Part 1, ch. 1)

Bank 'Bank' or 'banking' is used in educational measurement to mean collections of questions or *items* which can be used to construct *tests* or examinations. There is a trend for the term to be used increasingly to mean collections where the items have been calibrated (*calibration*). Collections of uncalibrated items are then known as item pools. (See Part 1, ch. 6)

Banking This large service industry includes the clearing, merchant, commercial and private banks. The majority of banks have highly developed training programmes, dealing not only with the specialised techniques of the industry but also with general job-related skills, such as people management. In addition, there are two major professional institutions in the UK.

The Institute of Bankers provides examinable qualifications with the following entry levels. Stage 1: new entrants with 4 or more O–levels (which must include English) take an Ordinary *National Certificate* in *Business Studies* by *day release*. Entrants with A–levels take a one-year conversion course. Stage 2: graduates and those who successfully complete Stage 1 can take Section A either through the Institute's examinations or through an approved Higher *National Certificate* in Business Studies Course. Section B is set by the Institute. Successful completion of the programme leads to the Diploma in Banking and Associate membership of the Institute (AIB). The Institute also runs a Trustee Diploma and a higher-level qualification, the Financial Studies Diploma.

Anyone employed in banking can become an ordinary member of the Institute. Non-bankers can take the examinations but are not eligible for membership. Fellows are elected from Associates of managerial status.

The Institute of Bankers in Scotland runs a Diploma programme. There are two membership grades: Associate and Fellow.

Several universities offer degree courses that include subjects approved for exemption to the Institute. It is also possible to study by research for higher degrees in Banking and Finance. All these courses have applications to sectors other than banking, such as public finance and economics generally. Further information is available from: The Institute of Bankers, 10 Lombard Street, London EC3 V9AS; 01–523 3531; The Institute of Bankers in Scotland, 20 Rutland Square, Edinburgh EH1 2DE; 031–229 9896. (See Part 1, ch. 2)

Battery When a number of *tests* are presented together and normed on the same *population* the collection is called a test battery. (See Part 1, ch. 6)

Behavioural studies/sciences This is the general heading for all those disciplines that deal wholly or partly with the study of the responses of organisms to an experience and/or environment. It includes ethnology, psychology, sociology and anthropology and, increasingly, economics and ecology. (See 'The Manager's Guide to the Behavioural Sciences', Industrial Society, 1979.) (See Part 1, ch. 12)

Behaviourism A major theoretical approach in psychology that has greatly influenced the discipline. It defined psychology as the study of behaviour. Its adherents have attempted to discover the general laws that describe behaviour, both human and animal, by using objective experimental methods and by relying exclusively upon unambiguous, observable data.

Further reading

Rachlin, H., 'An Introduction to Modern Behaviourism', W. H. Freeman, San Francisco, 2nd ed., 1976. (See Part 1, ch. 14)

Beloe Report 'The Report of the Committee on Secondary Schools Examinations other than the GCE' (HMSO, 1960) drew attention to the fact that schools, seeking an alternative to the General Certificate of Education, were entering pupils for a wide variety of examinations that were unsuitable for school purposes. The examinations were set by boards that did not necessarily have the needs of school candidates in mind and marked by examiners with little or no recent teaching experience. The recommendations of the report led to the setting up of the *Certificate of Secondary Education*. (See Part 1, ch. 10)

Block release This refers to educational courses arranged in full-time blocks of up to 12 weeks. Increasing use is made of this system where *modular training/education* is used. (See Part 1, ch. 2)

Bloom's taxonomy Bloom's 'Taxonomy of Educational Objectives' has had a major influence upon curriculum development. Bloom suggested that educational objectives can be classified hierarchically within three major domains. These are the cognitive domain, concerned with knowledge and its use; the affective domain, concerned with the emotional responses and values that are taught; and the psycho-motor domain, concerned with physical and manipulative skills.

Further reading

Gronlund, N. E., 'Measurement and Evaluation in Teaching', 3rd ed., Collier-Macmillan, 1976. (See Part 1, ch. 14)

Board of Governors Boards of Governors were established under the 1944 Act, but in many areas a system prevailed whereby one governing body assumed responsibility for a large number of schools. This was changed in the Education Act 1980, which lays down that every school shall have its own governing body except that – at the LEA's discretion – the sharing of a governing body by two primary schools is permissible. Other exceptions require the specific approval of the Secretary of State.

Membership of a Board of Governors of a county school is largely determined by the LEA, which decides how many members it shall have (and who they are); how many a minor authority may have (at least one on primary school boards) and whether other categories of persons and interests (school pupils, industrialists, etc) shall be represented.

In voluntary aided schools the foundation managers constitute a majority of two where the membership does not exceed 17, and three otherwise; in controlled schools they have one fifth of the places. The remaining places are filled by representatives of the LEA and other groups.

The 1980 Act made it a statutory requirement that teachers and parents be represented on a school's governing body. In schools of 300 or more pupils there are two teacher governors (otherwise only one) elected by the school's staff. In county schools the parents elect two parent governors, in voluntary schools they elect one but one of the foundation managers must also be a parent of a child at the school. Every headteacher is a governor ex officio unless he or she elects otherwise.

The Rules or Articles of Government define the powers of the LEA, of the Board and of the headteacher. They usually say; 'The LEA shall determine the general educational character of the school and its place in the local educational system. Subject to this the Governors shall have the general direction of the conduct and curriculum of the school. . . . Subject to the provisions of these articles the Headteacher shall control the internal organisation, management and discipline of the school.

In practice the *curriculum* of a school is determined by the headteacher and staff, and the influence of the governors is negligible. Perhaps their most important role had been their involvement in the appointment of teachers to their school, although practice varies between Authorities in this respect. However, the Taylor Report 1977 on the government of schools saw a more positive role for them where the curriculum of a school, and its performance generally, were concerned. Hitherto theirs has been a reserve authority exercised (if at all) only if something were amiss. (See Part 1, ch. 1)

Books Books are at present the most useful way of storing and retrieving information. They contain information in a compact form, can be skimmed for range of content or read as a whole. They can be taken up or put down, the information they contain being accessed at any point. They can be read and re-read. They are portable and convenient and need no supplementary equipment for their use. Books can be used to present introductions to a subject, as texts for the main body of a subject, as supplementary reading, for literary purposes, as well as purely for pleasure.

With the advent of new technology there are increasing possibilities in the storage and retrieval on microform and microfiche, on video discs and by computer storage devices such as floppy discs, bubble memories, etc. All of these latter require supplementary equipment to access the information, and apart from microform and microfiche all use video screen displays which do not have sufficient resolution and clarity to allow high definition images of any amount of print on the screen at any one time.

Further reading

Hills, P. J. (ed.), 'The Future of the Printed Word', Frances Pinter, 1980.
Erickson, C. W. H. and Curl, R. H., 'Non-projected Visual Media' (Ch. 4), in 'Fundamentals of Teaching with Audio-Visual Technology', 2nd ed., Collier Macmillan, 1972. (See Part 1, ch. 9)

Brain and behaviour All human behaviour and experience is ultimately under the control of the brain and the central nervous system. The sum total of all the brain processes operating together determines consciousness. The brain is so complex that it will be a long time before we have more than a very imprecise understanding of its full influence on human behaviour, but much is already known of its role in emotional behaviour, perception and memory.

The brain is made up of three concentric layers. The central core includes the medulla, which regulates breathing and bodily posture; the cerebellum, which is concerned with the co-ordination of physical activities; the thalamus, which appears to act as a relay station for incoming sensory information; the hypothalamus, which is involved in emotion as well as in maintaining the body's homeostatic processes such as water balance and blood sugar level; and the reticular activating system, which controls the individual's level of arousal. The next layer contains the limbic system. In conjunction with the hypothalamus this influences behaviour such as eating, fleeing from danger, and aggression. It is also involved in emotional behaviour and memory. The third and outermost layer is the cerebrum. This is divided into two cerebral hemispheres; the highly convoluted outer part is called the cerebral cortex. The cerebral cortex controls activities such as the discrimination of sensory information, including vision and hearing, motor control of specific parts of the body, purposeful activity, speech and the comprehension of language and other cognitive activities. In the majority of people the left-hand hemisphere is dominant in controlling verbal skills, whilst spatial skills seem to be controlled by the right hemisphere. See also: *heredity and environment, motivation, attention and perception.*

Further reading

Pribram, K. H., (ed.), 'Brain and Behaviour', 4 vols, Penguin, 1969.

Wright, D. S. et al., 'Introducing Psychology: An Experimental Approach', Penguin, 1970. (See Part 1, ch. 14)

British Association for Commercial and Industrial Education (BACIE) BACIE is a voluntary organisation with individual as well as organisational membership. A very wide range of organisations subscribe, including private and public industry, Government bodies, professional and trade associations, and trade unions. It was founded in 1919 and specialises in all aspects of vocational education and training in the UK.

Probably the most significant contribution that BACIE has made was during the discussions and consultation period that preceded the Industrial Training Act 1964. BACIE was a major pressure group for this, and through its conferences of interested parties focused a great deal of the hitherto unspoken desires of industry, commerce, government and the unions for better training in the UK. It is perhaps unfortunate that the high ideals of the period 1962–3, as epitomised by the BACIE conference reports of the time, were not reached in practice; and that what success the 1964 Act had tended to erode BACIE's position in the training field. However, BACIE continues to offer its members an excellent service, including the most comprehensive library of training documents in the country, backed up by a good information service. It is now heavily involved in the training of trainers. It is one of the major publishers of training subjects and offers a wide range of courses in training.

BACIE has recently acted as editor of a vocational 'Training Information Booklet' (published quarterly), published for the European Community by the European Centre for the Development of Vocational Training. For further information: BACIE, 16 Park Crescent, London W1N 4AP. (See Part 1, ch. 2)

British Broadcasting Corporation The BBC carries 'Education' as one of the three main responsibilities within its charter. Though there is often an educational aim in its general broadcasts, the BBC, through its educational broadcasting departments, provides programmes for all ages of pupils and students from pre-school to tertiary education and beyond that into informal adult education. To reach this wide audience the BBC broadcasts some 170 series of radio and television programmes, most of which are backed by teachers' notes and pupils' pamphlets. Though these programmes are eventually produced by writers, directors, actors and a whole host of craftsmen and technicians, the BBC has set up a number of mechanisms whereby they can receive educational guidance from the relevant sectors of education.

The *Schools Broadcasting Council* guides the BBC in programming policy for educational broadcasts throughout the UK. Representatives from the *Department of Education and Science* and the local education authority together with other professional bodies make up the Council. Because of differences of system, national interests and broadcasting provision, separate schools broadcasting councils have been set up in Scotland, Wales and

Northern Ireland. All of these are represented on the United Kingdom body. A series of programme committees gives more detailed consideration to programmes within selected age bands.

Broadcasts for continuing education are transmitted during the day alongside the schools broadcasts. Those of a wider, and perhaps less formal, educational interest are accompanied by publications. Contact with further education both formal and informal is maintained through the Continuing Education Liaison Section, which acts as a feedback mechanism to the programme producers, and more formal advice from this sector is obtained through the Continuing Education Advisory Council which, in helping to formulate policy, has two programme committees covering: Vocational Education and Training, Education/Non-Vocational Education and Training.

Open University Broadcasts are the third main sector of the BBC's direct provision of support service to education, through the transmission of radio and television broadcasts supporting the courses of the *Open University*. The number of students enrolled in the Open University has risen dramatically since the inception of this method of distance learning, and the total transmission time of OU programmes now equals that of the combined schools and further education broadcasts. (See Part 1, ch. 7)

British Correspondence Colleges, Association of 4/7 Chiswell Street, London EC1Y 4UR; 01–330 5837. This was founded in 1955 and in 1962 incorporated as a non-profit-making body. It aims to promote sound educational standards and ethical business practices, in the interests of postal tuition. It has an information and advice centre. (See Part 1, ch. 2).

British Film Institute (BFI) In addition to the many aspects of film culture that are the responsibility of the BFI, such as the setting up of Regional Film Theatres in England and Wales, the Institute is actively involved in the promotion of media education and provides direct support through the Educational Advisory Service. (See Part 1, ch. 7)

British Institute of Management (BIM) The British Institute of Management was established in 1947, as an independent, non-profit-making body. It aims to promote more efficient management and to help managers at all levels and in all management functions to be more effective. It had in 1979 more than 50,000 individual members, and support from some 12,000 subscriber organisations. These latter subscribe to the BIM foundation and are drawn from industrial and commercial companies, nationalised industries, various trade associations and federations, employers' associations, trade unions, professional institutions and associations, management consultants, various educational establishments, national and local government and the armed services.

Policy is made by the National Council, which is elected by the membership but can also co-opt. There is a Director General and a staff to carry out policy. Recently, BIM has become more active in promoting the interests of management generally and the idea of wealth generation in particular. There are seven Regional Advisory Boards, serviced by BIM Regional Managers, and over 75 branches in the major cities and towns.

Individual members are expected to commit themselves to attaining high professional management standards. Senior members are expected to help the development of the skills and professional standards of junior members. Full voting members are graded Fellow, Member and Associate Member (FMBIM, MBIM, AMBIM) depending on qualifications, experience and election, except for FMBIM, which is by invitation of the Board of Fellows,

B

for 'eminent achievement in the practice of management'. Details of membership requirements are available from BIM.

BIM publishes a monthly journal 'Management Today', a quarterly Review and Digest, and Management Reading Lists. Its other services include an excellent library, an information service on management courses, and education and training through seminars, courses and conferences.

Since there are probably 2–2½ million managers in the UK, the BIM's 50,000-plus membership can be placed in proportion. It does not however represent British management in the way that the TUC can be said to represent British employees. Most British managers' first allegiance is to their specialism and therefore their professional institution or association. For further information: BIM, Management House, Parker St, London WC2B 5PT, 01–405 3456. (See Part 1, ch. 12)

Broadcast organisations One of the major supports to education in Britain is that provided by the Broadcast organisations. The contributors to education are the *British Broadcasting Corporation*, the *independent television* companies and *local radio*. (See Part 1, ch. 7)

Bruner's strategies in concept formation Bruner found that not all individuals adopt the same strategy or plan of action, when attempting to solve problems that involve identifying the attributes of a concept. Some people use simultaneous or successive scanning strategies which involve working out and testing hypotheses based on the information given. Others use conservative focus or focus gambling strategies. These do not involve testing hypotheses; instead the individual alters one or more attribute values at a time.

Further reading

Bruner, J. S., Goodnow, J. J. and Austin, G. A., 'A Study of Thinking', Wiley, 1965. (See Part 1, ch. 14)

Bureaucracy Sociological analysis employing the concept of bureaucracy has been dominated by the thought of Max Weber, who closely interrelates the concepts of bureaucracy and of *authority*. Bureaucracy, in Weber's view, entails a hierarchy of officials in which the lowest officials are under the authority of those immediately above them, and so on upwards to the top. Each official, moreover, has a sphere of competence in which his judgments are authoritative. In the rational form of bureaucracy, appointment to office is conditional upon the possession of technical qualifications, and typically involves passing examinations; and the hierarchy offers a career whereby an individual can climb from level to level.

Weber sees any *organisation* as involving relations of authority; and for him the development of bureaucracy has been part of the rationalisation of the modern world, during the course of which the authority relations of the organisation have become increasingly based on the rational principle of technical specialisation.

Schooling can be seen both as (1) itself affording an instance of bureaucratic organisation, and as (2) taking its shape from the demands of the bureaucratic organisation of the wider society. Studies in the more traditional sociology of education have tended to conduct both kinds of analysis on Weberian lines. The *'new' sociology of education*, on the other hand, is more in sympathy with the approach of the American study by Samuel Bowles and Herbert Gintis, 'Schooling in Capitalist America' (1976). This uses both kinds of analysis together in a critical way, interpreting the concept of bureaucracy from a Marxian standpoint that sees it in terms both of the hierarchical division of labour and of *alienation*, and arguing a connection between bureaucratic organisation and the *social control* of the work-force.

Further reading

Albrow, M., 'Bureaucracy', Macmillan, 1970.

Bowles, S. and Gintis, H., 'Schooling in Capitalist America', Routledge & Kegan Paul, 1976.

Musgrove, F., 'Patterns of Power and Authority in English Education', Methuen, 1971. (See Part I, ch. 15)

Burnham Committee Teachers' salaries are negotiated in the Burnham Committee, so named after its first chairman in 1919. Prior to 1963 the representatives of the Local Authority Associations and of the teacher unions met under an independent chairman, and the salary scales they agreed were submitted to the Secretary of State for his approval or rejection.

Approval was forthcoming until the 1960s, since when successive Secretaries of State have assumed interventionist roles, reflecting the fact that teachers' salaries are the largest single item in the cost of the education service. The Remuneration of Teachers Act 1965 amended previous practice by including representatives of the Secretary of State in the Burnham Committee, making provision for arbitration in default of agreement, and by giving the power of retrospective payment.

Salary scales are set out in the Burnham Reports which are published after every agreement or arbitration. The various scales payable in a school depend on the size of the school and the ages of the pupils, the older ones counting for more points than the younger. The total number of points determines how many posts on various scales a school may have.

The salaries of teaching staff in the further education section are negotiated similarly after the school teachers' agreement, and salary increases are usually of the same percentage order. (See Part 1, ch. 1)

Business Education Council (BEC), Scottish Business Education Council (SCOT-BEC) BEC is an independent body, established in May 1974 by the Secretary of State for Education and Science. It has responsibilities to establish, promote and maintain a structure of awards for the whole of the United Kingdom (except Scotland) in non-degree business education. It is also required to devise and approve courses leading to such awards and generally to promote advances in non-degree business education in England, Wales and Northern Ireland. Such courses are offered, after BEC has given approval, in the further education sector, and can be on a variety of study bases (part-time to *full-time* study). The awards require evidence of disciplined attendance on an appropriate course, as well as success in examinations. There are currently three levels of award: BEC, General Certificate/Diploma; BEC National Certificate/Diploma; and BEC Higher National Certificate/Diploma. These provide a progressive route for students to higher awards in the BEC system and elsewhere. Diploma and Certificate courses are at the same level but Diploma courses cover a wider range of the relevant subjects.

SCOTBEC was established in 1973. It is the national examining body in Scotland for courses in business, secretarial, computer, administrative and distributive studies. It replaces the Scottish Council for Commercial Administrative and Professional Education (SCCAPE).

Further information available for BEC at 76 Portland Place, London W1; 01–580 3050; for SCOTBEC at 22 Great King's Street, Edinburgh; 031–556

4691. For courses available in a particular area, contact the local college of further education or college for higher education. (See Part 1, ch. 2)

Business school This is an American term, mainly used to describe very large, autonomous and self-financing institutions, usually with strong associations with leading universities. There are some that are so famous that most managers in the world would recognise them (Harvard, Massachusetts Institute of Technology, Stanford). These institutions have complete faculties of professors, assistants, researchers and student bodies at the post-graduate and doctoral level only. Other institutions offer graduate level courses. Entrance to post-graduate courses is by means of the Princeton Test of Admission, a rigorous and difficult examination of intellectual ability and practical fitness for such courses. This test is also used by the major UK schools.

In 1963 the Franks Report recommended the setting up of two business schools on the American pattern, presumably on the assumption that such institutions have been a key influence on American economic development. This has not been proved, but nevertheless, the London and Manchester Business Schools were founded, in association with the respective universities of these cities. There is also a Scottish Business School, in Glasgow. These three are the only business schools in the UK but there is in addition a plethora of other institutions, such as the business or management departments of universities, schools of management at universities or polytechnics, regional management centres, and so on. They are all attempts to answer what has been identified as a problem in the UK: the lack of able, highly trained managers. It will be some time before a balanced assessment of the contribution of the business schools and other institutions can be made, but the first signs are not encouraging, as the decline of the UK as an economy continues apparently unabated. Further information: London Business School, Sussex Place, Regents Park, London NW1 4SA; 01–262 5050; Manchester Business School, Booth Street West, Manchester M15 6PB; 061–273 1228; Scottish Business School, 69 St George's Place, Glasgow B2 1EU; 041–221 3124. (See Part 1, ch. 12)

Further reading

The Franks Report: 'British Business Schools', British Institute of Management, 1963.

Mant, A., 'The Experienced Manager: a Major Resource', British Institute of Management, 1970.

Business studies This term covers a wide range of activities in education and training. It usually means all those activities that educate and train people at all levels who work in organisations that deal in the purchase and sales of goods and services. (See Part 1, ch. 2)

Calibration This is the process by which the graduations or intervals on our measurement scale are fixed and checked. A blank thermometer is calibrated when marks are put on the side to show the level of mercury when placed in ice and when placed in steam. In educational measurement a traditional test is calibrated when the *mean* score obtained by a reference *population* is made equal to an arbitrarily chosen reference score (often taken to be 100) and when a measure of the spread of scores on the test (usually the *standard deviation* (see *measure of dispersion*) is made equal to another arbitrarily chosen standard deviation (often taken to be 15). This results in a *distribution* with mean score 100 and standard deviation 15, which allows for direct comparability of scores on different tests as long as the reference population remains the same in a statistical sense.

Calibration is the end result of a *standardisation* procedure, and one of the mathematical methods for transforming the scores can be found in 'The British Journal of Psychology' (Statistical Section), Volume III, part II, June 1950, in an article by D. N. Lawley called 'A Method of Standardising Group Tests'. Other methods for calibration exist, such as those based on *item characteristic curve theory*.

Further reading

Angoff, W. H., Scale, Norms and Equivalent Scores, in 'Educational Measurement', R. L. Thorndike (ed.), 2nd ed., 1971.

Childs, R., 'Norm-Referenced Testing and the Standard Scores', National Foundation for Educational Research, 1978. 'Journal of Educational Measurement', special issue on Latent Trait Models, vol. 14, no. 2, Summer, 1977. (See Part 1, ch. 6)

Capitation allowance The amount of money, related to the number of pupils on roll, which is allowed to a school annually by the LEA. for the purchase of books, stationery and equipment. (See Part 1, ch. 1)

Career development and planning A process by which individuals plan or have planned their future careers, together with the means by which they will gain experience and training to equip them for the jobs they expect to achieve. There exist independent agencies to help individuals with this as well as the management development departments of organisations. (See Part 1, ch. 12)

Careers education Careers education is a school-based activity, mainly concerned with group teaching, closely associated with the school's curriculum and having as its aim the widening of the career horizons of pupils. It is complementary to the *careers service's* responsibilities for vocational guidance with its emphasis on individual careers counselling. (See Part 1, ch. 1)

Careers organisations in education Under the Employment and Training Act 1973 all Local Education Authorities in England and Wales were made responsible for the careers service. The Manpower Services Commission opened the Careers and Occupational Information Centre (COIC) in 1974, having merged the Careers Information Division of the former Central Youth Employment Executive and the Occupational Information Section of the Employment Service Agency. The Centre is responsible for the preparation, publishing and distribution of information about jobs and careers and related careers, education and guidance material.

In Northern Ireland this function is carried out by the employment service, a branch of the Department of Manpower Services. In Scotland, the Careers Service Advisory Council was established to advise the Secretary of State on the conduct of the education authority careers services and matters relevant to the requirements of the Employment and Training Act 1973. (See Part 1, ch. 7)

Careers service The Employment and Training Act 1973 requires Local Education Authorities to appoint careers officers to administer a careers guidance and employment service for persons attending or leaving educational institutions other than universities, although university students may use the service if they wish. Local Education Authorities also have the power and may be called upon to make the service available to any other person who has ceased full-time education and who wishes to use or continue to use the service. Under a Principal Careers Officer, each Authority has a team of professional careers officers appointed to specialise in different aspects of the work. Some officers advise statutory school-leavers; some advise A–level pupils and students in colleges of further education; some deal with students in colleges of education and polytechnics; some help the physically or mentally *handicapped*. Local authorities are required to provide school pupils whom their officers advise with a written summary of the vocational advice given.

The main functions of the careers service are: to work with careers and guidance teachers in schools and colleges in the *careers education* of young people, and to provide them and their parents with information on educational, employment and training opportunities; to give continuing vocational guidance to pupils and students in their later years at school or college, and to help them to reach informed and realistic decisions about their careers; to help young people to find suitable training and employment and employers to find suitable workers; and to offer help and advice to young people on problems connected with their settlement in employment. (See Part 1, ch. 1)

Central Advisory Council The 1944 Act created two Central Advisory Councils, one for England and one for Wales, to be appointed by the Secretary of State with the duty of advising him on educational theory and practice and upon any matter referred to them by him. The major publications include 'The 15–18s' (Crowther, 1960), 'Half our Future' (Newsom, 1963), 'Children and their Primary Schools' (Plowden, 1967), and in Wales, 'The place of Welsh and English in the schools of Wales' (1953) and 'Primary Education in Wales' (Gittins, 1967). There has been no report since 1967. (See Part 1, ch. 1)

Central Bureau for Educational Visits and Exchanges Funded by the three UK Departments of Education, the bureau is the national office for information on educational travel and exchange. Schools and higher educational institutions are linked with other overseas bodies, and the Bureau places language assistants in appropriate schools and colleges, both foreign language assistants in Britain and English language assistants in other countries. (See Part 1, ch. 7)

Certificate of Secondary Education With an estimated top band of 20 per cent of children sitting the General Certificate of Education (see *examining bodies*) O–level examination, the CSE is intended for the next 40 per cent. Subject panels are drawn up on a regional basis and allow a variety of means of assessment. Schools may enter pupils for an examination in a subject for which the syllabus, examination paper, and marking are externally controlled (Method I). A school can offer a syllabus that is approved by the local board (Method II), or the school can set and mark its own examination papers subject to external moderation (Method III). A pass in the top grade of the CSE is counted as a pass in the GCE O–level examination. (See Part 1, ch. 10)

Certificate in Office Studies Offered in England and Wales as a two-year, part-time vocational course for young office workers. People who pass the examinations with sufficiently high marks may be eligible for entry to a course leading to the Ordinary *National Certificate* in *business studies*. (See Part 1, ch. 2)

Certified Diploma in Accounting and Finance This is intended to provide people who are not accountants with an understanding of finance and accounting. It aims to enable them to use their knowledge at a managerial level within their own functional specialism and in conjunction with their colleagues. (See Part 1, ch. 2)

Character-building industry A piece of jargon invented to give a degree of authenticity to those activities, projects, courses and experiences designed to improve the individual's understanding of himself and others and his ability to deal with highly demanding situations. Usually, character-building activities involve stressful physical and/or mental experiences in unusual surroundings by means of which self-learning is assumed to take place. There is little evidence of positive effects on work performance although there is no doubt the individual often changes. Examples include Outward Bound and survival courses for businessmen. Certainly, physical fitness is temporarily improved by such activities. (See Part 1, ch. 11)

Charity school Roman Catholics built the first charity schools in London during the reign of James II. Despite the 'Glorious Revolution' of 1688 Anglicans and dissenters, still fearful of a Roman Catholic counter-revolution, combined to form the Society for Promoting Christian Knowledge (SPCK) in 1699 as a co-ordinating body to aid the building of Protestant-controlled schools. Their emphasis on teaching children a useful trade and instilling the habits of industry was partly the product of a genuine concern to assist poor children to become financially independent adults. It also reflected the Puritan belief that charity should promote the glory of God by promoting the usefulness of man. In an age of slow economic growth such teaching contributed to social stability by not giving the pupils an education that would have made them discontented with their lot. Nevertheless the movement was attacked in a number of pamphlets, including B. Manderville's 'Essay on Charity and Charity Schools' (1723), for over-educating the children. The SPCK successively lost the support of dissenters during the High Church attack on them during the reign of Queen Anne and of the High Church itself with the collapse of Jacobite hopes. A return of 1729 shows 1,419 schools with 22,303 pupils, mainly in London and the large towns. By the late 1730s enthusiasm had waned. Many charity schools remained moribund until a revival of interest in popular education at the end of the century.

Further reading
Jones, M. G., 'The Charity School Movement', Cambridge University Press, 1938 (reprinted Frank Cass, 1963).
Simon, J., 'Was there a Charity School Movement?' in Simon B. (ed.), 'Education in Leicestershire, 1540–1940', Leicester University Press, 1968, pp. 55–100. (See Part 1, ch. 10)

Chief Education Officer The Chief Education Officer is the head of the LEA's education department. He is responsible for implementing the education committee's decisions and for conducting its business with the *Department of Education and Science* and with other bodies. Equally important is his role as the officer who advises the committee on the issues it has to deal with, which range from the annual budget and the priorities which that expresses, to future development plans, staffing standards, reorganisation of schools, and so on.

He is assisted by a professional staff, the usual pattern being one or two Deputy Chief Education Officers, and three or more Assistant Education Officers, each of whom is normally in charge of a branch of the service, such as schools, finance, further education, sites and buildings, etc. In addition there is a staff of advisory officers, headed by a chief adviser, who specialise in different aspects of education, either in various stages of education such as infant, nursery, etc., or in subject areas such as music, science, language, etc. Their role is to help schools to maintain and improve standards, and on occasion they may carry out formal inspections of schools. They also act as the eyes and ears of the Chief Education Officer and advise him on matters which may require decisions by the committee. See also: *education social worker, school psychological service*. (See Part 1, ch. 1)

Child development The study of child development is concerned to account for the way in which the relatively helpless new-born infant grows and develops into the complex adult. Developmental psychologists are interested in the systematic changes that occur as a child grows older. Both longitudinal studies, following the same group of children over a period of time, and cross-sectional studies, comparing a sample of children of different ages, are used.

Early studies in child development were largely descriptive, detailing the sequence of physical and motor development and establishing the average ages at which they occur. More recent work has seen the emphasis change to an interest in perceptual development, learning, cognitive development and *intelligence*, language development and the development of the child's *personality* and social skills.

The concept of development presupposes an orderly continuity in the changes that take place in the child. Such continuity has led to a concern with the innate, hereditary factors influencing maturation as well as with the environmental influences and learning. For example, the onset of puberty is a maturational phenomenon triggered by some internal mechanism; its onset may well have considerable influence upon the way in which the individual behaves. Other changes in behaviour, such as an increase in manual dexterity, will be the result of learning and dependent upon environmental opportunity.

Both inheritance and environmental influences are involved in most developmental processes. The onset of puberty, although a maturational phenomenon, can be delayed by malnutrition or anxiety, and likewise there may be an inherited aspect to the aptitude that the indivudal brings to his manual dexterity. See also: *Piagetian stages of development; heredity and environment; language and thought; maturation.*

Further reading
Mussen, P. H., Conger, J. J. and Kagan, J., 'Child Development and Personality', 4th ed., Harper & Row, 1974.
Mussen, P. H., (ed.), 'Carmichael's Manual of Child Psychology', 3rd ed., 2 vols, John Wiley, 1970. (See Part 1, ch. 14)

Chinese experience Uncritically the Chinese adopted various systems of education: in 1905 that of the Japanese, in 1922 the American, and in 1949 the Russian. All were disastrous.

Further reading
Hayter, R. and Jackson, R., The Changing Role of Teachers in China; post-Mao-Perspectives, 'British Journal of Teachers Education', 219–30, 1979. (See Part 1, ch. 3)

City and Guilds of London Institute In the mid-1870s the ancient City liveried companies were under strong political pressure to reform themselves and put their accumulated wealth to some socially acceptable use. By involving themselves in the development of technical education they reassumed one of their traditional roles. The Clothworkers' Company took the effective lead by giving £10,000 to the newly-formed Yorkshire College of Science, later the

University of Leeds, and contributing £500 for a chair in textiles. The City of London and the City companies formed the Institute in 1878; it was incorporated in 1882 and became a national body for encouraging and examining technical education. (See Part 1, ch. 10)

The Institute is an independent body which aims, in collaboration with the further education sector, to satisfy the demands of industry for technically qualified people. Operating under a royal charter, it provides nationally recognised standards at appropriate levels.

The Institute has a structure of advisory committees. These have representatives drawn from industry, education and the professions. They attempt to identify training and education requirements, and from them draw up syllabuses leading to examinations. Courses are run in *further education* colleges, usually on a part-time basis.

The major levels of examinable courses are as follows. City and Guilds Insignia Award (CGIA) is available to people who have already obtained appropriate certificates from the Institute. Candidates should have had suitable industrial experience, be able to demonstrate their understanding of the appropriate scientific principles and show a broad knowledge of their industry. The Full Technological Certificate (FTC) is awarded in some subjects to candidates who are over 21, have practical experience in their industry and have passed the necessary examination. Technician qualifications take some five to six years to obtain, with Part I taking two years, Part II two years, and Part III a further one or two years. Craft qualifications are similar in pattern to technician level, but Part I can be obtained after one year. The Institute also offers operative schemes, usually taking one or two years. There are some advanced operative examinations.

The Institute works closely with the *regional examining bodies*, and provides administrative services to a number of national bodies, among them the Joint Committees for National Certificates and Diplomas, the National Examinations Board for Supervisory Studies, the *Technician Education Council* and the *Business Education Council*.

It is now transferring much of its responsibilities for technician schemes to the Technician Education Council. Certain other schemes (such as distribution) are being passed to the Business Education Council. Examination arrangements will continue to be the responsibility of the Institute under the administrative systems mentioned above. The Institute provides some other services to industry, such as the Skills Testing Service. Further information: City and Guilds of London Institute, 76 Portland Place, London W1N 4AA, 01–580 3050. (See Part 1, ch. 2)

Classical conditioning Classical conditioning occurs when an association is established between a previously neutral stimulus and a stimulus that elicits an innate response. After a number of pairings the individual learns to respond to the neutral stimulus with the innate response. Classical conditioning can lead to behavioural problems such as the acquisition of school phobia and excessive anxiety towards school subjects. Pavlov did the pioneering work in this area of learning.
Further reading
Rachlin, H., 'An Introduction to Modern Behaviourism', W. H. Freeman, 2nd ed., 1976. (See Part 1, ch. 14)

Classification and framing Bernstein analyses the structure of educational knowledge at the twin levels of its classification, which concerns the strength of its subject divisions and sub-divisions, and its framing, which relates particularly to the degree of control exercised by the student over what is taught and how it is taught. He discusses the implications of differences in classification and framing with regard to the *socialisation* and *social control* of pupils and students of different *social class*.

Further reading

Bernstein, B., 'Class, Codes and Control', vol. 3, Routledge & Kegan Paul, revised ed., 1977. (See Part 1, ch. 15)

Classroom system To see *curriculum* and teaching as adapted to classroom systems, rather than vice versa, is to emphasise the extent to which schools as we know them were a socio-technical invention of the nineteenth century. Thus the cellular structure of classrooms and related methods of 'transmitting' knowledge were a solution to the problem of developing a common basic literacy, numeracy, and sense of order for the mass of the population. Views of children's acquisition of knowledge have become more sophisticated, but the difficulties of implementing more individualised or 'open' curricula can be seen as evidence of the durability of the older systems. (See Part 1, ch. 4)

Class struggle Where Durkheim and Parsons stress the need to understand the unity of society – its *consensus* – Marx stresses the need to understand the essential disunity of society – the *conflict*, the class struggle, that determines society's fundamental character. For Marx, the whole written history of mankind has been a history of class struggle in one form or another, though, in general, the real nature of the struggle has not been understood by the contestants.

Marx characterises societies in terms of their different modes of production, because he believes that relations of production hold the theoretical key to the final explanation of all human relations. From this point of view, the development of Western society over the last thousand years has been from the feudal mode of production, the essential feature of this being the class struggle between the feudal aristocracy and the serfs, to the capitalist mode of production, the essential feature of which is the class struggle between the bourgeoisie and the proletariat.

It is vital to appreciate the explanatory power which Marx attributes to the concept of the class struggle. The concept operates at quite a different level from either the common-sense concept of class or the Weberian concept of it. (See *social class*.) Marx sees the historical development of the class struggle as responsible for man's becoming thoroughly misled by *ideology*, led profoundly away from a true understanding of himself and his world. Again, the theory of *alienation* elaborated in Marx's early writings depicts the class struggle as the source of man's loss of his essential humanity. What is constant in Marx's thought is his belief that the concept of the class struggle is central to any genuine understanding of the human condition both as it is and as it should be.

Further reading

Wright, E. O., 'Class, Crisis and the State', New Left Books, 1978.

Holly, D. (ed.), 'Education or Domination?' Arrow Books, 1974. (See Part 1, ch. 15)

Clerical work Clerical work deals with the recording and collation of information, generally for other people to use. Clerical work is vital in any organisation, with the emphasis on speed and accuracy. Therefore, training and education for such skills is important, particularly as computerised systems handle more and more of the mechanics of the job. (See Part 1, ch. 2).

Cluster analysis When *data* have been collected over a range of learners and other factors, they may be displayed in a table (matrix). There may be similar effects or trends in the rows or columns: the clumping together of similar effects. The interpretation of what are similar effects is difficult. Using a computer it is possible to identify these clumps or clusters, using a mathematical technique called cluster analysis. (See Part 1, ch. 8)

Coaching This widely used technique involves the setting of real tasks for trainees by which their ability and experience is improved through continuous appraisal, advice and *counselling* of a supervisor. Its roots are in the traditional master/pupil learning system. (See Part 1, ch. 12).

Cognitive approaches to learning Cognitive learning theorists, in contrast to the behaviourists, maintain that learning comes about as the result of the restructuring of perceptions and thoughts within the individual. The restructuring enables the learner to perceive new relationships, to solve new problems and to gain understanding of particular areas of knowledge. They stress the importance of meaning in the learning of complex material such as school subjects.

Further reading

Ausubel, D. P., Novak, J. D. and Hanesian, H., 'Educational Psychology: A Cognitive View', 2nd ed., Holt, Rinehart & Winston, 1978. (See Part 1, ch. 14)

Cognitive style There is a wide variation in the styles that individuals adopt when they encounter a cognitive task. A number of factors have been investigated which appear to have an influence on cognitive style. For example, Bruner identified different strategies used in concept formation. With many of these aspects of personality difference it has been assumed that individuals can be placed somewhere upon a continuum that extends between the extremes of a pair of alternatives. Amongst the dimensions different theorists have advanced are Eysenck's *introversion-extraversion*, neuroticism-stability and psychoticism-normality. Hudson has developed the dimensions of *convergent and divergent thinking* and of syllabus-bound and syllabus-free approaches to study (*sylbs and sylfs*). Pask has distinguished between serialists and holists. The serialist approaches the study of new material by stringing a sequence of cognitive structures together; he builds up a total picture by stringing detail together. The typical holist attempts to gain an overview of an area of study so that the detail can fall into place. Witkin found that the perceptual characteristics of field-dependence and field-independence that he had identified related also to intellectual behaviour. The field-independent subjects were more analytic in their thought, did better on spatial tasks and performed well in mathematics and the sciences. Kagan has shown that some subjects are consistently impulsive when faced with problem-solving tasks. They blurt out the first possible solution that occurs to them although it is frequently incorrect. Other subjects are more reflective; they delay before venturing a solution and are then usually correct. See also: *Piagetian stages of development, personality, Bruner's strategies in concept formation.*

Further reading

Whitehead, J. (ed.), 'Personality and Learning', Vol. 1, 1975; Wolfson, J. (ed.), 'Personality and Learning', vol. 2, 1976; Hodder & Stoughton in association with the Open University Press. (See Part 1, ch. 14)

Cole, Sir Henry (1808–82) In public service from 1831 onwards, he assisted in the reform of the postal system before the introduction of the penny post and served on the managing committees of the London Exhibitions of 1855, 1862, 1871–4. British commissioner at the Paris Exhibitions of 1855, 1867. Joined the School of Design, Board of Trade, 1851, joint secretary with *Lyon Playfair*, Department of Science and Art, 1853–8, secretary, 1858–73. Played an active role in the development of the museums and the Royal Albert Hall on the South Kensington land bought with the proceeds of the Great Exhibition, 1851. Credited with designing the first Christmas card. (See Part 1, ch. 10)

College of higher education The report on Teacher Education and Training 1972 presented by the James Committee recommended inter alia that student teachers should study alongside students in other disciplines and that common curriculum courses should be prepared which would enable students to delay until a later stage the option as to final choice of career.

The Government endorsed the suggestion and proposed that colleges of education and technical and other colleges might either singly or jointly develop into major institutions of higher education with some degree of specialisation in the arts and human sciences. Consequently there developed during the 1970s the merger of colleges of this kind into institutions of higher education (though a few developed in their own right without amalgamation). It should be noted that technical colleges in assuming their new role as constituents of an institute of higher education often retained elements of their former function and continued to meet the demands of local industry for technician and craft training which might otherwise have been lost. Factors common to these colleges are courses of teacher training, degree courses approved by a university or by the *Council for National Academic Awards*, and other courses below degree level, such as the Diploma in Higher Education. (See Part 1, ch. 1)

College of Preceptors Founded in 1846, the College of Preceptors received a royal charter in 1849. It was established 'for the purpose of promoting sound learning and of advancing the interests of education, more especially among the middle classes' at a time when the standards of such schools were very low. By taking the College's examinations members could become fellows or licentiates. The College is still actively engaged in educational circles today. (See Part 1, ch. 10)

Commission of the European Communities Though not directly controlling education in the way that government departments of education do, the Commission of the European Communities can nevertheless be viewed as an administrative organisation which can influence educational development. Under a Commissioner responsible for Science, Research and Education, and through its Directorate of Education and Culture it has contact with all the members of the European Economic Community and covers education at primary, secondary and post-secondary levels; youth policy; co-ordination of vocational training; adult education and cultural matters. (See Part 1 ch. 7)

Committee of Enquiry If advice is required on a specific kind of issue the Secretary of State may constitute an ad hoc Committee of Enquiry to investigate and report. Examples include the enquiry into higher education (Robbins Report 1963), teacher education and training (James Report 1972), the pay of non-university teachers (Houghton Report 1974), the teaching of reading and the use of English in schools (Bullock Report 1975) and the education of handicapped children and young people (Warnock Report 1978). These reports are as influential as those issued by the Central Advisory Councils. (See Part 1, ch. 1)

Committee of the Privy Council on Education Popularly known as the Education Department, this Government office was established in 1839 to supervise the distribution of the annual grant (£20,000 in 1833 and £30,000 between 1834 and 1839) that the Treasury made available to the National Society and the British and Foreign School Society (see *religious societies*) for the building of new schools. With its wide brief 'the consideration of all matters affecting the education of the people' it posed a threat to the established church's claim to a monopoly of control over the education of the people. After a protracted dispute the terms on which schools in receipt of a grant were to be inspected were finally agreed between church and state. The new inspectors (HMIs) soon found much wrong with the schools and teachers. By the mid–1840s the National Society, which had run into financial difficulties, proved readier to negotiate over the terms on which the Education Department would subsidise the training of teachers than it had been in the 1830s when the idea had been first mooted. *Sir James Kay-Shuttleworth* was able to introduce a scheme whereby a 13-year-old boy or girl could go through a five-year apprenticeship in a school and then a one- or two-year course in a training college with state assistance. He later offered grants for the purchase of books and scientific apparatus. These grants, together with a capitation grant based on attendance offered from the early 1850s, were swept away by the *Revised Code*. The Board of Education took over the work of the Education Department in 1899. See also: *Robert Lowe, W. E. Forster*.
Further reading
Bishop, A. S., 'The Rise of a Central Authority for English Education', Cambridge University Press, 1971.
Hurt, J., 'Education in Evolution: Church, State, and Popular Education, 1800–70', Rupert Hart-Davis, 1971.
Sutherland, G., 'Policy Making in Elementary Education, 1870–95', Oxford University Press, 1973. (See Part 1, ch. 10)

Commonwealth Secretariat It is an international body at the service of all member countries of the Commonwealth, established in 1965. It publishes abstracts of current resarch, conference papers, reports, books and the CELC Newsletter, in addition to the Education in the Commonwealth series. Address: Commonwealth Secretariat, Marlborough House, Pall Mall, London SW1. (See Part 1, ch. 3)

Community school The concept of the community school was pioneered by Henry Morris, Chief Education Officer of Cambridgeshire, with the establishment of its village colleges in the 1920s. The college housed not only the school, but the village hall, the branch of the county library, the club room for old-age pensioners, and so on; and the facilities available to the school for example those in the workshops and gymnasium, were also available to the community. The college was the place not only where children went to school but also where their parents and elder brothers and sisters went to concerts, attended evening classes or meetings of the Women's Institute. 'We'll raise the school-leaving age to 90,' Morris wrote.

The idea has spread to many other parts of the country, including towns and inner-city areas. From the mid-1960s there developed the concept of joint provision between the LEA and another local council to provide facilities which would be used by school and public and which would be better

101

than either Authority could afford individually. Thus, some community schools make special provision for sport and recreation, others have opened up courses during the daytime which are attended by adults and older pupils. The advocates of the community school, however, regard it not only as an intensively used building, but also as a means of promoting community and social awareness among the pupils. (See Part 1, ch. 1)

Comparative education courses These are sometimes part of initial courses for teachers. Such courses include a survey of the history and methodology of comparative education, the contributions of sociology, history and demography, the difficulties concerned with language policies such as the problem of the *phonetic script* in China, problems of racial and religious minorities, the reform of education, educational difficulties in developing countries such as those connected with *localisation*, an analysis of the effects of industrialisation and of urbanisation on education. Courses leading to BEd, MA, MPhil, and PhD degrees are also available.

Other teaching and research centres now established include the Comparative Centre at Chicago University, the Max Planck·Institute for Educational Research in Berlin, the universities of Reading (UK), Michigan, Wisconsin and Pittsburgh (USA) and La Trobe, Macquarie and Monash (Australia).
Further reading
Bereday, G. Z. F., 'Comparative Method in Education', chs. 10, 11, 12, Holt, Rinehart & Winston, 1964. (See Part 1. ch. 3)

Comparative education societies Once they were established, a series of aims was adopted for these societies, and was broadly accepted by most comparativists. The founders of these societies sought to satisfy that interest in comparative education which had been manifested by many educators. They also wanted to encourage the extension of studies and to promote research in the comparative field. Others were interested in promoting educational reform or in increasing international understanding.

The first Comparative Education Society was established in New York in 1956 by W. W. Brickman and others. It organises conferences, workshops and meetings at international, national and regional level and also publishes a learned journal bi-annually, 'The Comparative Education Review'. By 1961 the Comparative Education Society in Europe had been founded, initially with branches in Britain and Germany. Subsequently branches have been set up in the Netherlands, France and Spain. The parent body holds conferences every two years and publishes a newsletter as well as conference proceedings. Other societies have been founded in Canada, Japan and South Korea, and, more recently, the Australian and International Comparative Education Society was established.

Since by the 1970s the number of comparative education societies had increased and a growing number of comparativists were convinced that the time was ripe for a global organisation, the World Congress of Comparative Education Societies was founded in 1972. Professor Brian Holmes of the Institute of Education, University of London was elected as its first President. The Congress, like other societies, maintains close links with the *International Association for the evaluation of Educational Achievement (IEA)*. (See Part 1, ch. 3)

Comprehensive secondary school Comprehensive schools provide for the educational needs of all normal children of secondary school age irrespective of their level of attainment. A few Authorities established schools of this type in the 1940s and 1950s, but the period of their great development was in the decade after 1965.

A major reason for the growth of comprehensive schools was growing dissatisfaction with the selective system whereby at the age of 11 children were divided into separate kinds of secondary school, the belief that the *eleven-plus examination* was not predictive of a child's ability and development, and that in any case the line between entry to one school or another was, to a significant degree, arbitrary.

A first principle which might command acceptance is that a comprehensive school should regard the educational needs of every child as being of equal importance. This principle has profound implications for the way learning is organised, the allocation of resources and the distribution of teachers, as well as the more peripheral matters such as school reports and the award of prizes. It will also influence attitudes towards the assessment of pupils, systems of *pastoral care*, option structures, parental involvement, and so on. Even so it does not mean that every child is capable of meeting whatever academic demands are made on him, but it does lead to higher expectations of children's attainments, and to attaching value to all achievements, not merely 'academic' ones. From this principle too will develop the aim of ensuring that every pupil has every opportunity of realising his full potential over as wide a range of activities and skills as possible. (See Part 1, ch. 1)

The policy of separating children in different schools according to their perceived ability has been historically a short-lived phenomenon. The nineteenth-century elementary school knew no such segregation. Even the three-tier system advocated by the Taunton Commissioners 1864–7 was based on a father's ability to pay, not his son's intellectual capacity. *Public Schools* were, and many still are, comprehensive schools in that they cater for pupils of widely differing ability. Even in the 1920s, the period of the development of the *tripartite system*, advocates of *multilateral schools* included the conservative Associations of Assistant Masters, Headmasters, and Headmistresses, as well as the National Union of Teachers, and the National Association of Labour Teachers. Despite the move to tripartism after 1944 a number of predominantly rural authorities (Anglesey is one example) found it administratively expedient to reorganise their schools on comprehensive lines. Although at the local level Conservative councillors raised little objection to such plans at this time, attitudes hardened at the national level during the Conservative period of office 1951–64, with the result that educational arguments became inextricably confused with political ones. Hence the Labour Government's Circular 10/65 requesting local authorities to prepare plans for reorganising their schools on non-selective lines was greeted with procrastination in some quarters. Recent legislation will undoubtedly still further delay the move away from the tripartite system.

Further reading
Rubinstein, D., and Simon B., 'The Evolution of the Comprehensive System 1926–72', Routledge & Kegan Paul, 1973. (See Part 1, ch. 10)

Compulsory school attendance A child is deemed of compulsory school age from the beginning of the term following his fifth birthday. For pupils who attain the age of 16 between 1 September and 31 January (inclusive) the school-leaving date is the end of the Easter Term. For pupils who attain the age of 16 between 1 February and 31 August (inclusive) the school-leaving date is the Friday before the last Monday in May.

It is worth noting that the duty of parents is to ensure that the child is educated 'either at school or otherwise'. If parents choose to educate their child at home the Local Education Authority has the responsibility to ensure that such education is efficient, having regard to the age, ability, and *aptitude* of the child. (See Part 1, ch. 1)

Computer Computers are being found of use increasingly in educational applications. Main uses at present are for:

1 Information retrieval.
2 Mathematical calculation.
3 The manipulation of mathematical models.
4 Simulations of a variety of situations, for example, of difficult or dangerous experiments.
5 Problem-solving and information-giving of the type associated with computer-assisted learning.

Computers are being linked in networks which allow information from a number of data bases to be available. This means that information is becoming much more easily available to anyone having access to a suitable computer *terminal*. More and more micro-computers are coming into use in schools, colleges and universities. These offer much more flexible, individual use than main-frame computers.

Further reading
Rushby, N., 'An Introduction to Educational Computing', Croom Helm, 1979.
Hooper, R. and Toye, I., 'Computer-Assisted Learning in the UK', Council for Educational Technology, 1975. (See Part 1, ch. 9)

Computer-aided learning (CAL) computer-assisted learning (CAL), computer-assisted training (CAT); CAL and CAT are relatively new techniques, with their roots in programmed learning, involving the use of a *computer* as a teaching medium or learning resource. As a teaching medium, learning is controlled by the computer programme as it reacts to the trainee's responses. As a learning resource, the computer is a tool for the learner, providing information. Thus, in this case, the computer is not a direct teacher (e.g., as in a flight simulator). (See Part 1, ch. 12)

Computer-managed learning (CML) The *computer* manages teaching and/or learning by performing tasks such as marking/analysing tests, the management of trainees through a course of study using other resources (e.g., by referring them to books, teachers, etc.), keeping records, and even preparing reports on attendance, achievements, and so on. (See Part 1, ch. 12).

Concept formation and attainment For meaningful learning to take place the learner must have relevant concepts available within his existing cognitive structure. A concept is a system of learned responses which facilitate the organisation and interpretation of *data*. Concepts are usually associated with specific words or phrases, but it is possible to have concepts without verbal labels. Words are not concepts, they only stand for concepts. It is possible to know many words without any understanding of the concepts that they stand for.

Two conditions are essential for concept formation. First, the learner must be able to recognise and abstract the common elements or attributes from a number of objects, events or situations in order to form generalisations. This recognition may come about by the learner abstracting these attributes for himself or through a teacher describing the attributes for him in some way. Second, the learner must be capable of discriminating between relevant and irrelevant attributes of the concept. For example: wheels, engine, steering, brakes, and seats are all relevant attributes of the concept 'car', whereas colour, kerb-side weight, size and shape are irrelevant attributes of the concept. Concept formation requires both classification and discrimination. The relevant or critical attributes enable the learner to make his classification; the ability to discriminate between relevant and irrelevant attributes enables the learner to recognise the limits of his classification.

The attainment of concepts by young children takes place so quickly and inevitably that it has been suggested that the young child has an innate predisposition to organise his perceptions into concepts. It is almost as if the child had a built-in *language acquisition device*. Much of Piaget's work has been concerned with the development of the child's competence in using concepts. Bruner has investigated adult concept formation. See also: *Piagetian stages of development; language and thought; learning, retention and recall; Bruner's strategies in concept formation; Gagné's conditions of learning.*

Further reading
Thomson, R., 'The Psychology of Thinking', Penguin, 1959. (See Part 1, ch. 14)

Confederation of British Industry (CBI) The CBI, which represents the interests of industrial and commercial concerns, sponsors a number of educational activities. 'Understanding British Industry' is sponsored by the CBI Educational Foundation and sets out to provide source material and audio-visual resources to education to explain the roles of commerce and industry in the social and economic life of the nation. Its Education and Training Committee is the main CBI education committee. Activity in the various education sectors is carried out through a series of joint committees with universities and polytechnics, colleges of further education and schools. The CBI operates through thirteen Regional Offices, those in Wales and Scotland having their own Education and Training Committees. (See Part 1, ch. 7)

Conflict The concept of conflict theory in sociology has tended to take shape in opposition to the focus upon *consensus* in *structural-functionalism*. Various theorists have called attention to important elements of conflict in society which structural-functionalism is claimed to ignore. However, the term 'conflict theory' can be misleading. Marx can be called a 'conflict theorist', and so can Ralf Dahrendorf. Yet to draw the inference that their theories are of a similar kind would be to make a serious mistake.

In 'Class and Class Conflict in an Industrial Society' (1959), Dahrendorf, following Max Weber, maintains that every *organisation* involves leadership, and so the giving and the acceptance of commands. He argues from this that, however complete the recognition of *authority* may be, there is bound to be a conflict of interests when one party is required to submit to another's commands. Therefore every organised group will present a conflict situation. In relation to the sociology of education, Dahrendorf's theory fits well with Willard Waller's analysis of conflict within the American school in his classic study, 'The Sociology of Teaching' (1932).

However, Marx, as a 'conflict theorist', is putting forward a quite different form of argument. He is claiming to demonstrate the existence of a *class struggle* that arises from the organisation of material production within society. Conflict is not to be explained in terms of separate, local relations of authority and subordination, but in terms of one overriding set of social relations that permeates every sphere. Furthermore, whereas Dahrendorf is proclaiming the inevitability of conflict, Marx is maintaining that it can and should be eradicated through a change in the mode of production.

Further reading

Dahrendorf, R., 'Class and Class Conflict in an Industrial Society', Routledge & Kegan Paul, 1959.

Waller, W., 'The Sociology of Teaching', John Wiley, 1932. (See Part 1, ch. 15)

Consensus Sociological theories which, like those of Durkheim and Parsons, posit the existence of a moral order or a *normative* order binding the whole of society together are often called consensus theories. Contrasts between consensus theories and *conflict* theories tend to hinge on the claim that consensus theories leave out of consideration conflicting interests and conflicting sets of values within society that are of fundamental importance.

Further reading

Wrong, D., The Oversocialised Conception of Man in Modern Sociology, 'American Sociological Review', vol. 26, pp. 183–93, 1961. (See Part 1, ch. 15)

Consultants and private organisations Consultancy in business education and training has been one of the major growth industries in the UK in the last few years. The Industrial Training Act 1964 made large sums of money available; and this, coupled with a chronic shortage of experienced and skilled trainers, produced a boom. The recession of the late 1960s and early 1970s applied the usual market constraints, and those firms that have survived obviously offer a reasonable product and service. There remains, however, a large number of them. The *National Training Index* lists most of them, together with some information on what they have to offer.

Anyone seeking to select training offered by consultancy organisations or privately run training centres needs to pose both himself and his clients the following questions. First, what are the real training needs of the individual concerned? What does the organisation/individual/his boss want him to be able to do on his return? Second, what are the constraints (time, cost)? Third, what organisation offers programmes most nearly matching requirements? Fourth, what have other users said about the programme and its organisers? Even after this, it is still worth seeing if the needs can be better met internally and preferably on-job through a properly constructed coaching programme. (See Part 1, ch. 2)

Consultative Committee on the Curriculum, Scotland The Consultative Committee (CCC) was established in 1965 to advise the Secretary of State for Scotland on matters related to the curriculum. Reconstituted in 1976, the CCC has now a strengthened developmental role in that it is charged with a continual review of the *curriculum*. This it does through working parties which investigate particular aspects of the curriculum. Standing central committees have been set up for each of the main subject areas of the curriculum; these supervise the development of new curricula and the development of courses and materials by working parties.

The CCC has committees responsible for all aspects of curriculum development in primary and secondary education: the Committee on Primary Education (COPE) and the Committee on Secondary Education (COSE). An integrated Scottish Curriculum Development Service has been established, consisting of three centres for secondary education, one also housing the Primary Education Support Service. All three centres are attached to colleges of education. (See Part 1, ch. 7)

Contingent statement Contingent statements could be described as those which just 'happen' to be true. Thus, the term is contrasted with *necessary statements* where the statement must be true. Thus 'cats like fish' is contingent, but 'a triangle has three sides' is necessary.

Further reading

Hamlyn, D. W., 'Theory of Knowledge', Macmillan, 1971.

Hospers, J., 'Introduction to Philosophical Analysis', 2nd ed., Routledge & Kegan Paul, 1967. (See Part 1, ch. 13)

Contribution of education to economic growth A number of attempts to measure the contribution of education to economic growth have been made, because of the belief that by increasing educational expenditure governments can accelerate the process of economic growth. The measurement cannot be accurate, since the relationship between education and economic growth is a complex one.

Some of the earliest attempts to analyse the link between educational expenditure and economic growth simply involved international comparisons of national income, educational expenditure, and the literacy and school enrolment rates. Bowman and Anderson (1963) were able to demonstrate that there were clear correlations between a country's level of national income per head and its level of literacy or educational expenditure. However, the fact that rich countries spend more on education than developing countries may be a result of their economic development, rather than the cause of it.

Denison (1962), in a different approach, attempted to measure the contribution of education to the growth of national income in the USA between 1910 and 1960. His conclusion that education accounted for about 23 per cent of the total increase in national income between those years was widely reported. This conclusion rests on a number of questionable assumptions about the process of economic growth and the way in which various factors, including educational change, interact. When Denison attempted to apply his method to various European countries, the results were very unclear. Few economists now believe that it is possible to measure precisely the contribution of education to economic growth. It is widely accepted, however, that there are important links between a country's educational system and its economy. See also *production function* in connection with this.

Further reading

Bowman, M. J. and Anderson, C.A., Concerning the Role of Education in Development, in 'Old Societies and New States', Geertz (ed.), reprinted in UNESCO Readings in the Economics of Education, UNESCO, Paris, 1968.

Denison, E. F., 'The Sources of Economic Growth and the Alternatives Before Us', Committee for Economic Development, New York, 1962.

Denison, E. F., 'Why Growth Rates Differ: Postwar Experience in Nine Western Countries', Brookings Institution, New York, 1967. (See Part 1, ch. 5)

Convention of Scottish Local Authorities (COSLA) The Secretary of State for Scotland is responsible to Parliament for education in Scotland. The regional authorities are responsible for the administration of public education. Scotland has in large measure its own legislation covering education. The principal Act from which current practice is derived is the Education (Scotland) Act 1972. COSLA draws representatives from each of the education authorities and is the body with legal responsibility, through its members, for education, subject to a series of regulations laid down by act of Parliament. (See Part 1, ch. 7)

Convergent and divergent thinking Some cognitive tasks, including most intelligence test items, require convergent thinking in order to produce a specified correct response based upon the information given. Other cognitive tasks require *divergent thinking*, sometimes loosely equated with *creativity*, which is best judged in terms of the quantity, variety and originality of the ideas produced. Hudson found that boys studying sciences tended to favour a convergent style of thought, whilst arts students favoured divergent thought. *Further reading*

Hudson, L., 'Contrary Imaginations: A Psychological Study of the English Schoolboy', Methuen, 1966.

Hudson, L., 'Frames of Mind: Ability, Perception and Self-perception in the Arts and Sciences', Methuen, 1968. (See Part 1, ch. 14)

Core curriculum The three terms, common curriculum, common core curriculum and core curriculum, are so frequently used interchangeably that it might seem academic to distinguish differing conceptions which can underlie their use. But to disinter these conceptions may reveal competing assumptions and beliefs about how schooling should reflect and influence society and culture. Whereas a common curriculum usually implies a compulsory pattern of learning for all pupils, a common core curriculum suggests rather an essential minimum of learning opportunities with much scope for variation and choice around it. Whereas a common curriculum tends to emphasise syllabuses and time allocations, a common core curriculum, though probably stipulating basic standards in reading and mathematics, tends to emphasise a common framework of aims. Within such a framework individual schools would exercise considerble *autonomy* in curriculum organisation and design. They could draw flexibly upon the disciplines of knowledge (rather than follow subject syllabuses), thus co-ordinating rather than separating areas of experiences (DES, 1977).

In contrast to either of the first two terms, the intention originally underlying the term 'core curriculum' was to shift attention from 'essential knowledge' to 'fundamental social values' (Smith, Stanley and Shore, 1957). Hence the core curriculum was built around problems common to everyone's cultural experience, like the effect of technology on life styles. The idea has recently been expressed as a 'cultural map' curriculum (Open University, 1976) in which core activities include work experience, community service, integrative projects in housecraft and craft and design, as well as orthodox academic studies.

These interpretations of the core concept had impinged little on school priorities until recently. In so far as schooling is seen in cultural perspective, the most influential view is that the school has a duty to ensure that all pupils have access to a 'selection from culture' in which the basic disciplines of knowledge are deemed most significant.Thus it has been argued that a 'common culture curriculum' (Lawton, 1975) with adequate coverage and balance should be based on five essential 'cores' of study: in mathematics, physical and biological sciences, humanities and social studies, expressive arts, moral education.

See also: *disciplines of knowledge, culture, ideology, curriculum organisation, areas of experience.*

Further reading

Department of Education and Science, 'Curriculum 11–16', 1977.

Department of Education and Science, 'The School Curriculum', 1981.

Lawton, T., 'Class, Culture and Curriculum', Routledge & Kegan Paul, 1975.

Smith, B. O., Stanley, W. and Shore, J. 'Fundamentals of Curriculum Development', Harcourt Brace & World, 1, 2, 14, 1957.

Open University, Course E 203, Units 3 and 4, Culture, Ideology and Knowledge (M. Skilbeck), Open University Press, Milton Keynes, 1976. (See Part 1, ch. 4)

Correlation Correlation is a method for seeing how two attributes vary together. If our two attributes were the ages of a group of children and the weight of these children, we would expect the older children to tend to be heavier than the younger ones. The extent to which this is true is described by our index of correlation.

There are numerous correlation indices, but the ones that are commonly accepted all have a range of values from -1 to $+1$. An index of $+1$ in the above example would indicate a perfect relationship between both attributes such that the older the child the heavier the child, by a proportionate amount. This kind of correlation is never achieved in practice, but an index value of $+1$ represents perfect systematic variation between attributes, and an index value of zero represents no systematic variation at all. A value of -1 represents perfect systematic variation but in reverse. Thus in our example it would mean that the older a child the lighter he was.

It may therefore be apparent that the index of correlation also gives us information about how well we can predict one attribute, given a value on the other. With perfect correlation we can predict exactly what value someone will have on a second attribute if we know his score on the first.

The principle behind the most commonly used correlation index, the product moment correlation coefficient, is essentially very simple. It is useful to multiply the following two columns of numbers together:

Individual	X	Y
A	1	1
B	2	2
C	3	3
D	4	4
E	5	5

The result of adding the cross products (X times Y) is $1 + 4 + 9 + 16 + 25 = 55$

If the Y column is now inverted we get:

Individual	X	Y
F	1	5
G	2	4
H	3	3
I	4	2
J	5	1

The sum of the cross products is now
$5 + 8 + 9 + 8 + 5 = 35$

We find that, no matter what the order of X and Y, these two values for the sum of the cross products give us the maximum and the minimum possible values. The product moment correlation coefficient uses this fact but introduces methods for controlling for the number of cross products (by finding the average cross product) and controlling for the absolute size of the values concerned (by dividing by a measure of spread, the standard deviation). This gives a formula for the coefficient as follows:

$$r = \frac{\Sigma \, x.y}{n \, (S.D_x).(S.D_y)}$$

$$\begin{aligned}
\text{where } x &= \text{score on one attribute} \\
y &= \text{score on other attribute} \\
\text{E}xy &= \text{sum of cross products} \\
n &= \text{number of people} \\
S.D_x &= \text{standard deviation for x score} \\
S.D_y &= \text{standard deviation for y score}
\end{aligned}$$

The value of r is now bounded between +1 and −1. Other measures of correlation include the biserial, point-biserial, tetachoric and phi coefficient, all of which are either derived from the product moment correlation or are estimates of it.

Further reading

Crocker, A. C., 'Statistics for the Teacher', ch. 6, 2nd ed., National Foundation for Educational Research, 1974.

Guildford, J. P and Fruchter, B., 'Fundamental Statistics in Psychology and Education', 2nd ed., ch. 6, McGraw-Hill, 1978. (See Part 1, chs. 6, 8)

Cost analysis Several methods of cost analysis have been devised. The term 'cost' does not necessarily imply financial cost; it can be expressed in units of time (e.g., man hours). The purpose of a cost analysis can be to demonstrate: (a) financial viability (e.g., an investment of money for future financial savings); (b) effectiveness related to main resource (e.g., investment of staff time for later saving of staff time); (c) net resource implications (e.g., solving organisational or resource problems); (d) educational outcome from long-term resource costs (e.g., a major curriculum development); and (e) improvement with reallocation of existing resources. The five types are not mutually exclusive. It can be seen that for some, evidence of a qualitative educational outcome is necessary, whilst for others it is a financial or resource outcome. The analysis requires a clear distinction between financial and other resources (e.g., learners' time). In order to estimate financial implications it will be necessary to define clearly the assumptions made (e.g., are buildings, rent, furnishing included?).

The errors of estimates also need clear definition. For conventional classroom teaching it is possible to deduce a figure of cost per student per hour, which gives a comparison basis. For independent and self-instructional learning materials it is more useful to compare cost per student per use, because the time dimension can have large variations across learners. The report needs to be written carefully bearing in mind the intended audience. For many analyses it may be necessary to write two reports, one aimed at teachers with the basic units in man hours, and another for administrators in financial terms. Often omitted from such analyses is the learner's time and its financial implications.

Further reading
Fielden, J. and Pearson, P.K., 'Costing Educational Practice', Council for Educational Technology, 1978. (See Part 1, ch. 8)

Cost-benefit analysis The techniques of cost-benefit analysis are used by economists to measure and compare the costs and expected monetary benefits of an investment in order to provide a measure of its profitability. The recognition that education is an important form of investment in *human capital* has resulted in a number of attempts to apply cost-benefit analysis to education in order to assess the profitability of expenditure on education, as an investment for society as a whole or for the individual student. The American economist, Becker (1964), was one of the first to apply cost-benefit analysis to education. Psacharopoulos (1973) later reviewed calculations of the costs and benefits of education in over 30 countries.

The way in which most of these cost-benefit studies measure the profitability of investment in education is by calculating the social or private *rate of return*. This expresses the relationship between the costs of education (including the value of pupils' time, as measured by their *forgone earnings*, as well as direct costs of tuition) and the direct and indirect economic benefits of education.

Direct monetary benefits of education are usually measured by comparison between the average lifetime earnings of workers with different levels of education. Thus, the extra lifetime earnings of graduates, compared with workers with secondary education only, are used as an estimate of the economic benefits of higher education, after allowances have been made for the influence of other factors, such as ability, or the earnings of graduates. See *age-earnings profiles* for more on this.

Ideally, cost-benefit analysis should also take into account the indirect 'spill-over' benefits (see *alpha-coefficient*) which are not reflected in relative earnings. This remains an unsolved problem, and indeed many of the assumptions of cost-benefit analysis are still matters of controversy and continuing research.

Further reading
Blaug, M., 'The Rate of Return on Investment in Education in Great Britain', The Manchester School, September 1965.
Psacharopoulos, G., 'Returns to Education: an International Comparison', Elsevier, 1973. (See Part 1, ch. 5)

Cost-effectiveness analysis Cost-effectiveness analysis attempts to measure in quantitive, but not monetary terms, the relationship between the cost of a project and its outcome. It differs from *cost-benefit analysis*, which is concerned with benefits which can be measured in monetary terms. Cost-effectiveness analysis has been applied to education in a few studies which attempted to measure effectiveness in terms of examination grades, test scores, etc. and to relate these measures to the costs of education. Wagner (1972), for example, compared the Open University and conventional universities in terms of cost-effectiveness analysis, and Layard and Oatey (1973) examined the cost-effectiveness of the new media in higher education.

The purpose of such research is to compare different methods of teaching, or different types of institution, in terms of the ratio between costs and various measures of output, such as examination results. The main problem in applying cost-effectiveness analysis to education is to define the objectives of education, and measure outcomes in terms of these objectives.

C

Further reading

Wagner, L., The Economics of the Open University, 'Higher Education', I, 2, pp. 159–82, 1972.

Layard, R. and Oatey, M., The Cost-Effectiveness of the New Media in Higher Education, in 'British Journal of Educational Technology', IV, 3, pp. 158–76, 1973. (See Part 1, ch. 5)

Costs of education The term 'cost' refers to two concepts in economics. The first refers to money which is spent to purchase goods or services. In this sense the costs of education means the total expenditure by Local Authorities and central Government on the provision of education. In 1979–80 this amounted to £10,623 million. During the 1960s and 1970s educational expenditure rose faster than many other forms of Government spending, and so education absorbed an increasing share of national income. In 1979–80 the proportion was over 5 per cent, compared with only 3 per cent in 1950.

Money spent on education is obviously of great importance, but economists find just as important the real resources which money can buy. In the case of education, the resources used by schools and universities include time (of teachers and non-teaching staff, pupils and students), buildings, equipment, books and materials.

Economists use the term *opportunity costs* to refer to real resource costs, as opposed to money expenditure. It is not simply the money which is spent but the real resources which are devoted to education, rather than to health, transport, or manufacturing industry. In many cases, resources can be measured in terms of money expenditure; for example, the real resource costs of teachers' time can be measured by expenditure on teachers' salaries. Where students are concerned, however, measurement is not simple. Here *forgone earnings* are used to measure the cost.

Not all economists accept the validity of this concept of costs, but it is used in *cost-benefit analysis*, when the benefits of education are compared with opportunity costs. Most analyses of educational costs, however, are concerned with expenditure, with the extent and causes of variations in costs between different levels of education, and with the difference between *average cost* and *marginal cost*. Cumming (1971) looked at educational expenditure in Scotland to discover why costs varied in different schools, and Hough (1981) examined costs in schools in England and Wales. Selby-Smith (1970) analysed costs of further education, and Glennerster and Wilson (1978) examined expenditure in the independent schools. Fielden and Pearson (1978) show how to estimate the costs of new educational technologies, such as teaching machines.

Further reading

Vaizey, J. and Sheehan, J., 'Resources for Education', Allen & Unwin, 1968.

Cumming, C., 'Studies in Educational Costs', Scottish Academic Press, 1971.

Selby-Smith, C., 'Costs of Future Education: A British Analysis', Pergamon, 1970.

Glennerster, H. and Wilson, G., 'Paying for Private Schools', Allen Lane, Penguin Press, 1978.

Fielden, J. and Pearson, P. K., 'Costing Educational Practice', Council for Educational Technology, 1978. (See Part 1, ch. 5)

Council for Educational Technology (CET) Formed in 1973 from the former National Council for Educational Technology, CEG acts as the central organisation for promoting the application and development of educational technology at all stages of education and training throughout the United

Kingdom. The Council operates in an advisory role to other bodies, initiates and assists in developmental programmes in the various sectors of education and training, supports and conducts innovative activity in new areas of educational development. In recent years CET has conducted major programmes in *computer-assisted learning*, the creation of learning materials for in-service training in educational technology and the development of computer-controlled media cataloguing.

Much of the work of CET emerges as publication of books, pamphlets and audio-visual media. Developmental programmes such as those directed towards the improvement of resource organisation may take the form of documents designed to stimulate further enquiry and provide support guidelines, CET also publishes the 'British Journal of Educational Technology'. The Council itself is representative of all sectors of education and training from all the areas of the United Kingdom, and where appropriate CET provides a link to international organisations. (See Part 1, ch. 7)

Council for National Academic Awards CNAA acts as the controlling board for awards given by polytechnics and central institutions and some of the courses offered by colleges of education and colleges of *further education*. In order to validate an award the CNAA assessors view the proposed *curriculum*, the methods of running a course and the methods of *assessment*. By this method the CNAA can affect the maintenance of standards in further and higher education. (See Part 1, ch. 7)

Council of Engineering Institutions This federal body, consisting of 15 chartered engineering institutions in the UK, received its royal charter in 1965, with the main function of establishing standards of professional engineering qualifications. The individual institutions are responsible for their own entry requirements and may ask for more than the Council requires. The Council sets standards to which corporate members of the member institutions must conform to be able to use the designation Chartered Engineer (C Eng). By and large, entry to C Eng is restricted to graduates in engineering of a British university, although CEI still provides an alternative route through its own examinations structure.

The Privy Council in 1971 approved changes to the charter of CEI to allow the creation of the Engineers' Registration Board (ERB) and Composite Register. This allows Chartered Engineers, Technician Engineers and Engineering Technicians of the organisations making up ERB to be registered and use designatory letters. Examples of member institutions are: The Royal Aeronautical Society, 4 Hamilton Place, London W1V 0BQ; The Institution of Chemical Engineers, 165–171 Railway Terrace, Rugby CV21 3HQ; The Institution of Civil Engineers, 1–7 Great George Street, London SW1P 3AA. (See Part 1, ch. 11)

Council of Europe Through its Directorate of Education and of Cultural and Scientific Affairs the Council of Europe can both draw on and influence the educational work in its 20 member nations. The main co-operative and consultative committee between governments is the Council for Cultural Co-operation, which was established in 1962. On it all the member governments are represented, together with Finland and the Holy See, the Consultative and Parliamentary Assemblies of the Council of Europe and the *European Cultural Foundation*. The Council's Education Committee was founded in 1949, and sponsors projects, commissions and publications, maintains a documentation centre and issues yearbooks, bibliographies, indices and guides to educational literature. (See Part 1, ch. 3)

113

Council of Local Education Authorities With the reduction of the number of direct grant schools and with the exception of the independent schools, Local Education Authorities are responsible either wholly or in some measure for the provision of education for all pupils. They have therefore the most significant role in both the day-to-day practical provision and administration and in the implementation of DES policy. In England and Wales these Local Education Authorities have as their central co-ordinating body the Council of Local Education Authorities. Full representation across England and Wales is secured by membership from both the Association of County Councils and the Association of Metropolitan Authorities. (See Part 1, ch. 7)

Council of Technical Examining Bodies (CTEB) The CTEB co-ordinates national and regional policies and standards for technical examinations. It is an advisory and consultative body consisting of representatives from the *City and Guilds of London Institute*, and the six *regional examining bodies*. The *Department of Education and Science* is represented through assessors. The Concordat is an agreement between CGLI and the six regional examining bodies that regulates their relationship on the courses in which each may examine for operatives, craftsmen and technicians. The Concordat states that in their own geographic areas the regional examining boards examine operatives' courses and the lower levels of craftsmen and technicians' courses. CGLI examines at the higher levels in these geographic areas and at all levels in England and Wales where there are regional examining bodies. All syllabuses issued by the parties to the Concordat include a statement indicating the effects of the agreement on those particular examinations. The regional examining bodies are recognised as agents for examinations for National Certificate courses. Much of their work is gradually coming under the aegis of the *Technical Education Council* and *Business Education Council (BEC)*.

The CGLI is deeply involved in technical education in the UK. The identification of educational and training needs together with the preparation of suitable syllabuses is achieved through the Institute's structure of Joint Advisory Committees with membership from relevant industrial, educational and professional interests. A very wide range of technical occupations is covered, but CGLI has agreed to withdraw progressively as the TEC develops, although the Institute will continue to supply administrative and examining services. (See Part 1, ch. 11)

Counselling Counselling aims to help an individual to achieve more satisfaction and achievement either socially or at work. The counsellor can be in a direct personal relationship through which knowledge and experience are available to the client. Or the counsellor can be someone who makes himself available permanently or temporarily to clients. (See Part 1, ch. 12)

Courses The range of courses for business is so vast that use must be made of specialised sources of information, such as the *National Training Index*, or publications such as 'British Qualifications'. Organisations like the *British Institute of Management* can be useful sources of information. (See Part 1, ch. 2).

Courses: entry requirements Entry requirements vary so much it is not possible to generalise, except to say that appropriate educational qualifications (CSE, GCE) are necessary for most academic/educational courses, while for training courses not leading to qualifications, a judgment has to be made of the individual's capabilities and the likely benefits to him and/or his organisation. (See Part 1, ch. 2)

Coverdale training The late Ralph Coverdale (whose company continues his work) devised a training system whereby trainees perform tasks in groups to develop a systematic problem-solving and task-achievement approach. There is no special emphasis on inter-personal behaviour and learning results from the individual and group experiences. (See Part 1, ch. 12)

Creativity The criticism of many educational exercises is that learners are required to give a correct answer. The expectation of a correct answer leads learners to conform. Such learning patterns provide problems for other learners who can see all the difficulties in determining or defining such an answer, and who can see lots of new ideas. This latter kind of learner is exhibiting creative or *divergent thinking* In recent years there have been attempts to measure this *creativity* by asking learners such questions as 'Write as many different (unusual) uses as you can think of for a tyre'. The convergent thinker will incline towards uses such as 'putting on a wheel, to prevent boats bumping into quays'. The divergent or creative thinker will include novel uses such as 'cut into sections to make knee guards for crawling, put soil in to have a circle of plants, use sections as rocking cradles for dolls', and so on. This sort of open-ended stimulus can be applied with or without time limit.

The problems which have arisen in measuring creativity are related to the diffuse definitions of the concept and to methods of scoring responses. A variety of strategies for scoring have been used, but all are laborious. In addition it is not clear whether creativity is an innate ability, one that can be developed, or one that can be constrained, although some work in the USA would confirm this last possibility.

Further reading

Hudson L., 'Contrary Imaginations: A Psychological Study of the English Schoolboy', Methuen, 1966.

Getzels, J. W. and Jackson P.W., 'Creativity and Intelligence', John Wiley, 1962. (See Part 1, ch. 8)

Criterion-referenced instruction (CRI) A learning system developed by Mager and Pipe that uses a detailed specification of what a learner is expected to be able to do at the end of an education or training programme in order to design the appropriate learning content and methods. Most trainers, without realising it, use this technique. (See Part 1, ch. 12)

Criterion-referenced measurement In recent years work has concentrated on the use of *objectives* and measuring whether learners have achieved those objectives. In its simplest naive form criterion-referenced measurement assumes one question or test item for each objective. E.g.:

Objective: Learners will discriminate between countries which were involved in colonising South America (most colonisation was carried out by Spain) by selection from a list.

Question: Most of South America was colonised by people from: Britain, France, Netherlands, Portugal, Spain.

The distribution of total marks before learning will be *skewed* to the bottom end of the range and the total marks after learning will be heavily skewed to the top end of the range. (Most other educational measurements compare one learner with another. Tests are devised to distribute learners' responses into an assumption of a *normal distribution*.) A modified form of criterion-referenced measurement has considered groups of items and groups (or domains) of objectives related together; such measurement is called *domain-referenced* measurement. Both types of criterion-referenced measurement have had enthusiastic response from teachers, who see their potential as diagnostic assessment procedures. For research workers the scene has been less attractive because the available statistical technology has been limited. It is now possible, by sampling from the learning criteria, to predict performance on a wider sample. In addition a further sample-free model has been developed where questions are arranged in a hierarchy and only a sample of questions need to be used. This type of question grouping is called the Rasch model, after its inventor.

Further reading

Popham, W. J., 'Criterion-Referenced Measurement', Prentice Hall, 1978.

Sumner, R. and Robertson, T. S., 'Criterion-Referenced Measurement and Criterion-Referenced Tests', National Foundation for Educational Research, 1977 (See Part 1, ch. 8)

Criterion-referenced test A CRT is just one name given to a host of *tests* which have in common that their main purpose is not to measure people relative to one another. They are therefore contrasted with norm-referenced tests which are constructed in order to produce a reliable rank order of people along the attribute.

As the name suggests, the principle aim of CRTs is to determine whether someone has reached criterion or not. There are immediate problems of definining a criterion and secondary problems of determining the error associated with such a measure, since classical reliability theory does not provide the right framework for calculating meaningful error coefficients.

The problems of defining a criterion are many. Some CRTs are designed to judge whether someone is adequately prepared to follow a certain course. If the course requires competence at the four rules, what percentage pass mark on a test of computation would be required? Empirical validation of various pass levels for each particular situation should be carried out to establish such a 'mastery' level. Such tests are therefore sometimes called mastery tests, but it is not uncommon for tests with this name to have an arbitrary percentage as the mastery or criterion level.

Some tests in this line rely on a *domain* sampling model, where the test is a random sample of *items* from a strictly defined domain. Results can then give an estimate of what a person can do from a particular domain. Such tests therefore allow interpretation in terms of what a person can do in contrast to norm-referenced tests which show how much better or worse he is than someone else. Such tests are often called domain or content-referenced.

The tests considered here under the name of CRTs are much more amenable to interpretation in terms of real behaviour, but it has proved very difficult to construct such tests except for very specific and limited areas of behaviour. (See Part 1, ch. 6)

Cross-disciplinary approach This approach involves four stages: (1) description; (2) interpretation through application of relevant disciplines; (3) juxtaposition (establishing criteria, formulating hypotheses); (4) simultaneous comparison, by rotation or fusion, to test hypotheses.

Further reading

Bereday, G. Z. F., 'Comparative Method in Education', chs. 1, 2, Holt, Rinehart & Winston, 1964. (See Part 1, ch. 3)

Cross-disciplinary nature of comparative education This had been a characteristic of recent approaches to comparative education. Earlier studies tended to be descriptive rather than analytical and interpretive. They also assumed that education was divorced from the rest of society and could be studied, as it were, in a vacuum. With the advent of the *historical-humanistic school* during the predictive stage more attention was paid to the factors and forces which influenced educational institutions and programmes, although these studies were given a particularly historical interpretation. As the attention of comparativists was increasingly directed to the methodology of the social sciences, so comparative education became more cross-disciplinary in approach.

It is axiomatic that the comparative researcher using such techniques should have had a rigorous training in at least one of the social sciences and that this parent discipline should be the predominant methodology used in his study, so that rigorous academic standards may be maintained.

Valuable perspectives into the relationship of school and society may be provided by the *sociologists'*, the *economists'* and *political scientists' contribution*. Recently comparative studies have been attempted by psychologists, and it is hoped that they may be joined in the near future by experts in the physical sciences and literature.

Further reading

Bereday, G. Z. F., 'Comparative Method in Education', Holt, Rinehart & Winston, 1964.

Fischer, J., 'The Social Sciences and Comparative Study of Educational Systems', ch. 1, Scranton. (See Part 1, ch. 3)

Cultural capital Pierre Bourdieu, one of the contributors to 'Knowledge and Control', considers the conventional distinction between calculating economic activity and disinterested cultural activity to be misleading, and argues that both alike should be analysed as, in a wide sense of the term, economic practices aimed at maximising material and symbolic profit. Capital in the sphere of material production gives its owners power over non-owners, and so does cultural capital. Both can be inherited. Bourdieu's allied concept of linguistic capital connects with Bernstein's concept of *linguistic codes*. Michael Apple makes extensive use of Bourdieu's concept of cultural capital in 'Ideology and Curriculum' (1979).

Further reading

Apple, M., 'Ideology and Curriculum', Routledge & Kegan Paul, 1979. (See Part 1, ch. 15)

Cultural deprivation The concept of cultural deprivation centres on the claim that some children are unable to benefit from schooling as much as others because of family, ethnic, *social class* and environmental restrictions upon their capacity to assimilate the culture of the school. One remedy proposed, especially in America, has been compensatory education. There has been much controversy not only about the efficacy of this remedy but also about the cogency of the basic claim itself.

Further reading

Keddie, N. (ed.), 'Tinker, Tailor . . . The Myth of Cultural Deprivation', Penguin, 1973. (See Part 1, ch. 15)

Culture Culture can be defined as the established ways of sharing and regulating experience that communities and groups evolve through common forms of expression and means of controlling and adapting to their material lives. Thus it can be argued that any thinking about *curriculum* content cannot help but incorporate some view of what elements of cultural experience, as expressed in a community's systems of beliefs, values and action, should be emphasised. For example, Lawton (1975) has suggested that the content of a 'common culture curriculum' should be based on the knowledge made available by the established disciplines. Other writers (Open University, 1976) see curriculum priorities in relation to a more general process of 'cultural mapping', whereby fundamental forms of experience, including work and leisure, social and political transactions, etc., are delineated. Similarly, Entwistle (1978) recommends analyses of what he calls 'shared' or 'mainstream' culture, as opposed to the 'high culture' of the social elite and academically-minded which has so far dominated the secondary school curriculum.

The idea of culture can also be used to focus less on the content of the curriculum than on the (socio-cultural) processes whereby practical curriculum decisions are influenced and made. If culture evolves through the values, understandings and meanings created, reinforced and reproduced in social interaction, the process of curriculum planning should be a form of 'cultural reconstruction'. Hence effective curriculum reform should involve corporate action centring on the reinterpretation of the general ideas teachers think with and implicitly transmit (see Reynolds and Skilbeck, 1976, chs 2, 8). Such thinking can be interpreted as an optimistic, 'reformist' view of the function of curriculum planning in the wider process of the transmission and reproduction of culture. Recent writings in the sociology of curriculum stress the ineffectiveness of curriculum change in the face of economic forces and embedded assumptions. It is argued that the academic culture into which both children and teachers are socialised in school is restrictive and, as such, a form of implicit social control (Open University, 1977). See also: *core curriculum, disciplines of knowledge, ideology, hidden curriculum, school-based curriculum development.*

Further reading
Entwistle, H., 'Class, Culture and Education,' Methuen, 1978.
Lawton, D., 'Class, Culture and the Curriculum', Routledge & Kegan Paul, 1975.
Reynolds, J. and Skilbeck, M., 'Culture and the Classroom', Open Books, 1976.
Open University, 'Culture, Ideology and Knowledge', Units 3 and 4 of Course E 203, (M. Skilbeck), Open University Press, 1976.
Open University, 'Culture, Class and the Curriculum', Unit 16 of Course E 202 (M. MacDonald), Open University Press, 1977. (See Part 1, ch. 4)

Cumulative-part method The operation to be learned is divided into an appropriate logical structure of parts. Instruction, then practice, is first given in part one only, then parts one and two together and so on, until the whole has been learned. It is an effective technique in building stamina. See also: *part-method* (See Part 1, ch. 11)

Curriculum Educationalists' definitions of the curriculum have tended to shift, in this country at least, from the content of discrete courses of study to the much wider notion of the curriculum as all the learning experiences offered to pupils under the aegis of the school. The shift in definition emphasises that what the pupil undergoes and learns at school is influenced by more than the subject matter taught. It also depends on the learning tasks set, their coherence and balance in the total school programme, and on how reflectively the pupil is led to engage in them; which depends in turn on teachers' values and aims; which are bound up in turn with how they evaluate pupils' learning and are themselves evaluated. Thus a simple way of considering the curriculum is to see it in terms of four facets: content, methods, purposes, evaluation.

Within this perspective, therefore, a whole school curriculum is not only extremely complex; it is also an idealised entity, for the definition refers to what is official and intended. Any school also has a 'hidden curriculum', the largely unintended effect of its social milieu; while the 'actual curriculum', whether interpreted as what pupils actually experience or teachers actually teach, may differ markedly from what is formally planned. This gap between 'curriculum-as-intention' and 'curriculum-in-use (or in-transaction)' underlines the need for a concrete view of the basic things that pupils should do and learn at school, an agreed 'public curriculum' (Becher and Maclure, 1978). Many countries have curriculum specifications that embody such a view. If not, as in this country, the curriculum-in-use is dominated by how pupils' work is assessed; the older view of curriculum, as course content, returns through the back door. The problem is how to make a sophisticated overall view of the curriculum effective and meaningful to the public at large.

Two particular approaches to this problem can be noted. The first is to see it as a problem more of research into the teaching of particular courses of study than of general planning. A curriculum is seen as a specification of content and principles to be investigated within classroom realities (Stenhouse, 1975). The second approach retains strong concern with the curriculum as a whole and as intention, for example, as a 'cultural map', but aims to translate such integrative conceptions into hard-headed analyses of constraints upon teachers and schools, and to link theorising about the curriculum with long-term social strategies for changing it (Reynolds and Skilbeck, 1976). See also: *hidden curriculum, curriculum organisation, whole curriculum, curriculum-in-transaction, culture, ideology.*

Further reading

Becher, T. and Maclure S., 'The Politics of Curriculum Change', ch. 1, Hutchinson, 1978.

Reynolds, J. and Skilbeck M., 'Culture and the Classroom', chs. 1, 2, 9, Open Books, 1976.

Stenhouse, L., 'An Introduction to Curriculum Research and Development', ch. 1, Heinemann, 1975. (See Part 1, ch. 4)

Curriculum analysis When a curriculum has been conceived, it is useful to identify clearly what are the intentions, methods, sequence, cost, etc. In order to derive this information a pre-specified procedure is commonly used to analyse the curriculum. There are several such procedures available which enable the types of information listed above to be elicited, e.g., flowcharts, network analysis and information mapping. (See Part 1, ch. 8).

Curriculum control Curriculum control can be initially seen as the process by which decisions about the curriculum made within the school or the teaching profession are limited by outside interests, those of parents, employers, the local community or society at large. This control may have formal administrative manifestations: for example, curriculum specifications in the case of countries with clear and centralised curriculum policies, as in Sweden, or administrative protocols on the duties of inspectors in countries with decentralised and piecemeal curriculum traditions, as in England and Wales. However, such administrative and legal instruments may seem to matter less in practice than tacit conventions and direct or indirect financial regulation of key curriculum resources. In England and Wales, for example, the autonomy of schools and teachers is profoundly ambiguous. Although unwritten, there is a shared view of the 'public curriculum', of basic skills to be taught; and teachers generally comply with the informal pressures that headteachers and advisers can bring to bear. Conversely, though in theory its governing body oversees each school's curriculum, its members usually feel, as amateurs, too ill-informed to question headteachers' judgments, which in turn are severely constrained by the staff available.

The actuality of control may be interpreted as follows. The nature of children and classroom demands that teachers have considerable 'discretionary space' in choice of curriculum emphases. Notwithstanding official curriculum statements, teachers' implementation of change is usually cautious and incremental in scope rather than radical and comprehensive. In any case, the curriculum has to balance a plurality of interests. What seems particularly important is the extent to which broad social pressures on schools are mediated through specific processes, such as question-setting by examination boards and testing agencies. This conditions the assumptions and *hidden curriculum* within which teachers and pupils work. Hence, though curriculum control is real enough, the term has a too mechanistic connotation. It operates rather through a shifting balance of internal and external interests, which shifting balance has major implications for conceptions of curriculum change and planning. See also: *hidden curriculum, implementation, styles of curriculum development, accountability, curriculum planning models.*

Further reading

Glatter, R., 'Control of the Curriculum', National Foundation for Educational Research.

Jenkins, D., and Shipman M., 'Curriculum: an Introduction', Open Books 1976, chs 3, 4. (See Part 1, ch. 4)

Curriculum deliberation Inasmuch as curriculum development is basically concerned with reconciling what is desirable with what is feasible, curriculum deliberation is the process of adapting both considerations into a working agreement on what is to be done and how it is to be done. Deliberation is thus an instance of 'practical reasoning' (Reid, 1978). More precisely, it is a type of rational discourse in the course of which, problems are defined, proposals suggested for their resolution, and arguments for and against the proposals weighted and compared (Walker, 1975). The composition and working style of those involved in such deliberation is crucial. For example, a curriculum planning group should be able to risk and contest assertions and to arrive at a defensible consensus, as well as to design teaching materials. Skills of 'bargaining', that is the trading of value-positions and the pooling of individual knowledge, are central. Stress on the role of deliberation highlights the inadequacies of rigid adherence to rational-deductive or sequential approaches to curriculum planning. In particular, the idea that curriculum decisions are negotiated refocuses thinking on the effective adoption and implementation of curriculum ideas within and between schools, providing a rationale for teachers' preference for continuity and gradual change.

Further reading

Reid, W. A., 'Thinking About the Curriculum: the Nature and Treatment of Curriculum Problems', Routledge & Kegan Paul, 1978.

Schwab, J. J., The Practical 3: Translation into Curriculum, in 'School Review', vol. 81, no. 4, pp. 501–22, 1973.

Walker, D. F., Curriculum Development in an Art Project, in W. A. Reid and D. F. Walker (eds), 'Case Studies in Curriculum Change', Routledge & Kegan Paul, 1975. (See Part 1, ch. 4)

Curriculum design A curriculum design is a set of abstract relationships embodied in the materials and learning activities of a course in use. It is the way that the critical variables of subject matter, pupils, teacher, and milieu are brought together. Thus the process of curriculum design is distinct from the broader social process, extending over time, of curriculum planning. The feasibility and educative potential of a finished curriculum design can be rationally analysed, but its formulation or synthesis is an art. (See Part 1, ch. 4)

Curriculum evaluation Curriculum evaluation is the gathering and analysis of evidence so as to inform judgments in relation to the qualities of courses of study. The particular framing of this definition brings out what is common to both homespun in-school evaluations and professionalised approaches, which now range from intensive anthropological-type case studies to analyses of curriculum data from possibly hundreds of schools. The definition also enables refinement of popular conceptions of evaluation, which may conflate it with assessment, the testing of pupils to rank or select them, or may restrict it to the comparison of measures of pupil performance with explicit curriculum objectives, as in the Tyler or 'classic' model of evaluation. But what distinguishes curriculum evaluation from the impressionistic, informal appraisals that teachers have always made in steering their work, is that it entails as critical and systematic a concern for evidence as is appropriate to the particular decisions to be guided and the resources (of time, money, etc.) available.

For example, an evaluation study might be commissioned to guide administrators' long-term decisions about the contribution of a curriculum to social policy, in which case full-time evaluators will probably make extensive but selective and precise observations to get objective and representative measures of the effect of the curriculum. They will probably interpret and present their findings so as to help policy-makers to generalise from them across a variety of school situations. But the need may be rather to generalise to a situation. For instance, evaluation may feed teachers' judgments in improving a course in a particular school. In this case their scrutiny and analysis may focus on the wholeness of the interactions concerned, their balance in operation. They may re-interpret and adjust practices and teaching materials in a way which, though unquantified, is certainly critical and defensible. But in the final analysis the defensibility of a curriculum decision depends on the application and justification of a standard of educational worth. Curriculum evaluation has tended to blur such issues either through over-absorption with measurement and techniques or through over-sensitivity to the anxieties and conflicts which it may generate among teachers and curriculum workers.

Thus there has recently been much differentiation of approaches to evaluation to do justice, for example, to its different functions in decision-making (see *summative evaluation*), to the relation between curriculum situations, audience concerns, and the communication of findings (see *illuminative evaluation*), and to the implications of curriculum control and influence (see *democratic evaluation*). See also: *accountability, behavioural objectives, self-monitoring, Tyler rationale.*

121

Further reading
Stenhouse, L. 'An Introduction to Curriculum Research and Development',
ch. 8, Heinemann, 1975.
Open University, 'Curriculum Evaluation' (D. Jenkins), Units 19–21 of
Course E 203, Open University Press, 1976. (See Part 1, ch. 4)

Curriculum-in-transaction Accumulating evidence of the ineffective implementation of curriculum policies and programmes has led to sharper analyses of
the transactions prior to or within teacher/pupil interactions. There is much
horse trading and impression management which is unacknowledged by
traditional curriculum models. Recent case studies and *illuminative evaluation* expose some of the neglected logic of transactions in decisions, and the
'coping strategies' by which teachers balance progressive aims and maintenance of classroom control. (See Part 1, ch. 4)

Curriculum organisation Though curriculum organisation often means the management of timetables, staff deployment, etc., its commoner reference in the
curriculum literature is to basic organisation of teaching/learning tasks: to
the general principles by which it is decided to organise the curriculum in
one way rather than another. For example, the curriculum can be structured
by any, or several, of the following organising principles or concepts; *disciplines of knowledge* or subjects; pupils' activities and interests; problem-
solving; themes; areas of experience; *core curriculum*. Ideally, the organisation should be such that learning activities reinforce one another. Their
vertical organisation over time should ensure continuity and sequence; their
horizontal organisation should foster integration of experience from one type
of activity across to another. Traditional subject-centred organisation is well
suited to the former but badly suited to the latter. (See Part 1, ch. 4)

Curriculum planning model Curriculum planning is a complex social process
which requires several types and levels of decision-making. The need to
discuss and co-ordinate the process requires the use of models to represent
its key aspects, though these representations inevitably simplify many aspects
and exclude others. As with models of decision-making in general, the
formulation of a planning model discloses 'rationality assumptions', that is,
assumptions about what counts as intelligent processing of information (for
example, about subject matter and pupils) when both the environment
(schools and classrooms) and outcomes (pupil learning) of the tasks to be
managed have many uncertainties. For example, the rational-deductive planning model, or *Tyler rationale*, emphasises the apparent logic of deriving
curriculum programmes from clear specifications of goals and objectives but
tends to discount what is problematic in the 'task environment'. The model
can be applied at all levels of decision-making; for instance, to rationalise
and explain the work of development projects which produce courses for
teachers in general; or to guide a 'planning-by-objectives' policy within a
department. It tends to commend itself to countries with centralised educational systems or planning elites where the curriculum is seen as a means to
the end of social and economic development.

Alternatively, the rational-interactive model sees rationality as requiring
negotiation between the different viewpoints of those affected, following no
overriding logical sequence. Curriculum planning is seen as a problem more
of 'planning with' than 'planning for'. Sometimes it is called the situational
model; its rationality assumptions emphasise flexible responses to curriculum
dissatisfactions and initiatives at school or local level. This may reflect an
ideological belief in community democracy or school-based curriculum de-

velopment; or recognition that the crucial phase in curriculum development is the implementation of plans, hence mutual adaptation between planners and curriculum users.

A third planning model, the 'disciplines model', emphasises the rationality of teachers themselves planning the curriculum when guided by systematic consideration of the relevance of philosophical knowledge (to issues of worthwhile knowledge, etc), of sociology (to tighten arguments on social trends, etc), and of psychology (to inform judgments about sequences of content, etc) (Lawton, 1973). A fourth or non-planning model is that in which teachers' intuitive judgments within individual classrooms are the main form of decision-making, with little attempt either to specify objectives, or to formalise the exchange of views, or intellectual analysis.

These four emphases represent 'ideal types' rather than models of actual curriculum planning. Much planning has aspects of all four; but to distinguish them is to be better equipped to analyse the variable appropriateness of planning practices. Their rationality assumptions affect so many interests that we need to be aware how ways of processing information may reflect the social positions or ideologies of those who regulate curriculum planning. See also: *school-based curriculum development; curriculum deliberation; styles of curriculum development; curriculum control; ideology; knowledge utilisation; implementation.*

Further reading

Becher, T. and Maclure, S., 'The Politics of Curriculum Change', ch. 2, Hutchinson, 1978.

Skilbeck, M., School-based Curriculum Development, in J. Walton and J. Wetton (eds.), 'Rational Curriculum Planning', especially pp. 157–8, Ward Lock, 1976.

Lawton, D., 'Social Change, Educational Theory and Curriculum Planning', University of London Press, 1973. (See Part 1, ch. 4)

Curriculum process The curriculum process includes all the experiences within an educational environment, both planned and unplanned, which have an impact upon the learning and personal development of each individual student. The conscious, planned aspect of the curriculum process has been called the intentional curriculum. The unplanned aspect, such as the effects of streaming, has been called the unintentional curriculum; these unexpected consequences often follow from the implementation of the intentional curriculum.

There are four interrelated elements to the curriculum process. First, decisions must be made about the aims and objectives that the educational institution is trying to achieve. These lead to the second stage, when decisions about suitable course content must be made to ensure that the objectives can be achieved. Work in the area of *concept formation and attainment, language and thought* and different *theories* of *learning* all have a significant contribution to make to the decision-making at this stage. Once the course content has been determined the third stage comes, when teaching methods appropriate to the organisation and presentation of the content must be selected and used. These methods will determine the educational experiences that the students will undergo. These experiences are a product of the interaction between what is taught, how it is presented and the way in which the students learn. Studies of *motivation, attention and perception, personality, cognitive style* and *social aspects of learning* all have guidance to offer at this stage. Once the teaching-learning process has taken place the fourth

stage is reached. Evaluation, using the various techniques of *educational assessment*, is necessary in order to establish whether the objectives have been achieved, so that the findings can be taken into account in future decision-making about objectives, content and teaching methods. See also: *learning, retention and recall; social aspects of learning; educational assessment; educational objectives; streaming; Bloom's taxonomy.*
Further reading
Golby, M. et al., 'Curriculum Design', Croom Helm for Open University, 1975. (See Part 1, ch. 14)

Data Data is the plural form of the word 'datum'. A datum results from the reduction of information to a single recorded unit. Thus 'John is 10 years old' can be reduced to age, sex or both depending on what is of interest. The collection and recording of data requires that we are able to classify into meaningful and mutually exclusive categories. Our data can then be expressed numerically by counting the numbers in each category.

Data collection is therefore the process of allocating to categories and counting, and such data are then usually presented as a data matrix. This matrix can have any number of dimensions but for simplicity the two dimensional matrix will be represented here. This is a common enough situation in educational measurement where a group of persons are asked to complete a group of *items* (i.e., a *test*) which can be *scored* as right or wrong. The following would be our data matrix:

Item	1	2	3
person 1	✓	✓	X
person 2	✓	X	X
person 3	✓	✓	✓

It is easy to see that complicating our response pattern so that several scores are obtained from a single item would necessitate the extension of the matrix into three dimensions. For analysis purposes, however, it is usual to condense our two (or more) dimensional matrix into one dimension by making certain assumptions. For example, if we can assume that our test items are measuring a uni-dimensional attribute we can condense this dimension into a score of rights and wrongs. We thus obtain a one-dimensional data matrix:

	Score
person 1	2
person 2	1
person 3	3

If our assumption of uni-dimensionality is not correct our data will be misrepresented in the one-dimensional matrix, and so there must be methods for checking dimensionality whenever a matrix is reduced. Such checks can be carried out using correlation methods such as: standard *item analysis*, *factor analysis*, or other methods such as *item characteristic curve* (ICC) analysis.

Further reading

Guilford, J. P. and Fruchter, B., 'Fundamental Statistics in Psychology and Education', ch. 2, 6th ed., McGraw-Hill, 1978. (See Part 1, ch. 6)

Data bank This is a central collection of data held available for use. The term is often used in connection with a store of data available via a computer network. (See Part 1, ch. 9)

Data processing/information services This rapidly expanding work sector demands abilities of logical thought, stamina, speed and accuracy in repetitive operations through to a very high level of systems thinking. There are many means of preparation for jobs in the field. (See Part 1, ch. 2)

Day release Employers release employees without loss of basic pay for *further education*, usually in colleges of further education and technical colleges. Most employers pay employees' fees, providing the course is appropriate to the employees' job. The DES recommends that all young employees (16–18 years old) are given day release. Many industrial apprenticeship schemes use this system. (See Part 1, ch. 2)

Deductive reasoning A piece of reasoning is deductively *valid* if the conclusion follows necessarily from the premises. A deductive argument makes explicit in the conclusion what is implicit in the premises. To assert the premises and deny the conclusion would therefore result in a contradiction. See also *inductive reasoning*. (See Part 1, ch. 13)

Degrees: advanced: post-graduate and post-experience First-degree graduates, it is often evident, require further study in a specialised area of job performance if they are to be really effective in an organisation. For example, the increasing complexity of manufacturing machinery requires a much higher level of engineering expertise than can be had from a first-degree course. Thus, many graduates in business or management subjects now proceed to post-graduate study.

Where this is an entirely new field, the post-graduate course can be regarded as a second first-degree. Most of these 'higher degree' courses are for Master's qualification (MA, MSc, MBA, etc.) increasingly available from *business schools* or the business/management departments/centres of universities (such as the Cranfield School of Management). Most of these courses (from one to two years) include a rigorous classroom programme together with dissertations or theses based on research study. Some courses at this level are called diplomas, but they are generally less demanding academically and tend to concentrate on a narrower range of study.

Doctoral degrees (PhD, D Litt, DSc, etc.) are a further award stage. They are at the peak of the structure of academic awards in the UK and require at least two years' more study after a Master's degree. They consist usually of a closely supervised research study with the presentation and often publication of a thesis. Since management in particular does not yet have a body of knowledge as a separate subject area, many doctoral courses in management also include a proportion of classroom studies of academic subjects, particularly in economics and its associated disciplines. This class work is examined.

Many of the specialist functions in organisations, especially in areas like corporate planning, are now filled by people with advanced degrees in business and management. It has been said that the present structure of advanced degrees in business in the UK produces very well trained advisors but very few true managers. There have been attempts (such as the Engineering Industry Training Board's fellowship scheme for manufacturing management) to correct this. (See Part 1, ch. 12)

Degree in business and management Degrees are awarded to students who successfully complete an examined course of study or who submit research theses to the standards required by the regulations of the university or other body concerned. The demand for degree recognition has become so great in the UK that the *Council for National Academic Awards* was created to enable non-universities to award degrees at, it is said, university standards. CNAA degrees are approved by the appropriate advisory committee, whilst each university is responsible for maintaining its own degree standards with the assistance of external examiners.

First degrees are at the bachelor level (BA, BSc, etc.) achieved after three or four years' study, usually covering more than one subject but with some taken at an honours level. The most common in business or management studies is the BA CNAA degree run at many polytechnics. Most of these studies are run on a sandwich-course principle requiring an extended period (three to twelve months) of industrial experience during the course. Many courses now include a large measure of project work of a consultancy kind with local organisations. These first degrees are no guarantee of practical competence but are sound evidence of the ability to pursue a disciplined effort over an extended period. They also indicate a sufficient theoretical grasp of elements of management to enable the graduate to contribute to solving organisational problems.

Some universities now offer similar courses. It is worth pointing out that the University of London has offered for many years its courses leading to BSc (Econ) and BSc (Com). Others now follow where London leads. Entry standards vary considerably. Many courses offer elective subjects that help entry to a professional association or institution.

For further information, consult the CNAA Compendium of Degree Courses, local careers advisory services, or the publications of the Careers Research and Advisory Centre, Bateman Street, Cambridge. (See Part 1, ch. 12)

Delinquency Three major influences have been identified which may lead juveniles to become delinquent and commit offences. Sometimes family influences such as emotional conflict, broken homes, poverty and child-rearing practices are responsible; sometimes it is situational influences such as city sub-cultures and membership of gangs that leads to delinquency. The third influence is *personality* deviance such as psychopathic conditions. Most juvenile delinquents do not persist in crime into adult life.

Further reading
Wilkins, L. T., Juvenile Delinquency: a Critical Review of Research and Theory, in 'Educational Research', vol. 5 (1963), pp. 104–19; reprinted in Child, D. (ed.), 'Readings in Psychology for the Teacher', Holt, Rinehart & Winston, 1977. (See Part 1, ch. 14)

Demand for education Economists use the term 'demand' to refer to the relationship between the price of a commodity and the quantity which consumers are willing to purchase at a particular price. One of the fundamental tools of economic analysis is the *demand function* which is used to analyse the relationship between demand and supply and the price of goods and services. According to classical economic theory, the price of goods determines the level of both demand and supply.

Economists therefore emphasise that demand for education is dependent on the 'price' that is charged, including the level of fees and the *forgone earnings* of pupils and students who continue their education. The demand for higher education by individual students is measured by the number of qualified school-leavers who choose to enter higher education; economists have tried to analyse trends in private or individual demand for higher education by means of a demand function. This relates the number of students who wish to enrol in colleges or universities to various factors which determine the level of demand. One of these factors is the 'price' of education. Other factors are also important, including the extent to which a university education will influence the future employment and earnings, etc.

The level of private demand for higher education is occasionally referred to as 'social demand', and most non-economists use the term 'demand for education' without any reference to price. Similarly, the term 'demand for manpower' is used to refer to the number of highly qualified workers who will be employed in the future, and forecasts of student numbers or manpower requirements are often concerned with numbers of students or numbers of skilled workers without any reference to 'price'. One of the central themes, however, of the economics of education is that demand for education is partly determined by 'price'.

Further reading

Open University, 'Economics and Education Policy', Course ED 322, Block 1, 'The Planning of Higher Education: The Private Demand', Open University Press, Milton Keynes. (See Part 1, ch. 5)

Demand function A demand function is a statement of the relationship between the quantity of a product which consumers are willing to purchase, and the factors which determine the level of demand, notably price. A demand function for higher education identifies the factors which determine the number of qualified school-leavers who choose to enrol in higher education. These factors include the 'price' of education, that is, the costs which the individual must bear, such as fees, and *forgone earnings*, taking into account the average value of student grants. Other factors which determine the level of demand for higher education include employment prospects for graduates, and the expected lifetime earnings of graduates, compared with those who leave school at 16 or 18. (See Part 1, ch. 5)

Democratic evaluation Inasmuch as curriculum evaluation informs decisions about educational practice, the evaluator cannot avoid adopting some stance towards how his work is to be used; and to the intimate relationship between access to information and location of power over the curriculum. Thus democratic evaluation stresses the rights of parents, teachers, pupils, etc., not just the initiators of an evaluation, to its findings, and in forms which the former will find understandable and suggestive. But assertion of this principle may make teachers and administrators reluctant to disclose information and views unless the democratic evaluator negotiates his intentions with all those his report may affect, anticipating sensitive issues of confidentiality. This ideal derives much of its appeal from its contrast with other tendencies: bureaucratic evaluation, in which methods and findings are oriented to the requirements of the government agencies which control re-

127

sources: or autocratic evaluation, in which curriculum enquiry may be externally financed but steered by the values and esoteric language of the academic research community (MacDonald, 1976).

These distinctions have arguable applicability to this country, where there are few professional evaluators, and curriculum power is diffuse and ambiguous, unlike countries such as Sweden or the USA. But the concept of democratic evaluation helps to heighten consciousness of the sense in which any involvement in curriculum development entails social relationships which are amenable to ideological or political analysis. See also: *curriculum evaluation, illuminative evaluation, ideology, curriculum control, politics of the curriculum.*

Further reading

MacDonald, B., Evaluation and the Control of Education, in D. Tawney (ed.), 'Curriculum Evaluation Today', Macmillan, 1976.

Lawton, D., 'The Politics of the School Curriculum', ch. 7, Routledge & Kegan Paul, 1980. (See Part 1, ch. 4)

Department of Education for Northern Ireland Though responsible to the Westminster Parliament, Northern Ireland has a much clearer separation of organisation and administration than does the Welsh Education Office from the Department of Education and Science. The Northern Ireland Department is divided into a number of divisons, namely: Finance Division; Schools I Division, which deals with school building, school development, primary school administration, special education administration and special education policy; primary schools policy and nursery schools; Schools II Division, responsible for secondary intermediate schools administration, grammar schools administration and finance, transfer procedure, secondary schools policy and schools management; Higher Education and Teacher Training Division; Professional Educational Development Division; Departmental and Area Boards Division; Teachers' Salaries and Conditions of Service Division; Further Education Division; Sports and Community Divisions; Youth, Arts and Libraries, Museums and Legislation; and of course an Inspectorate Division.

In addition to this wide range of responsibilities grouped under the Department of Education it is of note that on 1 October 1973 Northern Ireland regrouped its Education and Library Boards covering five areas and overlapping the existing county boundaries. The boards are Western, Southern, North-Eastern, South-Eastern and Belfast, and are designed to give a more even and logical spread of resources and administrative responsibilities. (See Part 1, ch. 7)

Department of Education and Science (DES) Though considered here as an administrative organisation, the DES, as with the other government departments of education, is also the main policy and executive body in education. The DES has responsibility for those levels of education specified in the 1944 Education Act, namely: primary education, which comprises infant schools (5–7 years), junior schools (7–11), and combined junior and secondary (11–16) education; and further education (all post-school education and training with the exception of universities).

The DES has responsibility for the administration of education for England and Wales and for Her Majesty's Inspectors of Education for England only. The range of administrative functions can be seen in the branch structure of the Department: Finance, Architects and Building, Arts and Libraries, Higher Further Education Branches (three), Division 'D' Computer Board,

Establishments and Organisation, Legal, Pensions, Schools (three branches), Planning and Research, Statistics Branch, Teachers' Branch (Salaries and Qualifications), Teachers' Branch (Supply and Training), Science and International Relations, and the Advisory Board for the Research Councils. H. M. Inspectorate are considered as a branch, but, as in the normal pattern of Civil Service organisation, provide professional 'specialist' input to the administrative branches.

The schools, nursery (for children below formal school age), primary, middle (operated by some LEAs) and secondary are run directly by the Local Education Authorities. In addition the LEAs run colleges of *further education*, most of the colleges of education, colleges or institutes of higher education and *polytechnics*. The DES has, in co-operation with particular industries, established a number of national colleges, most of which have now been amalgamated with universities or polytechnics. (See Part 1, ch. 1)

Deschooling The main name associated with deschooling is that of Ivan Illich. Illich argues that in Western society the threefold role of the teacher as custodian, preacher and therapist makes him an all too potent agent of *social control*. Through the *hidden curriculum* contained in the very structure of schooling, consumer-pupils are led to adopt the pernicious values of a consumer society. Liberation from this control could, Illich suggests, be achieved through the disestablishment of schools and their replacement by non-manipulative learning webs consisting of skill exchanges, a peer-matching network, and reference services to educational objects and educators.

The movement is interesting principally because it centres on points such as freedom and compulsion, *indoctrination*, and the responsibility of the state in *education*. Although the deschooling movement is regarded as very radical, many of its arguments are to be found in nineteenth-century liberalism.

Further reading

Illich, I., 'Deschooling Society', Calder & Boyars, 1971. (See Part 1, chs. 13 and 15)

Determinism Determinism is the theory that everything in the universe is controlled by causal laws. It is these causal laws which 'determine' what will happen. Once an event A has happened, it can be predicted that another event, B, will also occur. It is this assumption which has encouraged the development of physical science. But what of the social sciences? Can the same assumptions be made there, and if so what are the implications for the notion that man has free will or that he can behave with *autonomy?* There are, of course, people who do not object to seeing themselves as creatures of their environment, but on the whole most people prefer to think that they have some degree of autonomy.

How then can the social sciences and determination be squared with the assumption of free will and autonomy? There are several possible answers:

1 The social sciences, like other sciences, rely on observation. They are only observing what people do – they are not observing what people are 'forced' to do.

2 All that is meant by causation is that one event, A, precedes another, B. This idea of A actually causing B is a relic of anthropomorphism.

3 The proposition 'every event must have a cause' does not apply to human beings, who are motivated not by causes but by reasons.

4 Unless there were patterns in human behaviour one could not sensibly talk of being autonomous at all. As a human being one must know

129

what actions to do in order to bring about the desired end. Determinism is therefore essential for choice of actions.

Other writers have denied the appropriateness of the social sciences' adopting the causal model of the physical sciences, and believe other models should be sought. See also: *metaphysics; empirical and empiricism.*

Further reading

Hume, D., 'Treatise of Human Nature', Bk. 1, P. III (1739–40) edited by L. A. Selby-Bigge, revised by R. H. Nidditch, 2nd ed., Oxford University Press, 1978.

Mill, J. S., 'A System of Logic' (1843), vols 7 and 8, ed. J. M. Robson, Routledge & Kegan Paul, 1974. (See Part 1, ch. 13)

Diagnosis Diagnosis is the process of determining the nature of a problem. In education the problem is often to do with low *attainment*, and diagnostic *tests* attempt to measure the various aspects of the area concerned to determine whether any basic skills are particularly weak. This would then be linked to some remedial or corrective action. It is not always the case, however, that diagnosis combines both description and prescription. Some so-called diagnostic tests are entirely descriptive. (See Part 1, ch. 6)

Diagnostic branching This self-instruction (or teach yourself) system presents the trainee with alternative answers amongst which he must choose. Wrong choice identifies lack of understanding and therefore directs the trainee to an appropriate part of the programme. Then the original problem is put again. It is a particularly useful way of overcoming the training problems of people who are unwilling to admit publicly that they do not understand what they are supposed to learn. (See Part 1, ch. 11)

Difficulty This is the opposite of the term *facility*. An *item* with a facility of 10 per cent or 0.1 would have a difficulty of 90 per cent or 0.9. The facility value of 0.1 is the proportion getting the item right. The difficulty value of 0.9 is the proportion getting the item wrong. (See Part 1, ch. 6)

Diffusion of curriculum innovation Curriculum development involves innovation, that is, planned, deliberate changes of practice, rather than spontaneous change or casual initiatives. Thus diffusion of curriculum innovation is the process by which changes to the curriculum get adopted by teachers over time and place. The process is more problematic than it seems, reflected in the distinction between 'diffusion' and 'dissemination': whereas the former refers to the way in which curriculum ideas, textbooks, etc. actually spread, sometimes unintendedly, the latter refers to deliberate attempts, perhaps ineffective, to communicate and distribute them. Thought about curriculum dissemination tends to assume that innovations (for example, integrated science) exist fully realised prior to diffusion, and thus that the task is to 'move' innovations, seen as 'products', from a centre to dispersed adopters. But though this implicit model fits some innovation processes (for example, agricultural innovation or sales of educational hardware) most curriculum development requires teachers to incorporate new skills and knowledge into their practice within school milieux where incentives to change are low, but professional isolation and risks to self-esteem are high. In short, diffusion of new curriculum ideas depends as much upon the social relationships involved as upon effective 'transmission' of information. Thus informal 'personal contact networks' and official or unofficial 'change agents' have key influences (House, 1974).

In theory three modes of diffusion of curriculum innovation are possible: from centre to periphery, where dissemination is by a single (government) agency; from periphery to periphery, through localised and adaptable secondary centres, for example, teachers' groups; or embodied in social movements, like the women's movement or environmental concern, which, though lacking stable centres or messages, may be more pervasive and potent (Schon, 1971). Ideally, curriculum development should entail all three modes of diffusion. See also: *knowledge utilisation, strategies of curriculum change, styles of curriculum development, implementation.*

Further reading

House, E., 'The Politics of Educational Innovation', McCutchan, 1974.

MacDonald, B, and Walker, R., 'Changing the Curriculum', Open Books, 1976.

Schon, D., 'Beyond the Stable State', Penguin, 1971. (See Part 1, ch. 4)

Diploma in Management Studies (DMS) The DMS is the major national award of its kind. It was formerly run by the Department of Education and Science but in 1976 became a responsibility of the *Council for National Academic Awards.* Candidates must normally possess a degree from a British university, a Higher *National Certificate* with endorsement, a Higher *National Diploma*, a suitable grade of membership from a professional institution or association approved for DMS entry, or an equivalent qualification. It is possible but exceptional for a candidate aged more than 27 with at least four years' management or administrative experience to gain entry. The DMS in its early years was accessible under the experienced manager regulation to a large number of otherwise unqualified people, but with the alleged rise in academic standards this appears now to be much more difficult.

Courses are available throughout the country on a bewildering variety of bases, from three years' part-time through day release, half-day and evening, or evening only, to six months' full-time study. There are two parts. Part 1 deals with the role of management, behavioural studies, environmental studies, and quantitative studies. Part II covers human behaviour, operational studies, more on quantitative methods, project work and an elective subject (such as retail management, personnel management, and so on). Principles and practices of management are included throughout the course, as are human aspects, leadership, decision-making, and so on.

Where the course is intensely practical and uses teachers with industrial experience it appears to be beneficial. Unfortunately, as has been mentioned elsewhere, there is no accepted body of knowledge called management, so the tendency is to use specialised subject teachers for each segment of a DMS programme. The course attempts to deal with this by including a subject area called integrative studies. The course is available in a large number of *further education colleges, polytechnics*, and *regional management centres*. In Scotland the Diploma is administered by the Scottish Joint Committee for Diplomas in Management Studies, 8 George Street, Edinburgh, EH2 2PF. (See Part 1, ch. 12)

Directed private study This is the basis on which correspondence courses (and other forms of *distance learning*) work. However, many organisations have their own internal service using the technique, whereby learning materials are made available to individuals, with a support system run jointly by the education and training department and the individual's boss. Such systems offer considerable advantages, such as individualisation, and are therefore becoming widely used. (See Part 1, ch. 2)

Direct grant school As established under the 1944 Act these schools were independent of the LEAs but not entirely detached from them. As their name implies, they were financed, in part at least, by a grant direct from the Secretary of State based mainly upon the number of pupils on roll. In 1975 the total number of these schools was 176. The great majority were *grammar schools* selecting pupils on the basis of ability. In return for the grant they had to make a quarter of their places available without charge to pupils who had spent at least two years in maintained primary schools. The entry might be selected by the school or by the LEA on the basis of its normal selection procedures, the places being paid for by the LEA. In addition, the LEA had the power to reserve at a direct grant school up to a further 25 per cent of the places if it needed to increase its provision of secondary school places in the area, these fees again being payable by the LEA. The allocation of the remaining places was determined by the school, and the fees paid privately.

In 1975 the Government announced that as part of its policy of implementing comprehensive secondary education, direct grant schools would be phased out. No grant would be payable in respect of pupils admitted after July 1976 unless the Governors had declared their intention of joining the maintained sector as a non-selective school, it being open to them to seek voluntary status as either aided or controlled schools. Alternatively, they might decide to become *independent schools*. In fact 119 former direct grant schools became independent and 57 (all but three of them Roman Catholic schools) opted to joint the maintained sector. (See Part 1, ch. 1)

Direct training services These are provided by the *Training Services Division* of the *Manpower Services Commission* to organisations with particular training needs they cannot meet from their own resources, or where they need specialist help unobtainable elsewhere. (See Part 1, ch. 11)

Disciplines of knowledge In its everday sense discipline is activity guided by submission to rules. The same general conception underlies the idea of a discipline of knowledge. On the surface it refers to a body or domain of knowledge where precision of meaning and depth of analysis are achieved by the use of distinctive concepts. More basically, a discipline, such as history, philosophy or physics, can be seen as activity committed to the refinement or extension of knowledge in accordance with conventions about how intellectual enquiry should be conducted and its outcomes evaluated. In some disciplines scientific methodologies are inappropriate. Nonetheless, historians, philosophers, etc. are pressed by collegues to provide evidence and arguments which support their claims to knowledge in a far more stringent way than everyday thinking requires.

Thus the disciplines as such have a dual significance for the curriculum. First, they offer a suggestive model of learning communities bound together by a concern for truth, full membership of which depends upon a lengthy but civilising initiation. It can be argued that although school subjects rarely reflect these qualities of parent disciplines, they can do so when their characteristic 'traditions of enquiry' are systematically fostered. Second, it can be argued that the products of the main disciplines, bodies of structured, tested (hence 'public') knowledge should provide the main content of the curriculum; and that because the full spectrum of the disciplines displays mankind's most developed, disinterested striving for truth, they are the basis of a balanced 'liberal education' (Hirst, 1974).

This view permits varying emphases in the classification of disciplines and their organisation in the whole curriculum. Geography and engineering, for instance, may be termed 'fields' because they take concepts from several disciplines, which serves to emphasise their greater logical complexity. Cognate disciplines, such as history and social sciences, may be seen in whole curriculum planning as parts of a more general 'form of knowledge', the human sciences. Hirst's delineation of seven such fundamental 'forms of knowledge' is much disputed, though the idea of disciplines is widely accepted as a viewpoint from which to revitalise existing subject-based curricula (for example, Holt, 1978). There is a danger, however, that the more central concept of disciplined activity be 'colonised' by academic interests, with the implication that practical pursuits which promote craftsmanship, social competencies, etc. are marginal to the curriculum (Open University 1976, pp. 79–82). See also: *structure, core curriculum, areas of experience, curriculum organisation, culture.*

Further reading

Hirst, P., 'Knowledge and the Curriculum', Routledge & Kegan Paul, 1974.

Holt, M., 'The Common Curriculum: its Structure and Style in the Comprehensive School', Routledge & Kegan Paul, 1978.

Schwan, J. J. (1964) Structure of the Disciplines: Meanings and Significances, in M. Golby, 'Curriculum Design', pp. 249–67, Croom Helm, 1964.

Open University, 'Culture, Ideology and Knowledge', Units 3 and 4 of Course E 203, Open University Press (M. Skilbeck), 1976. (See Part 1, ch. 4)

Discovery learning (discovery method) This method of learning is designed to allow the learner to achieve his own understanding of the subject by means of successfully solving a carefully structured sequence of problems. It proceeds from examples to principles, rather than vice versa, which is the expository method. Its major advantage is that it tends to be participative rather than passive, so the learner achieves a feeling of ownership of the knowledge 'discovered'. (See Part 1, ch. 12)

Discrimination Discrimination requires that there is an observable difference between individuals or groups. In everyday usage the term has a meaning which requires that the observable difference(s) is used as the basis for making decisions more favourable to one individual or group than the other. In educational measurement, however, the term is used to describe how well certain measures can emphasise the specific differences in which we are interested. This is quantified by using an index of discrimination.

There are many possible indices of discrimination. All, however, are concerned with the differences between people on a defined dimension. Thus if we have a *test* of ability the discrimination index will be high for those *items* which best separate those with high ability from those with low ability. On ability tests we can say that those with high ability are the high *scorers*. The discrimination index for any item in such a test could therefore be the numerical value obtained by subtracting the number of low scorers who get an item right from the number of high scorers who get the item right. If as many low scorers as high scorers get the item right our discrimination will be zero, since the item is not separating the high scorers from the low scorers.

Such an index has severe limitations and so the most commonly used indices of discrimination are derived from statistical methods and usually involve a *correlation* coefficient between an item and a measure of the dimension of interest. (See Part 1, ch. 6)

Distance learning This term covers education and training (indeed, any form of learning) in which tutor and pupil are not in the same place. Correspondence courses are the most obvious examples, and it is possible to obtain a very wide range of skills and qualifications in this way. The *Open University* is probably the UK's leader in the technique of distance learning, although it is in a relatively favoured position because it uses BBC TV and radio. It also provides summer schools to support the system. A development of distance learning, open learning, is providing opportunities for those excluded from traditional systems. Such exclusion could arise from administrative, educational, psychological or social reasons. This system is centred on the student's needs and therefore each programme is an attempt to give individually based instruction.

Distance learning has progressed dramatically in the last few years, from the traditional home study materials (textbooks, exercises with a marking feedback) to the use of home experimental kits, *television, radio,* cassette kits and new microprocessors and other forms of *computer* learning. It is expected that the advent of very cheap, very small electronic computers will revolutionise home study, and experiments are already showing how effective such methods can be. However, the old practical problems of student motivation remain to be solved. Further information can be had from: The Council for Educational Technology, 3 Devonshire Street, London W1N 2BA; 01–580 7553.

Further reading

Holmberg, B., 'Distance Education: A Survey and Bibliography', Kogan Page, 1977. (See Part 1, ch. 12)

Distractor A number of options are presented to a testee as the possible right answer to each item in a *multiple-choice test*. Only one option is correct. The other options are called distractors, since they are intended to be plausible answers unless the person has confidence in his choice of the correct answer. (See Part 1, ch. 6)

Distribution Numerical *data* are available to us in two main forms. There are the type we are familiar with from the physical sciences which represent points on a scale of measurement. These give us what are known as 'metric values'. The other type are more familiar from the social sciences and involve number counts of certain attributes or number counts of different levels of the same attribute, and these give us frequency values. We can obtain frequency values of anything we can categorise. Thus a biologist may see how many of the different kinds of insect visit certain plants, or a road traffic researcher may check how many cars, lorries, vans and motor-bikes pass a certain set of traffic lights every day. The result is a distribution and this can be represented pictorially using a *histogram* as shown in the diagram.

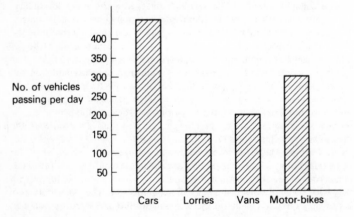

The result is quite obviously a visual representation of numerical data giving us information about the frequency of occurrence of the different vehicles. However, the classification of vehicles has not been done on any scale of measurement. There is no way we can say that a motor-bike is 'more than' or 'less than' a car. On the whole a motor-bike is less heavy than a car but this is not always so. Alternatively a motor-bike is not always less powerful than a car. They are not quantitatively different on an acceptable and consistent attribute. They are qualitatively different. The significance of this can be appreciated by rearranging the order of presentation of the data in the histogram. This is quite acceptable and does not alter our interpretations of the data. This would not, however, be acceptable for a distribution based on a quantitative classification. For example, a histogram showing the number of children at different heights has a certain logical order of presentation which cannot be violated without changing the clarity of the picture being presented.

There are numerous kinds of distribution based on quantitative categories, and the differences between them are important to understand when carrying out a statistical analysis of the data.

Further reading

Guildford, J. P. and Fruchter, B., 'Fundamental Statistics in Psychology and Education', ch. 3, 6th ed., McGraw-Hill, 1978. (See Part 1, ch. 6)

Divergent thinking A style of thinking which produces new or unusual ideas. The idea of divergent thinking is usually associated closely with *creativity*. Much learning design conflicts in expectation with divergent thinkers, because there is an expectation of agreed style or correct answer. See also: *convergent thinking*.

Domain The everyday usage of the word refers to an area of land or territory which has clear boundaries. In educational measurement the term refers to an area of educational interest which is also defined and bounded. Ideally we would have clear boundaries about which there would be little disagreement as to what behaviours fall within the domain. However, educational domains are not always like that. As usual, *'intelligence'* is a good example of a domain where the boundaries are not clearly defined, whereas addition of whole numbers is a clear domain with clear rules for deciding whether something belongs to the domain or not.

Specification of the domain is an important first stage in developing *tests* since it enables the test constructor to judge the suitability of the *items*. A well-defined domain will also contain rules for generating all the possible items, although it would usually be wasteful to do so. Once the domain is defined, measurement of it usually relies on a test which is made from a sample of the possible items which have been selected to represent the total domain.

Even in those areas where the domain cannot be clearly defined, it is often useful to view a test as being a sample from a domain since it helps in considering the issues of precision and *validity* of measurement.

Further reading

Bloom, B. S. et al., 'Handbook of Formative Evaluation of Student Learning', ch. 2, McGraw-Hill, 1971. (See Part 1, ch. 6)

Domain referenced measurement Because problems have arisen in showing a one-to-one relationship between test items and objectives, clumps of items are related to clumps (or domains) of objectives. (See Part 1, ch. 8)

Durkheimian sociology The French sociologist, Emile Durkheim, whose works belong to the end of the last century and the beginning of this, sees man as having a double nature. He has an individual being centred upon egoistic desires, and a social being that participates in a higher life, the intellectual and moral order of society. *Socialisation* for Durkheim is the process whereby each egoistic young child comes to develop a distinct social being: it thus takes in the entire sphere of social existence.

Durkheim defines education as a methodical socialisation of the young, presenting two aspects. First, it fosters in them the special beliefs and values appropriate to the particular milieux in which they will be called upon to act. Secondly, it fosters in them the common beliefs and values appropriate for all members of society. Above all, though, the goal of socialisation is that of making each individual a moral being. The voice of society is the voice of moral *authority*, an authority that is absolute and sacred. Durkheim's emphasis, in so far as he is a sociologist of education, is therefore upon education as moral education, and upon the teacher's authority as having its source in the authority of society. Where socialisation fails to achieve its goal, the result is a condition of anomie, or lack of moral regulation.

Parsons converted Durkheim's concept of the moral order of society into the structural-functionalist concept of the normative patterns of culture; and it is mainly through the grid of structural-functionalism that Durkheim's thought has influenced the sociology of education. There are exceptions, however, and, amongst sociologists of education in Britain, it is Basil Bernstein whose work most clearly shows the direct influence of Durkheim, particularly in its development of Durkheim's concepts of *mechanical and organic solidarity*.

Further reading

Giddens, A., 'Durkheim', Harvester Press, 1978.

Lukes, S., 'Emile Durkheim: His Life and Work', Allen Lane, 1973. (See Part 1, ch. 15)

Ecological approach This involves selecting the methods appropriate to the purpose of the study, and the co-operation of the scholar and administrator on issues of policy formulation guided by considerations of the ecological context.

Further reading

King, E. J., 'Other Schools and Ours', Holt, Rinehart & Winston, 4th ed., 1973. (See Part 1, ch. 3)

Economies of scale The term 'economies of scale' refers to a situation where an increase in the scale or volume of production causes the *average cost*, that is the cost of one unit of production, to fall. This means that the *marginal cost* of producing one extra unit of production is less than the average cost, so that an increase in the volume of production will result in lower unit costs.

In education economies of scale occur if the cost per pupil is lower in large schools than in small schools. This means that in large schools, the marginal cost of adding one additional pupil is less than the average cost per pupil, and in such circumstances it will be cheaper to expand large schools than to enrol additional pupils in small schools. Similarly, economies of scale may occur in the production of educational materials. The cost of producing school textbooks, for example, is often dependent on the scale of production. If a large number of books is produced, the cost of each book may be much lower than if the publisher produces a small number of highly specialised books.

There have been a number of attempts to discover whether there are economies of scale in education. Cummings (1971) showed that expenditure per pupil was related to the size of school in Scotland, and Laidlow and Layard (1974) demonstrated that economies of scale are significant in the Open University. In general, however, there does not seem to be a simple, clear-cut relationship between average costs and school size, and it is often difficult to measure the effects of variations in class or school size on the quality of education. The concept of economies of scale is, therefore, relevant to education, but research in this area has so far produced fairly ambiguous results. (See Part 1, ch. 5)

Economists' contribution Economists are likely to further our comparative investigation of relationships like those between wealth/poverty and education; *manpower planning* and labour activities; methods of production and schooling, etc. (See Part 1, ch. 3)

Education Education has in most societies two principal roles: that of passing on *knowledge* from one generation to the next, and that of providing people with *skills* that enable them to analyse, diagnose and thus question.

The use of education to pass on knowledge has led in the UK to a particular structure. It is by and large accepted that there are certain general areas of knowledge and skills everyone should have. Included in these are literacy and numeracy. Beyond that, the sum of human knowledge is so vast that specialisation is necessary. In most societies, the knowledge that is taught in education includes the teaching of generally accepted value systems. This is particularly true of moral codes; certainly for children, such teaching is an integral part of the education structure.

Since, however, education also works on skills, we find that the process involves teaching people to think analytically. This leads to questioning of what is being taught and the ways in which it is taught. From this there develops a whole attitude of education, and possibly even to society at large, whereby all is questionable and very little is certain. It is not possible to educate a person and then deny the right to question. This produces a great deal of social tension about the role of education, encourages political intervention and stimulates intense debate between educators and the providers of resources.

From these views of education, it is necessary for our purposes to derive a definition. It is suggested that education is a process of learning aimed at equipping people with knowledge and skills. These are to be enough to equip people sufficiently well so as to enable them to live satisfactorily, continue to learn and pursue a career. Business education deals with these aspects of knowledge and skills needed for a career in an organisation. Within education in general and business education in particular increased emphasis is now placed on linguistic, analytic and diagnostic skills. Social skills do not perhaps receive as much attention. (See Part 1, ch. 2)

Tracing the *logical geography* of the concept of education has received considerable attention and has helped to spell out some of the qualities that might be demanded of an educational system. How does education differ from training and what are the criteria for describing someone as an educated person? Peters believes that some of the distinctive qualities of education could be appointed by examining the way in which the words 'educate' and 'education' functioned in various contexts. Education, unlike training, is not concerned with the transmission of any particular skills. It is 'inseparable from talk of what is worthwhile, but with the additional notion written into it that what is worthwhile has been transmitted into a morally unobjectionable manner'. Thus though education does not point to a particular activity, certain activities would have a better chance of possessing the criteria of education. What are these criteria? The conditions of 'being educated' are summarised by Peters as being the central requirement of the concept:

1 Education implies the transmission of what is worthwhile.
2 Education involves *knowledge* and understanding and cognitive perspective. Educational knowledge – Peters suggested – is 'propositional'.
3 The process of education rules out any kind of coercion. It is for this reason that sleep learning might be excluded from the concept.

See also: *growth, moulding.*
Further reading
Archambault, R. D., 'Philosophical Analysis and Education', Routledge & Kegan Paul, 1965.
Peters, R. S., 'The Concept of Education', Routledge & Kegan Paul, 1967.
Peters, R. S., 'Ethics and Education', Allen & Unwin, 1966.
Warnock, M., 'Schools of Thought', Faber. 1977. (See Part 1, ch. 13)

Education Act 1902 In 1900 school boards with higher-grade schools, the new county and county borough councils providing technical education, the Board of Agriculture, the Charity Commissioners, and the Science and Art Department were all involved in secondary education. The opportunity to reform this muddle was provided by Mr Cockerton, a local government district auditor, who surcharged the London School Board for providing science and art teaching in its schools. The London School Board, in common with other large boards, had taken advantage of the failure of the *Elementary Education Act 1870* to define elementary education and expanded its activities into the secondary field.

The 1902 Act abolished the school boards and made county and county borough councils responsible for the provision of secondary and technical education. The same authorities, with the exception of the larger non-county boroughs and urban districts within their boundaries (the Part III authorities) also managed elementary education as well. The voluntary schools (see *religious societies*) had their maintenance costs met from the rates, a provision that aroused bitter nonconformist opposition and rent strikes in some areas, but which led to improved standards in rural areas. Nonconformists, however, secured one great advantage. Local Education Authorities could now open training colleges. As these were non-sectarian, the established Church lost the near monopoly it had previously enjoyed in this field.
Further reading
Eaglesham, E., 'From School Board to Local Authority', Routledge & Kegan Paul, 1956. (See Part 1, ch. 10)

Educational abstracting systems There is such a large range of journals in the field of education that it is difficult to locate papers relating to a specific area of research. As a result a number of abstracting systems exist. The abstracting system produces abstracts or summaries of papers in a specified list of journals. The papers are classified according to a key list of words or groups of words. Further sub-divisions are identified by a second set of words. When using an abstracting system it is essential to know the key words being used, for the styles of different abstracting systems vary. The larger abstracting systems produce a thesaurus of synonyms.

Abstracting systems usually have author indices. Recent developments use computer data systems. In this way not only can the monthly abstracts be consulted, but by using the appropriate key words all papers from, say, the last five years can be located interactively at a terminal. The original system using this computer base was ERIC (Educational Resources Information Center) in the USA. Other systems are now being developed in Europe. In the UK there is the British Education Index. The contents of current journals can be found in a non-computer system in the appropriate section of Current Contents, made up of the contents pages of new journal issues which have appeared that week. (See Part 1, ch. 8).

Educational/academic courses: applications For degree level courses: at universities, through University Central Council for Admissions, P. O. Box 28, Cheltenham, Glos; Cheltenham 59091; at polytechnics: to the appropriate polytechnic. For other courses: to the appropriate institution. (See Part 1, ch. 2).

Educational assessment The process of assessment plays a central role in education. The main emphasis in educational assessment is on the student and his learning progress. Information obtained through assessment is used in making a whole range of educational decisions. Assessment provides the teacher with the means of evaluating the extent to which his teaching methods are enabling him to achieve his *educational objectives* with his students. It also provides the student, other teachers, parents and, on occasions, employers with an estimate of the student's attainment and educational strengths and weaknesses. The range of assessment procedures and methods is now very extensive and includes standardised tests of achievement and aptitude, simple and *multiple-choice* objective tests, as well as tests suitable for measuring complex achievement through essay-type answers, projects, vivas and tests of practical ability.

Most *aptitude* tests, designed to predict success in some future learning activity, and achievement tests, designed to indicate level of success achieved in some past learning activity, are intended as measures of maximum performance. They are concerned with how well the individual can perform when he is motivated to give of his best. Other tests, for example those designed to measure interests, attitudes and aspects of personal-social adjustment, attempt to assess the student's typical behaviour. The result of assessment procedures can be interpreted in two basic ways. The *norm-referenced* approach describes the performance of an individual on a test in terms of its relationship to the performance of others in some known group (e.g., can solve verbal reasoning problems better than 80 per cent of his age group). The *criterion-referenced* approach compares the individual's performance with some performance standard (he can take shorthand dictation at 90 words per minute without error). See also: *intelligence, vocational development and guidance, curriculum process, mental testing, intelligence quotient, validity and reliability, objective test.*

Further reading

Gronlund, N. E., 'Measurement and Evaluation in Teaching' 3rd ed., Collier-Macmillan, 1976.

Rowntree, D., 'Assessing Students: How Shall We Know Them?' Harper & Row, 1977. (See Part 1, ch. 14)

Educational borrowing The expansion of the national systems of elementary education during the nineteenth century created a need to devise the most effective schools programmes. A number of educational administrators, many of them exceptional men, visited foreign schools to see at first hand what their colleagues were doing. They were interested in all aspects of teacher training, the organisation and financing of schools and the *curriculum*. Amongst these was Leo Tolstoy. In the USA Calvin Stowe, Barnard, and Mann, in Britain Kay, Arnold, Morant and Sadler, and in France, Cousins, visited foreign schools and wrote extensively about their impressions. The 'movement' was not solely reliant on individual efforts. For example, in 1867, Horace Mann in the USA established the Bureau of Education. In France the Musée Pedagogique was set up in 1879, and in Britain during 1895 the Office for Special Inquiries and Reports was established and presided over by Sadler.

All the institutions mentioned above became national agencies for the collection and dissemination of information about education. The reports mentioned earlier were designed to promote in certain aspects reform of the educational system in the writer's own country. The studies tended to be uncritical, descriptive, highly selective and, with the possible exception of Arnold and Sadler, ignored the normative, institutional and environmental influences on the schools. The penalties for uncritical borrowing from foreign educational practices may be severe, as has been demonstrated by the *Chinese experience*.

Further reading

Fraser, S. E. and Brickman, W. W. (ed.), 'A History of International and Comparative Education: Nineteenth Century Documents', Foresman, 1968. Holmes, B., 'Problems in Education: a Comparative Approach', pp. 5–18 and the list of reports on p. 310. Routledge & Kegan Paul, 1965. (See Part 1, ch. 3)

Educational communication The communications model of Shannon and Weaver (1949), although originally applied to the development of electrical systems, can be applied to human and educational communication. In essence this model is illustrated in the diagram.

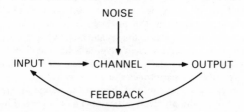

Educational input can best be described in terms of a communication between society and the individual. Society is concerned with transmitting its knowledge, skills, values and standards to the coming generation to preserve and safeguard that society. In this, the learner is central and has access to a number of resources which in the formal educational process include teachers, *books, audio-visual media* and a range of resource materials.

The 'channel' of communication should convey the message to the student accurately. 'Noise' in the system is one factor which can hinder this.

The output received by the student is not always that intended by the teacher who has designed the input. What is received will vary, depending on a number of factors, including the student's previous knowledge of a subject. *Feedback* is an important factor which enables the teacher to modify the input depending on the student response.

Further reading

Berlo, D. K., 'The Process of Communication: an Introduction to Theory and Practice', Holt Rinehart & Winston, 1960.

Hills, P. J., 'Teaching and Learning as a Communication Process', Croom Helm, 1979. (See Part 1, ch. 9)

Educational Disadvantage Unit (EDU) The EDU, a unit in the DES, was established to consider the special problems and needs of the educationally disadvantaged learner at all levels of education, especially those in immigrant populations. The Unit sets out to influence the use of resources to assist those who are identified as being educationally disadvantaged. In establishing criteria for this, assistance is given to the *Assessment of Performance Unit.* (See Part 1, ch. 7)

Educational evaluation A naive and simple discrimination made between educational research and educational evaluation is that research is looking for truth and evaluation for worth. Although the distinction may be useful in other disciplines, the boundaries are too blurred in education. Educational evaluation usually refers to research carried out in relation to curricula or institutions which enable educational or administrative decisions to be made on the basis of the report. The styles of evaluation can be heavily biased towards the collection of quantitative data on a large scale, leading to the use of statistical procedures such as *factor analysis* and *cluster analysis*. On the other hand, the information may be largely subjective based on interviews, observation and questionnaires (see *illuminative evaluation*). Evaluation data can be collected whilst a curriculum is developing to enable the developers to make decisions about their strategies. In addition data may be collected after the development is complete (e.g. *curriculum analysis*) to inform prospective purchasers, teachers and administrators about the performance of the materials in a real situation. In the American context educational evaluation is also used to describe the collection of data and information about individuals in order to make decisions on their needs and progress. Data and information collection for this purpose is not usually included under evaluation in the United Kingdom, where it would be called assessment. There is some confusion in the literature about the terms evaluation and assessment.

Further reading

Popham, W. J., 'Education Evaluation', Prentice Hall, 1975.

Hamilton, D. et al., 'Beyond the Numbers Game: A Reader in Educational Evaluation', Macmillan, 1977. (See Part 1, ch. 8)

Educational Foundation for Visual Aids EFVA, a non-profit-making body, produces learning resources and operates both the National Audio-Visual Aids Library and the National Audio-Visual Aids Centre through which courses are run. Supply and maintenance of audio-visual equipment is carried out through eleven regional centres in England and Wales. (See Part 1, ch. 7).

Educational objectives A teacher must first identify, in as much detail as possible, what it is that is to be learned by his students. The broad statement of what is to be learned represents his aims for the course, the fine detail of what is to be learned represents his educational objectives. Once his aims and objectives are established he can plan his teaching sequence; and once this has been carried out he will use various appropriate forms of *educational assessment* to evaluate whether his objectives have been achieved. This is a significant part of the *curriculum process*.

There is a considerable difference of opinion about how objectives should be stated. Mager maintains that objectives should be written by identifying as precisely as possible the new behaviour the learner should be able to produce after the learning experience. Only clearly defined behavioural objectives permit efficient course evaluation. Behavioural objectives are expressed in terms of what the learner will be able to do as a result of his learning. Behavioural objectives can easily be written for some subjects, where, for example, the student should be able to list or state facts or carry out a routine process. It is less easy to identify behavioural objectives for more open-ended and creative activities, such as carrying out historical research or writing a play. With some subjects it seems unhelpful and unrealistic to state more than the outline of the main course objectives. Bloom has attempted, with only partial success, to produce a taxonomy of educational objectives. See also: *Curriculum process, Bloom's taxonomy*.

Further reading

Beard, R. M., 'Teaching and Learning in Higher Education', 3rd ed., Penguin, 1976.

Golby, M. et al., 'Curriculum Design', Croom Helm for Open University, 1975. (See Part 1, ch. 14)

Educational planning Because of the heavy involvement of governments in the finance and provision of education throughout the world, there is an obvious need for educational planning: to attempt systematically to forecast numbers of pupils, students and teachers, as well as the level of educational expenditure, and to allocate resources efficiently between different levels of education. Educational planning is not new, but literature on educational planning has proliferated enormously in recent years, largely because there has been a new interest in linking educational and economic planning and in using techniques such as *manpower forecasting, cost-benefit analysis* or the development of mathematical models for educational planning.

The literature shows three approaches to planning; they should be regarded as complementary to each other and not as alternatives. The Robbins Report exemplified one approach: the attempt to forecast private *demand for education*, in the sense of the number of qualified school-leavers who wish to enter universities or other institutions of higher education. It explicitly rejected the other two approaches, manpower forecasting and cost-benefit analysis, on the ground that both presented too many problems to be an accurate guide to planning decisions. Since the Robbins Report there has been considerable research in both these areas, as well as on the factors which determine the private demand for education. Mathematical models have been developed for projecting student numbers, and there have also been various attempts to improve analysis of educational costs and expenditure.

Further reading

Blaug, M., Approaches to Educational Planning, in 'Economic Journal', LXXVII, No. 306, June 1967.

Lauwerys, J. A. and Bereday, G. Z. F., 'Educational Planning: World Yearbook of Education', Evans, 1967. (See Part 1, ch. 5)

Educational Television Association An agency for bringing together those who work with or are interested in educational television and other educational media. The association publishes the 'Journal of Educational Television'. (See Part 1, ch. 7)

Education and training techniques There is now a bewildering array of techniques and methods available for management studies. This entry can do no more than introduce a proposed classification from which the reader can identify those of interest to pursue in more depth. Further short entries expand some of the terms herein mentioned.

The most useful way of classifying the various learning techniques is by means of the major schools of thought on organisations, because by and large what managers are taught reflects the basic assumptions the teachers (and trainers) have about the work that managers do. The scientific school of management, as exemplified by the work of men such as Taylor, Fayol, Urwick and Treck, leads to assumptions that if only managers could learn the appropriate scientific skills and knowledge, they could manage effectively. Probably the most advanced educational technique deriving from this assumption is the *case study*. This assumes that the detailed study of other men's mistakes and successes is a satisfactory foundation for avoiding the one and achieving the other. The Tavistock School has produced the theory known as the socio-technical system. From this has come a series of learning techniques on groups. There is no doubt that learning in groups produces considerable benefits to the individual members; whether this translates into effective action in the work-place remains debatable.

During the 1960s Burns and Stalker and Woodward developed the contingency theory, which holds that all depends on the situation. From this has emerged the situational theory of management learning, whereby it is agreed that managers learn by having to manage the situation, even if they have never encountered it before. This leads further to the idea that there are certain managerial skills of analysis and synthesis applicable to any situation.

There are probably no absolutes in any of these, and contemporary thinking has moved towards a mixture. There are some things best learned through, say, *case studies*, an understanding of self may be achieved through group techniques like the *T-groups*, and *activity learning* may well succeed with some people at some time. All that the careful trainer will say is that the organisation, the manager, the task and the relationships involved need careful analysis before any decision can be reached on the right way in which to teach an individual what he is to do and how he is to do it; and he avoids panacea. (See Part 1, ch. 12)

Education finance Local Authority spending on education is of two kinds: capital expenditure and revenue expenditure. Capital expenditure relates largely to the purchase of assets which will be of use for a number of years; the acquisition of land, the building and equipping of a new school, etc. Expenditure of this sort is financed very largely from loans, so that effectively the cost is spread over the number of years during which the asset is in use. Before a Local Authority raises loans, however, it needs the consent of the appropriate Government department, and a variety of controls exists which virtually ensures that the overall volume of capital expenditure is kept within margins set by Parliament.

Revenue expenditure is concerned with annually recurring costs: salaries and wages, capitation expenses, repair and maintenance of buildings, heating, lighting, cleaning, etc. Enormous sums of money are involved and the education service accounts for about 60 per cent of all Local Authority spending. The three sources of income which provide the finance necessary to meet these costs are the user, the taxpayer and the ratepayer:

(i) The user: certain 'services' are charged for. Examples are *school meals, evening class* fees, hire of premises, etc. Only a very small proportion of total costs is met from this source.

(ii) The taxpayer: by far the largest source of Local Authority finance is Government grants, which currently account for over 60 per cent of total net expenditure. There are certain specific grants – towards mandatory awards, urban aid schemes, etc. – but the bulk of the taxpayer's contribution is distributed through the Rate Support Grant system, block grants which are in aid of rates generally rather than being specifically aimed at particular services or particular facets of a service.

(iii) The ratepayer: the balance of costs is met from rates. This is a tax levied by rating authorities which is based on the value of properties within their area and is calculated so as to equate with Local Authorities' total net requirements after taking account of the users' and the taxpayers' contributions. (See Part 1, ch. 1)

Education social workers They are on the staff of the *Chief Education Officer* (exceptionally, on the staff of the Social Services Department) and were formerly known as Education Welfare Officers. They are in linear descent from the old school attendance officer, although the job has broadened considerably since those days. A major role is still to ensure that children are attending school; and in addition to help children and families who need assistance, which involves liaison with health and social services departments and other caring agencies. (See Part 1, ch. 1)

Education vouchers The term 'education voucher' refers to a coupon or voucher of a specific monetary value which could be used to purchase education in state or private schools. This idea has been advocated by economists in the USA and in Britain by Peacock and Wiseman (1964) and West (1965). Instead of receiving all their funds directly from Local Education Authorities, schools would receive them through vouchers given to parents to purchase education for their child at the school of their choice. Central or local government would then provide funds for that school to the value of the voucher.

Advocates of vouchers argue that it would stimulate competition between schools, encourage diversity, give parents a degree of choice, and make schools more responsive to parents' wishes. Opponents argue that vouchers would be socially divisive, encouraging richer parents to 'top-up' the value of the voucher to send their children to schools charging higher fees. According to West and some American advocates, one way to overcome this problem would be to give lower-income families vouchers of higher value, or forbid 'topping-up'. Clearly the proposal to finance schools by vouchers is, in fact, a series of proposals, since different authors have suggested very different schemes.

In the school district of Alum Rock, California, vouchers were used experimentally for a few years to finance elementary schools. The experiment demonstrated that, although vouchers for education are feasible, they do present a number of problems.

Further reading
Peacock, A. and Wiseman, J., 'Education for Democrats', Institute for Economic Affairs, 1964.

West, E. G., 'Education and the State', Institute for Economic Affairs, London, 1965. (See Part 1, ch. 5)

Efficiency This term refers to the relationship between outputs and inputs. It may refer to either economic efficiency or technical efficiency. A process is described as technically efficient if it produces the maximum output from a given combination of inputs; this relationship between outputs and inputs is dependent upon the *production function* which the process uses. It will be economically efficient if it produces the output at the lowest possible cost. This is dependent on the relative price of the different factors of production.

Both these concepts are relevant to education. One of the objectives of government economic policy is to ensure that resources are allocated efficiently; resources must be allocated in such a way as to produce the maximum benefits for society, at the lowest cost. Techniques such as cost-benefit or cost-effectiveness analysis are used. Even if such techniques are not used, the economics of education suggests that decisions about the allocation of resources should be based on some assessment of the economic efficiency of alternative policies.

At the level of the individual school or university the concept of technical efficiency is relevant. For example, what effect would expenditure on teachers rather than on books have on the quality of education provided? A few attempts have been made to study the relationship in universities between outputs and inputs, but little has been done at school level to analyse technical efficiency because of the problem of defining and measuring output and quality of education.

Further reading

Lumsden, K. G., 'Efficiency in Universities: the La Paz Papers', Elsevier, 1974.

Bottomley, J. A. et al., 'Costs and Potential Economies', OECD, 1972. (See Part 1, ch. 5)

Elaborated and restricted codes Bernstein suggests that different language forms are used according to social class and that these may influence the way the user organises and responds to experience and learning. An 'elaborated code' with accurate grammatical and syntactical structure in complex sentences that convey their meaning with precision is used almost exclusively by the middle classes. A 'restricted code' with grammatically simple, unfinished sentences with a poor syntactical structure is used by both working and middle-class people.

Further reading

Lawton, D., 'Social Class, Language and Education', Routledge & Kegan Paul, 1968. (See Part 1, ch. 14)

Elementary Education Act 1870 *Forster*, the architect of this Act, created the dual system in elementary education by building a state one to complement the existing voluntary one (see *religious societies*). School boards were set up in those districts where the Education Department found an insufficiency of school places. School boards had the power to levy a rate, build schools, and require children to attend school (see *compulsory school attendance*). Boards consisting of five to fifteen members were elected annually. School board elections transferred the sectarian struggle from Westminster to the provinces. The winning party influenced not only the form of religious instruction, within certain limits, to be given in the board's schools, but could also safeguard its denominational interests through its control over local policy. It was, for example, in the Anglican interest to boost the numbers in

145

church schools by restricting the building of new board schools. The boards of the major cities were able to use their superior financial resources to provide a wide range of facilities for their schools. Their achievements made a sharp contrast with those of the poverty-stricken rural boards, whose members often had little interest in, if they did not openly oppose, the education of the agricultural labourer's children. The *Education Act 1902* swept away more than 2,500 school boards, ranging in size from the London School Board, whose boundaries were coterminous with those of the present Inner London Education Authority, to rural boards serving a population of under a hundred. (See Part 1, ch. 10)

Eleven-plus examination This is an examination used by LEAs which have a selective secondary school system, on the basis of which children are allocated either to grammar schools or secondary modern schools. Now (1980) it is used only in those areas which have retained grammar schools. Children sit the examination in the school year in which they attain the age of eleven. Each LEA is responsible for its own examination, but it is usual to have tests in English and in arithmetic and to set an intelligence test. Most Authorities also refer to a pupil's primary school record. The percentage of pupils qualifying for grammar schools used to vary from one LEA to another, and was usually in the range 20–30 per cent. (See Part 1, ch. 1)

Emotive Some words not only describe, but are used so as to raise particular emotional attitudes to what is being described; e.g., 'I am firm. You are pig-headed.' Some philosophers would maintain that concepts in *ethics* are of this nature. Educational discourse provides many examples of terms which are part emotive and part descriptive. *Indoctrination* and 'educated' are of this type.

Further reading

Ayer, A. J., 'Language, Truth and Logic', Gollancz, 2nd ed., 1946.

Stevenson, Charles L., 'Ethics and Language'. Yale University Press, 1944.

Hare, R. M., 'The Language of Morals', Oxford University Press, 1952.

Hudson, W. D., 'Modern Moral Philosophy', Macmillan, 1970. (See Part 1, ch. 13)

Empirical and empiricism The terms 'empiricist' and 'empirical' occur frequently in philosophy because they convey (a) how a statement was derived, i.e. from sense-perception, or (b) what reliance can be placed on the statement in view of its origin. British philosophers have tended to be empiricists. They have maintained that most of our *knowledge* is derived from sense-perception, or more strongly that observation is our only source of knowledge. Locke asks how the human mind comes by its 'vast store of knowledge' and replies; 'from EXPERIENCE. In that all our knowledge is founded; and from that it ultimately derives itself'. Hume made a similar point, though his empiricism was more thoroughgoing than Locke's. He insisted that all our ideas were derived from impressions (immediate experiences). If we wished to examine the trustworthiness of these ideas, we should ask ourselves 'from what impression is that supposed idea derived'. If we cannot find this 'impression' then the 'idea' should be viewed with suspicion.

The acceptance of sense-perception as a reliable source of knowledge would not be accepted by all philosophers. It would not have been accepted by *Plato*, who believed that our senses were misleading vehicles of *knowledge*. This was mainly because he took mathematics as his *paradigm* of knowledge, and mathematical truths are reached by *deduction* and not by observation. But empiricism (i.e., the belief that knowledge is largely gained

146

by sense-perception) was given practical vindication by the success of physical science. Empirical statements, therefore, must be justified by appeal to observation. How much observation, or how many tests, are needed for the establishment of an empirical statement is an important principle of methodology in sociology and psychology The educationalist is concerned with distinguishing genuine empirical statements from *prescriptions* and value judgments. See also: *theory, rationalism.*

Further reading

Locke, J., 'An Essay Concerning Human Understanding', ed. P. H. Nidditch, Oxford University Press, 1975.

Ayer, A. J., 'The Foundations of Empirical Knowledge', Macmillan, 1940.

Hamlyn, D. W., 'Theory of Knowledge', Macmillan, 1971. (See Part 1, ch. 13)

Empirical approach This envisages a 'scientific' approach, involving problem identification, hypothesis formulation, defining indicators and concepts, selecting cases, collecting and manipulation and interpretation.

Further reading

Noah, H. J. and Eckstein, M. A., 'Towards a Science of Comparative Education', Macmillan, 1969. (See Part 1, ch. 3)

Endowed school The term 'endowed school' indicated not the level of teaching available but how the school was financed. Thus an endowed school could be one teaching only Latin and Greek grammar, one offering the three Rs to poor children, or one offering a mix of subjects. When Nicholas Carlisle published his 'Concise Description of the Endowed Grammar Schools in England and Wales' (1818) he found that many schools in small market towns had abandoned the teaching of the classics because local business men and farmers saw little point in providing such an education for their sons.

A Royal Commission to survey educational charities appointed in 1819 helped to persuade many schools to bestir themselves during the course of its investigations extending over the next generation. Nevertheless the Taunton Commission (1864–7), which included girls' schools within its brief, uncovered many scandals. Five hundred and fifty of the 782 grammar schools inspected sent no boys at all to university; only 40 sent three a year. The report was instrumental in the passing of the Endowed Schools Act 1869 which set up the Endowed Schools Commission, whose work was transferred to the Charity Commissioners in 1874. By 1895 only 546 of the 1,448 schools that came within the scope of the 1869 Act had been left untouched by these reforming agencies. Despite this many of the smaller schools still faced financial difficulties and competition from the higher-grade schools of the school boards and private commercial schools. The *Education Act 1902* offered them the chance of a financial stability that they had previously lacked.

Further reading

Archer, R. L., 'Secondary Education in the Nineteenth Century', Cambridge University Press, 1928; reprinted Frank Cass, 1966.

Tompson, R. S., 'Classics or Charity? The Dilemma of the Eighteenth-Century Grammar School', Manchester University Press, 1971.

Crook Z. and Simon B., 'Private Schools in Leicester and the County, 1789–1840'; and Simon B., Local Grammar Schools, 1780–1880, in B. Simon (ed.), 'Education in Leicestershire, 1540–1940', Leicester University Press, 1968. (See Part 1, ch.10)

Entry requirements for professional institutions and associations These vary considerably, depending on the status aspired to by a particular professional institution or association. Generally, at the highest (or most restrictive) levels a degree of a British or equivalent university is required, and at the lowest (or least restrictive) the ability and willingness to pay an annual subscription. (See Part 1, ch. 2)

Equality The desire for greater equality has been one of the motivating forces of educational thought and practice. But the concept of equality is a very confused one, which only makes sense in conjunction with other notions such as 'justice' and 'fairness', as people having 'equal worth'. The slogan 'All men are equal' cannot be interpreted descriptively.

If 'equal' is understood as a predicate then the 'category mistake' of Orwell's famous phrase inevitably results. The slogan must therefore be interpreted *prescriptively*, meaning 'that all men count for one and no one more than one' (Bentham). The implication is that no person should be supposed to have more *intrinsic* value than another person. Within the context of law it means that no one should receive preferential treatment.

Outside the law, 'treating people equally' is fraught with difficulties. Aristotle was aware of the injustice of treating 'unequals equally'. Phrases such as a right to an 'equal share of the cake' come to mind. But the refusal of cake to a diabetic would scarcely be 'unjust'! So, this becomes revised to 'treating people equally unless there are relevant reasons for not doing so'. Deciding what these relevant differences are can only be discovered *empirically*. In the case of *education*, the difficulties become greater, for there is a tendency to confuse the claim that everyone has an equal right to education with the claim that everyone has a right to an equal education. Providing that education is regarded as a good then 'equality in education' can only mean that everyone should be given an equal opportunity to obtain the education. See also: *positive discrimination*.

Further reading

Benn, S. I. and Peters, R. S., 'Social Principles and the Democratic State', Allen & Unwin, 1959.

Warnock, M., 'Schools of Thought', Faber, 1977. (See Part 1, ch. 13)

Errors of measurement All measures contain a degree of imprecision. It is often important to know how much imprecision is involved. In certain circumstances it is possible to ignore the fact that errors occur at all. An example would be measuring the diameter of a drain-pipe with a micrometer. We know the instrument is more precise than is required for the task. Educational measures are never in a position to ignore the errors associated with any obtained scores.

Where known impression exists in physical measurement, such as measuring a person's height with a ruler, it is usual to quote the obtained height and to quote a range within which the person's true height is likely to be. Thus we might say that John is 6 feet tall, plus or minus an inch. We are really saying that John's most likely height is between 5 ft 11 inches and 6 ft 1 inch. The same is done in educational measurement. Each *score* is quoted as a range. The problem is to determine the size of the range which should be used.

Statistical methods are used to provide a unit called the standard error of measurement (SEm). The calculation of this unit is such that it enables us to say how likely it is that a person's true level of performance lies outside the range quoted. If the range is 1 SEm either side of the obtained score, we can say that 32 times out of a hundred is the person's true score likely to fall outside the range. If this range is increased to 2 SEms this drops to only 5 times in every hundred. Therefore if we need to make a decision on the basis of someone's score we can estimate the likelihood of making a wrong decision. The SEm is calculated from the *reliability* coefficient. The more unreliable the test, the greater is the likely variation in score, and therefore the greater the SEm. A formula commonly used is:

$SEm = S.D_x\sqrt{(1-r_x)}$

where $S.D_x$ is the standard deviation of the scores obtained on a *test*

r_x is the reliability coefficient for the test

It is therefore not possible to calculate the SEm without the test being administered to a group of people such that the SD and reliability can be calculated.

Further reading

Ferguson, G.A., 'Statistical Analysis in Psychology and Education', 4th ed., McGraw-Hill, 1976. (See Part 1, ch. 6)

Establishment and discontinuance of schools Under the Education Act 1980 an LEA proposal to establish a new school, close an existing school, or vary the size of an existing school by one-fifth or more requires that a public notice be published. The LEA may proceed with the proposal unless there are objections, in which case the Secretary of State will determine the issue. Proposals involving voluntary schools require the Secretary of State's approval, regardless of objections. (See Part 1, ch. 1)

Ethics Educational discourse contains many references to 'moral education' and the development of 'moral concepts'. The philosopher is concerned with the justification and elucidation of these concepts. The main difficulty is that people are genuinely concerned with moral questions and seem to assume the autonomy of ethics. Put briefly, when we talk of 'morally acceptable conduct' or 'behaving morally', what is the force of the 'moral'?

David Hume suggested that we use the word 'good' to describe a feeling of approval we experience when witnessing certain acts. However, he did not explain how a feeling of moral approval would differ from gastronomic approval and consequently how a good action differed from a good wine. G. E. Moore, arguing for the autonomy of ethics, insisted that moral good could not be explained in terms of anything else: 'Good is as unanalysable as yellow'. The *positivists* continued Hume's line. To say that an action is good is not to describe it but shows the speaker's attitude towards it. Thus, to say 'murder is morally wrong' would be to say 'murder' in a tone of disgust. This became known as the 'boo and hurrah view of ethics'. But the *theory* does not explain what kind of disgust the speaker feels or why the speaker should want to boo such actions.

In an influential book, Hare pointed out that ethical terms are used *prescriptively*. That is, by calling an action good we are commending some kinds of action and rejecting others, and reasoning that all things are *relative*.

Further reading

Hudson, W. D., 'Modern Moral Philosophy', Macmillan, 1970.

Hare, R. M., 'The Language of Morals', Oxford University Press, 1952.

Warnock, G. J., 'Contemporary Moral Philosophy', Macmillan, 1967.

Ayer, A. J., 'Language, Truth and Logic', Gollancz, 2nd ed., 1946. (See Part 1, ch. 13)

Ethnomethodology Harold Garfinkel, who coined the term 'ethnomethodology' soon after the Second World War, published its basic text, 'Studies in Eth-

149

nomethodology', in 1967. Aaron Cicourel, another leading ethnomethodologist, characterises ethnomethodology as probing beneath the level of analysis at which concepts like those of *status, role* and *norm* are operative, in an attempt to discover the tacit base-rules or interpretative procedures that provide people with the competence actually to decide what constitutes an appropriate status or role for a particular social interaction and what the appropriate norms are.

Further reading

Garfinkel, H., 'Studies in Ethnomethodology', Prentice Hall, 1967. (See Part 1, ch. 15)

European Cultural Foundation This independent organisation was founded in 1954 for projects in science, education and the arts. Eighteen countries participate and 13 have national committees. In 1960 an agreement on consultation and co-operation was made with the *Council of Europe* and an Institute of Education for research into higher education was established at the Université Dauphine in Paris in 1975. Many other organisations have been established within the context of the European movement. Of particular note within this section are the Centre for Educational Research and Innovation within the manpower and education division of OECD in Paris, and the European Educational Research Trust in London. (See Part 1, ch. 7)

European Research Group on Management (ERGOM) The European Research Group on Management is an organisation that encourages the use of specific exercises in organisational and managerial psychology, first developed in the US by Bass. The exercises are simulations that by developing in complexity and depth become confrontation rather than merely simulation. Only qualified people approved by ERGOM can use these powerful training tools. (See Part 1, ch. 12)

Evaluation Evaluation is often used interchangeably with assessment (see *educational assessment*). This is because there is considerable overlap in their meanings. Both involve measurements designed to describe the amount of certain attributes. Both involve procedures for obtaining these measurements which can involve *tests* as well as less objective instruments such as rating *scales*. There is a tendency, however, for evaluation to be used in a more general way, involving a wider range of measures with a greater acceptance of subjective judgments. There is also a tendency for evaluation to be used more when the subject of the evaluation is not a person (or group of persons) but the success of a course of teaching or method of teaching. Assessment is therefore used more usually in situations where the procedures involve more objective instruments, and when these instruments are measuring personal attributes. (See Part 1, ch. 6)

Cronbach (1963) describes evaluation as the 'collection and use of information to make decisions about an educational programe'. There are many different types and forms of evaluation which can be used. Some of these are described in Eraut's article 'Strategies for the Evaluation of Curriculum Materials' (Eraut, 1976). Three methods in particular are worthy of note: the agricultural-botany method, the objective method, and *illuminative evaluation*.

The agricultural-botany method draws its name from comparing seedlings subjected to different treatments. The danger in comparing groups of students subject to different educational methods is that although groups of plant seedlings may be similar, no two people react in exactly the same way to any given situation. The objective method asks the question: is the educational method doing what it is designed to do? This type of evaluation is based on specifying the *educational objectives* and the finding out if these objectives have been achieved. Illuminative evaluation takes account of a wide context before focusing on specific issues. More details will be found in the entry under its name.

Further reading

Cronbach, L. J., Evaluation for Courses Improvement, in 'Teachers College Record', vol. 64, 1963.

Eraut, M., Strategies for the Evaluation of Curriculum Materials, in 'Aspects of Educational Technology VI' (Austwick, K. and Harris, N., eds), Pitman, 1976.

Hamilton, D., 'Curriculum Evaluation', Open Books, 1976. (See Part 1, ch. 9)

Evaluation of management training 'Management training has had more money spent on it, with less known return, than any other kind of training' (David Wright, in 'Encyclopaedia of Personnel Management', ed. D. Torrington, Gower Press, 1974). There has been no completely satisfactory answer to the problem of the evaluation of training in general, and even less so for management training. Trainers may set learning objectives, they may identify with precision-targeted outcome behaviour, they may with clarity state programme aims, but all too often they must sell management training as an act of faith, because we have no adequate ways of measuring achievement against objectives, budgets, or aims.

Hamblin, in 'Evaluation and Control of Training', has suggested that there are five levels of evaluation, on the basis of the research so far available. First, reactions of the trainees to the training experience. Means are devised to test reactions like how useful, how enjoyable, opinions of sessions, views on speakers and so on. Such means usually ask for views on content (what to leave in, what to take out) and so on. Second, the learning that has taken place can be measured through the behaviour that occurs in the period following immediately after training. Third, job behaviour after the training can be observed, to see if trainees are applying learning to their work. Fourth, if there are changes in job behaviour, their organisational effects can be observed. Fifth, to see if the organisation has benefited in terms of better growth, greater profitability or even survival. Hamblin suggests this is a chain: training produces reactions, which lead to learning, which leads to job behaviour changes, which lead to organisational changes, which lead to changes in goals achievement.

Evaluation can be carried out at any level but the fourth and fifth levels are in the long term the two that the trainer must concentrate on if he is to continue to be able to persuade his organisation to invest in training.

Further reading

Kenny, J. P. J. and Donnelly, E. L., 'Manpower Training and Development', IPM, 1972.

Hamblin, A. C., 'Evaluation and Control of Training', McGraw-Hill, 1974. (See Part 1, ch. 12)

Evening class This was in the past a major route to qualifications, particularly for professional institutions. It is now less widely used as day and block release has grown. However, many institutions in further education continue to offer the possibility of vocational education through evening classes, although very often part of a half-day release system. (See Part 1, ch. 2)

Examinations Examinations are both a subject of research and the basic data

151

for research. Research about examinations attempts to resolve a range of dichotomies: a big range of marks in one subject (such as mathematics) and a small range of marks in another subject; the measurement of actual attainments against the need to provide a form of rank order for gradings (in technical terms these can be related to *validity and reliability*); the ease of measurement using short questions (*objective tests*) against the difficulty of using longer essay-type questions. Much of the research on examinations has investigated styles of question, marker variations, multiple marking, and statistical procedures for utilising the data available. Recent examination systems in the United Kingdom where schools can set their own examinations on their own syllabus have provided further complications in ensuring comparability between schools. Scores can have a technique called *scaling* applied.

Examination data as a basis for research also provide problems. Because of the difficulties mentioned in the previous paragraph, examinations are only limited in their usefulness in indicating attainment. Certainly scores on scripts are very difficult to use. Detailed analysis of questions avoided and poorly answered may identify particular learning (or examining) problems. Unless the raw scores are accessible, the grades allocated by examining boards are not a useful basis for research, except as a crude measure of a particular school, district, or authority's performance from year to year. Attempts are now being made to develop measurements which incorporate (a) items which are independent of one another, and (b) items which are independent of the people taking them.

Further reading

Rowntree, D., 'Assessing Students: How Shall we Know Them?' Harper & Row, 1977.

Wood, R. and Skurnik, L. S., 'Item Banking: A Method for Producing School-based Examinations and Nationally Comparable Grades', National Foundation for Educational Research, 1969. (See Part 1, ch. 8)

Examining bodies Closely tied to the official conduct of education are those organisations that set and assess examinations. However much autonomy is given to an educational institution, once examinations are administered by an outside body that body does to some extent shape educational objectives and control standards of achievement. Thus those organisations responsible for examinations play significant roles within the structure of education. In most cases there are close links with the official departments of education and with bodies such as the *Schools Council for the Curriculum and Examinations* or the *Consultative Committee on the Curriculum, Scotland*.

In secondary education in England and Wales the General Certificate of Education is administered by seven different boards in England and the *Welsh Joint Education Committee*. The alternative *Certificate of Secondary Education*, which differs from the GCE in that examinations are set and conducted by the schools rather than being set centrally by a board, is validated by one of a series of regional boards. Twelve boards in England and the Welsh Joint Educational Committee carry responsibility for the CSE examinations. In Scotland the examinations for secondary education are the Scottish *Certificate of Education* and the Scottish Certificate of Sixth Year Studies. These are set and administered by the Scottish Certificate of Education Examination Board. There is no direct Scottish equivalent of the CSE examination. Northern Ireland, however, does follow the pattern of England and Wales by having both the GCE and CSE examinations, both of which are administered by the Northern Ireland Schools Examinations Council.

Post-secondary education presents a more diffuse pattern of examining bodies, as the interests become more specialised. Many further and higher education establishments offer courses leading to certificates and diplomas awarded by the *City and Guilds of London Institute*. For a long time this has been one of the main examination bodies for further education. Recently there has been a change in some subjects to courses (in England and Wales) which are set by institutions or groups of institutions and validated by either the *Technical Education Council* (TEC) or the *Business Education Council* (BEC). A similar pattern has developed in Scotland through the Scottish Technical Education Council (SCOTEC) and the Scottish Business Education Council (SCOTBEC), though in both these cases the courses are established centrally rather than by institutions.

A number of other bodies set and conduct examinations covering broad ranges of subjects, amongst which are the Joint Committees for Higher National Certificates and Diplomas in Mathematics, Statistics and in Computing and Computer Studies, the College of Preceptors, the London Chamber of Commerce and Industry, and the Royal Society of Arts Examination Board. When considering those organisations which make up this part of the structure, consideration must be given to the large number of organisations which are not as clearly connected with the official education system yet have a major effect on post-school education. These are the professional and vocational organisations that not only form the point of contact and information for members of a profession or trade but also set the standards of entry and advancement (see *professional organisations*). See also: *public examinations*. (See Part 1, ch. 7)

Exemption (levy) The *Industrial Training Act 1964*, as amended by the Employment and Training Act 1973 provides that a firm may apply to be exempt from training levy. If the *Industry Training Board* (ITB) concerned finds that the firm's training meets the board's criteria, a certificate of exemption from levy for a period of time is given. There are now only seven ITBs. (See Part 1, ch. 11)

Expressive objectives As contrasted to behavioural objectives, expressive objectives do not specify what the student should be able to do after the learning activity. Instead, an expressive objective delineates an 'educational encounter', for example, with a work of art, or in a situation to which children are to respond. By providing the teacher and pupil with information to explore, an expressive objective is evocative rather than prescriptive. However, it can be argued that this conception of an objective is mildly contradictory, illustrating the tendency within orthodox curriculum thinking to try to accommodate traditional thought in education within an end-means framework. (See Part 1, ch. 4)

Facility Facility in educational measurement is used to describe the ease with which a certain task can be done. For example, if only 10 per cent of 10-year-old schoolchildren get an item right, then its facility, expressed as a proportion, is 0.1 for that group. Obviously the facility index is meaningless without describing the population from which the index was obtained. (See Part 1, ch. 6)

Factor A factor is a *trait* which has been identified using the procedure called *factor analysis*. The word can also be used more generally to cover any identifiable or hypothesised cause of variation. In both cases it is assumed that there is an underlying dimension which helps to 'explain' the events observed. It is wrong, however, to assume a causal relationship between the underlying factor/trait/dimension and the observed events on the basis of factor analysis alone. (See Part 1, ch. 6)

Factor analysis When many factors are taken into consideration over a large sample of the population, it is difficult to see relationships between the factors. Statistical techniques can be used in association with computers to compare factors. One such statistical technique is called factor analysis. (See Part 1, ch. 8)

Our world is continually changing with different things happening in every moment. In order to cope with this bombardment of information we simplify the world by grouping together similar events under a single heading. There are many different reasons for grouping things, but factor analysis is a method for helping us to decide what events should or should not be combined.

Factor analysis is based on the idea that things which change together have something in common. Thus in medical science it is known that certain symptoms such as a runny nose, headaches and a sore throat often appear and disappear together. They, in fact, occur in such a way that the appearance of one can warn us about the imminent appearance or disappearance of another. Where a consistent relation between different symptoms occurs they are grouped together as a syndrome and it is usual to connect the syndrome with an underlying cause. In this example it would be a virus. The problem is that it is often difficult to determine whether there is a truly consistent relationship between symptoms because of the many other influences on the situation, such as another illness contracted simultaneously.

Factor analysis therefore helps to sort out the extent to which we can say that there is a consistent relationship between variables. A *correlation* between two variables gives a measure of the extent to which they vary together. Factor analysis uses this fact by taking all the correlations between any number of variables and grouping those that correlate most highly together. Such a grouping is called a *factor*. Such a factor may then be used to describe how a number of variables relate to each other in much the same way as we use the lines of latitude and longitude. They merely provide a framework with which to work. Some people go beyond this and postulate some psychological or educational reality for their factors. Such claims require further experimental evidence to be substantiated and the role of factor analysis is to suggest certain groupings of variables rather than others.
Further reading
Child, D., 'The Essentials of Factor Analysis', Holt, Rinehart & Winston, 1970.
Nunnally, J. C., 'Psychometric Theory', Part 3, ch. 9, 2nd ed., McGraw-Hill, 1978. (See Part 1, ch. 6)

Factor approach This approach seeks to establish evidence of the common origins of educational institutions by examining natural (race, language, environment), religious (Catholic, Anglican, Puritan) and secular factors (Humanism, Socialism, Nationalism). (See Part 1, ch. 3)

Factory children From 1802 onwards Parliament passed a series of Factory Acts to limit the hours worked by children and to provide schooling for them in their spare time, towards which they had to pay fees from their earnings.

At first these Acts covered children working in textile factories only, but from the 1840s children in other industries also received protection. It is unlikely that the number of children who alternated between school and work under these acts ever exceeded 100,000. By 1914 the number was down to 30,000, most of whom were working in the textile mills of Lancashire and the West Riding of Yorkshire. The Education Act 1918 abolished the part-time system as from 1921. The standard work on this topic is A. H. Robson, 'The Education of Children Engaged in Industry in England 1833–1876' (Kegan Paul, 1931). (See Part 1, ch. 10)

Falsification Popper uses this notion in two ways: (a) He suggests that physical science proceeds by 'conjecture and refutation', or falsification; (b) Falsification is used as a criterion for demarcating *empirical* statements from *metaphysical* statements; empirical statements are open to falsification, but metaphysical statements are saved from falsification by addition and qualification. See also: *verification*.

Further reading

Popper, K. R., 'Conjectures and Refutations', Routledge & Kegan Paul, 1972.

Popper, K. R., 'The Logic of Scientific Discovery', revised, Hutchinson, 1972.

Medawar, P. B., 'Induction and Intuition in Scientific Thought', Methuen, 1969.

Swinburne, Richard (ed.), 'The Justification of Induction', Oxford University Press, 1974. (See Part 1, ch. 13)

Feedback Feedback is an important part of any self-regulating mechanism, e.g. the thermostat on a radiator which feeds back information on the surrounding temperature and regulates the supply of electricity to keep the surrounding air at a constant temperature. Human beings are largely self-regulating mechanisms, as for example when they perspire or shiver to maintain the body heat against extremes of temperature. In the context of *educational communication* feedback from a student on how the teacher's messages have been received is an essential part of the exchange. (See Part 1, ch. 9).

Film By projecting a series of pictures in rapid succession a motion picture can give the impression of movement. Film has been described as an edited version of reality. It can duplicate reality by using colour, sound and even the use of three dimensions. Film can bring the past, present or a series of possible futures into the classroom. It can speed up, slow down or freeze time sequences. It can enlarge or reduce size, it can record processes that would not be visible to the unaided eye. Film can simply record events as they happen or it can be used to change attitudes and promote learning. *Television* is a similar medium, but differs in certain fundamental respects. (See Part 1, ch. 9)

Finance of education Research on this topic has taken two different directions. Firstly, there have been a few studies which have tried to analyse and explain the complex chain of financial flows between individual taxpayers and central and local government, between central government departments (including the Department of Education and Science and the Department of the Environment and the Local Education Authorities), and between LEAs or the University Grants Committee and individual schools, colleges and universities. The purpose of such studies has been to explain the existing methods of financing education, and to examine the implications of the methods of financing.

A rather different approach has been adopted by economists such as West (1965) and Maynard (1975) who advocated radical changes in the way in which education is financed. Most suggestions for changing the methods used by central or local government to fund education have involved three proposals: the introduction of education vouchers, student loans, and raising the level of fees for students in higher education. Such changes have been advocated on the grounds of efficiency, equity, and freedom of choice. Such proposals attracted fierce opposition by those who believe that all these financial changes would reduce equality of opportunity.

Another important issue is the balance between public and private finance for education. Glennerster and Wilson (1970) examined the finance of private schools and showed that private schools accounted for a declining share of pupils and educational expenditure. In post-compulsory education of all kinds, the individual student or his family bears part of the costs of education, through *forgone earnings*, and proposals to replace student grants by loans, as for example, *income-contingent loans*, to raise the level of fees, or to impose a *graduate tax* would involve a shift in the burden of financing, away from government funds towards the individual student. In 1980 an important new policy was introduced when the government announced 'full-cost fees' for overseas students. The implications of this have been analysed by Williams (1981).

Further reading

Peacock, A. T., Glennerster, H., and Lavers, R., 'Educational Finance: its Sources and Uses in the United Kingdom', Oliver & Boyd, 1968.

Glennerster, H., and Wilson, G., 'Paying for Private Schools', Allen Lane, Penguin, 1970.

Maynard, A., 'Experiment with Choice in Education', Institute of Economic Affairs, 1975.

West, E., 'Education and the State', Institute of Economic Affairs, 1965.

Williams, P. (ed.) 'The Overseas Student Question', Overseas Students Trust, 1981. (See Part 1, ch. 5)

Forgone earnings The forgone earnings of pupils or students represent the earnings which they give up, while they are in school or university, rather than in employment. Earnings forgone are used as a monetary measure of the value of students' time. For the individual, forgone earnings are a measure of the income which the student sacrifices while he continues his education; for society, they are a measure of lost output. (See Part 1, ch. 5)

Forster, W. E. (1818–86) By upbringing a Quaker until his marriage to Matthew Arnold's sister, he served in Gladstone's first administration as Vice-President of the Committee of the Privy Council. In this capacity he was admitted to the Cabinet in July 1870, thus becoming the first 'Minister of Education' to be so admitted. He was MP for Bradford from 1861 to 1886 and also served as chief secretary for Ireland from 1880 to 1882. (See Part 1, ch. 10)

Free answer Free answer describes a response mode used in *tests*. The Test consists of a number of *items* each one consisting of a 'stem'. The stem can be a question, a statement, a series of figures or anything else that can require the testee to work out a suitable response. The essence of free answer is that the testee has to generate a correct response from the information available to him. (See part 1, ch. 6)

Full-time study Most major national qualifications are offered on a full-time basis. Generally, full-time means anything over 12 weeks in length, and for people in employment necessitates a release from work, often on a secondment or sponsored basis. Nevertheless, because of employment pressures, most courses are available somewhere on almost any time basis that best suits students. Full-time study, especially in colleges of further education, has expanded rapidly in the recent past, as the demands of organisations for qualified people have become greater. (See Part 1, ch. 2)

Funding for education/training These are various: self, through Local Education Authority grants, the *Training Opportunities Scheme*, various grant bodies, such as Social Science Research Council, and so on. Grants may also be available for specific courses from Industry Training Boards. Generally, the institution providing the course will be in the best position to advise on possible sources of funds. Most employers nowadays support financially people undergoing education and training that is job-related. (See Part 1, ch. 2)

Further education and technical colleges These are colleges maintained by LEAs which provide courses of a vocational or academic nature. Vocational courses are designed to lead to a qualification acceptable in a defined field of employment, and are available at three broad levels: operative, craft and technician. (Technologist courses would be available at institutions of higher education.) Some courses are available only to apprentices or people in employment, whose employers release them, on pay, for one day a week (day release) or for a period of several weeks at a time (block release). The areas of vocational study are diverse and include commerce (secretarial, banking, accountancy, etc.), catering (bakery, hotel keeping, institutional catering, etc.) and engineering and construction (technical skills for all branches of industry). Colleges usually provide courses to meet the specific needs of local industry, and to this end technical colleges may sometimes provide specialist advanced courses normally found only in colleges of higher education. The academic courses provided can include those leading to GCE O and A level. To avoid wasteful duplication of courses and expensive resources there are regional committees to co-ordinate the provision of advanced courses. (See Part 1, ch. 1)

Further education: major establishments These provide full-time, sandwich and part-time courses of education, almost completely vocational, to post-school students. The term excludes evening institutes and adult education centres. The further education system covers a wide variety of instituions and provides courses leading to several levels of qualification. Local Authorities maintain nearly all further education establishments, which range from *polytechnics* to small technical colleges. The recent reorganisation of teacher training has brought colleges of education into the further education sector.

The institutions have four major roles in higher education.

(i) They provide full-time and sandwich courses leading to degrees of the *Council for National Academic Awards*, and in some cases external degrees of universities. Generally, these courses deal with the application of knowledge rather than knowledge for its own sake.

(ii) They provide full-time and sandwich courses at a level less rigorous than degrees for people likely to become the technicians and managers who support scientists, technologists and top managers.

(iii) They provide teacher training.

(iv) They provide part-time courses at advanced levels to supplement other qualifications. These courses also provide opportunities to those who have missed the full-time route.

In Scotland, almost all advanced education (except for the universities and colleges of education) is 100 per cent grant-aided by the Secretary of State for Scotland. In Northern Ireland responsibility for further education is exercised by the Education and Library Boards. (See Part 1, ch. 2)

Further Education Staff College The college, maintained by the Local Authorities of England, Wales and Scotland, and in receipt of a grant from Northern Ireland, is concerned with means of increasing the efficiency and effectiveness of higher and further education in the public sector, and with the relationship of that education to industry, the universities and other major national and international agencies. It conducts workshops, study conferences and seminars, publishes reports and undertakes investigations, and brings together senior members of the education service to facilitate the development of organised thought concerning problems facing them and their institutions. (See Part 1, ch. 7)

Future of comparative education Studies in comparative education are likely to focus on the relationship between school and society rather than solely on inter-educational issues. Therefore the number of studies involving the use of the methodologies of the social sciences are likely to be more numerous in the future than those in which an historical approach is used. New developments in the methodology of history are such as to ensure that historians have still much to offer comparative education. The methodologies mentioned above will increasingly have to face a challenge from the comparative studies of the radical anthropologists whose emphasis lies in producing illuminative, holistic works. The latter are differentiated from the studies involving the methods of the social scientists in so far as they are hermaneutic in purpose; that is, they seek to describe and understand and not to interpret. Thus an exciting, if yet unproved, dimension is added to the methodologies available to comparativists. It is hoped that educational planners will increasingly in future utilise the expertise of comparativists who have improved their research techniques. Thus discussions between comparativists and planners about the alternative strategies available to educational administrators, and the possible outcomes of policy decisions may be of immense benefit to the development of viable educational developments. (See Part 1, ch. 3)

Gagné's conditions of learning R. M. Gagné suggests that there are eight types of human learning, and seven of them are related together in a hierarchical fashion. Signal learning, or *classical conditioning*, he places outside the hierarchy. His typology integrates *operant conditioning* with the more complex processes of discrimination learning, concept learning, rule learning, and problem-solving. Each level in his hierarchy, after the first, has as its prerequisite appropriate learning at each of the lower levels of the hierarchy.
Further reading
Gagné, R. M., 'The Conditions of Learning', 3rd ed., Holt, Rinehart & Winston, 1977. (See Part 1, ch. 14)

Games and simulations Simulations are designed to model reality. Often a real-life situation may be too complex or too dangerous to be used in an educational setting. A simulation can focus on specific aspects of the situation and provide an essentially non-threatening environment for the learning experience. Educational games are usually simulations of reality which introduce the competitive element.

Types of simulation and game which have been used in education include case studies, in-training exercises, *role-playing*, card games, board games, etc. Monopoly is an example of a board game which simulates reality. Although this is more for entertainment, other competitive games of this kind have been designed to model situations in industry, government and other situations where decision-making is required.

Further reading

Tansey, P. J. and Unwin, D., 'Simulation and Gaming in Education', Methuen, 1969.

Megarry, J., Developments in Simulation and Gaming, in 'International Yearbook of Educational and Instructional Technology. 1978–79' (A. Howe and A. J. Romiszowski, eds), Kogan Page, 1978. (See Part 1, ch. 9)

General Teaching Council for Scotland The GTC is the sole overseeing body in Scotland of the registration of teaching staff, and the implementation of conditions of service as agreed between the employers and the teaching unions. The Council is also the body which makes recommendations to the Secretary of State on matters relating to teachers in Scotland. The Council has elected members from primary, secondary and further education, together with the colleges of education. Fifteen members are also appointed from the *Convention of Scottish Local Authorities*, the *Association of Directors of Education in Scotland*, universities in Scotland, central institutions and both the Roman Catholic Church and the Church of Scotland. Four additional members are nominated by the Secretary of State for Scotland and SED assessors are appointed. (See Part 1, ch. 7)

Girls' education The issue of the education of the working-class girl was settled without the controversy that surrounded the schooling of her wealthier sister. She followed much the same syllabus as her brother. The one act of sex discrimination in the *Revised Code* was that she had to learn needlework. Since schoolmistresses in turn had to teach this subject in school, the girl pupil-teacher in her apprenticeship had to sacrifice her algebra and geometry to concentrate on needlework. She suffered a similar deprivation at training college.

Middle-class girls had a greater struggle than their brothers, whose fathers dispensed with the private tutor and sent the boys away to boarding school but kept the governess for the girls and babies. By the middle of the nineteenth century a combination of humanitarian, economic and vocational considerations promoted change. In 1848 Charles Kingsley helped to found Queen's College, Harley Street, London, for governesses; it had amongst its early pupils Miss Frances Buss and Miss Dorothy Beale, who later became headmistresses of the North London Collegiate School and Cheltenham Ladies' College respectively. In 1868 Cambridge University made its school examinations (see *school examinations*) available to girls' schools, a step Oxford took shortly afterwards. Pioneers of girls' education then used the examination system to demonstrate that girls could be academically as successful as boys, a point well made by Philippa Fawcett when she was placed above the senior wrangler at Cambridge in 1890. Despite her success and the founding of Girton (1869), Newnham (1871), Lady Margaret Hall (1878), and Somerville (1879), girls were not admitted to degrees at Cambridge until 1948, some 28 years after Oxford, and long after other universities had begun conferring degrees on them. See also: *Girls' Public Day School Trust*.

Further reading

R. Deem, 'Women and Schooling', Routledge & Kegan Paul, 1978.

Kamm, J., 'Hope Deferred: Girls' Education in English History', Methuen, 1965.

Kamm, J., 'Indicative Past: One Hundred Years of the Girls' Public Day School Trust', Bodley Head, 1971.

White, C. L., 'Women's Magazines', 1693–1968', Michael Joseph, 1970.

Burstyn, J. N., 'Women's Education in England during the Nineteenth Century', in History of Education, vol. VI (1977), 11–19.

Dyhouse, C., 'Girl's growing up in late Victorian and Edwardian England', Routledge & Kegan Paul, 1981. (See Part 1, ch. 10)

Girls' Public Day School Trust Founded in 1872, the GPDST became the largest organisation of girls' *direct grant schools*, with 23 schools containing 15,000 pupils as members. The ending of the direct grant as a means of financing schools in the autumn of 1976 forced the schools to become completely independent of state assistance. (See Part 1, ch. 10)

Goal One of a series of terms often used loosely to indicate intent. Goals are sometimes placed in between *aims* and *objectives*, which may be considered as the extremes of specificity. Goals are also associated with attempts to specify performance expectations on changes in attitude. (See Part 1, ch. 8)

Grade A grade is a position on a graded *scale*. However, since this would cover all the standard *scores* used in *testing*, its use in educational measurement is more specific. It is used for broad graduations based on *percentile* positions in a *distribution*. The most commonly used grades are A B C D E, where grade A denotes scores obtained by the top 10 per cent of the population, grade B denotes scores obtained by the next 20 per cent, grade C denotes scores obtained by the middle 40 per cent of the population, grade D denotes scores obtained by the 20 per cent of the population below grade C, and grade E denotes those scores obtained by the bottom 10 per cent of the distribution. The choice of what percentage of the population should be represented by each grade is, however, arbitrary, and other percentages are in use. (See Part 1, ch. 6)

Graduate tax This is the term given to a system by which the costs of higher education would be partly financed by means of an extra tax imposed upon graduates who had benefited from higher education in the form of higher life-time earnings. Such a scheme has occasionally been advocated in Britain or the USA as a more equitable method of financing education than the present system, which uses the income taxes paid by the average tax-payer to finance the education of those who in the future will have higher than average incomes as a result of their higher education. A graduate tax would differ from a system of *student loans* in being compulsory, rather than optional. (See Part 1, ch. 5)

Grants to students LEAs have the duty to make awards in accordance with the Secretary of State's regulations, to students attending university or comparable courses, undertaking training for teaching or pursuing full-time courses for the Diploma of Higher Education or the Higher *National Diploma*. These are full-value awards designed to cover the full cost of the student's fees and maintenance. They are based on scales determined by the Secretary of State and are related to the student's or parents' means. The LEA has discretion to give full value awards to students pursuing courses comparable to the above, and also lesser-value awards to students over the school-leaving age attending full or part-time courses of further education. The scales in this case are determined by the LEA.

Grants for post-graduate courses leading to higher degrees are funded by the DES and various research councils and normally administered by the establishment at which the course is based. (See Part 1, ch. 1)

Group method Often the group method in education is thought of as one teacher engaging a small group of students in discussion. There are many varieties of group interactions, both for large and for small groups. Bligh et al. have listed a number of these in their book 'Training Students'. Group methods are useful for students to encourage them to share and discuss their ideas with others, and to see how others receive and interpret information.
Further reading
Bligh, D. et al., 'Training Students', Exeter University Teaching Services, 1975. (See Part 1, ch. 9)

Group Training Scheme Group Training Schemes provide for some aspects of the training function to be carried out on behalf of or by several organisations. They employ at least one training specialist and often have a training centre. (See Part 1, ch. 11)

Growth The 'growth' metaphor has been important to the advocates of child-centred *education*. The child is encouraged to develop his own innate qualities, rather than those prescribed by authority. The metaphor tends to break down, as not all qualities and potentialities can be developed consistently. See also: *moulding*.
Further reading
Dearden, R. F., 'The Philosophy of Primary Education', Routledge & Kegan Paul, 1968.
Scheffler, Israel, 'The Language of Education', Blackwell, US ed., Thomas, 1960. (See Part 1, ch. 13)

Handicap: intellectual, emotional, social and physical A number of children suffer from intellectual, social, emotional or physical disabilities which prevent them from learning successfully in normal educational settings. Typically an individual with one major handicap will suffer in other ways as well. For example, a brain-damaged child may be mentally backward, have poor language skills, and so come to have social and emotional problems all as a result of his initial disability. Slow learners may either be mentally dull, with a limited intellectual ability which requires a special education, or mentally retarded. Retarded children have had their achievement depressed by causes other than a lack of intellectual ability. Once their problem has been accurately assessed they require appropriate remedial education. *Intelligence tests* can be used to discriminate between slow learners who are mentally dull and those who are retarded.

Many social factors can interfere with a child's educational performance, including poverty, the language codes used in the child's home, lack of sensory stimulation, parental attitudes, family size and emotional deprivation. Compensatory programmes concentrate on providing a safe, stable environment where the development of language and perceptual and social skills can be encouraged.

When emotional handicaps become serious enough to interfere with a child's development the term maladjustment is used. Six areas have been identified as associated with maladjustment: nervous disorders, such as excessive anxiety; habit disorders, such as tics or speech defects; behaviour disorders, such as *delinquency*; organic disorders, such as brain damage; psychotic disorders, such as hallucinations; and education and vocational difficulties, such as slow learning. Treatment for maladjustment is usually through the child guidance service.

Physical handicap can take many forms and may often lead to other psychological problems. Severe physical handicap may require attendance at a special school where appropriate medical and educational provision is available. See also: *intelligence, brain and behaviour, autism.*

Further reading

Gulliford, R., 'Special Education Needs', Routledge & Kegan Paul, 1971.

Shakespeare, R., 'The Psychology of Handicap', Methuen, 1975. (See Part 1, ch. 14)

Handicapped child Voluntary agencies, concerned to teach the indigent blind, deaf and physically handicapped a trade by which they might support themselves, pioneered this field from the middle of the eighteenth century onwards. General education was usually rudimentary. From 1870 onwards school boards (see *Elementary Education Act 1980*) in major cities started providing special classes for these children. Such provision, owing nothing to legislation, was piecemeal in its incidence. The Report of the Royal Commission on the Blind and Deaf produced the Elementary Education (Blind and Deaf Children) Act 1893 which required school authorities to provide for these two categories of children and made their attendance at school compulsory to the age of sixteen. A year after the Committee on Defective and Epileptic Children had reported in 1898, a further act gave school authorities power to provide for these two further groups.

In 1914 Local Authorities were required to make teaching provision for mentally defective, but educable, children. Other mentally defective children became the responsibility of mental deficiency committees. Similarly the Education Act 1918 required Authorities to provide for physically defective and epileptic children. The 1924 Mental Deficiency Committee (the Wood Committee) pressed for the closer association of mentally defective children with the rest of the education service. Not until 1970 were the mentally deficient and 'ineducable' children removed from the control of the local health authorities, thereby making educational provision for children who had previously languished at home or in private or other institutions. The opportunity for integration with the rest of the community seemed to come a stage further in 1976, when a new act required local authorities to arrange for the special education of all handicapped children.

Further reading

Pritchard, D. G., 'Education and the Handicapped. 1760–1960', Routledge & Kegan Paul, 1963.

'Special Educational Needs', Report of the Committee of Enquiry into the Education of Handicapped Children and Young People (The Warnock Report), Cmnd. 7212, HMSO, 1978, pp. 8–35.

Harmonisation An attempt to promote international co-operation by creating equivalent entry requirements, length of courses and qualifications for educational programmes. (See Part 1, ch. 3)

Headteachers Headteachers are appointed to their posts by the LEA after interviews in which representatives of the *Governors* normally participate. In aided schools, the Governors make the appointment. Short of professional misconduct or criminal acts it is virtually impossible to remove them from office. They are responsible for the organisation, internal management and discipline of the school subject to requirements which the LEA might lay down but which, in practice, infringe little on the head's authority.

The head is the key figure where the teaching organisation is concerned and can take new initiatives in such matters as *streaming by ability, team-*

teaching, systems of *pastoral care*. He controls the disposition of staff as well as the internal allocation of the *capitation allowance*. He has a voice in the appointment of teaching staff, and promotion within the school depends upon his recommendation. Unless the LEA has forbidden it, he can determine the school policy on corporal punishment. He can dictate what clothes pupils must wear and even how long they may grow their hair.

This model of the head as a constitutional autocrat bound by usage is seldom encountered, however. The increasing size of schools has made the delegation of authority necessary and the new salary structure has recognised this by creating subordinate posts of responsibility. Consequently, heads consult with their staffs, but the manner of consultation varies, ranging from consultation with a 'cabinet' of senior colleagues to a formal structure of staff consultative committees. Nevertheless, the ultimate responsibility for the school rests with the head. See also: *mixed ability grouping, setting, banding*. (See Part 1, ch. 1)

Health Education Council The Council provides assistance to local education authorities through its resources centre, which houses a reference collection of audio-visual aids and book-lending library. The information service runs an enquiry service and produces source lists for selected topics. A range of free materials is available. When requested the Council can provide advice and assistance with in-service training courses for LEAs. The Council regularly publishes bulletins and journals and supports research and development in the field of school health education in collaboration with the *Schools Council for the Curriculum and Examinations*. (See Part 1, ch. 7)

Heredity and environment Both heredity and environment influence human behaviour, but the investigation of their relative influences is an extremely difficult and probably ultimately fruitless task. The direct manipulation of heredity through selective breeding or the direct control of the environment is not possible with human subjects. Genetic characteristics cannot be measured directly and no precise measures of environmental differences exist. In spite of these difficulties considerable debate has surrounded the relative influence of heredity and environment, or nature and nurture, in determining human behaviour and especially *intelligence*.

The issue is an important one: are all humans born equally endowed with the potential for intelligent behaviour and do differences develop exclusively as the result of environmental inequalities? Alternatively, if differences in genetic potential for intelligent behaviour do exist can they be compensated for by positive discrimination in educational programmes? The answers to these questions have profound implications for the fulfilment of human potential.

Studies of genetically identical twins and research using family trees have offered a partial answer to the problem. Heredity, it seems, does have an important role to play in determining intellectual abilities, but it is clear that exclusively genetic or environmental explanations are too simplistic. All human characteristics are influenced by both genetic and environmental factors. The genotype determines the potential, the environment determines how much of this potential will be realised. Any polarisation of heredity from environment is misleading. Any theory to be useful must concern itself with the interactions between innate potential and environmental opportunities. See also: *child development, intelligence, intelligence A, B and C.*
Further reading
Halsey, A. H. (ed), 'Heredity and Environment', Methuen, 1977.

163

Kamin, L., 'The Science and Politics of I Q', Penguin, 1977 (See Part 1, ch. 14)

Her Majesty's Inspectors HMIs are normally recruited from the teaching profession and are specialists in various spheres of education. They are attached to the DES and allocated to regional divisions of the country. They inspect schools and other educational institutions and report on what they find. There is strong moral and other pressure on LEAs and schools to take account of HMIs' recommendations. A prime role is their continuing dialogue with schools, LEAs, and the DES on such matters as curriculum, the development of education policy, and related matters.

They are an important source of advice both to the Secretary of State and, by means of reports, courses, and personal contact, to schools and LEAs. (See Part 1, ch. 1)

Hidden curriculum The suggestiveness of the idea of a hidden curriculum should be an embarrassment and challenge to the curriculum planner. It brings out the many aspects of learning which go on alongside or even in contradiction to the intended or official *curriculum*. It has also been termed the unwritten or latent curriculum, or even the paracurriculum (Hargreaves, 1978). In part, it is the outcome of the institutional press of the school, an unintended effect of our will to marshal children towards bookish tasks within bounds of time and space; and the need to induce their compliance, punctuality, etc. Through recurrent classroom interactions and the rituals of testing teachers may subconsciously modify or displace their claimed educational ideals. Instead they reinforce more pervasive 'cultural messages' about social behaviour. What pupils actually learn from the 'underlife' of schooling may be how to adapt to surveillance and competition, and how to 'play the system'; or perhaps belief in their own inabilities, for example, to fathom the 'mindless rulery' of mathematics (Ormell, 1978) plus deference to those who can and are thereby destined for superior occupational status.

The hidden curriculum remains a provocative but diffuse concept. It draws attention to the ways in which authority and definitions of significant knowledge are maintained in schools, but leaves their source and nature unclear. Are they internal to the school, or are they aspects of wider processes of *socialisation* inherent in industrial society? It is certainly true that many curriculum planners have taken the *classroom system* itself for granted, overlooking its latent influences. But generalised critiques of the hidden curriculum imply that it is similar everywhere, whereas there can be different hidden curricula in different schools and classrooms. Where teachers and parents conjointly acknowledge the problem, they may be able to minimise it (Martin, 1976). But it is an unavoidable implication that if the formal curriculum includes aims like critical-mindedness, social integration, etc., their realisation demands much harder-headed diagnoses and longer-term treatments of the social forces within schools than usually accompanies such aims. See also: *culture, ideology, curriculum control.*

Further reading

Hargreaves, D., Power and Paracurriculum, in Richards, C. ed., 'Power and the Curriculum', Nafferton, 1978.

Martin J., 'What should we do with a hidden curriculum when we find one?', in Curriculum Inquiry, 6.1. 1976. (See Part 1, ch. 4)

Histogram A histogram is a bar chart which shows the frequency of different events. Thus the number of cars, bicycles and lorries passing a point can be represented by a histogram (see *distribution*). This can be used in educational measurement to show the numbers of people falling into various *score* categories. (See Part 1, ch. 6)

Historical approach This involves an examination of educational systems against a common historical and cultural background. The work is merely descriptive and few attempts have been made to generalise.

Further reading

Ulich, R., 'The Education of Nations: A Comparison in Historical Perspective', Harvard University Press, 1961. (See Part 1, ch. 3)

Historical-humanistic school The mere collection of educational data from foreign systems and the uncritical incorporation into one's own system led to considerable difficulties for the adopters. The thesis that education was autonomous and existed in a vacuum, completely divorced from the rest of society, found little acceptance in the Historical-humanistic school. These people argued that a more sophisticated methodology for studying educational systems was needed, and they offered a solution involving the use of historical techniques. Their accounts were not merely descriptive but sought, when writing about past events, to identify the various factors which shaped educational norms, institutions and practices.

In general, the writers of this school, such as Kandel, Hans, Schneider and Rosello, not only described the educational system that they found, but also interpreted and explained the phenomena as they understood them. These writers were not completely objective since they entered the field with pre-determined values by which they judged the systems they studied. *Kandel's approach* indicated his passionate commitment to Western-style democracy and his implacable hatred of Communism and Fascism. Kandel's study of comparative education gave administrators indications of the factors and forces which could help the development of democracy or, alternatively, those which would further totalitarian ideologies and practices. Similar views were held by Ulich, who used an *historical approach* and Hans, who used the *factor approach*. While it is not certain to what extent they were influenced by Sadler, what was common to all of them was their commitment to the concept of *national character*, a feature which prompted much criticism.

Further reading

Kandel, I. L., 'Comparative Education', Houghton Mifflin, 1933.

Ulich, R., 'The Education of Nations: a Comparison in Historical Perspective', Harvard University Press, 1961.

Hans, N. A., 'Comparative Education', Routledge & Kegan Paul. (See Part 1, ch. 3)

Human capital Economists make a fundamental distinction between consumption expenditure which consists of the purchase of goods and services that bring immediate, but short-lived, benefits, and *investment*, which consists of the purchase of capital assets, such as buildings or machinery, that will generate income in the future. In the past there was a certain amount of fruitless dispute among some economists about whether expenditure on education should be classified as consumption or investment. It is now widely recognised that spending on education brings immediate satisfaction and increases the productive capacity of educated workers in the future. In other words, like many other items of social expenditure, education represents both consumption and investment. Today such a statement is accepted as self-evident, but in the late 1950s the idea that spending on education represents an investment in human capital, which increases the productivity of workers by providing them with the *skills*, *knowledge* and *aptitudes* needed in the market, had never been fully explored by economists. The decision to treat investment in human capital as analogous to investment in physical capital has been described by Bowman (1966) as 'the human investment revolution in economic thought'.

This new approach not only led economists to revise traditional theories about what determines earnings differences, or the economic justification for subsidies for education, such as scholarships or student grants; it also led to a re-appraisal of the need for educational planning and the contribution of education to economic growth.

The idea that education is a form of investment in human capital has been attacked. One common argument is that education simply acts as a convenient 'filter' which enables employers to select workers, the most recent challenge. In its mildest form this implies that education fulfils more than providing knowledge and skills. In its extreme form the *screening hypothesis*, as Layard and Psacharopoulos (1974) call it, is presented as being in direct opposition to the concept of human capital.

Further reading

Becker, G., 'Human Capital,' Princeton University Press, 1964.

Bowman, M. J., The Human Investment Revolution in Economic Thought, in 'Sociology of Education', pp. 111–37, Spring 1966.

Layard, R. and Psacharopoulos, G., The Screening Hypothesis and the Returns to Education, 'Journal of Political Economy', September 1974. (See Part 1, ch. 5)

Humanistic psychology A recent school of psychology, influenced by existentialism, which rejects the mechanistic, dehumanising approach of *behaviourism* and emphasises man and his natural tendencies towards the actualisation of his potentials. It is concerned with subjective experience, with the individual's perception of himself and his world and with human values.

Further reading

Rogers, C. R., 'On Becoming a Person: A Therapist's View of Psychotherapy', Houghton-Mifflin, 1970.

Maslow, A. H., 'Motivation and Personality', 2nd ed., Harper & Row., 1970. (See Part 1, ch. 14)

Human resources This generic term covers the potential of people in organisations. It is analysed and developed through organisation analysis, *manpower planning*, education and training, development, pay and conditions, and so on. Formerly, these were collectively called personnel management, but human resources management is becoming the contemporary term. (See Part 1, ch. 11)

Ideology The term 'ideology' is often used in a loose way to refer to any coherent body of beliefs shared by a number of people and governing their practice; for example, their political or religious practice. The Marxian use of the term, however, carries the implication that the beliefs held are out of touch with the reality that Marxian theory itself brings to light.

In Marx's view, the beliefs people hold are determined by the conditions of material production existing in their society (see *sociology of knowledge*). Relations of production which involve the oppression of one class by another give rise generally to sets of beliefs presenting a distorted and misleading view of society. These ideologies not only arise out of the *class struggle*, but they also mask the true nature of that struggle. One method of attempting to combat such ideological distortions is by a critique of them.

A view of ideology that has been widely influential in the sociology of education, though subjected to criticism within the *'new' sociology of education*, is that put forward by the French philosopher, Louis Althusser, in his study of 'Ideology and Ideological State Apparatuses' in 'Lenin and Philosophy and Other Essays' (1971). Althusser here argues that the educational system is one of several ideological state apparatuses, and that in capitalist society it is the dominant ISA. It, above all, serves to achieve the reproduction of the work-force needed for capitalist production by causing the right proportion of pupils in school to acquire the appropriate ideology. One of the aims of Paul Willis's 'Learning to Labour' (1977) is to show this process actually occurring in a particular school, though his analysis of the ideology acquired is based on a different position from Althusser's.

Further reading
Centre for Contemporary Cultural Studies, 'On Ideology', Hutchinson, 1978.
Willis, P., 'Learning to Labour', Saxon House, 1977. (See Part 1, ch. 15)

Illuminative evaluation An indication of the meaning of evaluation has already been covered under the section on *educational evaluation*. Illuminative evaluation is a deliberate attempt to change the style of evaluation away from quantitative data towards descriptive information. All quantitative data is effectively a form of shorthand. The shorthand has become so sophisticated, because of the development of statistics, that the interpretation of the data is difficult. In addition each step of mathematical manipulation removes another detailed level of information. Education is a human activity usually involving interaction between human beings. The protagonists of illuminative evaluation argue that information about the actual learning process and environment is vital and important – the descriptions and the reactions of individuals. A variety of styles can be used. One style is to go into the milieu with no preconceived ideas (on *aims* or *objectives* for the evaluation, or *aims* and *objectives* of the learning situation). By observation and interaction the objectives are derived: this style is called '*goal*-free evaluation'. The collection of information is from informal meetings, interviews and observation and on the basis of the initial ideas formulated by the evaluator a strategy for more in-depth follow-up is feasible. The ideas develop from the learners and the participants in the learning situation to identify the questions to be asked, rather than the evaluator having a preconceived model of the evaluation questions to be answered.

Further reading
Hamilton, D. et al., 'Beyond the Numbers Game: A Reader in Educational Evaluation', 1977.
Kraft H. P. et al, 'Four Evaluation Examples: Anthropological, Economic, Narrative and Portrayal', AERA Monograph Series on Curriculum Evaluation No. 7, Rand McNally, 1974. (See Part 1, ch. 8)

During the expansion of curriculum development in the USA in the 1960s it became apparent that teachers were unresponsive to the then dominant modes of curriculum evaluation, which emphasised analysis and measurement of selected curriculum inputs and outcomes. It was argued that teachers' curriculum practice depended upon their perception of total curriculum situations, rather than empirical reports, and thus that evaluation should 'portray' new curricula and consequent changes as complex wholes, including the aspirations of the participants and difficulties encountered. The evaluator should use a panoramic viewfinder rather than a microscope (Stake, 1967). In the UK this view was translated into the idea of 'illuminative' evaluation (Parlett and Hamilton, 1972) and gained support through its more explicit critique of traditional (unilluminating) evaluation; and its articulation of the neglected role in education of anthropological and historical styles of research. It follows that curriculum processes should be interpreted as profoundly influenced by the culture of the school or learning milieu through which teachers and students interact, and by their unacknowledged but distinctive concerns. Thus an evaluator needs many ways of gathering evidence, especially interviews and participant observation, before he can understand what really matters to the participants, and what measurements may have most meaning. The breadth of observation minimises any tendency for the evaluator's findings to be channelled by the course designer's or administrator's expectations.

But to digest and summarise such varied forms of evidence the curriculum evaluator needs exceptional skills of interpretation. In practice there is a danger that illuminative evaluations turn out to be unacceptably subjective or banal, though much progress in disciplined curriculum case study is now being made (Shaw, 1978). Moreover, such approaches complement rather than supplant larger-scale, quantified approaches. See also: *curriculum evaluation, process model of curriculum design.*
Further reading
Parlett, M., and Hamilton, D., Evaluation as Illumination in D. Tawney (ed.), 'Curriculum Evaluation Today', Macmillan, 1976.
Stake, R., The Countenance of Educational Evaluation, 'Teachers' College Record', 68, 52340, 1967.
Shaw, K., Understanding the Curriculum: The approach through Case Studies, 'Journal of Curriculum Studies' 10.1. 1975. (See Part 1, ch. 4)
Implementation Implementation is a curiously ugly term for a curiously ill-articulated aspect of human experience, that of translating a complex conception or plan into new patterns of action. Its commonest use in the curriculum field has been to diagnose failures of curriculum innovations, shifting attention from their design and diffusion to the difficulties which teachers encounter, after their decision to adopt innovations, in applying them in their working situation. Thus implementation has been defined as the actual use of an innovation, or what an innovation consists of in practice (Fullan, 1977), This conception enables two perspectives on implementation to be distinguished. The first analyses the degree to which an idea, method or course is put into practice, and its eventual 'fidelity' to the initial intention. Thus major influences on implementation might be: characteristics of the innovation (its complexity, explicitness, etc.); the strategies for change used; characteristics of the adopting unit (how decisions are made in a particular school, etc.); the nature of external incentives, such as promotion, and political influences. The second perspective highlights the changes made both to the innovation itself and to the practice and thinking of the adopters. Frequently the adopting school or teachers do not change; they 'knock the edges off' the innovation to fit embedded practices. However, there is much evidence that mutual adaptation is crucial in effective implementation (McLaughlin, 1976). This has major if neglected implications, not only for externally-sponsored innovations, but also for modest curriculum changes initiated within the school. See also: *dissemination, styles of curriculum development, change-agent, practicality ethic, rational-interactive planning.*

Further reading
Fullan, M. and Pomfret A., Research in Curriculum and Innovation Implementation, in 'Review of Educational Research', 47/2, pp. 335–97, 1977.
Holt, M., 'Schools and Curriculum Change', McGraw-Hill, 1980.
McLaughlin, M., Implementation as Mutual Adaptation, in 'Teachers College Record', 77/3, 1976. (See Part 1, ch. 4)

Incident method (process) This variation of the *case study* can be of two forms. In one form trainees are given a short description of an event or incident and then must ask questions to secure sufficient information to propose solutions. In the other form the participants describe real-life incidents, which the group attempts to answer. Their answers are compared and contested with the real-life events. (See Part 1, ch. 12).

Income-contingent loan This is a type of loan which might be offered to students, on condition that they promised to pay a fixed proportion of their income in the future until the loan was repaid. The amount which a graduate would pay each year would, therefore, depend on his rate of earnings. Such a system differs significantly from the type of *student loan* scheme in operation in the USA or in some Scandinavian countries, under which graduates repay their loans in fixed instalments, in the same way as mortgages are repaid in this country. There has been only one small-scale experiment with income-contingent loans in the USA. Their wider use has been advocated by several economists. (See Part 1, ch. 5)

Independent management education and training institutions It is impossible to state how many of these exist in the UK. The most comprehensive listing is in *National Training Index*, Course Organisers Section, although there are many other sources of information. They all have a number of things in common. First, they are concerned with the provision of education and training for experienced people, usually of managerial level but also at lower level (supervisory). Second, they provide an enormous range of activities, of almost any duration, on almost any subject. It is possible to find a course on anything from accounting through sensitivity to working methods, with a length of one day up to three months, for generalists or for specialists. Third, they are all commercial and need to make profits, and must thus deliver a product the client needs, wants and is satisfied with.

Some have been in existence long enough, and have achieved enough good work, to possess a kind of momentum based on recommendation. Rarely does a client organisation examine closely the value received. Some spring up overnight with the latest fashionable product (often presented as a panacea) to disappear as rapidly.

Any intending user must ask himself some questions before committing himself, his organisation, his manager or his money. First, what needs does the particular manager have? Second, what is it that we want him to be able to achieve after the course? Third, what content, what methods and what style must the course possess to achieve what is wanted? Only then should considerations be made of cost, time and the particular institution. Unfortunately, most British managers go on a course because of one or all of: they liked the look of it; their boss/colleague/subordinate went and enjoyed it; their boss decided it was good for them; they have a friend/contact/ex-colleague at the institutions; and so on. Only rarely is a proper analysis made.

Most of the institutions in this sector offer in-company, allegedly client-

I

based, services. The normal business criteria (of cost against benefit) used to select consultants should be applied.

Independent school An independent school is any school at which full-time education is provided for five or more pupils of compulsory school age, not being a school maintained by an LEA or a school in respect of which grants are made by the Secretary of State. These schools are fee-paying; most of them are boarding schools; and with some exceptions there is division at the age of 13 between preparatory schools (age 8–13) and what are usually known as *Public Schools* (13–18).

The independent schools are subject to the provisions of part 3 of the Education Act 1944 (which became fully effective in 1959) and the Education Act 1980. All such schools must be registered, and it is illegal to establish and maintain a school which is unregistered. The Secretary of State may refuse to register a school if the buildings, the staff or the education provided are unsuitable. There is provision for the school to appeal against the Secretary of State's decision to the Independent Schools Tribunal. (See Part 1, ch. 1)

Independent television The educational output of the independent television companies is co-ordinated through the Independent Television Programme Planning Secretariat (Education), which also co-ordinates the print back-up to the broadcast output. Under the Independent Broadcasting Authority Act 1973 the IBA is required to appoint an advisory body to give advice on policy and planning related to educational programmes. This it has done through the Educational Advisory Council, a Schools Committee, and an Adult Education Committee. (See Part 1, ch. 7)

Individual differences Every person is different from every other. The science of individual differences, which gave rise to the current field called *psychometrics* attempts to classify and quantify these differences. Attributes are therefore defined and measures constructed so that they demonstrate (or even exaggerate) the differences between people on that attribute only. (See Part 1, ch. 6)

Individualised instruction Students differ from each other in the background knowledge they bring to a situation, in their learning habits, and in many subtle and complex ways. There is therefore a need to consider how teaching methods (instruction) can be adapted to the need of the individual.

Often current teaching practices ignore the need for individualised instruction and concentrate on merely displaying knowledge to a group of students. In this type of approach individual differences are often treated as a nuisance and the teachers try to get the group to conform to a common standard.

The good teacher has always recognised the need for what amounts to the personal touch and has encouraged students to think and act for themselves. There now exists a variety of methods and techniques (referred to at the end of the entry) which go towards the concept of individualised instruction. However, they do not provide a truly individual approach but merely a more efficient way of presenting the material or, for example, where testing is involved, a better way of letting the student and the teacher know that the material is being absorbed or learned.

True individualisation of instruction could provide a variety of ways of proceeding towards a given goal, and could enable the student to make an (albeit guided) choice of methods towards this. See also: *audio tutorial, individually prescribed instruction, Keller plan, self-teaching techniques.* (See Part 1, ch. 9)

Individually prescribed instruction It was developed by Glaser and others at the University of Pittsburgh in the 1960s. The students' work is guided by individual prescriptions of instructional activities. Detailed *educational objectives* are used and pre-tests are given before, and post-tests after, each unit of material. The *Open University* uses a similar system of objectives and self-assessment tests. (See Part 1, ch. 9)

Indoctrination Although it would be agreed that the word 'indoctrination' conjured up the idea of undesirable type of instruction, it is not easy to pinpoint the precise nature of this undesirability. Hence the differing criteria provided by different writers:

1. Wilson suggests that indoctrination occurs with certain types of subject matter. Similar methods used in politics and mathematics would amount to indoctrination in the former but not in the latter.
2. Hare argues that, as religion could be either indoctrinated or not, the difference must depend upon methods. The educator encourages criticism, the indoctrinator does not.
3. White is concerned with the place of intention in indoctrination. He also wonders whether facts could be indoctrinated. Could a teacher set about 'indoctrinating' that Australia was not an island?
4. Smart suggests that the indoctrinator and educator differ fundamentally in their attitude towards persons. The educator is committed to beliefs about the dignity of persons. The indoctrinator is not.

Criticism has centred on indoctrination in politics or religion. But why not extend the possibility to any area where more than one hypothesis is possible? The possibility of indoctrination in the area of health education has not been explored, but the deliberate suppression of knowledge of side-effects of drugs would seem to be an example.

Further Reading

Hollins, T. H. B. (ed.), 'Aims in Education', Manchester University Press, 1964.

Langford, C. and O'Connor, D. J., 'New Essays in the Philosophy of Education', Routledge & Kegan Paul, 1973.

Snook, I. A. (ed.), 'Concepts of Indoctrination: Philosophical Essays', Routledge & Kegan Paul, 1972.

Snook, I. A., 'Indoctrination and Education', Routledge & Kegan Paul, 1972. (See Part, 1, ch. 13)

Inductive reasoning Inductive reasoning states more in the conclusion than the premises strictly allow. Thus from the examination of a group of sample of Xs the investigator may go on to assert factors about all Xs. The result of such reasoning provides probability, but not certainty. (See Part 1, ch. 13)

Industrial Society The Industrial Society has grown into one of Britain's leading advisory bodies in people management and industrial relations. It also provides extensively for training in these subjects. It is independent and self-financing, relying on income from subscriptions and activities. It has some 14,000 member organisations, drawn from all sectors of the economy, including private and public industry, trade unions, government bodies and employers' associations.

It aims to promote the fullest involvement of all people in their work in order to increase the effectiveness of organisations and the satisfaction of individuals in creating the goods and services which the community needs. This has led the Society to specialise in leadership (the action-centred leadership ideas of John Adair), management/union relations and participation, communication and the development of young employees. In employee communications it is a strong advocate of the briefing group idea. It has a strong interest in training overseas nationals.

The Society has extensive advisory services for both members and non-members, in personnel and industrial relations, consultancy training and research. It publishes a well-received range of practical booklets under the general title 'Notes for Managers', as well as books, pamphlets and guides to current topics. It produces audio-visual programmes for training, mostly dealing with its specialised areas of interest. Further information from the Industrial Society, Robert Hyde House, 48 Bryanson Square, London W1H 1BQ, 01–262 2401. (See Part 1, ch. 2)

Industrial Training Act 1964, and Employment and Training Act 1973 In 1960 and onwards pressure grew from industry, commerce, the trade unions and eventually from Government for an overhaul of industrial training in the UK. *The British Association for Commercial and Industrial Education* (BA-CIE) played a significant part in providing both a platform and a focus for this pressure. Eventually, in 1964, the then Conservative Government introduced the Industrial Training Act. The objectives of the Act were: to ensure an adequate supply of properly trained people at all levels in industry; to secure improvements in the quality and efficiency of industrial training; and to share the cost of training more evenly between firms. The aims of the Act were carried through by the creation of the *Industry Training Boards* with powers to levy money from all firms in their industries and to pay grants to firms who carried out effective training.

By the early 1970s there was a great deal of discontent in industry with the levy/grant system in particular and the administrative burden of the ITBs generally. This led to pressure on the Government to review the workings of the Act, and the Conservative administration of 1970–4 undertook a detailed revision of the legislation. This led to the Employment and Training Act 1973 by which the Industrial Training Act 1964 was extensively modified. The *Manpower Services Commission* was created with under it the Employment Services Division and the *Training Services Division*.

Major revisions of the Industry Training Boards after 1973 have meant the introduction of the *exemption* system. Many small firms were removed completely from the levy/grant schemes, and a substantial proportion of the ITB's funding is now drawn from Government funds, routed throughout MSC. The Labour administration of 1974–9 used the 1973 Act to achieve through the MSC and its Divisions major interventions in employment and training, through social schemes, job-creation programmes, and so on. By 1979 the MSC cost over £200 million a year in administration charges and dispersed over £400 million of public money. Whether the nation receives value is debatable.

The government has recently produced a white paper, 'The New Training Initiative', proposing radical changes. Only seven Industry Training Boards remain as statutory bodies. The rest will be replaced by voluntary arrangements. (See Part 1, ch. 11)

Industrial Training Service This independent, non-profit-making but financially self-supporting (through its fees income) organisation was founded in 1960 by the former Industrial Training Council. It was at that time grant-aided by the then Ministry of Labour. Its aims were then to provide training development services with a strong emphasis on exploratory and innovatory work.

From 1964 to 1974 the ITS was sponsored by the former Central Training Council (dissolved by the Employment and Training Act 1973) and the Department of Employment. Following the re-structuring caused by the 1973 Act, the ITS has been sponsored since 1974 by the *Manpower Services Commission*.

While remaining true to its original aims, the work of the ITS has expanded considerably to deal now with all facets of training, manpower and organisational development. It concentrates primarily on issues relating to the problems and potential of people within organisations. In addition to the ITS public courses and seminars, it offers an excellent advisory and consultancy service based on a commissioning process by which a client asks ITS to solve problems rather than offer pre-determined solutions. The ITS also undertakes research, so it maintains a high degree of exploration and innovation in its work. ITS has developed a strong overseas base and has carried out assignments in a large number of countries in all the continents.

The Manpower Services Commission appoints the 14 non-executive directors, from industry, the unions, education and other sectors of UK society. ITS has 35 consultants based in the major industrial centres of the UK. Further information can be had from ITS's Head Office, 73–75 Mortimer Street, London W1N 8HX; 01–637 8876–7. The Director and Secretary is J. P. de C. Meade, OBE. Regional offices are in: North: Wetherby (0937) 63531; London and South-East: Head Office; Northern Ireland: Belfast (0232) 22471; Scotland: Glasgow (041) 221 4067; Wales and South-West: (0222) 43441; West Midlands: West Bromwich (021) 553 4408. (See Part 1. ch. 11)

Industry Training Board (ITB) These Boards were created by the Secretary of State for Employment under the *Industrial Training Act 1964*, as amended by the *Employment and Training Act 1973*. Boards consist of a Chairman with an equal number of members of employees and employers and a smaller number of educationalists. ITBs have responsibilities for: strategic views of the manpower and training needs in their industries, judged against national priorities; ensuring a sufficient amount of training is achieved; and effective standards of training. They are empowered to operate through *exemptions*, *levies* and grants. They may provide through special provisions like *key training grants*. They are able to offer direct training services, and they produce training recommendations which their industries are expected to apply. Of the 23 Boards 16 have now been established as statutory bodies. The industries concerned must however have satisfactory voluntary arrangements for training.

The Boards now report to the *Training Services Division* of the *Manpower Services Commission*. Most of the ITBs' funds are now derived from Government (i.e. tax-payers') money diverted through the MSC. Examples of training boards are:

Engineering Industry Training Board, P.O. Box 176, 54 Clarendon Road, Watford, Herts. WD1 1LB, Watford 38441.
Road Transport Industry Training Board, Capitol House, Empire Way, Wembley, Middlesex.

(See Part 1, ch. 11)

Information technology Information has in the past been largely paper-based. Now developing is a technology of information which has been described as 'a convergence of interest between electronics, computing and communications' (Barron and Curnow, 1979). Developments in this field involve *computers*, data banks and switching for the information networks which are being set up. View-data systems like *Prestel* in the UK give access to an interactive computer via the normal telephone system. The increased availability of information and the possibilities in the use of such interactive systems will have considerable implications for education. Also important will be the increased use of *microcomputers* and a closer look at *educational communication* in general.

Further reading

Barron, I. and Curnow, R., 'The Future with Microelectronics', Frances Pinter, 1979.

Hills, P. J. (ed.), 'Trends in Information Transfer', Frances Pinter, 1982. (See Part 1. ch. 9)

Inner London Education Authority The administration of education in London was changed in 1965 when the London Government Act 1963 came into force, creating the new unit of Greater London, which incorporated the former counties of London and Middlesex and parts of Essex, Kent, Surrey and Hertfordshire. Twenty of the outer London boroughs became Education Authorities but in the inner boroughs (in the area of the former London County Council) the Inner London Education Authority (ILEA) was created, which precepted on the GLC and, after the Local Government Act, 1980 received a block grant directly from central government. Membership of ILEA consists of the councillors of the Greater London Council who represent the inner London boroughs, together with one representative from each of the inner boroughs. It is the largest Education Authority in the country, with a population of some 3,000,000 people. (See Part 1, ch. 1)

Innovation strategies Innovation strategies imply the development of new ideas which are disseminated and utilised. As in the case of strategies for educational research, there are some simplified models. The first model assumes that by heavy central investment of funds to initiate a sequence of basic research, applied research and the trial versions of the ideas, a mass production of curriculum materials can be disseminated to a passive user. It is very much a model from the centre outwards. The other extreme model arises from a user having a need or a problem. The user then searches for ideas, tries and adapts the ideas to solve his problem; the outsider is an enabler. This model has no systematic dissemination and utilisation policy beyond the one user. Attempts at a middle road have been the basis of some recent curriculum development. Teams of teachers have been encouraged to meet together to solve a common problem. The teams try out innovations and modify them. When a viable innovation is available the dissemination phase is initiated. Each of the original teachers will act as a nucleus for a new group of teachers, who in turn will become disseminators. In this way a chain development brings about a more satisfying and real dissemination based on informal personal contact rather than on imposed formal contact. The advantage of the first model is the tight control from the centre. This control is difficult to maintain using the third model.

Further reading

Lippitt, R. et al., 'The Dynamics of Planned Change', Harcourt, Brace, 1958.

Rogers, E. M. and Shoemaker, F. L., 'Communication of Innovations: A Cross-Cultural Approach', 2nd ed. (New York), Free Press of Glencoe. (See Part 1. ch. 8)

Instructional specification This is part of the *systematic* approach to training and consists of a statement of the objectives, learning strategies, teaching aids and testing procedures of a particular course of training. It usually also contains notes on administration of the course, staff lists and timetable. (See Part 1, ch. 11)

Instruction schedule For the purposes of instruction it is often necessary to prepare a detailed breakdown of skills. Instruction schedules attempt to define the best learning sequence to bring the trainee to proper work standards as quickly as possible. (See Part 1, ch. 11)

Insurance (including actuarial work) Insurance covers the major branches of the industry: general, life, motor and liability, property and marine, and aviation. The Chartered Insurance Institute provides qualifications by examination leading to Associateship (ACII) and thence to Fellowship (FCII) for those wishing to pursue a career in insurance. In addition, the major companies provide in-service training. New entrants seeking qualification need an Ordinary *National Certificate* in Business Studies of 3 A-levels or 2 A- plus 2 0-levels. A pass in English is required and one A-level pass must be in an academic subject. The Corporation of Insurance Agents is a professional association of those people who are accredited agents of the insurance companies and who practise as agents in conjunction with other professions or occupations. Qualification (for Fellow or Associate) is by age and practice.

Actuarial work refers to those who are engaged in the statistical calculation of insurance risks and premiums. The Institute of Actuaries provides an examined route to Associateship, followed by practical experience for Fellowship. Examinations are grouped into A and B, and the Actuarial Tuition Service provides tuition, mostly by correspondence. Entrance standards are high, and include mathematics. For graduates, an honours degree in statistics or mathematics including statistics gives some exemptions.

The Faculty of Actuaries provides examinations leading to Fellowship (FFA). Tuition is available from the Actuarial Tuition Service. The Chartered Institute of Loss Adjusters has examinations leading to Associateship and then, by practical experience, to Fellowship. The entrance requirements are similar to those of the Chartered Insurance Institute. The Association of Average Adjusters is the professional institution for marine loss adjusters. It provides for membership through examinations and under articles, in 3 to 5 years depending on previous qualifications, or 8 years without articles.

Further information can be had from:

The Chartered Insurance Institute, 20 Aldermanbury, London EC2V 7HY; 01–606 3835.

The Corporation of Insurance Agents, 63 Great Cumberland Place, London W1A 7LJ; 01–723 9556.

Institute of Actuaries, Staple Inn Hall, High Holborn, London WC14 7QJ; 01–242 0106.

The Faculty of Actuaries, 23 St Andrew's Square, Edinburgh EH2 1AQ; 031–556 6791.

The Chartered Institute of Loss Adjusters, Manfield House, London WC2 0LR; 01–240 1496.

Association of Average Adjusters, Irongate House, Duke's Place, London EC3A 7LP; 01–283 7671. (See Part 1, ch. 2)

Integration (integrated studies) Integration is a way of organising learning in which engagement within an activity or problem draws upon more than one

175

subject or discipline. In higher education it is generally called interdisciplinarity. The immediate appeal of the idea at school level lies in its promise of an alternative to subject-centred curricula that seem abstract and fragmented. Thus curriculum integration has been most influential in primary schools, for example in the 'integrated day', in which children's work is organised around broad areas of study, and in some lower secondary schools, where integrated studies with 12- and 12+-year-olds may soften the transition from primary school without impairing the subsequent run-up in established subjects to examinations at 16-plus.

In practice, however, integration is an umbrella-term whose effective application depends upon solutions to major problems of its logic and its practicality. The particular problem of the former is: how exactly are different subjects to be 'integrated'? Different answers are possible: first, to accept the distinctness of subjects but to articulate cross-links between them when questions arise in one subject which entail recourse to another; second, integration through over-arching ideas, topics or themes, for instance, 'communication' as an idea to link language-teaching and expressive arts; thirdly, integration through study oriented to practical thinking, leading, for example, to decisions on courses of action, or designs for vocational or leisure activities, etc.; fourth, the integration that ensues as the pupil's personal interest, crystallised perhaps through project work, stimulates him to assimilate new perspectives to his interests. Problems of the practicality of integration give rise to organisational solutions with equally varying emphases, ranging from periodic liaison between departments to thorough-going *team teaching* or the merging of departments. These solutions invariably reflect their social contexts and act back on how decision-makers actually interpret the 'logic' of integration. For example, the adoption of integrated studies in the lower secondary school can be seen as dependent as much upon its weaker social constraints as upon teachers' curriculum aims and grasp of knowledge structures. See also: *structure, enquiry model, core curriculum, curriculum control.*

Further reading

Open University, Course 203, Curriculum design and development, Unit 12, 'The Integrated Curriculum' (R. Pring), 1976.

Schools Council Integrated Studies Project, 'An Introduction to Integrated Studies', 1972. (See Part 1. ch. 4)

Intelligence Many words convey a general meaning without being well defined. Intelligence is such a word. If one teacher says to another that 'Johnny is very intelligent while Paul is unintelligent', this will immediately convey certain ideas about how the two boys will progress in response to teaching. However, the amount of overlap between any two people's ideas about what is intelligent is not as great as this might suggest. On numerous occasions one will hear people talking about what a university student has done and how it didn't seem particularly intelligent of him to do so. Yet university students are supposed to possess a proportionately larger amount of what we call intelligence. The reasons for comments of this kind are due to the elusive nature of the concept. To some people intelligence is the ability to reason. There are definitions of intelligence based on adaptability or flexibility, whereas others emphasise the ability to persist and excel in one particular area. The ability to respond rapidly to new situations may sometimes be considered more important than the ability to converge to a correct conclusion regardless of speed. Concepts such as fluency, *creativity* and originality are all supposed to be aspects of intelligence. Given the diversity of these concepts, all of which are aspects of intelligence, it may seem pointless to try to group them under one heading. If forced to do so, however, it may be possible to abstract the common elements of each so that a definition would run something like this: 'Intelligence is an underlying attribute which describes the potential for changing behaviour or for selecting appropriate previously learned behaviours to be applied in a new situation with a minimum of wasted motion.'

This definition requires that there be change either in the behaviours of the person or the situation in which the person finds himself. Change is a necessary part of the definition because, no matter how complex certain behaviours are, merely applying them to familiar situations is not an expression of intelligence. Thus a person applying the skills of differential calculus to a well exercised problem is not showing intelligence. However, when learning to carry out differential calculus he was changing his capacity to behave in new ways. Therefore learning complex behaviours is an expression of intelligence. Applying these skills to familiar problems is an expression of attainment rather than intelligence.

The question of whether it is useful to have such a general concept of intelligence has been long debated. It may help to consider a simple analogy. People often talk about a general ability in sport, such as an 'eye for the ball'. However, 'eye for the ball' will not explain why some people are good at tennis and others are good at badminton or cricket. At times it may be useful to consider people's 'eye for the ball' in trying to explain or predict success in a number of sports. However, such a concept has severe limitations and other concepts such as 'athletic' or 'perseverant' may provide valuable alternative or additional explanations. Intelligence suffers from a similar problem of providing an easy overall explanation for certain events which often covers a host of other, more particular attributes. Current research generally refers to a number of factors which have been identified through *factor analysis*. Names given to some of the major factors which the reader may come across are verbal educational (V. ed), general intelligence (g), reasoning, verbal comprehension, spatial orientation, visualisation and induction. (See Part 1. ch. 6)

Intelligence is a term that came into wide use as a result of the growth in *mental testing* in the early years of this century. C. Burt defined intelligence as 'an innate, general, cognitive ability' which underlies all complex processes of reasoning. Intelligence soon came to be defined in operational terms for all practical purposes, defined in terms of the individual's performance on standardised tests of abstract reasoning: intelligence was what intelligence tests measured. The statistical abstraction of the *intelligence quotient* led some to the misconception of intelligence as a fixed and definable quantity like height or weight; such misconceptions led to many of the injustices of the eleven-plus system of selection.

Today most psychologists are more concerned with the study of intelligent behaviour rather than the reification of intelligence. The stress is upon the activity of the individual when he is exposed to certain kinds of experience. This change in emphasis has led to a reconsideration of the role of heredity in determining intelligent behaviour and an increased emphasis upon the influence of the environment. Deciding upon the criteria for specifying intelligent behaviour still poses considerable problems. Typical tests of intelligent behaviour include tests of reasoning requiring the ability to educe relations and correlates as well as memory items and word and number series. Other tests are designed to tap kinaesthetic and spatial abilities. Psychologists favour a profile of intelligent behaviours rather than a single global score. However, numerous forms of intelligent behaviour have proved far from easy to measure. Creative ability, musical talent and competence in coping with the practical situations of daily life can still not be adequately assessed. See also *heredity and environment, cognitive style, educational assessment.*

Further reading
Butcher, H. J., 'Human Intelligence: Its Nature and Assessment', Methuen 1968. (See Part 1, ch. 4)

Intelligence A, B and C Hebb distinguished between Intelligence A, the innate, genetically determined potential for intelligent behaviour which sets the limits to the individual's capacity to respond intelligently, and Intelligence B, the level of development which results from the interaction of Intelligence A with environmental influences. Neither A nor B can be directly measured. Vernon suggested that the term Intelligence C should be used to designate the sample of Intelligence B obtained from a standardised *test*.

Further reading
Child, D., 'Psychology and the Teacher', 2nd ed., Holt, Rinehart & Winston, 1977. (See Part 1, ch. 14)

Intelligence quotient The intelligence quotient, or IQ, is a measure of intelligence. It was originally calculated by dividing a subject's mental age, obtained from a test, by his chronological age and then multiplying by 100. IQ scores are now computed on the basis of how far the individual's score deviates from the mean score obtained by all individuals of his chronological age.

Further reading
Cronbach, L. J., 'Essentials of Psychological Testing', 3rd ed., Harper & Row, 1970. (See Part 1, ch. 14)

Intelligence tests Intelligence usually relates to cognitive and intellectual capacities such as: perceiving, thinking, imagining, learning, recalling. The main problem in attempting to measure intelligence is whether there is a basic common factor or a range of interrelated factors making up intelligence (for example, is spatial ability something special and different from 'general' intelligence?) Different psychologists have different opinions. One of the originators of intelligence tests, Binet, is quoted as saying 'To judge well, to comprehend well, to reason well, these are the essential activities of intelligence' (Vernon 1960). Many early intelligence tests were heavily dependent on language, which precluded their use with learners of limited experience in reading. Some tests are administered by individuals to individuals using equipment which may in turn give a bias to spatial abilities. Yet other tests attempt to mix language, mathematics and spatial ability. Again, earlier tests were heavily dependent on cultural background; more recent tests attempt to achieve a culture-free base. These tests are often designed to be administered to groups for economy of time. Many tests allow only a limited range of people to administer them because of the need to follow a fixed routine and to be able to interpret the data, which may be presented in standardised form (see *standardised score*). Such tests will have been administered to *samples* of the target *population*. Standardised tests are usually available through national agencies such as the National Foundation for Educational Research in the United Kingdom.

Further reading

Vernon, P. E., 'Intelligence and Attainment Tests', University of London Press, 1960.

Wiseman, S., 'Intelligence and Ability', 2nd ed., Penguin, 1973. (See Part 1, ch. 8)

Interaction analysis The idea of interaction analysis is to study the interaction between teacher and learner, learner and learner. The variables to be studied will depend on the purpose of the research. Some researchers go in with pre-specified ideas of what to look for and keep checks on a checklist or grid. (See Part 1, ch. 8)

Interactive skills *(inter-personal skills)* This is the general term for the skills involved in personal effectiveness, in person-to-person and person-to-group relationships. It revolves around personal sensitivity to the behaviour, with or without reasons, of others. Training methods include *T-group*, and increasingly the behaviour analysis school known as DIS (developing interactive skills).

Further reading

Rackham, N. and Morgan, T., 'Behaviour Analysis in Training', McGraw-Hill, 1977. (See Part 1, ch. 12)

Interest in comparative education Since the Second World War the number of comparative education courses being offered at universities and colleges of education has increased greatly. The earliest courses in this country were established by Kandel in 1905 at Manchester, and Hans in London in 1930. Eventually the major centres of comparative education proved to be at the University of London Institute of Education under J. L. Lauwerys, N. Hans and B. Holmes, and the Teachers College, Columbia University in New York under I. K. Kandel, R. King Hall, G. Z. F. Bereday and D. G. Scanlon. These two centres, separately before 1957 and jointly thereafter, published Yearbooks of Education. In terms of research the Yearbook was devoted to a different international theme each year, until 1974 when publication ceased. Themes covered included guidance and counselling, the secondary school curriculum, education in rural areas, etc. (See Part 1, ch. 3)

International Association for the Evaluation of Educational Achievement (IEA) This organisation, founded in 1959, arose out of a meeting of a group of respresentatives from 12 countries. These met during the 1950s in order to discuss the efficiency of the various educational systems.

At the first meeting a pilot study was launched under the direction of A. W. Foshay, the director of the Horace Mann Institute of School Experimentation. This study involved 10,000 13-year-old children in twelve countries. Tests were given to them in reading comprehension, geography, science, mathematics and non-verbal ability. This feasibility study convinced the members that such cross-national studies were viable, and a larger project designed to assess achievement levels in mathematics in 12 countries was developed. The results were published in 1967 and subsequently the IEA was made permanent. Studies to assess the relation between teacher behaviour and achievement levels, learning strategies and pre-school education have also been implemented. The projects were partly sponsored by UNESCO, the Institute of Education, Hamburg, and the Centre for Comparative Education, Chicago.

The influence of the *sociological* and the *empirical approaches* are marked. The attempt to provide cross-national variables which were viable proved to be difficult. Some comparativists have not always shown as much appreciation of the IEA's efforts as they might have done, since qualitative assessments are often valued in preference to the empirical and quantitative data on which IEA studies place such high reliance.

Further reading

Foshay, A. W. et al, 'Educational Achievements of thirteen-year-olds in Twelve Countries', UNESCO Institute, 1962.

Husen, T., 'International Study of Achievement in Mathematics', 2 vols, John Wiley, 1967. (See Part 1. ch. 3)

International Association of Universities (IAU) Founded in 1950 to promote co-operation between academics and to aid universities; co-operates with IEA and UNESCO on projects.

Further reading

Bowles, F., 'Access to Higher Education: the International Study of University Admissions', UNESCO, 2 vols, 1963, 1965. (See Part 1, ch. 3)

International Bureau of Education (IBE) The International Bureau of Education was established in 1925 in Geneva and came under UNESCO in 1969. It is now the major documentary section of UNESCO. Its store of data includes the computerised indices which contain details of documents concerning major policy changes, reform and innovatory procedures effected in many countries.

The IBE distributes a Newsletter giving details of the activities of comparativists, listing appropriate books and journals, and providing synopses of reports and governmental papers. Other work undertaken by IBE includes acting as the Liaison Office for Comparative Education and linking the academic community and international agencies. This office co-operates with the World Congress of Comparative Education Societies in sponsoring the Newsletter, selecting bibliographies on topics such as 'Innovation in Secondary School Curricula', and in publishing case materials of various projects, for example, 'Innovation in Singapore' and 'A Community School in Yugoslavia'.

Further reading

Tretheway, A. R., 'Introducing Comparative Education', ch. 8, Pergamon, 1976. (See Part 1, ch. 3)

International Council for Educational Media (ICEM) ICEM is an international organisation whose members represent national organisations responsible for the production and dissemination of educational films and other audio-visual materials. More than 30 nations are now represented on the General Assembly of the Council. Since each of the members, representing a country, carries out a variety of support activities to education, ICEM becomes an enormous set of channels of communication through which members can have access to information or help from other members.

Operating through an Executive Committee and sub-committees on innovation and development, co-production, and international exchange, ICEM holds an annual week of screenings of educational films and an annual conference. Under contract from UNESCO, the Council has carried out a number of research contracts on national and international media organisation (See Part 1. ch. 7)

International Institution of Educational Planning (IIEP) The International Institute of Education Planning is the UNESCO centre which offers advanced courses in educational planning and research and publishes studies and bibliographies devoted to these topics. Address: 7–9, Rue Eugene-Delacroix, 75016, Paris. (See Part 1, ch. 3)

Intervention Among the several schools of *organisation development* is that of the intervention theory, based on the work of Argyris. It deals with the actions taken by a third party (the so-called change agent) in influencing the processes of an organisation.

Further reading

Argyris, C., 'Intervention Theory and Method', Addison-Wesley, 1970. (See Part 1, ch. 12)

Intra-regional study Deals with comparisons between two or more regions in one country. The reference given below makes comparisons between education in Northern and Southern Ghana. See Foster, P. J., 'Education and Social Change in Ghana.' (See Part 1, ch. 3)

Intrinsic (contrasted with extrinsic) This term is frequently used by educationists who wish to emphasise that some pursuits are valuable in themselves and not as means to a desirable end. The difficulty lies in the justification of such 'intrinsically worth-while pursuits'. (See Part 1, ch. 13)

Introversion-extraversion Introversion-extraversion is a personality dimension along a bipolar continuum that is favoured by Eysenck. The introvert is shy and private, plans ahead and has tight emotional control. He is reliable and sets high ethical standards. The extravert is sociable and outgoing, his emotions are given free play. He is impulsive and quick to lose his temper. He likes action and is not particularly reliable.

Further reading

Eysenck, H. J., 'The Structure of Human Personality', 3rd ed., Methuen, 1970. (See Part 1, ch. 14)

Investment An important distinction is drawn in economics between investment, representing the purchase of capital assets which are expected to provide benefits in the form of income or output in the future, and consumption, which is expenditure on goods and services intended to provide immediate but short-lived benefits.

There has been considerable debate in the past about whether expenditure on education should be classified as investment or consumption. Some writers have tended to distinguish between vocational education and training, which they classify as investment, since it increases the future working capacity of educated workers, and 'education for its own sake', which they classify as consumption. It is now argued that expenditure on education has both a consumption and an investment aspect, since it provides both immediate and long-term benefits for the individual and for society. (See Part 1, ch. 5)

Ipsative Ipsative is a form of measurement where a person's mean *score* is used to anchor his other scores. Thus each score reflects the individual's own strengths and weaknesses, without showing how strong or how weak he is in relation to another person. This form of measurement is often used for measuring *attitudes*, where we want to know, for example, those attitudes which a certain person holds most strongly. It would be possible for another person with identical scores to be much stronger in his attitudes. (See Part 1, ch. 6)

Item The word 'item' is used in educational measurement for the basic unit which is marked 'pass' or 'fail' in a *test*. To most people this will be identified with the questions in a test, and in many cases the words are interchangeable. However, the units in a test need not necessarily be actual questions in the sense that they require a question mark at the end of the sentence. For example, some test items are statements which require the testee to indicate whether they are true or false. Another reason for not using the word 'question' is that examinations often set questions which require long answers and are complex to *score*. An item is a much smaller unit which has strict and relatively easy instructions on how to be scored, such that individual judgments are minimised. (See Part 1, ch. 6)

Item analysis When deciding what *items* should be included in a *test* there are many considerations to make. Even an experienced item writer cannot be sure that all the items he writes will be problem-free. Questions such as whether the items are too difficult or too easy or whether they are free from any ambiguities cannot be answered by scrutinising the content. It is necessary to see how people respond to the item in real life. To do this items are administered to relevant groups of people whose answers become the data which can then be analysed.

A standard item analysis assumes that the group of people can be considered to differ only along the attribute measured by the items. We can then obtain a score for each item (i.e. number of people who passed it) which is the opposite of the usual procedure where a score is obtained for each person (i.e. number of items passed by each person). The score for each item can be converted to a percentage to give an index of difficulty. What is appropriate will depend on the purpose for which the test is constructed, but decisions at this stage will determined the shape of the distribution of scores we would expect on the final test. We can therefore tailor our test in order to provide the kind of distribution we require.

The second major index in a standard item analysis is the discrimination index (described separately). Further refinements can be added to the item analysis such as discarding the worst items and recalculating the indices thus reducing the 'noise' produced by these items. It is also possible to look at the errors that are made in order to understand better how the item is being approached. In multiple-choice items, for example, it is sometimes found that certain of the alternative choices distract the better pupils because there is a subtle way in which it could be considered correct. It may therefore be possible to improve the item by changing this distractor.

Item analysis does not select or reject items. It provides more information so that the item writer can understand what is happening when pupils answer it. The decision to select items must remain with the test constructor to ensure that aspects such as the balance of different items in the test remains suitable. Item analysis merely provides a certain kind of feedback which is added to the test constructor's information about the items and helps him to select appropriate items.

Further reading

'Short cut Statistics for Teacher-made Tests', Educational Testing Service, Princeton, 2nd edn., 1964.

Guilford, J. P., 'Fundamental Statistics in Psychology and Education', McGraw Hill, 1978, pp. 493–509. (See Part 1, ch. 6)

Item characteristic curve theory (ICC theory) Classical test theory is based on the *test* as the main unit. Where individual *item* characteristics are scrutinised it is generally to help to produce desirable characteristics for the entire test. The way in which the items are scrutinised is based entirely on describing how the items have performed in a specific situation.

Item characteristic curve theory differs in both these respects. First, the theory is based on the individual item as the main unit. Test characteristics are the summations of the individual item characteristics. Second, the items don't just describe how people have responded; they also predict how other people will respond. This is because ICC theory makes assumptions about how people interact with the items they are asked to attempt. These assumptions are defined as a mathematical model which relates person parameters to item parameters. For example, the simplest such model relates the person's ability to the item's *difficulty* and makes the assumption that when a person's ability is equal to the item's difficulty, the probability of the person passing the item is 50 per cent. This can be written mathematically like this:

Probability of person x passing item y = $\dfrac{a/d}{1+a/d}$ a = ability

    d = difficulty

Thus when a = d then a/d = 1 and the probability is therefore ½ or 50 per cent. This model defines its own item characteristic curves as follows:

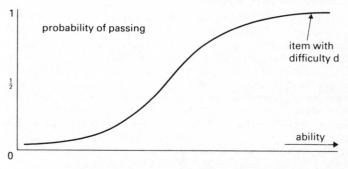

As ability increases, the probability of passing the item increases, and the curve displays this relationship graphically. Different models have different item characteristic curves and can involve greater numbers of parameters. Such models provide scope for investigating dimensionality of attributes and for providing flexible testing procedures, since the unit is now the item rather than the test.

Further reading
'Journal of Educational Measurement', No. 2, vol. 14, Summer 1977. (See Part 1, ch. 6)

J

Job analysis This process, by which a job is examined in detail, aims to identify component tasks. It is used for purposes other than training (although this is most frequent) such as work-place design, bench layouts and so on. It is one of a group of techniques including *Training within industry* and *skills analysis*. (See Part 1, ch. 11)

Job enrichment/enlargement Job enrichment holds that increased satisfaction at work derives from greater responsibility. The theory owes much to the work of Herzberg. Job enlargment suggests that restructuring to introduce greater variety into work produces satisfaction. This ignores the fact that five rotten jobs may still when put together form a rotten job. (See Part 1, ch. 11)

Jullien's Plan Early comparative studies were carried out by philosophers and travellers; and during the nineteenth century educational borrowing was practised by administrators whose writings and recommendations bore the imprint of the expert in the field and were more systematic than the studies of their predecessors.

The changeover from the first group to the second was marked by the appearance in 1817 of Jullien's plan. M. A. Jullien de Paris, moved by the moral turpitude of the French public, tried to help the situation through a thorough reform of the French educational system. To further this aim he published 'L'Esquisse et Vues Préliminaires d'un Ouvrage sur L'Éducation Comparée'. His plan was based on three assumptions:

(1) that to reform one's own system one had to look to the example of others;
(2) that a piecemeal examination of other systems would not be effective in providing viable data for reform; and
(3) that the successes and failures of foreign systems could only be evaluated thoroughly when a systematic and comprehensive collection of educational data had been completed.

An Educational Commission would be established, charged with the task of collecting facts and observations about education in foreign countries. These data would be categorised according to certain principles and arranged in analytical charts to facilitate easy comparison. In this way a system of comparative education, analogous to comparative anatomy, would be established. The data would be collected by means of questionnaires sent out to other countries, which would provide information of various types. The Educational Commission would be responsible for disseminating their findings. Jullien showed little interest in what happened outside the school, but did recommend the creation of a Normal College charged with improving teacher education and promoting appropriate innovations in educational practice.

Further reading
Fraser, S. E. (translator), 'Jullien's Plan for Comparative Education 1816–17', Teachers College, Columbia University, 1964.
Kazamias, A. M. and Massialas, G. B., 'Tradition and Change in Education', Chs. 1–2, Prentice Hall. (See Part 1, ch. 3)

Kandel's approach In his monumental work 'Comparative Education' Kandel dealt with a fundamental problem felt by democratic countries. This problem concerned the reconciliation of the rights of the individual with his position as a member of society and the state. These rights were dependent on the interaction of educational norms and processes with nationalism. The two forces were reconciled by the school acting out its key function; namely, that of developing national character. Guided by these reference points Kandel dealt with the relationship of the state and education, the organisation of elementary education, secondary education and teacher education. He examined these topics in Britain, France, Germany, Italy, the USA and the USSR, all of which he viewed as the leading educational laboratories. His methodology consisted of a description of the theory and practice of the educational system in question listed under the categories given above.

These descriptive accounts were the essential first stage of any research.

Then followed an explanation or interpretation of the forces which gave rise to that educational system. The third stage was a comparative analysis of the differences between educational systems and their antecedent causes. The fourth and final stage sought to establish general principles based on the recurring patterns which had been identified by the researcher.

In order to cope with the difficulties of such a vast undertaking Kandel utilised a broad historical approach backed by comparatively few references indicating his sources. Furthermore, the comparative element in his work was usually given at the beginning of each chapter and consequently much of his work achieved a level of generality not acceptable to comparativists today.

Further reading

Kandel, I. L., 'Comparative Education', Houghton Mifflin, 1933. (See Part 1, ch. 3)

Kay-Shuttleworth, Sir James Phillip, first baronet (1804–77) James Kay assumed the name Shuttleworth on marriage in 1842 and was created a baronet in 1849. He trained as a doctor in Edinburgh. On returning to his native Manchester, he acted as honorary physician to the Ardwick and Ancoats Dispensary, and was active in establishing the Manchester Provident Society and the Manchester Statistical Society. In 1835 he became an assistant poor-law commissioner in East Anglia, where he promoted the education of workhouse children. As Secretary of the Committee of the Privy Council on Education, 1839–49, he introduced a series of grants to encourage school managers to extend and improve the voluntary schools.

Further reading

Tholfsen, T. R. ed., 'Sir James Kay-Shuttleworth on Popular Education', Teachers College Press. (A recent critical assessment.) (See Part 1, ch. 10)

Keller plan This is also known as the personalised system of instruction. In its original form it consists of a set of self-study units taken by the students at their own pace. Mastery of a unit must be demonstrated before going on to the next one. A completed test is discussed with a tutor and if a student fails a test it must be repeated.

Further reading

Keller, F. S., Goodbye Teacher . . . ., in 'Journal of Applied Behaviour Analysis', 1 (1) Spring 1968, pp. 79–89. (See Part 1, ch. 9)

Key results Key results analysis is a definition of the key tasks that must be performed in a job with the necessary standards and methods to measure achievement. Key results areas (KRA) define the task or tasks where improvement significantly increases and/or where failure produces severe diminishment in organisational effectiveness. KRA is a major element in the practice of *management by objectives*. (See Part 1, ch. 11)

Key training grants The *Manpower Services Commission* and the *Industry Training Boards* decide from time to time to provide grants to promote and support particular training activities, usually aimed at specific and vital skills. It is difficult to establish their effectiveness in achieving their aims. (See Part 1, ch. 11)

Knowledge The evaluation of knowledge claims has long been regarded as an important task of the philosopher. But others interested in educational problems have also given considerable time to the analysis of knowledge. It may therefore be useful to see how a philosopher and sociologist would differ in approaching the question: what is knowledge?

Ayer has defined knowledge in the following manner:

S can legitimately claim to know P if
    S accepts P,
    S has adequate evidence for P,
    P is true.

Thus the philosopher is laying down the formal conditions of knowledge; 'feeling sure' is not sufficient. The notion of knowledge is tied to that of evidence. Also, it is suggested, if P were not really true, one would be in the position of having to say that one did not 'really' know P. Knowledge could therefore be defined as 'justified true belief'. But there are difficulties here. It frequently happens that the evidence which was adduced in favour of P is insufficient. One can only be confident in an assertion to 'know P' if one is also confident about the strength of the evidence. The philosopher is insistent that there are standards distinguishing knowledge from belief. But he may well be sceptical about whether these standards are applicable in particular cases.

The sociologist of knowledge would be less precise in his differentiation between knowledge and belief. But the chief difference would be in his analysis of standards, as he would be less willing to admit the existence of any precise standard of knowledge, and any absolute way of distinguishing knowledge from belief, and truth from falsity. See also: *sociology of knowledge*, *relativism*, *objectivity*.

Further reading

Hamlyn, D. W., 'Theory of Knowledge', Macmillan, 1971.

Ayer, A. J., 'The Problem of Knowledge', Penguin, 1967.

Phillips, A., 'Knowledge and Belief' (ed. Griffiths), Oxford University Press, 1967.

Popper, K. R., 'Objective Knowledge', Oxford University Press, 1972. (See Part 1, ch. 13)

Knowledge utilisation The general idea of knowledge utilisation serves to focus analysis on the complex relationship in curriculum development between 'knowledge producers' (for example, research agencies) and 'knowledge users' (for example, teachers). Why does the interaction between the two tend to be ineffective? The problem has been clarified by the recognition of three main models of knowledge utilisation and dissemination which can describe and guide the interaction (Havelock, 1971). The first model exhibits a rationalised or highly planned sequence, that is, a research, development and dissemination model (RD and D). For example, a central project staffed by curriculum specialists systematically tests and improves a new course of study, then mass markets it as high quality, user-proof product. The process seems efficient but in practice may induce a hostile or passive response from users (teachers) unable or disinclined to adapt the product to the circumstantiality of their teaching situations. In the second, social-interaction model, the take-up of curriculum ideas or materials depends upon teachers' informal contacts, for instance, through a teachers' group or subject association. Although this leaves the quality of the products and predictability of the process uncertain, it often results in greater receptivity to new ideas. The crucial characteristic of the third model, the problem-solving model, is that it starts from the teacher's own need and active search for solutions appropriate to a 'felt' problem. Thus utilisation of ideas will be critical and sustained, though the educational merits of the problem solution (for example, a new teaching method) depend upon whether the teacher had access to valid knowledge.

It is possible to combine the strengths of each of the three models through a 'professional centre' in which teachers and researchers are brought together at appropriate times and places by co-ordinators or change-agents. But so far few educational systems have given this fourth 'linkage' model much priority. See also: *diffusion of curriculum innovation, support system, strategies of curriculum change, styles of curriculum development.*

Further reading

Dalin, P., 'Limits to Educational Change', Macmillan, 1978.

Havelock, R., The Utilisation of Educational Research and Development, in 'British Journal of Educational Technology', 2.2, 1971, pp. 84–97. (See Part 1, ch. 4)

Kurtosis Kurtosis is a description of the shape of a *distribution* with respect to how flat or how peaked it is. A normal distribution is taken as having no kurtosis. If the distribution is flatter than the normal distribution it is called platykurtic and if it is more peaked it is called leptokurtic. An index of kurtosis can be obtained using the following formula:

$$k = \frac{(x = \bar{x})^4}{(x - \bar{x})^2} - 3$$

x = individual values

$\bar{x}$ = mean value of x

This value is 0 for the normal distribution. If k is greater than 0 it is leptokurtic, and if k is less than 0 it is platykurtic. (See Part 1, ch. 6)

Labour market Economists use the term 'labour market' to refer to the complex set of relationships and mechanisms by which the supply of labour and the demand for labour are regulated and brought into equilibrium. Economic analysis of the labour market therefore includes analysis of the effects of wage and salary levels on demand and supply, the influence of employers' hiring practices, and the influence of educational qualifications and other factors on the selection of workers by employers. (See Part 1, ch. 5)

Language acquisition device (LAD) Chomsky maintains that all children show such competence in acquiring linguistic skills that they must have an innate potential to master language. He has suggested an hypothetical, innate facility–the language acquisition device–which enables children to process, comprehend and respond to incoming linguistic signals and which leads them to develop for themselves the rules of language.

Further reading

Lyons, J., 'Chomsky', 2nd ed., Harvester Presss, 1977.

Herriot, P., 'An Introduction to the Psychology of Language', Methuen, 1970. (See Part 1, ch. 14)

Language and thought Animal studies have shown that language is not essential for thought to take place. For example, monkeys, who have no language available, can learn to solve complex discrimination problems which must require some inner representation. The interaction between language and thought has been an important concern of psychology and psycholinguistics.

Some theorists, such as Whorf, have argued that language is essential for thought and determines the way that the world is viewed. The evidence does not wholly support this extreme view. Experiments in perception suggest

L

that all see the world in the same way. However, the concepts that are available in a particular language may well determine which aspects of experience are attended to. This view is exemplified by Bernstein's work on restricted and elaborated linguistic codes.

Piaget's view is that thought precedes language and is necessary for its development. It is necessary for the child to have mastered the underlying concept before he can understand the verbal expression of the concept. Piaget's stages of development illustrate the way this understanding comes about.

Vygotsky's view is that language and thought are initially quite separate. In very young children thought takes place without language; and equally the babbling of the young infant, he suggests, is language without thought, a proto-language used to attract attention and to please adults. At about 2 years of age the pre-linguistic internal thought and the pre-intellectual external communication through sounds combine and thought becomes verbal and speech rational. Over the next few years the child can be observed talking aloud about his internal thoughts as he uses the egocentric speech noted by Piaget. According to Vygotsky it is only after about 7 that the child learns to restrict his overt use of language to social communication and his internal use of language to his thoughts. See also: *Piagetian stages of development, concept formation and attainment, language acquisition device, elaborated and restricted codes.*

Further reading

Greene, J., 'Thinking and Language', Methuen, 1975.

Vygotsky, L. S., 'Thought and Language', MIT Press, 1962. (See Part 1, ch. 14)

Language game Words derive *meaning* from their function in specific contexts or 'language games'. The sense of an expression can only be established by examining the 'language game' in which the word occurs. This is a reaction against the *logical postivist* inclination to label terms such as 'God' as 'nonsense' because they lack a definite denotation.

Further reading

Pihler, G. (ed.), 'Modern Studies in Philosophy', Macmillan, 1968.

Wittgenstein, 'The Philosophical Investigations', 3rd ed., Blackwell, 1967. (See Part 1, ch. 13)

Learner-controlled training This is a development of *discovery learning*, which in addition to discovery techniques allows the learner to determine his own programme at his own pace using methods that suit him best (in his judgment). It is based on the assumption that the learner understands his own capabilities best. (See Part 1, ch. 12)

Learning curve Work performance is plotted against time to show the rate of progress of an individual or group in achieving the accepted level of performance. It possesses certain characteristics, showing early rapid progress, a plateau, followed by another rapid improvement to accepted performance. For manual skills, repetition and therefore stamina is critical. (See Part 1, ch. 11)

Learning, retention and recall Much of education is concerned with encouraging remembering. The process of remembering can be broken down into three interrelated phases: learning, retention of the learned material over a period of time, and recall, when the learned material is brought back into attention out of *long-term memory*.

The simplest cognitive learning involves the formation of a link between two or more items. For simple associations to be formed between words they must be presented very close together so that they can both be in *short-term memory* at the same time and can then go forward associated together into *long-term memory*. It is possible for such an association to be established as the result of only one presentation, but normally the more frequently the association has been repeated the more durable it is likely to be in long-term memory. When there is no meaningful learning to support the establishment of an association, then plenty of repetition and revision are called for. With plenty of practice such rote-learned material can be retained for long periods. Once rote-learned material has been partly forgotten it cannot be reconstructed from other material in long-term memory.

Meaningful learning is far more efficient. No learner ever comes to a learning experience with a completely blank memory. Most cognitive learning involves building upon a structure of existing concepts that are already within the long-term memory. If learning is meaningful and draws upon already established concepts in the cognitive structure, then even if part of the detail is lost during the retention period it can be reconstructed from the concepts with which it was associated in long-term memory at the time of recall. Recall involves an active reconstruction rather than a playing back of some fixed memory trace.

Unfortunately, existing concepts can lead to distortion in learning during retention or at the time of recall. This is especially likely to happen when new learning is inappropriately classified using existing concepts. See also *Concept formation and attainment, attention and perception, cognitive approaches to learning*.

Further reading

Gregg, V., 'Human Memory', Methuen, 1975.

Hunter, I.M.L., 'Memory: Facts and Fallacies', Penguin, 1957. (See Part 1, ch. 14)

Leicestershire plan The pattern of secondary education which was developed in Leicestershire in the 1950s involved the transfer of all children at the age of 11 to a junior high school. At the age of 14 they could transfer to grammar schools on condition that they stayed on at least to the age of 16 to complete a two-year course. The ones who did not opt for a two-year course at the grammar school remained for a further year at the junior high school until they reached the then statutory school leaving age of 15. (See Part 1, ch. 1)

Libraries The best library on training and education generally in the United Kingdom is at the *British Association for Commercial and Industrial Education*. Most large public libaries contain sections on business, commerce and so on. (See Part 1, ch. 2)

Likert scale In a Likert scale of attitude measurement statements are used as a basis for getting the respondent to agree or disagree. The number of points on the scale can vary. An even number of points is used where there is a clear decision required, an odd number to allow an overall neutral stance. (See Part 1, ch. 8)

Linear programme In *programmed learning* a linear programme is one where the programme consists of a number of steps or frames through which the student proceeds one after the other. Each frame consists usually of some information, together with a question or problem for which the student is required to construct an answer. The next frame of material gives the answer to the previous frame and poses a new question. Seee also: *multiple-choice programme, Skinner, Pressey*.

L

Further reading

Markle, S. M., 'Good Frames and Bad', John Wiley, 2nd ed., 1969. (See Part 1, ch. 9)

Linguistic code Basil Bernstein's work on linguistic codes is probably the best-known feature of the sociology of education in Britain. Apart from his own studies, a number of associated studies have been produced under his direction by the Sociological Research Unit at the University of London Institute of Education.

Bernstein claims that *social class* differences in forms of speech need to be understood as governed, at a level not directly observable in consciousness, by different linguistic codes carrying different sets of base-rules for language-use within social interactions. Members of the working class tend to use a restricted code, and members of the middle class an *elaborated code*. One of the key features of speech regulated by a restricted code is that it is context-dependent: it is embedded in a local social context in terms of which part of its meaning has to be supplied. Speech regulated by an elaborated code is context-independent: its meaning can be explicit. Communication in schools is characteristically based upon an elaborated code, and this, Bernstein argues, presents a barrier to working-class children to the extent that their preference is to employ a restricted code. His argument here has been mistakenly linked with *cultural deprivation* theory, but his point is rather that if these children, although competent to use either kind of code, remain indifferent or resistant to meanings based on an elaborated code, they will be forfeiting access to the languages of control and innovation that can lead them to an understanding of the grounds of their own *socialisation*; and the extent of their readiness to use an elaborated code to gain such access will depend largely on the strength of their schooling's *classification and framing* of educational knowledge.

Further reading

Bernstein, B., 'Class, Codes and Control', vol. 1, Routledge & Kegan Paul, 1971.

Bisseret, N., 'Education, Class Language and Ideology', Routledge & Kegan Paul, 1979. (See Part 1, ch. 15)

Link course Schools and *further education* institutions run joint courses for students in their last year of full-time schooling, to help to ease the transfer from one learning system to another, start people on courses related to their intended careers, and provide some introduction to the adult world. (See Part 1, ch. 11)

Literacy rates The extent to which people could read and write was keenly debated in the nineteenth century both by protagonists of the voluntary system (see *religious societies*) and those who wanted to see it supplemented, if not supplanted, by the state. Economic historians, interested in the inter-relationship between economic growth and literacy, and historians of education, abandoning their earlier narrow institutional approach, have begun to share this interest. In such studies the nineteenth-century historian starts with the advantage that the Registrar General began to publish data about the numbers of brides and grooms signing the marriage register. Moreover, the Births, Deaths, and Marriages Act 1836 required the contracting parties to state their condition, allowing the data to be analysed in terms of occupational, regional, and chronological variables.

The difficulties of interpreting the evidence are considerable. Marriage took place some ten to fifteen years after the people concerned left school, that is if they ever attended. The ability to sign one's name on a particular day does not provide evidence of fluent literacy, nor does a mark in the register prove life-long illiteracy. There are, however, strong grounds for believing that those who could write could also read. Historians attempt to quantify reading ability mainly by analysing the output and content of the printing trade, books, newspapers, chap-books, tracts, and pamphlets. However, the sale or free distribution of much ephemeral literature does not necessarily indicate that it was read.

Further reading

Hartwell, M., 'The Industrial Revolution', Metheun, 1971.

Perkin, H. The Origins of the Popular Press, in 'History Today' VII, July 1957, pp. 425–35.

Stone, L., Literacy and Education in England, 1640 – 1900, in 'Past and Present', No. 42, February 1969, pp. 69–139.

Webb, R. K., 'The British Working-Class Reader, 1700 – 1848', Allen & Unwin, 1955.

West, E. G., Literacy and the Industrial Revolution, in 'Economic History Review', 2nd series, XXXI, 1978, pp. 369–83. (See Part 1, ch. 10)

Localisation This term refers to the policies of newly independent states who were concerned to replace expatriate administrators, technicians and educators by their own people. (See Part 1, ch. 3)

Local radio Local radio stations, of which there are now more than 20, broadcast both formal and informal educational programmes. (See Part 1, ch. 7)

Logical geography 'Exploring the logical geography' of a concept, or a group of concepts was a phrase used by Ryle to illustrate the way in which concepts such as 'the mental' and 'mind' function. The method has been used by philosophers of *education* in analysing the relationship of such various concepts.

Further reading

Ryle, G., 'The Concept of Mind', Hutchinson, 1949. (See Part 1, ch. 13)

Logical positivism In logical positivism the problem of *verification* was linked with that of *meaning*: 'We say that a sentence is factually significant to any given person if and only if he knows how to verify the proposition which it purports to express, if he knows what observation would lead him to accept the proposition as being true or reject it as being false.'

Ayer is correct in insisting that only empirical evidence can justify an empirical statement – that is, after all, what we mean by an empirical statement – but the additional claim that it is only statements of this kind which are significant is a different matter. What are the consequences of this for *ethics*, religion or *aesthetics*? Statements of value are either empirical, or 'expressions of emotion which can be either true or false'. The concepts of ethics are 'pseudo-concepts'. To say 'you acted wrongly in stealing money' is to say 'you stole money' (a factual statement). The 'wrongly' could be expressed by saying 'you stole that money' with a particular tone of horror. Similarly 'by the same criteria, no sentence which purports to describe the nature of a transcendent God can possess any literal significance'.

However, far from sounding the death-knell of ethics, etc., logical positivism effected a fruitful revival. The movement provided philosophers with useful insights into the way in which language functions in ethics and aesthetics, and the philosophy of religion. *Positivism* has also probably had a beneficial effect on philosophy and *education*, testing the necessity of distin-

L

191

guishing the different ways in which educational concepts are used. (See Part 1, ch. 13)

London polytechnics By 1900 London possessed twelve polytechnics built to enable young men and women who had left school to start work to obtain technical education in an atmosphere that offered opportunities for a wider cultural education as well. The academic work, conducted mainly on a part-time basis at night, ranged from the top level of an elementary school to that of a London University degree, for which candidates could study as external students. In addition there were classes in such trades as carpentry and bricklaying. Many of these London polytechnics formed the nuclei of the five polytechnics in the London area today, set up after the publication of the White Paper, 'A Plan for the Polytechnics', Cmnd 3006 (HMSO, 1966). (See Part 1, ch. 10)

Long-term memory The long-term memory is a hypothetical third stage in the memory process. It has an unlimited capacity and information can be stored there for indefinite periods of time. One unit of information can be transferred to long-term memory from *short-term memory* about every five seconds. The size of the units of information that can be stored is dependent upon the existing knowledge of the learner.

Further reading

Gregg, V., 'Human Memory', Methuen, 1975.

Baddeley, A. D., 'The Psychology of Memory', Harper & Row, 1976. (See Part 1, ch. 14)

Lowe, Robert, first Viscount Sherbrooke (1811–92) Educated at Winchester and University College, Oxford. In Australia, 1843–50, where he acquired a distaste for democracy that was reflected in his opposition to parliamentary reform later. Leader writer of 'The Times'. As vice-president of the Committee of the Privy Council on Education, 1859–64, he introduced the *Revised Code*. Chancellor of the Exchequer, 1868–73; Home Secretary 1873–4. (See Part 1, ch. 10)

Management Management is defined by the 'Concise Oxford English Dictionary' (6th edition) as: persons managing a business; administration of business concerns or public undertakings. It also indicates that in the verbal sense the word can mean deceit or trickery. For the purposes of this section, we shall use the word to indicate that we are talking of the people who control and direct the affairs of an organisation. The term 'manager' will be taken to mean someone who is responsible for the work of others. It can therefore be taken to include the owner-managers of businesses and supervisors. Often, there is a distinction made between the duties of supervisors and managers. Managers are usually concerned with the setting of objectives and determining priorities, finding and implementing means to carry them out, and assessing the results achieved. Supervisors are usually in charge of a particular area of work.

A number of censuses in the last few years used a narrower definition than above and discovered that there are probably about 2 to 2½ million managers in Great Britain. Managers have been subject to a great deal of attention in recent years, as it has become realised that they are key people in any organisation. This is because managers use resources, often very large, and the effectiveness with which they do this directly affects the results of the organisation and ultimately the economy as a whole. The most important resource most managers have is people. Henri Fayol argues that the manager plans, organises, controls and directs, and while we know this is too simplistic, by and large it is those four things a manager must somehow achieve if people are to be able to apply their skills to their jobs.

Alongside the manager's responsibilities inside the organisation must be put his duties towards the community. All managerial work produces social effects, some of them potentially damaging (such as pollution from a manufacturing plant). The nineteenth-century attitude of laissez-faire (or its modern equivalent: as long as it is not illegal, we can do it) is far too narrow a view, and unacceptable. Therefore, management has today to try to meet the demands of employer, employees and society. The skills and knowledge needed have to be learned. (See Part 1, ch. 12)

Management by objectives (MbO) This technique is attributed to Humble, although Drucker is probably the true author of the idea. It is a technique by which targets are determined for individual managers in order to achieve greater effectiveness in contribution to organisation results. It enjoyed considerable popularity in the 1960s, but the paperwork required was so extensive that most managers eventually rejected it. (See Part 1, ch. 12)

Management centres This item includes business departments of universities and other higher educational institutions.

There is now a very wide range of management and business courses available, including *National Diplomas* and *National Certificates*, honours and ordinary degrees, masters and doctoral programmes (either general, like the business schools' MBAs or specialist such as the MSc in Operational Research at some universities), and post-experience diplomas and certificates. There are many courses leading to membership of professional institutions and associations.

While the major parties involved in the development, financing and use of these centres and departments (government, industry, the individual student and the educationalists) may differ in their aims, all are agreed that the primary and common aim is to develop the capacity and performance of the individual manager. However, how this can be achieved remains a matter of contention. Most of the difficulties facing the educational institutions arise from the comparative youth of management education as an academic discipline. We do not know yet its value in economic terms. The quality of courses varies considerably, largely because of rapid expansion without adequate resources, especially teachers. The mix of theory and practice in courses is not easily determined.

There are at least 20 leading institutions, and a very large number of others, offering management education leading to qualifications. Any good reference book ('Personnel and Training Management Yearbook', published by Kogan Page, for example) lists most of them. The *National Training Index* is also helpful. (See Part 1, ch. 12)

Management consultants The Institute of Management Consultants, Alfred House, 23–24 Cromwell Place, London SW7 2LG (01–584 7285) aims to achieve recognition, respect and acceptance for the profession. Potential clients of management consultants may accept that a member of the Institute has been recognised as possessing experience or knowledge, or both. (See Part 1, ch. 2)

Management development A survey of the literature on management reveals no common agreement on the meaning of this term, and it is unlikely that this entry can do more than reflect the writer's own views. Management

193

M

development suggests by its words that we are concerned with the development of the management of an organisation as a whole. It can thus be argued it is a set of procedures or processes by which the organisation, its objectives and the required performance of the managers is analysed; systems by which managers are trained to achieve that performance; and means by which performance, both of the organisation and its management, is assessed and evaluated. We are therefore concerned with developing the competence, abilities, skills and knowledge of management as a whole in order to improve organisational performance. This view suggests that team development is an important element of management development. Within this, manager development (that is, the development of the individual) is important, as is management training and education and planned experience. *Appraisal* is often the system by which individual performance is examined.

Some careful distinctions need always to be made by the person responsible for management development in an organisation. First, it is critical to design any procedures so that they deal both with improving performance in current jobs and developing individuals for future jobs. The first is for all managers: the second only for those who can demonstrate their potential, either through the excellence of current performance or through the use of techniques like those used at *assessment centres*, or a combination of both. Second, individual attributes and personality characteristics, although important in terms of personal relationships, must not cloud the judgment of performance. Third, the only practical and value-free way of assessing managerial performance is the maintaining of progress against agreed *objectives* and targets. Fourth, no management will willingly inspect itself and its performance unless it is convinced that there is benefit (usually personal) in the process. Management development has to be sold.

Further reading

Humble, J. W., 'Management by Objectives in Action', McGraw-Hill, 1970.
Farnsworth, T., 'Developing Executive Talent', McGraw-Hill, 1971. (See Part 1, ch. 12)

Management development adviser This role first emerged strongly during the popularity of the *management objectives* movement. An MDA is a person specifically responsible for the management development process, either wholly or in part, in an organisation. (See Part 1, ch. 12)

Management game (exercise) This usually consists of a controlled situation requiring responses from participants to deal with an environment to attain predetermined objectives. The environment and controlling rules may use modelling techniques to try to represent business realities. Games and exercises should accurately reproduce organisational realities. (See Part 1, ch. 12)

Managerial grid This technique is part of an organisational development approach produced by Blake and Mouton. It places managers on a two-dimensional chart (one axis for concern for production, the other concern for people) from low to high on each dimension in an attempt to help people to identify their managerial styles (the behaviour they use in achieving work). Reddin has extended this to a 3-D theory by adding an effectiveness dimension.

Further reading

Blake, R. R. and Mouton, J. S., 'The Managerial Grid', Gulf Publishing, 1964.

Reddin, W. J., 'Managerial Effectiveness', McGraw-Hill, 1970. (See Part 1, ch. 12)

Manpower forecasting During the 1960s the idea became prevalent, particularly in developing countries, that it was desirable to plan the expansion of a country's education system to satisfy the future demand for educated or highly qualified manpower, and to avoid shortages or surpluses of manpower, which would either cause a slowing-down of economic growth or a waste of scarce resources. Whether or not it is possible to forecast the future demand for specific categories of educated workers accurately is a controversial point.

The idea of forecasting rests on the assumption that there are a number of fixed and rigid relationships between education and employment. The terms 'manpower requirements' and 'needs' assume there is a fixed and unchanging link between the number of workers employed and the level of output they produce. However, several research studies suggest that it is possible to produce the same level of output with many different combinations of manpower and capital, and that the link between the level of education of workers and their level of output is a flexible rather than a rigid one.

Similarly, there is dispute about whether it is possible to speak of the educational requirements of a job, since the same job is often performed by people with very different educational qualifications and on-the-job training is often employed. See the item on *substitutability* for further discussion.

In the U.K. there have been no attempts to plan the whole of higher education in the light of manpower forecasts, as attempted in the Mediterranean Regional Project (OECD 1963). However, attempts to forecast the demand and supply of teachers, doctors, and scientists and engineers have had considerable influence on the planning of higher education in Britain. These and other attempts at manpower forecasting have been assessed by Ahamad and Blaug (1973); they are highly critical of the value, and of the central assumptions of forecasting for the *labour market*.

Further reading

Ahamad, B. and Blaug, M., 'The Practice of Manpower Forecasting', Elsevier, 1973.

Parnes, H. S., 'Forecasting Educational Needs for Economic and Social Development', OECD, Paris, 1962.

OECD, 'Planning Education for Economic and Social Development', 1963. (See Part 1, ch. 5)

Manpower planning As has been said in other entries (particularly under *training needs analysis*) manpower planning has a deep and close relationship with training and development. In its turn, manpower planning is part of a greater whole, *human resources*.

Manpower planning is a strategy for the acquisition, utilisation, improvement and preservation of an organisation's human resources. There are three principal activities involved. First, the organisation determines its needs for manpower, both short- and long-term, by categories and skills. This demand analysis is critical to the whole process and requires a high degree of discipline and skill from both managers and specialists in the organisation. Second, a careful supply analysis is carried out. It is sensible to begin by a 'stock-taking' of the manpower already in the organisation, by quantity, quality, age, length of service, skills, knowledge and qualifications and so on, in order to identify any gaps between demand and supply. Decisions must then be made about estimated availability from the market, including trend analy-

195

M

sis (such as the likely outputs from schools, colleges and universities). Third, an appropriate action plan is prepared, covering recruitment and selection, training and development, and so on.

If demand and supply cannot be brought into balance in an organisation, it rapidly falls into one of two conditions. It can become grossly over-manned, not only in quantity but in quality, with good men asked to do poor jobs. Such organisations will eventually experience heavy manpower losses as people leave for more satisfactory employment. On the other hand, the organisation may find itself under-manned, again both in quantity and quality. This can lead to over-promotion, over-stressing, with individual work demands greater than the individual can carry. In both cases, and when demand and supply are balanced, education and training have a vital role in helping the organisation and its members to deal adequately with the environment. Further information can be had from the Institute of Manpower Studies, University of Sussex, Brighton. (See Part 1, ch. 11)

Manpower Services Commission (MSC) The Employment and Training Act 1973 provided for the establishment of the Manpower Services Commission to operate the public training and employment services that were previously part of the Department of Employment. Some parts of these services were historically part of the Ministry of Labour, whose demise was so regretted by, amongst others, Ray Gunther.

The MSC is separate from Government officially, but is accountable to the Secretary of State for Employment for its activities in England, and to the Secretaries of State of Wales and Scotland, respectively, for its activities in these areas. Although it is supposed to be at arm's length from Government the majority of its staff are established civil servants, its personnel policies are controlled by the Civil Service Department, and the original concept of taking in, on contract, experienced practitioners from outside, sadly weakened. In addition, the Labour Governments of 1974–9 saw the MSC as a means by which they could intervene in the labour market to protect and create 'jobs'. Whilst the evidence of effects is mixed, the general view is that efforts like job creation schemes disguise the true extent of unemployment in the UK without necessarily contributing positively to economic results. It is easy to do good with other people's money.

The MSC has 10 members who serve for three years: the chairman, three members agreed with the TUC, three with the CBI, two with local authority associations and one with professional education interests. It is interesting to note the lack of provision for members from the personnel and training professions who might be thought to have a keen interest in the body responsible, through its three operating divisions (*Training Services*, Employment Services and Special Programmes), for spending large sums of money on employment and training.

The MSC through its operating division is responsible for Job Centres, *Industry Training Boards*, the Training Opportunities Scheme, and other schemes. In the financial year 1977–8 the MSC spent over £200 million on administration alone. (See Part 1, ch. 11)

Marginal cost The marginal, or incremental, cost of education is the extra cost incurred when one additional pupil or student is enrolled in a school or college. In some cases, the marginal cost may be the same as the *average cost*, but if there is any spare capacity in the school, and if the resources of teachers or buildings and equipment are not already fully utilised, then the marginal cost of enrolling one additional student may be less than the average cost, due to *economies of scale*. (See Part 1, ch. 5)

Maturation Human behaviour is partly the product of learning, which results from changes in environmental stimulation. There are, however, some aspects of behaviour where the patterning and sequencing are under genetic control. Maturation is the term used to refer to these biologically determined processes of growth, development and ageing.

Further reading

Wright, D. S., et al., 'Introducing Psychology: An Experimental Approach', Penguin, 1970. (See Part 1, ch. 14)

Mean The mean is a statistical term used for what is often loosely described as average. The term mean is specifically defined and is calculated by adding all the separate scores and dividing by the number of scores.

E.g., examination scores of 30, 40, 35, 50 and 45 would have a mean of
$$\frac{30 + 40 + 35 + 50 + 45}{5} = \frac{200}{5} = 40$$
(See Part 1, ch. 8)

Meaning The relationship of language to the world and the way in which words acquire meaning has become an important problem in recent philosophy. The main theories are the following: (1) That words stand for ideas in the mind (John Locke). Criticism: as people vary in their formulation of ideas, the same word would stand for different ideas. (2) A word means what is stands for: denotation. This view was criticised by Frege, who pointed out the difference between sense and reference. The phrase 'the morning star' does not mean the same as 'the evening star' though both denote Venus. Frege also pointed out the importance of use in establishing meaning, with the advice that if 'you want the meaning of a term look at its use'. This was developed further by Wittgenstein, who emphasised the importance of examining the use of a word within a given context. (See Part 1, ch. 13)

Measures of central tendency Since there are few *scales* in educational measurement which can be said to have a true zero, some other reference point is required for anchoring a scale. Measures of central tendency of a distribution provide such reference points. There are three main measures, called the median, the mode and the *mean*. The median is the score obtained by the person at the 50th percentile. The mode is the most common score in a *distribution*. The mean is the average score of the distribution and is therefore calculated by adding all the values (x) obtained by all the people and then dividing by the number of people (n). This can be written mathematically as follows:

$$\text{Mean } (\bar{x}) = \frac{\Sigma x}{n}$$

where Σx is the sum of all the values x.

These measures of central tendency have the same numerical value when the distribution is uni-modal and symmetrical. The 'normal distribution' is such an example as in Figure (a):

197

M

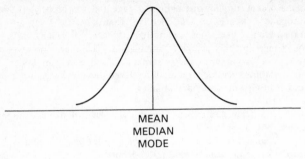

MEAN
MEDIAN
MODE

Figure (a)

The values diverge in the following manner when the distribution becomes *skewed* also in Figure (b):

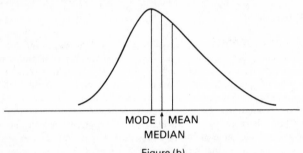

MODE ↑ MEAN
MEDIAN

Figure (b)

The mean is the most important measure of central tendency, since it lends itself most easily to mathematical manipulation and plays an important part in general statistical theory.

Further reading

Childs, R., 'Norm-Referenced Testing and the Standard Scores', National Foundation for Educational Research Publishing Co., 1978.

Crocker, A. C., 'Statistics for the Teacher', 2nd ed., National Foundation for Educational Research, 1972.

Guilford, J. P., 'Fundamental Statistics in Psychology and Education', ch. 4, 6th ed., McGraw-Hill, 1978. (See Part 1, ch. 6)

Measures of dispersion Given that our *data* are based on a quantitative classification it is both meaningful and useful to consider the extent to which values are dispersed along the measurement scale. For example, if our classification is based on people's height, it is interesting to have a measure which tells us how much people tend to be grouped around the central value, or how much they tend to be spread out between a certain range of values.

One of the crudest measures of dispersion is the range of *scores* in the *distribution*. However, it would only take one dwarf in a *population* to make the range very much greater. Such susceptibility to a single datum is undesirable, and so other measures of dispersion are used which reduce the effects of single results.

One such measure is the inter-quartile range, which is simply the difference in score between the lowest scorer in the top quarter of the distribution and the highest scorer in the bottom quarter of the distribution. This can be portrayed using the normal distribution, as follows in Figure (c):

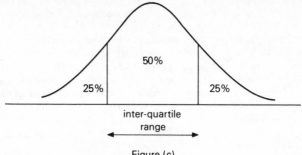

Figure (c)

More commonly used measures of dispersion are based on a different concept than range. This concept is the extent to which the scores in the distribution deviate from the mean. Thus we could subtract the mean score from every obtained score (resulting in negative values as well) and summate these values without regard for the negative signs involved. Dividing by the number of people (n) in the distribution gives the average deviation from the mean. Since ignoring the signs is highly non-mathematical, however, it is usual to obtain the squared value of all the deviations, which makes all the values positive. Summing these squared deviations and dividing by n gives the average squared deviation which is usually called the *variance*. The square root of the variance gives us what is commonly known as the standard deviation (SD). The formula for the SD is therefore:

$$SD = \frac{\sqrt{(\Sigma (x - \bar{x})^2)}}{n}$$

where x = each observation
     x̄ = mean value
     Σ = the summation of these values
     n = number of people in the distribution.

Further reading
Crocker, A. C., 'Statistics for the Teacher', 2nd edition, National Foundation for Educational Research, 1974.
Guilford, J. P., 'Fundamental Statistics in Psychology and Education', ch. 5, McGraw Hill, 1978. (See Part 1, ch. 6)

Mechanical and organic solidarity Durkheim argues that in a society in which the division of labour has not advanced far, there is a specific form of social solidarity – or bonding of its members into a social whole – that arises out of the uniform nature of their way of life and the reflection of that uniformity in their moral code. In a society with an advanced division of labour, there is a different form of solidarity associated with a moral code arising from the mutual dependence of its members. The first Durkheim calls mechanical solidarity; the second, organic solidarity.
Further reading
Durkheim, E., 'The Division of Labour in Society', Macmillan, 1933. (See Part 1, ch. 15)

M

Membership gradings There are for most institutions three main gradings, although these may contain subtleties peculiar to a particular institution or association. The three are: non-corporate, for those as yet unqualified; corporate, for those qualified and accepted; honorary, for distinguished members or outsiders. (See Part 1, ch. 2)

Mental testing Mental tests can take many forms, and are widely used as both diagnostic tools and as predictors of future performance. Some tests are intended to assess *intelligence*. whilst others measure particular *aptitudes*. Educational *tests* are used to measure levels of skill in areas such as reading, mathematics and comprehension; yet other tests are designed to identify aspects of *personality*. To be of value a test must be both *valid* and reliable.
Further reading
Cronbach, L. J., 'Essentials of Psychological Testing', 3rd ed., Harper & Row, 1970. (See Part 1, ch. 14)

Metaphysics
Metaphysics is the study of what lies beyond our immediate experience. An empiricist would doubt the usefulness of such an enterprise. But a more moderate reaction would be to say that it may be fruitful to postulate how things may be beyond experience, for our actual experiences to be of the kind we know. (See Part 1, ch. 13)

Methodological difficulties Investigators must be wary of the difficulties connected with research in comparative education. These difficulties concern relevant *data*, problem definition, comparability and terminology. The question of a relevant data is important: what are the sources of this information? How reliable is it? What ideological, institutional and personal bias is inherent in the data?

Politicians are often ideologically biased, while governments tend to give that interpretation which places their activities in the most favourable light. Similarly, the commentaries of individuals may be distorted by prejudice against ethnic religious and ideological groups. The question of problem definition also created difficulties and has been dealt with at length by a number of comparativists. Those favouring the anthropological approaches to comparative education generally hold that 'expert' investigators define problems according to their own preconceived value systems. These may have little or no semblance to the conceptions of the problematic situation held by the participants in the institution being investigated. Ideally the comparativist should be a participant observer.

Other difficulties concern comparativists: for example, is it feasible to compare France with Kenya or should comparisons be limited to cultures having common features, such as England and Scotland or Spain and Portugal? There are similar difficulties concerning choice of system and in points of terminology: for example, the term 'school-leaving certificate' has different meanings according to which educational system is being investigated. This has created problems of *harmonisation* within closely-knit groups of countries such as the European Economic Community.

Problems facing comparativists have only now been touched upon and much must be considered before research is attempted.
Further reading
Tretheway, A. R., 'Introducing Comparative Education', Pergamon, 1976.
Bereday, G. Z. F., 'Comparative Method in Education', Holt, Rinehart & Winston, (See Part 1, ch. 3)

Milk and meals The requirement placed on LEAs under the 1944 Act to provide meals suitable in all respects as the main meal of the day was withdrawn in the Education Act 1980. This Act gives Authorities the discretion whether to provide school meals or not, what kind of meal to provide, and its price. They must however make 'such provision . . . as appears to the Authority to be requisite', without charge, for children whose parents are in receipt of Supplementary Benefit or Family Income Supplement. Facilities must also be made available for children to eat the food brought to school by them.

Free milk used to be provided in schools, but in 1971 it was withdrawn from all children aged 8 and over except those in special schools. Under the 1980 Act an LEA is under no obligation to provide milk at all, but it has the discretion to do so and charge appropriately. (See Part 1, ch. 1)

Mixed-ability grouping This is the form of organisation where pupils are taught in classes which are not homogenous in academic ability. It is a reaction from the system of *streaming by ability*, which, it is believed, because of the well-researched phenomenon of the 'self-fulfilling prophecy', creates a hierarchy of excellence and develops feelings of failure and under-achievement even among those not of low ability. It avoids the situation in which staff tend to have preconceived notions of children's abilities, and allows for better social integration into the school. Equally important is that it reflects the fact that a school has other values apart from academic excellence, such as care and compassion for others, pride in one's work, consistency of effort and so on. In secondary schools mixed-ability classes are associated particularly with the earlier 'diagnostic' years. (See Part 1, ch. 1)

Mobile instructor service The *Training Services Division* of the *Manpower Services Commission* provides this service. Instructors from TSD provide in-company training in special skills, usually engineering, for firms with particular needs. An economic fee is charged, except in assisted areas where it is free. The training is tailor-made and can last from one to eight weeks. (See Part 1, ch. 11)

Modular training This, undoubtedly one of the few resounding successes produced by the *Industrial Training Act 1964*, was developed by the Engineering Industry Training Board. The term is generally used to describe separate training programmes designed as a series or a related group, from which selections are made according to need as a route to a qualification, usually at craft or technician level.

It is used specifically to refer to the engineering craft system developed by the EITB. The 'Glossary of Training Terms' (HMSO) states that it is a type of training based on the concept of building up skills and knowledge in units as needed by the individual. Each module is based on a skill or group of skills which analysis shows to be a visible unit in the job situation, and has a training element, an experience element, and where appropriate, a further education element. The satisfactory completion of a series of modules usually denotes a recognised level of qualification, and the satisfactory completion of further modules may lead to a higher level of qualification. The length of a module varies according to its content. The EITB pattern is that any trainee completing satisfactorily first-year basic training and a minimum of two appropriate modules is awarded a certificate of craftsmanship.

Other *Industry Training Boards* have developed similar schemes, and the basic pattern for craft training in the UK is now modular. Because of its success, the technique is now very widely applied by trainers in industry, even for programmes which do not lead to qualifications.

While accepting the great success of modular training, it is sensible to keep in mind the continuing shortage of skilled workers in the UK. The numbers entering such schemes (and others) is insufficient for national needs, partly because schools do not seem able to produce enough qualified candidates and partly because training is subject to economic influences. Many firms still cut training expenditures when times are hard; and suffer the subsequent shortages of output and efficiency when times are good. An attempt by the EITB in 1978 to introduce further changes as a part-answer was unhappily not well received.

Further reading Further reading can be found in the craft apprenticeship recommendations of the various ITBs and especially the EITB, P.O Box 176, 54 Clarendon Road, Watford, Herts WD1 1LB, Watford 38441; 'Glossary of Training Terms', HMSO, 1971. (See Part 1, ch. 11)

Monitorial system Both the Rev. Andrew Bell of the National Society and Joseph Lancaster of the British and Foreign School Society can claim credit for introducing the monitorial system on a large scale. By using young children as assistants and breaking a lesson down into its simplest elements for them to teach to small groups of children mechanically, Bell and Lancaster believed that one teacher could supervise a thousand children on his own. (See Part 1, ch. 10)

Motivation Motivation is the process which leads the individual to attempt to satisfy some need. The simplest model of the relationship between motivation and learning assumes that when a need exists it will lead to a drive which will energise behaviour. This will result in the individual engaging in some appropriate behaviour in his attempt to satisfy his need. If the activity does lead to a reduction in the drive the activity will be reinforced, or strengthened, so that it will be more likely to occur on future occasions. The reinforcement that results from the drive reduction causes learning to take place. This is Thorndike's law of effect in action.

In some instances the need which leads to the learning may be easy to recognise and have its origin in biological processes such as hunger or thirst; in other instances the need may be much more complex and have its origin in social processes and the self-concept which the individual has.

Maslow has advanced a theory of human motivation in which he identifies five basic needs, which are related to one another in a hierarchy. Lower-order needs must be at least partly satisfied before needs higher in the hierarchy influence behaviour. At the base of the hierarchy are physiological needs which arise from an imbalance in the body's homeostatic regulatory system, such as hunger and thirst. Next is the need for safety; then comes a need for love, affection and a sense of belongingness with others. When these needs are satisfied, a need for self-esteem and the esteem of others will arise. At the top of his hierarchy Maslow places the need for self-actualisation; the need to fulfil one's potentialities as a human being. Largely independent of the hierarchy of needs there are, Maslow suggests, needs to obtain knowledge and understanding. Maslow's work is an example of *humanistic psychology*. See also: *schools of psychology*; *theories of learning*; *learning retention and recall*; *attention and perception*; *social aspects of learning*; *achievement motivation*.

Further reading
Maslow, A. H., 'Towards a Psychology of Being', 2nd ed., Van Nostrand Reinhold, 1969.

Vernon, M. D., 'Human Motivation', Cambridge University Press, 1969. (See Part 1, ch. 14)

Moulding The 'moulding' metaphor in education is held to be the authoritarian approach. The educator is supposed to know what kind of person he wishes to produce and works towards that end. How authoritarian the notion need be in practice would depend on the kind of person the educator hoped to produce. Thus the 'moulding' and 'growth' metaphors tend to converge. See also: *education, growth, indoctrination*.

Further reading
Dearden, R. F., 'The Philosophy of Primary Education', Routledge & Kegan Paul, 1968.
Scheffler, I., 'The Language of Education', Blackwell (US ed.). (See Part 1, ch. 13)

Multilateral school The idea of a school with three sides, grammar, technical and modern, in the same building or in separate buildings on the same site, but organised separately, gained currency in the late 1930s. The bilateral school, grammar and modern, was a variation on the theme. For a while the multilateral school gained support as an alternative to the comprehensive school, defined in Circular 144/1947 as 'intended to provide for all the secondary education of all the children in a given area without an organisation in three sides'. (See Part 1, ch. 10)

Multiple-choice 'Multiple-choice' describes a response mode used in *tests*. The test consists of a number of *items* each one consisting of a 'stem' followed by a number of alternative 'answers'. The stem can be a question, a statement, a series of figures or anything else that can be followed by an 'answer'. The answer can equally be anything that can be related to the stem by certain rules. The essence of multiple-choice is that the correct answer is hidden amongst a number of other distracting answers. The person has to identify the correct answer or the answer which is nearest to being correct in order to obtain a *score* for that item. (See Part 1, ch. 6)

Mutiple-choice programme Unlike *linear programmes*, multiple-choice programmes do not generally require a student to construct an answer, but rather require him to select one from a multiple choice of answers provided. Selection of an answer is then followed by a frame of material which explains the correctness or otherwise of the answer. If the answer is correct, the student is directed to the next frame in the programme. If the answer is incorrect, the error is explained and the student then referred back to the next frame of the programme.

Further reading
Markle, S. M., 'Good Frames and Bad', Wiley, 2nd ed., 1969. (See Part 1, ch. 9)

Multi-skilling The term has two meanings.

First, it is used to describe the process by which operators are trained to undertake the full range of jobs in their section.

Second, it is used to describe the addition of skills to an individual initially trained in one (as an apprentice electrician may go on to take training in mechanical skills). It is often suggested as a route to increased job satisfaction and therefore is closely related to *job enrichment/enlargement*. (See Part 1, ch. 11)

Museums Education Services Museums throughout Britain make a direct input to the education system. Though the purpose of museums may always have been ostensibly educative, recent years have seen a major growth of a direct

M

educational development within museums with the appointment of educational specialists, the creation of new materials and a new approach to presentation and information provision. Several museums have established educational resource centres. Though each museum or group of museums within an authority is autonomous, the Group for Educational Services in Museums does act as a co-ordinating and promotional body through which information and ideas can be exchanged between museums. (See Part 1, ch. 7)

National Certificates National Certificates are awarded jointly by the Department of Education and Science (in Scotland, the Scottish Education Department) and the appropriate professional institutions. They now cover a vast range of subjects. There are two levels. Ordinary National Certificates (ONC) take two years, part-time and are about GCE A-level standard. They are accepted by many colleges of higher education as an entry qualification. Higher National Certificates (HNC) are about first degree level, but in a narrower range of topics. They are gained by part-time study.

It is intended that these will be gradually replaced by technician qualifications laid down by the *Business Education Council* and the *Technician Education Council*. (See Part 1, ch. 2)

National character This term refers to those characteristics common to certain national groups which differentiate them from other groups and which were shaped by their history, traditions, environment, and intellectual outlook. (See Part 1, ch. 3)

National Colleges These have been established to provide advanced courses relating to particular industries or technologies, are independently managed but are designated by the Secretary of State for Education and Science and receive grants from his department. The *Further Education Staff College*, Coombe Lodge, Blagdon, Bristol BS18 6RG (0761 – 62503) seeks to improve the effectiveness of higher and further education. (See Part 1, ch. 2)

National diplomas These are awarded on the same basis as *National Certificates*. Ordinary National Diplomas (OND) are awarded for success in two-year full-time or sandwich courses and are approximately at GCE A-level. They are as acceptable as entry qualifications as ONCs. Higher National Diplomas (HND) are awarded on the basis of two-years' full-time or three years' sandwich courses. Standards are about pass degree level, and usually give exemption from some parts of the qualifying examinations of some professional institutions. (See Part 1, ch. 2)

National Examinations Board in Supervisory Studies (NEBSS) NEBSS was set up in 1964 to stimulate and co-ordinate suitable courses for supervisors. It aims to ensure the provision of courses for supervisors at all levels over the entire range of trade, commerce and industry, and to provide and control examination standards to a nationally accepted level. A major feature of NEBSS work is the flexibility it offers course organisers, who may design syllabuses to cater for specialist groups of supervisory managers. It will also accept submissions from an educational institution for courses designed to cater for a specific organisation. This has led to the development of some very successful joint college/company courses, where the NEBSS examinations are an integral part of the company's manpower development plans.

The Certificate in Supervisory Studies covers the principles and practice of supervision, industrial relations, technical aspects, economic and financial aspects, and communications. It must include at least 240 hours of formal instruction, on a *day-release*, *block-release* or *full-time* pattern. A project is compulsory, and the report of this helps to determine final awards. There are no educational entry requirements, but obviously intending students must be capable of benefiting from such a course. The Diploma in Supervisory Studies is a more advanced course. It has no formal examinations, but a rigorous assessment procedure is used.

NEBSS recently introduced an introductory course, fulfilling a long-felt need for something to help people in supervisory jobs to re-enter the field of formal adult study. Many supervisors and managers are reluctant to undergo formal study, and this reluctance increases with age. The NEBSS introductory course is a sound, practical idea more institutions could with value undertake. Further information from: NEBSS, 76 Portland Place, London W1N 4AA; 01–580 3050. (See Part 1, ch. 12)

National Federation of Community Associations The Federation in its aim of promoting new community associations acts as a liaison organisation between appropriate professional training agencies and voluntary bodies. It also provides and promotes links with local statutory bodies that are pertinent to community associations. (See Part 1, ch. 7)

National Institute of Adult Education The Institute is a national centre of reference for all forms of adult education. As now constituted, it merges the former National Foundation for Adult Education and British Institute of Adult Education. Its governing council has representatives of local education authorities (appointed by the AMA, ACC, Welsh Joint Committee for Further Education and the ILEA), the universities, armed forces, Home Office and numerous national voluntary bodies. The Department of Education and Science appoints assessors. The BBC and IBA appoint observers. It may invite into associate membership national bodies promoting special purposes amongst the adult population by educational means, and there is provision for individual members. (See Part 1, ch. 7)

National Training Index This is published by Graduate Appointments Ltd., 7 Princes Street, London W1R 7RB, 01–629 7262. It provides a comprehensive guide to what is available not only in the UK but also on a selected international basis. It provides a guide to the providers of courses as well, both public and in-company. (See Part 1, ch. 2)

Necessary statements Necessary propositions are considered to be unconditionally and eternally true because they could not be otherwise. Empirically-minded philosophers have insisted that such necessity is solely dependent upon analyticity. (See *analytical statement*). Necessary statements are contrasted with *contingent statements*. (See Part 1, ch. 13)

New sociology of education In 'Knowledge and Control' (1971), the formative text of the 'new' sociology of education, Michael Young and his associates argue the need for the sociology of education to take it as one of its central tasks to investigate what the school or college curriculum presents as knowledge. Their claim is that, since this 'knowledge' has been socially constructed, it has to be assessed in the context of the social relationships that have shaped its content and the form of its transmission. (See *sociology of knowledge*.) Contemporary philosophers of education are criticised for encouraging the belief that what is taught can be judged to be true or false independently of any consideration of the nature of the society in which it has come to be taught.

The 'new' sociology of education has, by taking this stance, attracted a considerable amount of attention from the philosophers of education, and the philosophers have particularly singled out for attack what they see as the *sociological relativism* of the new movement. In 'Society, State and Schooling' (1977), edited by Michael Young and Geoff Whitty, the position taken in 'Knowledge and Control' is itself subjected to criticism, and a paper by Whitty specifically offers 'Notes towards a reconceptualisation of the "new" sociology of education'. The purpose of this reconceptualisation is to eliminate the dangers of a critique of knowledge based on Schutz's *phenomenological sociology*, such as the danger that the difficulties of effecting any radical change in education will be seriously underestimated. Educational change of a radical kind, it is now argued, can come only through the progress of the *class struggle*.

Further reading

Young, M. (ed.), 'Knowledge and Control', Collier-Macmillan, 1971.

Young, M. and Whitty, G. (eds), 'Society, State and Schooling', Falmer Press, 1977. (See Part 1, ch. 15)

Non-parametric statistics *Data* are collected where the number system does not have equal intervals (e.g., the difference between 2 and 3 is not the same as that between 18 and 19), or the numbers merely identify something (say question numbers). The statistics applicable are called non-parametric. (See Part 1, ch. 8)

Norm, normative On a *structural-functional* analysis, the basic structure of a normative system or a normative pattern of culture is made up of sets of value standards of three kinds: cognitive, appreciative and moral. Of these, the moral standards serve to integrate the social system most comprehensively. Value standards are held in common by all members of a social system or sub-system. Norms are more specific rules of conduct which can apply to one individual's *role* without applying to his partners. Parsons claims that there are a few basic normative decisions universally structuring interactions. These are either/or decisions, and he calls them 'pattern variables'.

Further reading

Parsons, T. and Shils, E. (eds), 'Toward a General Theory of Action', Part 2, Harvard University Press, 1951. (See Part 1, ch. 15)

Normal distribution A normal distribution is the name given to a mathematically defined *distribution* as shown in the diagram.

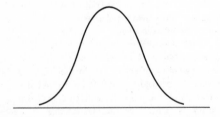

It is found that many real life distributions approximate to this shape (e.g.. heights of all British schoolchildren) and it is therefore often taken as the expected shape for educational attributes. Its mathematical properties make it useful for both interpretation and statistical analyses. The formula for the curve of the normal distribution is obtained from the binomial theorem and can be written:

$$Y = \frac{N}{\sigma\sqrt{2\pi}} \circ e \frac{-x-\mu)^2}{2\sigma^2}$$

where Y = height of curve for particular values of X
  π = 3.1416
  e = base of napierian logarithms = 27183
  N = number cases
  μ = population mean
  σ = standard deviation

(See Part 1, ch. 6)

Norm-reformed measurement If the height of a large group of people is taken, the graph of a number of people against heights of those people would be a *normal distribution*. This kind of distribution is commonly found in measurements. Statistics are used which enable predictions and comparisons to be made. In educational testing it is often assumed that ability (see *intelligence tests*) and attainments (see *examinations*) will also be normally distributed. It is not possible to prove that this distribution is a correct assumption, since we can neither directly observe ability and achievement, nor get consistent distributions using different questions or items. However, by using a normal distribution certain mathematical advantages accrue. For example, there is a precise relationship between the difference of a score x from the *mean* score and the proportion of people who score more or less than x. A convenient term to identify some score differences is called the *standard deviation* (for example, 34 per cent of scores lie within one standard deviation each side of the mean). From this type of distribution can be derived standardised tests (see *standardisation*).

By using the norm-referenced measurement it is possible to make comparisons between distributions that are obtained and a normal distribution. From these comparisons statistical conclusions can be drawn on the probability of the actual distribution occurring when related to a normal distribution. For further details a book on statistics relating to education, psychology or the behavioural sciences should be consulted.

Further reading
Garrett, H. E., 'Statistics in Psychology and Education'. Longmans, 1966.
Lewis, D. G., 'Statistical Methods in Education', University of London Press, (See Part 1, ch. 8)

Null hypothesis The null hypothesis is a formal procedure to test differences between two groups. For example, it is required to compare the reading ability of children in the east and the west of a country. A large *sample* of children from each *population* would be chosen in a manner to prevent bias (for example, the sample would not include all rich children in the east and all poor children in the west). A set of tests on reading would be administered to each sample. If the test results of one group had much higher scores than the other group we would probably conclude that group could read better. If there was little difference in scores we would conclude that there was no difference between the groups. The problem is deciding what constitutes a 'large difference' and a 'little difference'. A null hypothesis is a mechanism for testing the difference mathematically. The null hypothesis gives an exact base for mathematical testing because its base is the assumption that there is no difference between the populations. It is comparable with the legal decision of innocent until proved guilty. The basis of testing the null hypothesis in education often depends on the *norm-referenced measurement*, and the statistical techniques used would be *parametric statistics*. For other distributions and conditions the testing of the null hypothesis would use *non-parametric statistics* (see any book on non-parametric statistics for the distinction).

Further reading

Siegel, S., 'Non-Parametric Statistics', McGraw-Hill, 1959.

Garrett, H. E., 'Statistics in Psychology and Education', Longmans, 1966. (See Part 1, ch. 8)

Nursery school Nursery schools are educational establishments which cater for the needs of children between the ages of 3 and 5. They must be distinguished from day nurseries which meet the social need of caring for children when their parents are at work. The 1944 Act made it incumbent on LEAs to provide nursery education; but this section of the Act was not implemented because of the lack of accommodation and shortage of teachers in the post-war period.

The Plowden Report 1967 focused attention on nursery education and the formative part it could play in a child's early learning experiences. The nurseries provided verbal stimulus and opportunities for constructive play which were especially valuable to children coming from deprived or inadequate homes.

After Plowden new nursery projects were included in building programmes in educational priority areas, and there was further expansion after 1973 with the aim of providing a substantial increase in full-time nursery places for 4-year-olds and part-time places for 3-year-olds. Nursery education is still outside the statutory period of school attendance, however, and tends to be one of the first parts of the service to be cut back in periods of economic restraint. See also: *playgroup*. (See Part 1, ch. 1)

Objective 'Objective' has two meanings. One is to do with the goal to which one aspires. Thus competence in reading can be an objective. It also has a meaning to do with the nature of the measurement system. Some measurements are based on subjective judgments. Objective measurements reduce the effect of individual subjectivism to a minimum. Thus an objective test is one which can be scored by any person and the same result should be found. The system is 'outside' the person. It can be argued that total objectivity is impossible and that there is only a continuum from subjective to objective. (See Part 1, ch. 6)

Objectives A clear specification of intent for learning, which often includes the performance and the conditions under which that performance will be expected. It is usually a more detailed statement of intent than *aims* and *goals*. (See Part 1, ch. 8)

Objective test There are two interpretations: (1) each question in a test relates to a particular objective; (2) a style of question where the marks can only be allocated in one way. The second usage is more common and includes such questions as multiple-choice, e.g. most of South America was colonised by people from: (a) Britain; (b) France; (c) Netherlands; (d) Portugal; (e) Spain. The correct answer has to be underlined.

Further reading

Thyne, J. M., 'Principles of Examining', University of London Press, 1974. (See Part 1, ch. 14)

Objectivity *Knowledge* is assumed to differ from belief and opinion because the former is concerned with what is really the case and the latter with how things may appear to be. This may be summarised by saying that knowledge is concerned with what is 'objectively true' as opposed to opinion, which is concerned with the assessment of an individual or group. Knowledge, in this sense, assumes that there is an 'external world' and that this world can be known. Our knowledge is adequate or inadequate inasmuch as our ideas about how the world is, tally with how it really is. The main criticism of objectivity, expressed in this manner, is that of presupposing that we can experience the world 'as it really is' irrespective of our ideas and concepts about it. See also: *relativism*.

Further reading

Hamlyn, D. W., 'Theory of Knowledge', Macmillan, 1971.

O'Connor, D. J., 'The Correspondence Theory of Truth', Hutchinson, 1975. (See Part 1, ch. 13)

Observation schedules A whole range of observation schedules are used in educational research. Such schedules may, for example, assist the design of learning sequence, or enable systematic records to be kept of interactions between individuals or groups. An example of the simplest form of an interaction-schedule would be a list of statements to check whether certain activites have taken place (called a check list). Another simple form may be a plan of a room where the movements of individuals are plotted at fixed intervals of time. Others may list defined activities (e.g., teacher asks learner a question) and use boxes in which ticks are placed each time the activity takes place and/or the time at which it occurred. More sophisticated systems may use a table in which a complex range of interactions is recorded: an example is *interaction analysis*. For carrying out an observation to assist the design of learning materials, two common kinds of scheme are used. If the learning is going to relate to physical control a *skills analysis* may be carried out to identify the set of physical and co-ordination skills required. From the relationships between the skills a learning sequence can be derived. In other activities a mixture of decisions and skills may be needed to carry out a task. By asking an experienced person to talk through their activities a *task analysis* can be carried out. Again a learning sequence can be derived. For these kinds of activity such observation schedules are very powerful aids to the design of learning. A whole range of other analytical and observation techniques is used.

Further reading

Seymour, W. D., 'Skills Analysis Training', Pitman, 1968.

Flanders, N. A., 'Analysing Teaching Behaviour', Addison-Wesley, 1970. (See Part 1, ch. 8)

Occupational analysis This widely used technique examines job descriptions, job specifications and job studies to arrive at groupings of similar jobs to produce a common title as an aid to recruitment and selection, education and training, and employee relations. (See Part 1, ch. 11)

Open-plan This phrase describes the internal design of primary schools built in the 1960s and thereafter. The traditional layout of classrooms and corridors is replaced by a pattern of inter-connected teaching areas of various sizes and functions. The basic concept derives from the fact that a class of, say,

30 children will consist of individuals who vary in their interests, aptitudes and stages of development and who do not learn at the same pace. Consequently to have these 30 individuals engaged in the same learning activity at the same time is not the most effective way of organising the work. The aim is to tailor the curriculum more to the needs of individual pupils, so that the teacher will be dealing with individuals or groups, and only sometimes with the whole class together. There will be different learning activities being pursued concurrently, so the teaching area must be suitable for the relevant activities and the size of group likely to be engaged in them. For example, members of a class may be engaged in mathematics in the mathematics area, painting in the 'wet' area, project work in the resources area, or listening to a story on cassette at a listening post. The school will have areas suitable for these activities, some of them being shared between two or more classes. At the same time circulation spaces, instead of being corridors only, are organically linked and incorporated with teaching spaces, thus maximising the areas available for learning. (See Part 1, ch. 1)

Open University In 1966 a Government White Paper, 'The University of the Air', was published. The then Prime Minister, Harold Wilson, was strongly committed to the creation of an institution through which people could obtain qualifications through home study. In 1967, as a result of the White Paper, the Open University Planning Committee was formed; it reported in January 1969, and the University was granted its Royal Charter in May 1969. The first undergraduates were admitted in 1971, part-time undergraduates in 1972, and the first post-experience students in 1973.

The University aims to provide opportunities of higner education for those who, for any reason, were not able to enter higher education immediately on leaving school. It also aims to provide continuing education for adults, including the provision of higher degree programmes.

Many employers support employees taking Open University courses, not only because the course might be relevant to work but also because of a sense of social responsibility. Of particular interest to many employers has been the OU's development of associate student courses. These, based on the growing awareness that initial education and training are not sufficient to last for a whole career, provide opportunities for adults to pursue their knowledge into new areas. The courses concentrate not only on the acquisition but also on the application of new knowledge. The courses are particularly attractive to those who cannot be released from full-time work and who do not wish to pursue the award of a degree. There is now a wide range of associate student courses. Many of the subject areas (numerical computation, statistics, systems management, computing and computers are only a few) are directly applicable to work and thus provide excellent answers to some of industry's problems of re-training and re-educating. Further details from the Prospectus of Courses for Associate Students, the Associate Student Central Office, Open University, P. O. Box 76, Milton Keynes, MK7 6AN. (See Part 1, ch. 12)

The Open University was set up to provide higher education by home-study methods for adults in full-time employment or working in the home. Students are generally over the age of 21 and do not need academic qualifications in order to apply.

The University's undergraduate teaching programme began in 1971. The basic teaching material is specially written correspondence texts which the student uses in conjunction with BBC radio and television programmes. There is face-to-face tuition at local study centres and at residential summer schools. A large number of study centres have been established in 13 regional groups covering the whole of the United Kingdom. (See Part 1, ch. 7)

Operant conditioning The process of operant conditioning involves the modification of behaviour by its consequences. Typically a relationship is established between some form of voluntary behaviour and a reinforcement. A subject is operantly conditioned when he has modified his behaviour to obtain the reinforcement or reward. A knowledge of the pattern of reinforcement enables predictions to be made about the individual's behaviour. B. F. Skinner is the originator of work in this area of learning.

Further reading
Skinner, B. F., 'Cumulative Record', 3rd ed., Appleton-Century-Crofts, 1972. (See Part 1, ch. 14)

Operative This term refers to work people who possess degrees of skill and knowledge of a narrower and often lower kind than those needed by craftsmen. Operatives carry out specific operations involving machinery or plant. The range of operative jobs, often called semi-skilled, is very wide in most industrial organisations. Numerically, operatives are usually the largest group of people in manufacturing industry. Something like half the work-force in the engineering industry, for example, are described as operatives. In construction, the term is used somewhat more widely to include craftsmen.

After the Industrial Training Act 1964 most *Industry Training Boards* (ITBs) gave operative training a high priority. Whilst this reflected the numerical size of the group, the major reason was probably that operative training was highly developed already. The exigencies of the Second World War had produced *systematic training* systems as a route to the production levels required by the war effort. Employers therefore understand the need for and benefits of good training for operatives.

Most operative training systems aim to bring workers to *experienced worker standards* as quickly as possible. Therefore, wide use is made of *job analysis*, *skills analysis* and similar techniques. Most operative training is characterised by short learning times, standardised programmes, off-job, high manual-skill content, minimal education standards, and limited knowledge demands. There has been some development in further education for operatives, but it is limited to those jobs with a significant element of technical or supervisory skills. Because the effects of error can be so high for, say, an operative involved in a high-technology process, it is necessary that the principles of the technology are understood.

It is likely that as manufacturing becomes more computerised and automated many operative jobs will disappear and those that remain will need a much higher level of skills. *Re-training* is likely to become much more important in the near future. (See Part 1, ch. 11)

Opportunity cost The opportunity cost of education measures the value of all the real resources which are devoted to education by society. The measurement of opportunity cost must take into account resources, such as students' time, which are not bought or sold, and therefore are not included in money expenditure on education. The usual way of measuring the opportunity cost of students' time is by *forgone earnings* which represent the value of students' time in the alternative opportunity of employment, which the student gives up, when choosing to continue in education. (See Part 1, ch. 5)

Organisation Organisations, as Weber defines them, are social groups either closed to outsiders or open to them only in accordance with specific rules, and governed by a leader or an administrative staff, under whose guidance a specific form of regular purposive activity is conducted.

Analysis of the school as an organisation is possible from a wide range of perspectives. There can be, for example, a *structural-functionalist* focus on *roles*, *norms* and goal-attainment, a *symbolic interactionist* or *phenomenological* focus on members' meanings, a Weberian focus on *bureaucracy*, or a Marxian focus on *alienation* and *conflict*.

Further reading

Silverman, D., 'The Theory of Organisations', Heinemann, 1970. (See Part 1, ch. 15)

Organisation development (OD) The organisation development (OD) movement has enjoyed explosive growth over the last decade and has until now escaped the rigorous criticism extended to other, earlier movements such as *management by objectives (MbO)*. The multiplicity of meanings attaching to the term illustrates the present confusions, and hence explains the relative freedom from attack.

The central idea appears to be that interventions by a third party, designed to ensure an effective organisation, will cause the organisation to respond appropriately to changes, both within it and within its environment. Thus the organisation will use best the capacities of its members. From this five approaches have developed:

1 The structural approach: by analysing the implications of change, by implementing changes in structure, culture and management, the organisation will function effectively.

2 The integrative approach: this argues that it is necessary to find ways of satisfactorily integrating the diversities arising from growth and change.

3 Team development: this is highly thought of by senior managers with armed forces experience.

4 The planning approach: this suggests that if objectives are properly developed, people will know what they are to do and how to do it. This derives strongly from management by objectives (MbO). It has also led to the development of an instructional theory known as *criterion-referenced instruction* (CRI).

5 The scientific model: this is referred to in *education and training techniques*. It is a skill- and knowledge-based system and works largely through educational activities.

All these approaches require highly trained interventionists, and Argyris has described their skills.

Further reading

Stephenson, T. E., in 'Journal of Management Studies', October 1975.

Argyris, C., 'Intervention Theory and Method', Addison-Wesley, 1970. (See Part 1, ch. 12)

Organisation for European Co-operation and Redevelopment (OECD) OECD, like other international organisations such as UNESCO, the *Commonwealth Secretariat* and the *Council of Europe*, has influenced considerably the development of comparative education. Established in 1948 as the OEEC, the Organisation for European Economic Co-operation, it was primarily intended to aid Europe's post-war economic recovery. OEEC was replaced in 1961 by the OECD.

Its aims are to improve the standards of living of the citizens by promoting employment and investment policies which will contribute to economic expansion, productivity and increased world trade. Thus OECD has shown interest in educational and manpower policies. Its work in comparative education is carried out by the Education Committee. This is responsible for publishing reviews of educational policy which are reports of investigations into the educational systems of member countries.

OECD is engaged in the production of a 'Classification of Educational Systems', which offers a common presentation of educational data, classified under level of education, entry requirements and length of study. Countries are grouped together. Finland, Germany and Japan have already been covered, and other members are being surveyed preparatory to being included in subsequent volumes. Address of OECD: 2 rue Andre-Pascal, 75775 Paris, Cedex 16. (See Part 1, ch. 3)

P

Paradigm The term 'paradigm' has acquired considerable importance since the publication of T. S. Kuhn's 'The Structure of Scientific Revolutions'. Here Kuhn draws attention to what might be described as 'revolutionary changes' in our conceptual schemes. Although Kuhn's use of the term is not entirely consistent, it is possible to discern the following salient points.

The term 'paradigm' refers to our total view of a problem. It refers to a total outlook, not just a problem in isolation. From this Kuhn has inferred that it may be impossible for the people holding paradigm A to have any understanding of paradigm B. Someone maintaining the Aristotelian paradigm of science would be unsympathetic to the aims and methods of the Galilean approach. Thus some have inferred that there can be no rational way of choosing between paradigms. See also: *knowledge, relativism, sociology of knowledge, objectivity.*
Further reading
Kuhn, T. S., 'The Structure of Scientific Revolutions', Chicago University Press, 2nd ed., 1970.
Lakatos, I. and Musgrave, A. (eds), Criticism and the Growth of Knowledge, in 'Proceedings of the International Colloquium in the Philosophy of Science', vol. 4, Chicago University Press, 1970. (See Part 1, ch. 13)

Parametric statistics This is the style of statistics most commonly used in educational work. The techniques used make assumptions about the type of data collected. Some statisticians argue that these techniques are not applicable to much educational data, however many of the techniques are applicable over a fairly wide range of data. (See Part 1, ch. 8)

Parents' organisations The parents of those children receiving the benefits of education have formed a number of organisations, some of which provide both support for the development of schools within the education system, while others act as pressure groups striving to change aspects of the system. Many of the Parent-Teacher Associations, formed at individual schools, gather under the National Confederation of Parent-Teacher Associations, which itself is made up from affiliated federations representing most of the areas of England together with Clwyd.

Other organisations of parents include the Home and School Council, which incorporates members of teachers' unions, in observer status, thus forming a link between parents and the formal representative bodies of professional teachers. Of the pressure groups that put forward particular views perhaps the most publicly active is the Confederation for the Advancement of State Education (CASE). (See Part 1, ch. 7)

Part-method This method analyses a job into separate sections, each of which is then taught and practised separately. It is different from *cumulative-part method* in that steps are not repeated each time a new step is to be learned. In part-method, after all parts have been separately learned they are brought together and practised as a whole. (See Part 1, ch. 11)

Pastoral care This phrase describes a system, normally associated with *comprehensive secondary schools*, whereby responsibility is assigned to teachers to deal with the individual welfare of pupils. It also illustrates a school's role as a caring community. A school is divided into groups either on a mixed age ('house') basis or on a year basis, and teachers allocated to each. They will keep records of individual pupils, meet parents, liaise with other teachers, and generally ensure that no child goes through the school without a member of staff having a personal responsibility for his progress and welfare. (See Part 1, ch. 1)

Percentile ranks Subjects can be rated on a continuum from zero to 100 per cent either in comparison to a general *population* or to some specific population (e.g., 10-year-old boys attending state schools). A percentile rank is then a position on this *scale* which states the percentage of people falling above or below that point on the scale. (See Part 1, ch. 6)

Personal construct Recent work has looked at the possibility of teachers developing information about themselves. The idea developed from work carried out by Kelly (1955). He suggested that each individual has his own representation of the world so that events can be predicted and controlled. The representation consists of a limited number of constructs or categories. The constructs are used by that person for comparisons based on similarity or contrast. All the constructs have opposites as their extremes (e.g., attractive, repulsive). The repertoire of constructs is unique to a person. The constructs are elicited in a variety of ways. It is possible for a skilful interviewer to provide a basis for an investigator to listen carefully to a person's conversation and explore the ideas that are generated. Another method is to use a list of descriptions of people (e.g., a teacher you liked, a teacher you disliked) to generate names of people. Sets of three names are written on cards and presented. Usually people can use a word to describe how two of the names written are the same and one different (e.g., kind, cruel). These descriptions are used to derive the construct. A written essay is sometimes used, as for young children and less intelligent adults the procedure described is too complex. Whatever system is used, the analysis is checked by the investigator with the person. From the analysis a grid of relationships between the constructs and the source (e.g., the names of people) develops. These grids highlight the constructs which play a dominant role. The attraction of the method is that the person's unique experience and view of the world is used. The approach suggests a different set of values from conventional techniques (see, for example: *attitude assessment*, *personality assessment*). The data derived can be submitted to rigorous statistical procedures such as *cluster analysis*. It will certainly give different information from other methods. The information will be more difficult to generalise.

Further reading

Fransella, F. and Bannister, D., 'A Manual for Repertory Grid Technique', Academic Press, 1977.

Kelly, G. A., 'The Psychology of Personal Constructs', 2 volumes, 1955. (See Part 1, ch. 8)

Personality Although there is great diversity amongst people, most individuals are remarkably consistent over long periods of time in the way they think, experience the environment and behave towards it. These relatively stable ways of responding towards the world are all manifestations of the individual's personality. The task of attempting to describe, define and measure personality has proved very complex. Vernon has described three very different approaches to be found in the literature. He has called them the naïve, the intuitive and the inferential approaches.

Naïve interpretations of personality are subjective and tend to employ rigid stereotyping based upon superficial, face-value observations. The judgments we make of others in everyday life are usually in this category and they are of little value to the psychologist. Intuitive approaches are typified by the work of Freud and the psychoanalytic psychologists. They work within a coherent theoretical framework but still depend upon subjective assessments of human conduct. Inferential theories are based upon the assumption that the individual possesses personality traits that can be measured using standardised tests and that these traits or behavioural tendencies can be subjected to objective analysis using statistical techniques. Eysenck, working in this tradition, maintains that personality organisation can be described in terms of three basic dimensions: *introversion-extraversion*, neuroticism-stability and psychoticism-normality. Another psychometrician, Cattell, whose work is similar to that of Eysenck, has suggested that sixteen personality factors are necessary to describe the organisation of personality.

A fourth approach, not identified by Vernon, is that of the increasingly influential humanistic psychologists such as Maslow and Rogers. They stress the importance of the individual's self-concept and the importance of regarding the whole being as the pivot of the study of personality. The work of Kelly on personal construct theory has gone some way to an integration between the intuitive, the inferential and the humanistic approaches. See also: *schools of psychology, cognitive style, self-concept, humanistic psychology, psychoanalytic psychology*.

Further reading

Bannister, D. and Fransella, F., 'Inquiring Man: the Theory of Personal Constructs', Penguin, 1971.

Lyons, R., 'An Introduction to the Study of Personality', Macmillan, 1971.

Vernon, P. E., 'Personality Assessment: a Critical Survey', Tavistock, 1969. (See Part 1, ch. 14)

Personality assessment An important and often neglected facet of a learner is his or her *personality*. Many learning and curriculum development materials are designed for learners with a similar personality to that of the designer. Personality traits are dynamic and are often considered by characterising opposites such as Cattell's: reserved-outgoing, emotional-stable, humble-assertive, tough minded-tender minded, trusting-suspicious (Vernon, 1953). There are two ways of eliciting data as a basis for determining personality scores: one uses *self-rating* scores; the other uses ratings by others. A self-rating score uses questions from which the personality can be deducted. The questions may be direct such as: 'If you are in a group discussing a topic with which you are unfamiliar, do you (a) keep silent, (b) join in, (c) change the subject?' This sort of question is typical of those used in magazines, but will only give a superficial description. More sophisticated versions use less obvious questions such as 'Do you like surprises?' 'Do you enjoy an argument?'. A series of such questions, when carefully selected, can elicit answers which are used to chart an outline of personality structure. Probably the best known test in use in the United Kingdom is the Eysenck Personality Inventory, which uses the latter strategy. Rating by others is going to depend on the personality of the rater as well as that of the person being rated. (For example, a child at school may respond differently to different raters.) A way of reducing this effect is to use systematic rating schemes where the specific qualities to be observed are precisely defined. A helpful technique is to identify two extremes and to use a five-point scale in between them, the ends of the scale relating to the extremes (for example, 'extremely quick on the uptake' and 'does not always grasp the point'). Another way is to require a distribution of responses across the five points corresponding to a *normal distribution*.

Further reading

Vernon, P. E., 'Personality Tests and Assessments', Methuen, 1953.

Buros, O. K., 'Mental Measurements Yearbook' (7th issue), Gryphon Press (this yearbook appears at intervals, the first being published in 1938) 1972. (See Part 1, ch. 8)

Personnel and training Until recently the route into careers in personnel and training was by experience. Companies recognised as providing excellent training in personnel include the Ford Motor Company, Unilever and ICI. Many other organisations provide a sound grounding, particularly in manufacturing industry and the public corporations, because of the emphasis on sound industrial relations.

The Institute of Personnel Management was founded in the early years of this century. The two World Wars gave great impetus to the Institute, particularly because of the enormous expansion of welfare services as the population was mobilised for the war effort. The Institute now has over 18,000 members and a growing number of students. Membership is now by examination through the Diploma in Personnel Management. The Institute provides a large number of short courses to its members (and others). Qualification for the Diploma course is either through education or experience or a combination.

The Institute of Training and Development has emerged from the old Institute of Training Officers, and is a professional association for those engaged in training. It aims to promote training as a profession, and to this end has introduced the Diploma in Training Management.

Training for training is a rapidly expanding area as the *Training Services Division* of the *Manpower Services Commission* has taken an active interest in it, as part of its responsibilities under the *Employment and Training Act 1973*. The effects of this and of the activities of the *Industry Training Boards* on the nation's economy are awaited with interest. Further information can be had from: Institute of Personnel Management, Central House, Upper Woburn Place, London WC1H 0HX; 01–387 2844; Institute of Training and Development, 5 Baring Road, Beaconsfield, Bucks HP9 2NX; 04946 3994. (See Part 1, ch. 2)

Phenomenological sociology Central to phenomenological sociology is the thought of Alfred Schutz. Schutz's primary concern is to investigate what Berger and Luckmann call the social construction of reality. He attempts to do this by 'thinking away' every aspect of man's being that is social in origin and stripping him down to a skeletal 'ego'. What then becomes possible is an examination of the kind of interplay between different 'egos' that is required for each to become a member of a social world. This interplay is the process of *socialisation* as phenomenological sociology sees it.

To this end, Schutz adopts Edmund Husserl's philosophical method of phenomenological reduction, a method of suspending belief in the existence of an 'outside' world, and transforms it into a method of suspending belief in the existence of the social world specifically. This allows him to focus directly upon the kind of belief that any 'ego' must acquire if a social world is to exist at all.

It is an essential characteristic of beliefs operating at this profound level that they do not normally become the object of conscious scrutiny. They are part of everyone's taken-for-granted structuring of reality – part of what everyone 'knows' without question. The inverted commas round 'knows' come into being precisely when phenomenological sociology makes such taken-for-granted knowledge open to question – makes it problematic. It is this aspect of phenomenological sociology on which the *new sociology of education* is drawing when it recommends making the 'knowledge' in school and college curricula problematic.

Phenomenological sociology also links with *ethnomethodology* to probe background expectations of various kinds, and to make them visible.

Further reading

Filmer, P., Phillipson, M., Silverman, D. and Walsh, D., 'New Directions in Sociological Theory', Collier-Macmillan, 1972.

Esland, G., 'Schooling and Pedagogy', Open University Press, 1977. (See Part 1, ch. 15)

Phenomenology Phenomenology asserts that the categories by which we explain experience distort the experience itself. Husserl wrote, 'Thus all sciences which relate to this natural world . . . though they fill me with wondering admiration . . . I disconnect them all. I make absolutely no use of their standards . . . I do not appropriate a single one of the propositions which enter into their system.' The world must be taken 'free from all theory'. Thus the phenomenologist tries to revert to the primacy of experience by means of the epoché (a bracketing), putting the meaning of his experience into suspension, and the 'phenomenological reduction'.

The phenomenologist regards the following as important: (1) The individual's subjective experience. (2) The meaning the individual tries to place on this experience. (3) That there are specific structures within consciousness which can be intuited by reflection. (The precise nature of this is controversial among phenomenologists.)

Once the external structures have been 'peeled away', new meanings can be bestowed. The chief difficulty is the validity of the 'phenomenological reduction'. Has it been reached, is it the appropriate one?

Phenomenology has an appeal to those who feel that their subject needs to be freed from its incrustation, and to return to the basic experiences. Thus, phenomenology has an appeal in religious discourse because it is felt that much theology has distorted the 'religious experience'. An educationalist would similarly be concerned with the way in which the child attempts to put meaning on his experience of the world.

Further reading

Husserl, E., 'Cartesian Meditations: an Introduction to a Phenomenology', Heinemann, 1960.

Husserl, E., 'Logical Investigations', trans. J. N. Findley, 2 vols, Routledge & Kegan Paul, 1970.

Pivcevic, E., 'Phenomenology and Philosophical Understanding', Chicago University Press, 1975.

Curtis, B. and Mays, W., 'Phenomenology and Education: self-consciousness and its development', Methuen, 1978. (See Part 1, ch. 13)

Philosophical approach This approach enables comparativists to seek out the different modes of thinking or arguing inherent in each society and relate these to education.

Further reading

Lauwerys, J. A., Methodology of Comparative Education, in 'International Review of Education', V5, 285–7, 1959. (See Part 1, ch. 3)

Piagetian stages of development J. Piaget in his study of children's cognitive development has suggested that there are a series of stages in the development of every child's thought as it progresses from birth to maturity, and that each stage shows a progressive sequence from simpler to more complex levels of organisation.

The sensori-motor period extends from birth to about 2 years. At this stage the child can only perform motor actions, manipulating objects, but he gradually becomes aware of the effects of his actions on the environment and so begins to differentiate himself from the objects that surround him. He learns to construct the notion of the permanence of objects.

The period of pre-operational thought lasts from about 2 to 7 years. Although the child can now use language and is able to represent the world by images and words he is egocentric and cannot carry out reversible operations. He classifies objects by single salient features. Only towards the end of this period does he begin to develop some concept of conservation. Intelligent behaviour tends to be limited to overt actions and thought is dominated by perceptual factors.

The period of concrete operations lasts from about 7 to 11 years. During this stage the child becomes capable of logical thought. He develops conservation concepts for number, substance, weight and volume. He becomes more mobile in his thinking, able to reverse operations and take account of the views of others. He also begins to construct the view of time and space that he will live with as an adult.

The formal operational period starts at about 11 and extends into adulthood. The full attainment of logical cognitive operations comes. The child thinks in abstract terms beyond the present task and is able to form theories and hypotheses. He can isolate the elements of a problem and systematically explore all possible solutions. The full intellectual accomplishments of the intelligent adult become possible for the first time. See also: *child development, concept formation and attainment, language and thought.*

Further reading

Phillips, J. L., 'The Origins of Intellect: Piaget's Theory', 2nd ed., W. H. Freeman, 1975. (See Part 1, ch. 14)

Plato Plato wished to escape the conclusion of *relativism*, i.e., that an object was as it seemed to be to each particular individual. He therefore postulated the theory of forms. *Knowledge* was not concerned with individual instances of X but with X itself. Thus, appreciating beauty entailed appreciating Beauty itself and not beautiful things. This theory began in the earlier Socratic dialogues as a search for concepts. But later the forms took on a *metaphysical* status. They could not be known by sense-perception but only by reason, because they themselves were supra-sensible realities beyond the world of sense. Obviously, Plato's epistemology is based on mathematics, where the concepts themselves are not *empirical* concepts; they must be discovered by reason.

The epistemology has always appealed to those of a religious frame of mind, willing to believe that the real world lies beyond this world. In the 'Republic' Plato unites his epistemology with his thought on *education*. If the state is to produce a just society, then the education must be appropriate. By various methods children must be brought into contact with the Good. This has sounded so commendable that Plato enthusiasts seem to have been blinded to the undesirable aspects of his system. This education was not thought suitable for all people: only those who were the potential Guardians received it. The rest received an education more suitable for their lower status. A thorough criticism of these undesirable aspects of Platonic thought has been made by Popper. See also: *rationalism*.

Further reading

Plato, 'The Republic', Penguin.

Cornford, F. M., 'Plato's Theory of Knowledge', Routledge & Kegan Paul, 1935.

Popper, K., 'The Open Society and Its Enemies', vol. 1, Plato, Routledge & Kegan Paul, 4th ed., 1962. (See Part 1, ch. 13)

Playfair, Sir Lyon, first Baron Playfair (1816–98) Studied chemistry at Glasgow University and obtained his PhD under Liebig at Giessen, where he acquired an enthusiasm for scientific research. Helped to organise the Great Exhibition, 1851. Joint secretary with *Sir Henry Cole* of the Science and Art Department, 1853–8. Professor of Chemistry, Edinburgh University, 1858–69. MP, 1853–8. Leading advocate of the extension of scientific and technical education. Author of numerous scientific papers and propagandist works, which include, 'Industrial Instruction on the Continent' (1852), 'Science in its Relations to Labour' (1853), 'The Study of Abstract Science essential to the Progress of Industry' (1855), 'On Primary and Technical Education' (1870). (See Part 1, ch. 10)

Playgroup Playgroups are formed in the belief that opportunities should exist for children in the age range 3–5 to mix together and play, and that this is a valuable stage of a child's development before starting school. The lack of nursery facilities leaves a gap which the playgroups aim to fill. They usually meet in rented premises for a few mornings or afternoons a week, depending on local funds and availability of supervision, etc.

The Pre-School Playgroups Association (PPA) is a voluntary charitable body founded in 1964 which has done much to popularise the movement. It has received grants from both the DES and the Department of Health and Social Security; nevertheless the playgroups exist on a limited budget and rely on a great deal of voluntary work. (See Part 1, ch. 1)

Political scientists' contribution These are likely to illuminate our comparative knowledge of patterns of disadvantage, attitudes towards authority, the effects of private education and higher education, and access to political power. (See Part 1, ch. 3)

Polytechnic Recommendations made in the 1945 Report on 'Higher Technical Education' (the Percy Report) and endorsed by the 1946 Barlow Report ('Scientific Manpower') led to the setting up of the National Council for Technological Awards in 1953 to supervise the awarding of Diplomas in Technology in certain technical colleges. The Diploma, based on a four-year course with a year in industry, a sandwich course, was comparable to a university degree. Further fears concerning the output of technically trained personnel led to the decision to concentrate the relevant courses in a number of designated colleges that became known as colleges of advanced technology (the CATs) which were to be financed by the Ministry of Education. In accordance with a recommendation of the Robbins Report, 'Higher Education' (1963) the CATs became universities, an action that robbed the public-sector system of its apex. In turn a number of already existing technical colleges active in providing courses at university degree level were upgraded to form 30 polytechnics in the late 1960s. Their degree-awarding body is the *Council for National Academic Awards*. This body, granted a charter in 1964, has replaced the National Council for Technological Awards. It serves colleges of education and technical colleges, as well as the new polytechnics. With more than 1,000 undergraduate courses already approved and followed by 100,000 students, it has become the largest degree-awarding body in the country. The range of courses includes the arts and the social sciences, as well as the pure and applied sciences.

The wide variety of courses available lead to qualifications that include degrees (both first and higher), Higher *National Certificates* and *National Diplomas* and the qualifications of the major professional institutions. Courses may be *full-time*, sandwich, *block-release* or part-time. Thus, the polytechnics may be distinguished from other higher education establishments by the flexible modes of study and the breadth of the range of levels of courses offered.

Further reading
Burgess T. and Pratt J., 'Polytechnics: A Report', Pitman, 1974. (See Part 1, chs. 2 and 10)

Population When data are collected it is seldom possible to collect them from every person that goes to make up a population. For example, if information was required about how many 12-year-olds stayed for school lunches, the collection of data from all 12-year-olds would be formidable. 'All the 12-year-olds' is the population under investigation. (See Part 1, ch. 8)

The term 'population' is a sampling word used to refer to a well-defined group of people, objects or events. There is no implication of size, since a single class of children can be the population for certain studies. In educational measurement a population of interest may be all children aged between 10 and 11 years who attend state schools. *Test* results for individual children are then compared to the results obtained from this population – or more usually obtained from a *sample* designed to represent the population. (See Part 1, ch. 6)

Positive discrimination The demands of justice seem to require that persons should be treated equally. However, as Aristotle suggested, to treat unequals equally tends to exacerbate this inequality. Positive discrimination would therefore emphasise the necessity of rectifying this inequality, so that subsequent equality of treatment does not perpetuate injustice. See also: *equality*.

Further reading
Cohen, M. et al. (eds), 'Equality and Preferential Treatment', Princeton University Press, 1976.
Warnock, M., 'Schools of Thought', Faber, 1977. (See Part 1, ch. 13)

Positivism Positivists attempted to eradicate 'non-observable entities' from scientific explanation. The chemist Ostwald rejected the atomic theory in chemistry because he held that atoms were 'unobservable'. In psychology the movement encouraged the growth of *behaviourism* and attempted to avoid explanations involving entities like 'mind' or 'will'. The movement tended to be unsympathetic towards Freudian theory, with its emphasis upon 'the id', 'the ego', etc. In sociology, positivism concentrated upon strict observation and statistical method, avoiding 'functionalism' and any references to intention and purpose. (See Part 1, ch. 13)

Positivistic sociology Auguste Comte, who developed his 'positive philosophy' in the first half of the nineteenth century, believed scientific method to be the only basis of genuine knowledge. He fathered the positivistic claim that there is a universal method of investigation which should be applied whatever the object of study. On this view, the natural sciences and the social sciences should have an identical method. Critics of positivistic sociology consider it to be blind to crucial differences between physical reality and social reality. The term 'positivistic' is now commonly pejorative.

Further reading

Giddens, A. (ed.), 'Positivism and Sociology', Heinemann, 1974. (See Part 1, ch. 15)

Practicality ethic Teachers' 'practicality ethic' is the idea summarised in a framework developed to analyse teachers' decision-making in response to proposals for curriculum development. Teachers usually take a very sceptical stance, appraising the 'ecological validity' of a new course, method, etc. in terms of the complex demands of the classroom environment. Thus curriculum innovations should be informed by the following criteria which describe how the innovations can actually be applied to the classroom: congruence with teachers' self-image; cost to teacher in terms of time invested as opposed to satisfactions realised. (See Part 1, ch. 4)

Preparatory courses These aim to help people whose standards of literacy and numeracy limit their chances of getting or keeping a job or of entering formal training schemes. They are available to 17 and 18-year-olds who have been out of full-time education for at least a year or who missed at least a year in the UK full-time education system; and to 19-year-olds and over who have been out of full-time education for at least two years. The courses are promoted by the *Training Services Division* of the *Manpower Services Commission*. (See Part 1, ch. 11)

Prescriptive This refers to a theory in *ethics* which accounts for terms such as 'morally wrong' or 'good' by saying that such words are used as recommendations or 'prescriptions'. Thus by calling an action 'good' the speaker is recommending a certain kind of attitude towards it. The term is often contrasted with 'descriptive'.

Further reading

Ayer, A., 'Language, Truth and Logic', Gollancz, 2nd ed., 1946.

Sellars, W. and Hospers, J., 'Readings in Ethical Theory', Prentice Hall, 2nd ed., 1970.

Hare, R. M., 'The Language of Morals', Oxford University Press, 1952.

Hospers, J., 'Introduction to Philosophical Analysis', ch. 6, Routledge & Kegan Paul, 2nd ed., 1967. (See part 1, ch. 13)

Pressey Pressey of Ohio State University was concerned in the early 1920s with the need to find a rapid method of scoring and administering objective-type tests. He developed a number of devices which gave the student immediate

221

feedback on the correctness or otherwise of his answer. Pressey believed that an 'industrial revolution' in education would take place, bringing sweeping advances in the development of instruments for teaching. *Skinner*, commenting on Pressey's work, felt that the world of education was not ready for Pressey's machines. Pressey did, however, in proposing a system which not only gave immediate feedback of information, but also allowed the student to work at his own speed, lay the foundation for the development of the *programmed learning* movement.

Further reading

Pressey, S. L., A Simple Apparatus which gives tests and scores – and teaches, in 'School and Society', 23, pp. 373–6, 1926. (See Part 1, ch. 9)

Prestel Prestel is the Post Office's public view-data service. This system allows information to be displayed on a television screen; the viewer can interact with it, using a key pad to call up other frames of material, or he can send a message in reply to a response frame. Educational implications of the system have not yet been fully explored, but at its simplest it could be used for *multiple-choice programmes*. (See Part 1, ch. 9)

Problem approach This methodology, as developed by Holmes, is designed to facilitate educational planning and policy considerations, and to identify underlying laws and principles governing the education process. Holmes's approach is influenced by Dewey's analysis of reflective thinking, which followed this sequence: confusion, hypothesis formulation, problem analysis, specification of context, deduction of consequences, and practical verification of hypotheses.

From this Holmes develops four major research stages. The first is that of problem selection and analysis, which is guided by the researcher's experience, knowledge and interests. In order to sharpen the focus, the problem is then intellectualised. This leads to the second stage, the formulation of possible policy proposals or solutions. Here possible solutions are examined in terms of what success has been achieved in some of the educational systems with which the researcher is familiar. The third stage concerns the identification of relevant factors, which will involve the identification selection of relevant data and the weighting of contextual determinants. Realistic appraisal will be aided by reference to *critical dualism*, which has been modified for purposes of comparison to give the following framework: (1) ideological factors (norms, attitudes, values); (2) institutional factors (organisations, practices); and (3) miscellaneous factors (climate, terrain, natural resources). Disharmony between items (1) and (2) is a source of cultural problems known as *social lag*. The fourth stage is that of prediction, which gives an indication of the most likely solutions. At all these stages appropriate techniques are drawn from a number of the social sciences.

Further reading

Holmes, B., 'Problems in Education: a Comparative Approach'. Routledge & Kegan Paul, 1965. (See Part 1, ch. 3)

Process model of curriculum design Although the very concept of curriculum development is sometimes equated with the working out of the implications of schools' instructional *objectives*, many teachers feel that this approach puts their curriculum thinking within a Procrustean bed. Thus the process model of curriculum design articulates a 'humanistic' alternative to the means-end or objective model; a framework, it is claimed, which better reflects teachers' actual practices and values (Stenhouse, 1975).

In this model, specification and justification of curriculum programmes takes the form of delineation of the educative process to be offered, conceived in terms of general *aims*, the characterisation of the content to be taught, and the procedural principles of teaching to be followed. Underlying the concern for the nature of the content, rather than the objectives for which it is to be used, is the view that pupils' engagement with appropriate content, such as good literature or material illustrative of the humanness of experience, necessarily entails activities with built-in intellectual discipline; that is, standards for appraising experience, and for discrimination and refinement of meaning. For example, the key concepts and procedures within appropriate content are not the objects of mastery, rather the medium and focus of interpretations and speculation. Thus teachers' choice of content is more important than their definition of objectives. It follows that the teachers' task is open-ended but rule-guided, inasmuch as it is to exemplify the arts by which key concepts and procedures are critically explored, and to guide pupils in their critical exploration of them. This is a process of induction into a way of thinking in which the aim is rightly general: that the pupil develops the capacity to grasp and make relationships and judgments for himself (Hanley, 1970). In that sense, precise learning outcomes cannot be specified, though the process certainly entails rational application of criteria.

Thus the process model incorporates the distinction between instructional and expressive objectives (Eisner, 1969) but applies to the curriculum in general as well as to creative-expressive activities in the arts. Moreover it offers a way to link curriculum development with studies of teaching. See also: *objectives, disciplines of knowledge, structure, curriculum design.*

Further reading

Eisner, E. W. (1969), Instructional and Expressive Objectives, in Golby, M. et al. (eds), 'Curriculum Design', Croom Helm, pp. 351–4, 1975.

Hanley, J. P. et al. (1970), Curiosity, Competence, Community-Man: a course of study, an evaluation, in Golby (see above), pp. 467–79.

Stenhouse, L., 'An Introduction to Curriculum Research and Development' ch. 7, Heinemann, 1975. (See Part 1, ch. 4)

Production function A production function describes the relationship between inputs and outputs in a process, or in the economy as a whole. For example, if it were possible to identify the production function of a school, it would show how a given set of inputs, including pupils' and teachers' time, books, equipment and buildings were transformed into outputs, knowledge or attitudes acquired by school-leavers in the course of their schooling. It is, of course, impossible to measure the production function of an educational institution in any precise way, but studies of educational *productivity* or *efficiency* are all concerned with an implicit, though not an explicit, production function for education.

Attempts to measure the contribution of education to economic growth may also use the concept of a production function, for the economy as a whole. (See Part 1, ch. 5)

Productivity The term 'productivity' refers to the ratio of outputs to inputs in a process. Economists may be interested in labour productivity, which is measured by output per worker, or in total factor productivity, which relates output to the input of all factors of production. Productivity trends measure changes in the ratio of output to inputs over time.

There are two ways in which this is relevant to education. The knowledge and skills imparted by the educational system increase the future level of productivity of educated workers. When economists apply *cost-benefit analy-*

223

sis to education, they take account of the crucial assumption that educated workers have higher life-time earnings than those with lower educational qualifications, and that this reflects the superior productivity of the highly educated.

Equally important is the relationship between inputs (of teachers, students, equipment, buildings) and outputs in the education system. There have been a few attempts to measure trends in the productivity of education, for instance by Blaug and Woodhall (1968), or to compare the productivity of different institutions, such as the Open University and conventional universities (Wagner 1972). Such attempts involve a comparison of the 'outputs' of education, measured in terms of numbers of graduates or examination results, with the total inputs, measured in terms of costs or real resources.

Because of the considerable problems of defining and measuring the outputs of the education system, and particularly the difficulty of measuring differences in quality in different institutions or at different times, such attempts have been fiercely criticised as 'pointless' or 'insensitive', for example by Vaizey (1972). It is not necessary to view education in narrow terms as an 'industry' to believe that the concept of productivity is relevant to education, just as it is relevant to any activity which tries to use scarce resources as efficiently as possible.

Further reading

Blaug, M. and Woodhall, M., Productivity Trends in British Secondary Education, 'Sociology of Education', Winter 1968.

Vaizey, J. et al., 'The Political Economy of Education', Duckworth, 1972 (See Part 1, ch. 5)

Professional associations There is a very large number of professional associations and institutions, and it is necessary to make some distinctions before discussing the most important in any detail.

Many of the professional associations seek to control entry, although few have achieved this, by means of examinations of those who wish to be practitioners in a particular field. Some associations recognise qualifications of other bodies, and many grant exemption from some parts of their *entry requirements* to people qualified in some other way. Because of these variations, it is important to check entry standards with the appropriate body.

In this dictionary we are mostly concerned with those associations dealing with professional qualifications. By this, we mean those professions that offer a distinctive service, where admission to the full rights and privileges of corporate membership can come only through an examined standard of competence. A member of such a professional association accepts certain responsibilities for his conduct towards clients, colleagues and the community. Such membership usually allows designatory letters.

There is a number of professions regulated by law where the associations act as a register of authorised practitioners. Entry is controlled and discipline exerted by the associations. Misconduct can be punished, often by removal from the register and hence the impossibility to practise. The professions registered by statute are: architects, dentists, doctors, chiropodists, dieticians, medical laboratory technicians, occupational therapists, orthoptists, physiotherapists, radiographers, remedial gymnasts, midwives, nurses, opticians, patent agents, pharmacists, solicitors and veterinary surgeons.

There is also a number of closed professions. The Inns of Court, although not statutory, control Bar admissions. Merchant Navy Officers are certificated by the Department of Trade. Mine managers are certificated by the

Health and Safety Executive. Teachers must have their qualifications accepted by the Department of Education and Science before taking up a permanent post in a maintained school in England and Wales. Employers will often ask applicants for certain specialist posts to have the qualifications of the appropriate professional association if its standards are recognised as good. (See Part 1, ch. 2)

Professionality Professionality refers to the (teacher) practitioner's exercise of *autonomy* in applying distinctive (educational) knowledge and skills in the interests of his clients (pupils). These three elements (autonomy, valid professional knowledge, service to pupils) provide categories for analysis of teacher engagement in curriculum development. For example, *school-based curriculum development* often entails sacrifice of classroom autonomy. While *self-monitoring* fosters a more rigorous approach to classroom knowledge, it modifies personalised intuitive appraisals of pupils' needs. Thus 'extended' rather than 'restricted' professionalism is involved. (See Part 1, ch. 4)

Professional management associations Most of the institutions set professional standards and act as qualifying bodies through appropriate education and experience, upon which individual membership grades are awarded. Examples of these are: British Computer Society, 29 Portland Place, London, W1M 0BP. Founded in 1957. Over 20,000 members, covering all aspects of computer applications.

Hotel Catering and Institutional Management Association, 191 Trinity Road, London SW17 7HN. Has some 20,000 members. Entry by combination of academic qualifications and experience. Operates examinations.

Institute of Public Relations, 1 Great James Street, London, WC1N 3DA. Concerned with establishment standards through its educational scheme and code of conduct. (See Part 1, ch. 12)

Professional organisations There are many bodies representing a wide variety of trades and professions. Many of these have histories as long as the ancient guilds, as they were formed as protective groups for those who had developed or been trained in particular skills. It is natural to find accountants, librarians, nurses, physicians or valuers forming a professional body. Courses in professional studies may be offered by educational establishments, or where no satisfactory courses are available, the professional society may itself set up the required training facilities. Whatever the provision, for any group to maintain its own professional standards it is necessary to monitor the courses that are made available to aspiring students. Some bodies have opted to liaise with accreditation and examination boards such as the *City and Guilds of London Institute* or recognise passes in examinations from universities, polytechnics or colleges as acceptable for professional practice.

In many cases practice of a profession may not be carried out without this accreditation and the awarding of qualifications. In this way the professional bodies can not only maintain the standards of entry of their members but also keep a degree of control on the numbers of people entering the particular profession. It is also these bodies that take any action against members who fail to follow the agreed code of professional practice. Because of this natural desire to maintain standards and to promote the interest of a particular body many of the associations carry out active educational programmes, having educational officers, running courses and publishing much educational support material. Though many are directly linked to vocational education there are those that direct some of their efforts more widely back into the field of general education. In this latter case one could look at bodies such as: the

Royal Institute of British Architects, the Institute of Bankers, the Chemical Society, the Institution of Electrical Engineers, the Institute of Foresters of Great Britain, the Library Association, the Institute of Personnel Management, the Museums Association, the Royal College of Nursing of the United Kingdom, and the Institute of Travel and Tourism. There are, of course, many more professional bodies which, should they be relevant to a particular educational interest, can be contacted directly. Lists of such associations can be found in most educational yearbooks or almanacs.

In addition to the teachers' unions and linked in this schematic mode of educational organisations, there is one other body specifically concerned with the professional administration of education, that is the British Educational Administration Society Ltd, which is an association of people actively interested in the development of practice, teaching, training and research in educational administration.

Outside this group of professional bodies is another set of associations which, whilst not having the same degree of professional control, do have a major contribution to make to education. These are the subject teaching organisations. Generally these are associations of teachers having a subject within the curriculum in common, and the list of these is very long. The support given by these associations to their teacher members is valuable and varied, including many journals and newsletters. One body through which the majority of these associations liaise is the Council of Subject Teaching Associations.

Subject teaching associations cover not only separate subjects but also groups of subjects with a common basis, such as the teaching of languages or the various religious denominations that have an interest in teaching. Many of these groups or associations have large-scale organisations with regional secretariats. Through the meetings, publications and working parties organised by the subject teaching associations new ideas, techniques and educational developments can spread across the teaching profession. Here curriculum and educational development arises from the practitioners themselves. (See Part 1, ch. 7)

Programmed learning A form of learning materials which are highly structured and organised. The structure and organisation are related to the clear specification of *objectives*. Each step requires a response which is immediately checked, enabling the learner to move towards achieving the objectives. The steps can be sequential, or alternate routes may occur. (See Part 1, ch. 8)

Principles of programmed learning include active involvement of a student in a gradual progression through a programme of materials. The programme consists of frames of material, each frame typically containing three parts: (1) information on the topic, (2) a question on a problem, and (3) the answer to the question or problem. In such a programme simple ideas are related to previous knowledge, and more complex material is built on to this. By providing the student with knowledge of the right answers, reinforcement and learning of the right answers is promoted. Students can work through such a programme at their own speed. There are two main types of programme: *linear programmes* and *multiple-choice programmes*.

Skinner, one of the leading figures in the programmed learning movement of the 1950s, considered that students can be motivated by a controlled progression through structured learning material (Skinner, 1954). *Pressey* of Ohio State University is usually cited as the founder of the modern programmed learning movement, but it was the Second World War that gave the movement impetus in the USA. In the UK the programmed learning movement gathered momentum in the late 1950s and early 1960s. A useful commentary on these early developments is provided by Leith (1969).

Today the principles of programmed learning – active learning, feedback of information, the need to relate new knowledge to existing knowledge – have been extended and incorporated in curriculum development schemes and in developments in educational technology.

Further reading

Leith, G. O. M., 'Second Thoughts on Programmed Learning', National Council for Programmed Learning, 1969.

Markle, S. M., 'Good Frames and Bad', 2nd ed., Wiley, 1969.

Skinner, B. F., The Science of Learning and the Art of Teaching, in 'Harvard Educational Review', 24, 1954, pp. 86–97. (See Part 1, ch. 9)

Psychoanalytic psychology A system of psychology, developed by Freud, which stresses the dynamic nature of mental life and places special emphasis upon the influence of the unconscious. The development of a 'normal' adult personality is thought to depend upon the child's successfully negotiating a series of developmental phases which relate to oral, anal and genital erotogenic zones.

Further reading

Hall, C. S., 'A Primer of Freudian Psychology', World Publishing, 1954.

Freud, S., 'Two Short Accounts of Psycho-analysis', Penguin, 1962.

Wollheim, R., 'Freud', Fontana Modern Masters, 1971. (See Part 1, ch. 14)

Psychological measurement Psychology in its broadest sense is the science of human behaviour and conscious life. As such it subsumes educational measurement. However, it is useful to keep separate those aspects of behaviour which develop as a direct result of conscious teaching and those which develop by virtue of being an experiencing individual. The distinction can therefore be made between the measurement of educational *attainment* and the measurement of psychological attributes. The latter refer to underlying *traits* which influence or explain behaviour in numerous situations including educational ones. Educational attainment, on the other hand refers to overt outcomes which can be viewed as descriptive or surface traits since they do not specify or imply any underlying attributes. A test of mechanical knowledge would be measuring surface traits which were the result of an educational process (not necessarily within the formal educational system); and a test of mechanical ability would be measuring an underlying attribute.

It is clear from the above example that the theoretical distinction would not be easy to achieve in practice since a test of mechanical ability is difficult to conceive of without recourse to some mechanical knowledge. It is also clear that psychological measures can be and have been of great interest and value to educationalists.

Further reading

Cronbach, L. J., 'Essentials of Psychological Testing', 3rd ed., Harper & Row, 1970. (See Part 1, ch. 6)

Psychometrics Originally this word was used to describe the application of mathematical and measurement principles to psychological experiments and events. However, due to the enormous increase in the use of tests, the term has become predominantly used in relation to the statistical treatment of test results.

Today a psychometrician is someone who understands and handles test *data* in order to construct new tests, *standardise* or re-standardise old tests, to investigate the nature and function of tests, or to formulate new theories and methods for analysing and interpreting test data. (See Part 1, ch. 6)

Public examinations The General Certificate of Education (GCE) may be awarded by eight examining boards in England and Wales. This examination is set at two levels, the Ordinary level (O-level) which is normally taken at the age of 16 and the Advanced level (A-level), taken at 18. They are both single-subject examinations. The number of subjects set would not normally exceed eight at Ordinary level and three at Advanced level. The results are given in five grades (A to E). The GCE is the criterion often required for entry to higher education and the professions.

The Certificate of Secondary Education (CSE) is another single-subject examination taken at the age of 16. There are 14 regional examining boards which can operate only within their own regions. The examination is aimed at a spread of ability which excludes the most able 20 per cent and the least able 20 per cent. The results are given in five grades (1 to 5). It is accepted that CSE grade 1 is equivalent to GCE grade C.

The Certificate of Extended Education (CEE) is controlled by the CSE boards and is a post-16 single-subject examination usually taken after one year. Results are given in five grades (1 to 5), a grade 3 being equivalent to CSE grade 1.

CSE examinations are of three kinds or 'modes'. In Mode 1 the Board sets the syllabus and the questions. In Mode 2 the syllabus is the school's but the questions are set by the Board. In Mode 3 the schools draw up the syllabus and the questions, subject to the approval of the Board. (See Part 1, ch. 1)

Public School In the early nineteenth century the major Public Schools were few in number and financially insecure. Headmasters, reluctant to engage additional staff, relied on a number of labour-saving devices. These included daily compulsory games that had little or no supervision, prefects to act as substitute masters, the fagging system to cut down on servants, and severe corporal punishment to discourage malefactors when masters were few in number and discipline (as the number of rebellions in Public Schools attests) was hard to maintain. These devices were later considered to have character-forming values. The nineteenth-century expansion in the number of non-local independent schools giving a predominantly classical education raised problems of definition for the observer of the English social scene. The claims of the Clarendon Schools, Eton, Rugby, Harrow, Winchester, Westminster, Charterhouse, Shrewsbury, Merchant Taylors' and St Paul's, which were investigated in the early 1860s, are generally conceded. In contrast the 1965–8 Public Schools Commission was informed: 'For the immediate purpose of the Commission Public Schools are defined as those independent schools now in membership of the Headmasters' Conference, Governing Bodies' Association or Governing Bodies of Girls' Schools Association', some 288 schools in all. Yet while the Commission was sitting 20 new schools were admitted to these bodies and 9 left. In addition there were over 2,800 other independent preparatory and secondary schools. In this more egalitarian age Public Schools are anxious to break down their older image of social exclusiveness and point to the high academic standards they offer. Far from giving a predominantly classical education they have pioneered such curricular innovations as Nuffield A-level physics, and the teaching of economics and business studies.

Further reading

Bamford, T. W., 'The Rise of the Public Schools', Nelson, 1967.

de S. Honey, J. R., 'Tom Brown's Universe', Millington, 1977.

Mack, E. C., 'Public Schools and British Opinion, 1780–1860', Methuen, 1938.

Mack, E. C., 'Public Schools and British Opinion since 1860', Oxford University Press, 1951.

Public Schools Commission: First Report, HMSO, 1968.

'The Public and Preparatory Schools Yearbook', A. & C. Black, published annually. (See Part 1, ch. 10)

Purpose of comparative education Comparative education has a range of purposes. One, intellectual development, has two dimensions, personal and societal. On a personal basis some individuals have an insatiable curiosity, studying foreign systems because they want to improve their knowledge. On a societal basis intellectuals wish to improve their epistemologies regarding education. They want to know how education systems function, which knowledge elements may be combined to form the most appropriate curriculum pattern, etc. It is generally thought that a study of comparative education will sharpen one's ability to understand and analyse factors influencing one's own education system.

Another purpose is educational development, which may be advanced by appropriate comparative studies. It is now understood that *educational borrowing*, without serious consideration, is a dangerous practice, but a study of foreign systems, while not offering a panacea, may indicate what pitfalls one might have to face if a specific policy is adopted. Comparative education has also been a major contributor to international goodwill and to the promotion of international understanding among educators. Through the removal of ignorance of foreign practices, they have identified international and universal traditions in comparative studies which transmute and transcend parochialism and self-isolation.

Further reading

Tretheway, A. R., 'Introducing Comparative Education', ch. 3, Pergamon, New South Wales, 1976.

Kandel, I. L., 'Comparative Education', Houghton Mifflin, 1933. (See Part 1, ch. 3)

Qualifications There are many courses leading to qualifications in business or business-related subjects. It is usual to distinguish between those available through the further education sector and those available for membership of an appropriate professional institution or association. Often, the latter demand the former. The levels of courses determine the entry requirements.

The business schools award post-graduate degrees and normally require an honours degree as part of their entrance qualifications. Some universities offer higher degrees through their Schools of Management. The *Council for National Academic Awards* recognises a number of BA degree courses. These are often described as BA (Business Studies). London University offers through various colleges external degrees, such as BSc (Econ). Some colleges offer their own diplomas and certificate courses which give limited exemptions from the examinations of some professional bodies.

The major professional qualifications in business are dealt with in the professional institutions sector. The *Business Education Council* and the

Scottish Business Education Council award General Level Certificates and Diplomas, as well as National and Higher National awards. These awards provide the basis of vocational education in business related careers. Further details are in BEC publications. The *regional examining bodies*, in addition to courses that lead to national examinations, also offer their own awards. The range of business education and training is broadly similar in Scotland.

At the secretarial/clerical level the *Royal Society of Arts* and the London Chamber of Commerce, as well as private organisations like Pitmans or Speedwriting, offer awards, often with part-time or *evening classes*. There are also numerous private colleges offering courses. (See Part 1, ch. 2)

Questionnaire This is a popular method of collecting information; but the responses to questions are not only very dependent on careful design and trials of the questions, but also on the mood of the respondent when answering them. A further hazard is that response rates can be poor because the researcher may not be present to ensure that all the questionnaires are filled in. The attraction of using questionnaires is that they are economic in terms of cost, time and labour. A questionnaire may include items other than straight questions, such as *attitude scales*. Good questions are those derived by dint of careful consideration of the purpose, the characteristics of the target audience and pilot trials. The key to successful use of questionnaires is research. An important factor in designing questionnaires is considering how the responses will be analysed on completion of the questionnaires. A careful schedule is important in this context. The style of questions used is usually direct, allowing only a limited answer or answers to a question. Although this permits easier processing, it has the potential problem of getting the answers to the researcher's questions, whilst not allowing the respondent the opportunity to express opinions he has. Open-ended questions or sections for comments can be used, but these provide problems for processing and classifying the responses. The commonest error in designing questionnaires is to ask leading questions such as 'Is it practicable to abolish corporal punishment?'. Whilst it is possible to answer 'yes', the question expects the answer 'no'.

Further reading
Moser, C. A., 'Survey Methods in Social Investigation', Heinemann, 1958. Oppenheim, W. A., 'Questionnaire Design and Attitude Measurement', Heinemann, 1966. (See Part 1, ch. 8)

Quotient A quotient is obtained by dividing one quantity by another. The quotient scales used in educational measurement have all been obtained by dividing the person's 'mental age' (MA) by his chronological age (CA) and multiplying the result by 100. This results in a *scale* whereby a score of 100 is obtained by obtaining age-norms for a particular *test*. If the test measures reading skill then the scores obtained by this method are called reading quotients, and if the test measures *intelligence* then the scores obtained are called *intelligence quotients* (IQ). The problem with the quotient scales is that there is no standard unit of spread, so that differences between scores are not easily interpreted. (See Part 1, ch. 6)

Ragged school Ragged schools provided schooling and food for some of the poorest children of London, Bristol and Norwich. In London, where they date from at least 1835, the Ragged School Union was founded in 1844 and was assisting nearly 200 schools by the late 1860s. With the introduction of compulsory education their numbers declined. They offered a number of welfare facilities, including penny bunks and the Boys' Shoeblack Brigade, which was still giving poor boys employment fifty years later. (See Part 1, ch. 10)

Rate of return The rate of return to an investment is a measure of its profitability. It measures the relationship between costs and expected benefits, by showing at what rate of interest, or discount, the present discount value of future benefits is exactly equal to the present discount costs. The social rate of return to investment in education measures the profitability of education viewed as a social investment. The private rate of return measures the profitability from the point of view of the individual. (See Part 1, ch. 5)

Rationalism Rationalism is usually contrasted with *empiricism*. Rationalists take mathematics rather than physical sciences as their paradigm of *knowledge*. The importance of purely logical reasoning is emphasised and scientific knowledge considered of lesser importance.

Further reading

Hamlyn, D. W., 'The Theory of Knowledge', Macmillan, 1971. (See Part 1, ch. 13)

Rationality Most people would agree that the purpose of *education* is to encourage children (a) to behave rationally and (b) to believe in those proportions and beliefs which are 'rational'. However, some difficulties arise when attempts are made to establish criteria by which the rational may be distinguished from the irrational. An obvious criterion would be that 'rational beliefs are those which are in accordance with reality'. The distinction may not be as effective as it appears to be, because of the interlocking relationship which exists between ideas of rationality and ideas about what the world is like. It is considerations of this kind which have led some writers to suppose that witchcraft may be as rational as Western science! See also: *paradigm, relativism, sociology of knowledge, objectivity*.

Further reading

Winch, P., 'The Idea of a Social Science and its Relation to Philosophy', Routledge & Kegan Paul, 1958.

Wilson, B., 'Rationality', Blackwell, 1970. (See Part 1, ch. 13)

Reflexive sociology In so far as sociology presents a kind of 'knowledge', it can itself be investigated from the standpoint of the *sociology of knowledge*. Such an investigation constitutes the sociology of sociology, or reflexive sociology. From this viewpoint, the account given in Part I of the development of the sociology of education ought to have examined the social context of the various changes described, since these changes have their origins elsewhere than in the sphere of theoretical debate. Alvin Gouldner, in 'The Coming Crisis of Western Sociology' (1970), calls for a reflexive sociology capable of giving sociologists an historically new level of self-awareness.

Further reading

Gouldner, A., 'The Coming Crisis of Western Sociology', Basic Books, 1970. (See Part 1, ch. 15)

Regional examining bodies There are six of these in England and Wales. They deal with various examinations for courses in further education colleges and adult education centres. They work closely with the *City and Guilds of London Institute* and have a national agreement under which standards are maintained for those courses and examinations offered by both organisations.

The six bodies, together with their locations, are briefly outlined below.

East Midland Educational Union was founded in 1912, and consists of

Local Education Authorities and further education establishments in the East Midlands region. The Union's examinations are recognised for *National Certificate* schemes. Location: Robins Wood House, Robins Wood Road, Aspley, Nottingham NG8 3NH; 0602 293291.

North Western Regional Advisory Council for Further Education (incorporating the Union of Lancashire and Cheshire Institutes) is a co-ordinating body principally, but since the amalgamation with ULCI it provides further education examinations up to Higher National Certificate standard. The Council does not classify its certificates but grades, with Distinction, Credit or Pass. Location: Town Hall, Walkden Road, Worsley, Manchester M28 4QE; 061–702 8700.

The Welsh Joint Education Committee is a statutory joint Committee, set up under the Education Act 1944. Founded in 1948, it co-ordinates many of the functions of all the Welsh Education Authorities. The Department of Education and Science accepts the Committee as the Welsh Education Authorities' association, and recognises it as the advisory council for further education in Wales and as an examining board for Wales (GCE, CSE and further education examinations). Location: 245 Western Avenue, Cardiff CF5 2YX; 0222–561231.

The Northern Counties Technical Examinations Council was founded in 1920. It consists of five counties and five metropolitan districts and provides further education examinations for its region. It also conducts National Certificate examinations (and others of similar standards to CGLI). Location: 5 Grosvenor Villas, Grosvenor Road, Newcastle-upon-Tyne NE2 2RU; 0632–813242/3.

West Midlands Advisory Council (incorporating the Union of Educational Institutions) deals with examinations, mostly at craftsman and operative levels, in further education institutions. It works in close association with CGLI and the council of Technical Examining Bodies. It also provides examinations for certain commercial subjects. Location: Norfolk House, Smallbrook, Queensway, Birmingham, B5 4NB; 021–643 8924.

Yorkshire and Humberside Council for Further Education, founded in 1928, provides examinations to National Certificate levels. It also conducts examinations in various other fields, like distributive trades, mining, engineering and construction. The further education colleges involved with the Council are able, by their participation, to exert a strong influence on the maintenance of standards and determination of results. Location: Bowling Green Terrace, Leeds LS11 9SX; 0532 40751. (See Part 1, ch. 2)

Regional Management Centre (RMC) In March 1971 Margaret Thatcher, then Secretary of State for Education and Science, announced the decision to set up RMCs, 'to foster the best use of resources for management study in the further education sector and to encourage the development of high quality work'. They were expected 'to become focal points for management education in their region, contributing through industry-linked research and consultancy to the quality of management in practice'.

RMCs are based on *polytechnics* and other colleges with an established reputation for providing courses in management studies. There are 12 such Regional Centres of Management Education, and they are designated as the focal points for management studies within the *further education* sector. They have thus become part of the *higher education* sector, but continue to work at a wide range of levels of courses. The modes of study are also very wide, as most RMCs provide courses on *day release* to full-time bases, depending on the nature of the programme and the approval of any controlling or examining body. Most RMCs also offer consulting services to businesses and organisations within their region.

Many RMCs have developed close links with colleges of further education in their area, and act as sponsors and monitors of RMC-level courses in the colleges. This has helped to make certain courses, and in particular the *Diploma in Management Studies*, much more widely available. One of the major aims it was hoped RMCs would achieve was to strengthen links between colleges, industry and commerce. Experience suggests that the requirements of examining bodies, whether national, like the *Council for National Academic Awards*, or professional institutions, are more important to an academic sector than the demands of industrial organisations. However, many RMCs have adopted very flexible approaches to the provision of management education.

The Association of RMCs exists to promote the spread of good management studies practice of proved effectiveness, and collaborate with the Conference of University Management Schools. Further information on the services of particular RMCs is available from those RMCs. All RMCs hold occasional open days for potential clients within their geographical area. (See Part 1, ch. 12)

Relativism The concept of relativism seems to deny the possibility of *knowledge*, so that the belief that 'everything is relative' is another way of saying 'nothing can be known'. Relativism was examined by *Plato* in his dialogue 'Protagoras', and it was to combat relativism that the theory of forms was developed. Man was the measure of all things, and everything was as it was to each individual. The question 'But what is X really like?' could not be asked. Thus, water could be hot to one person and cold to another, and there was no means of saying which view was correct. Everything was as it seemed to be and the same object might be different to each individual. The main objection to the theory is that it excluded the possibility of truth. If X gives an account of P and Y gives an account of P, and the accounts differ, one could not ask 'But whose account is true?' The conditions of knowledge seemed to require that a certain object X has certain qualities and characteristics and that human knowledge is possible because it is possible to make statements and propositions about these objects and qualities. There must also be means of saying whether these propositions are true. If it is allowed that it is impossible to discriminate between accounts, or that each account is equally right, or equally wrong, then the whole possibility of knowledge seems to have been abandoned.

Moral relativism and the awareness of different moral systems seem to contradict the notion that there could be any absolute standards of morality. Each set of morals is the result of social conditions and there is no means of adjudicating between these.

Further reading

Hamlyn, D. W., 'The Theory of Knowledge', Macmillan, 1971.

Scheffler, I., 'Science and Subjectivity', Bobbs Merrill, 1967. (See Part 1, ch. 13)

Reliability If someone were asked to measure a desk every day with a ruler to the nearest centimetre, we should find that his results would be very consistent. It is unlikely that he would give us lengths which varied by more than 1cm if they varied at all. However, if this person were to use the same ruler to give us lengths for the same desk to the nearest millimetre, we should expect to get a small range of lengths, since we know that measuring in this way involves a degree of imprecision. We are, in fact, admitting that the measuring system is unreliable. It is the attempts to understand and quantify the extent of unreliability which has led to the body of knowledge known as 'reliability theory'.

Educational measures are particularly prone to imprecision because of the many variables affecting the outcomes. These variables can be divided into three kinds: those variables inside the person, those variables inherent in the *test*, and those variables exterior to both of these. Thus fatigue affects test *scores* in a way that does not reflect what the person can do when he is tested. Variables inherent to the test could be ambiguities in the test *items* such that they have different meanings to different people, and this would mean that the test would be measuring a slightly different attribute in each person. Variables exterior to both could be the style of the test administrator or the climatic conditions.

All these factors introduce variations in the test scores which are independent of the variations due to the attribute being measured. There is no single way to estimate how much imprecision they introduce. The most common methods all correlate two sets of scores obtained for each person. The way in which these two sets of scores are obtained falls into three main categories:

(a) Test re-test reliabilities

If it were only the attribute being measured that affected scores, a second attempt at the test would produce the same results. A test re-test *correlation* therefore gives an estimate of the reliability. However, in the time between testing a genuine change in the attribute may occur in each person. There are also memory and boredom factors which interfere with the pureness of the estimate.

(b) Parallel-form reliability

Well-constructed tests have a defined *domain* from which one or more tests can be drawn to measure the domain. The extent to which two such tests correlate gives information about how well the domain is defined, and therefore how well the tests can estimate the domain score. This is still an impure estimate of reliability since different factors can be present at both testing sessions, such as genuine change in the attribute. Memory and boredom factors should, however, be reduced since the test is different on both occasions.

(c) Internal consistency

This is similar to parallel-form reliability since the test is the defined domain and two halves of the test can be treated as parallel. If the test has a variety of items, however, any two halves could well not be parallel and therefore could produce discrepant scores. As such these estimates of reliability are known as internal consistency. By removing the effect of time differences between testing those estimates reflect fewer changes in the variables which would affect scores. As such they tend to give a picture of higher reliability. This may not be giving a more *valid* picture for interpreting individual scores, because certain factors may be strongly influencing a certain person's score on that one occasion, and a second opportunity to demonstrate his ability would therefore present a truer picture.

There are advantages and disadvantages for each of these estimates and it is advisable to consider more than one kind when evaluating a test's reliability.

Further reading
Crocker, A. C., 'Statistics for the Teacher', 2nd ed., National Foundation for Educational Research, 1974.
Guilford, J. P. and Fruchter, B., 'Fundamental Statistics in Psychology and Education', 6th ed., McGraw-Hill, 1978. (See Part 1, ch. 6)

Reliability is a technical term used in relation to the performance of a test. It indicates how consistent a test is in measuring what it is supposed to measure. The measure can be determined in several ways. The commonest methods are by administering a second time or by comparing results for the odd- and even-numbered questions. (See Part 1, ch. 8)

Religious education The Education Act 1944 gives detailed attention to religion in schools, a fact which is explained by reference to the history of popular education and the prominent part played in it in the first half of the nineteenth century by voluntary bodies (see *religious societies*) associated with the churches. The question of religious education in schools and the division between the voluntary schools and the non-denominational schools (Board Schools) established after the Education Act 1870 and financed from the rates continued to be a burning issue until the 1944 Act. From the compromise there emerged inter alia the designation of voluntary schools as aided or controlled, certain financial arrangements, and the provisions for religious worship and religious instruction.

The Act states that the school day in both county and voluntary schools shall begin with a collective act of worship, provided the accommodation for such assembly is available and subject to the parental right of withdrawal.

Religious education is also prescribed as part of the curriculum, again subject to the parental right of withdrawal. In county and controlled schools such education must be in accordance with an agreed syllabus to be drawn up by a conference convened by the LEA. The Conference is to be composed of four Committees: (1) those religious denominations the LEA considers ought to be represented (the Roman Catholic Church has declined invitations to participate), (2) the Church of England, (3) such teachers' associations as the authority considers appropriate and (4) the LEA itself. Each Committee in the Conference has one vote, and the decision of the Conference must be unanimous. If there is no agreement the Secretary of State must appoint another similar body to prepare an agreed syllabus.

In aided schools religious education must conform to the trust deed of the school. (See Part 1, ch. 1)

Religious societies There was widespread belief at the beginning of the nineteenth century that the education of poor children had to be based on the teachings of revealed religion, the basis of all morality. Unfortunately, as the number of conflicting faiths attests, there was no general consensus on these teachings. Moreover, at a time of high infantile und juvenile mortality, religious leaders saw life on this earth as a preparation for life everlasting. This was the most important task of the school. Hence as *Sunday Schools* attached to churches and chapels gradually developed into day schools, religious societies were founded to safeguard and propagate the tenets of different sects. The most important of them were the National Society for Promoting the Education of the Poor in the Principles of the Established Church throughout England and Wales, founded in 1811, and the nonconformist British and Foreign School Society, established in 1814 on the basis of the Lancasterian Society of 1808. Others included the Home and Colonial

235

Society (1836), the Wesleyan Education Committee (1840), the Catholic Poor School Committee (1847), the Congregational Board of Education (1847) and the Voluntary Schools Association. With the exception of the last two, who objected on grounds of conscience until the 1860s, all the other societies accepted help from the *Committee of the Privy Council on Education*. Their schools constituted the voluntary system which by 1870 had provided school places for nearly 2,000,000 children, but as the building of the schools had depended on local initiative and not social need the distribution of the school places did not match that of the population.

Further reading

Binns, H. B. A., 'A Century of Education', 1908, reprinted Kelley, USA, 1978.

Burgess, H. J., 'Enterprise in Education', S.P.C.K., 1958.

(See Part 1, ch. 10)

Research and advisory organisations Within the group of organisations which carry out research or have an advisory function there are several which are directly connected through financial support of government departments to the official education system. Because of the nature of their work a large measure of autonomy is given. Central to educational research, other than that carried out within universities or colleges, are three main bodies: the National Foundation for Educational Research in England and Wales, the Scottish Council for Research in Education, and the Northern Ireland Council for Educational Research.

Funding for other research bodies varies, and a number are housed within universities or polytechnics. Examples of these are: the Centre for Labour Economics at the London School of Economics; the Centre for Institutional Studies at the North East London Polytechnic; the Centre for Contemporary Cultural Studies at the University of Birmingham, the SISCON Project (Science in a Social Context) at the University of Manchester, and the Institute of Education of the European Cultural Foundation at the Université Dauphine, Paris. Here the advantages of close connection with an institution can be seen, since staffing and housing are provided by that body and the officers of the research organisations work in a stimulating environment.

A considerable amount of educational research is funded by charitable trusts, some of which have founded their own research organisations. Notable in this latter respect is the Nuffield Foundation, which has made such a direct impact on the development of materials for schools. The Calouste Gulbenkian Foundation supports a wide range of research with an emphasis on community aspects, whereas the Wellcome Foundation appears to emphasise sociological and anthropological research. There are many other trusts or foundations actively supporting educational research, often feeding back into the educational system personal or industrial wealth; lists can be found in many almanacs or yearbooks.

Several research units have been founded by sectors of industry or administration, such as the Industrial Training Research Unit Ltd or the Local Government Operational Research Unit.

With Government support a number of industries and professions have established research councils which, though not research bodies in themselves, co-ordinate and direct research within their own field. Some of the councils have selected boards specifically concerned with educational research. Included among the research councils are; Agricultural Research Council, Medical Research Council, Natural Environment Research Council,

Science Research Council, and the Social Science Research Council. These bodies are themselves represented on the Advisory Board for the Research Councils, which is an organisation serviced by the Department of Education and Science. (See Part 1, ch. 7)

Research trends in comparative education A survey of the writings of comparativists will indicate their interest and the development of the subject. Published books have been adequately dealt with by Bristow and Holmes, Bereday and Richmond. The reader is directed to these works for further consideration. In terms of articles an interesting review of comparative articles has been surveyed by Koehl. The survey involved articles in 'Comparative Education Review' (USA), 'Comparative Education' (Oxford, England) and the 'International Review of Education' (UNESCO Institute, Hamburg) over periods varying between ten and twenty years. A summary of the findings, admittedly highly selective, is given below. The reader is recommended to consult the source article for complete details.

It was noted that about three quarters of the articles in the CER and about half those in CE were defined as 'comparative'. About a third of the articles in CER were concerned with one country, while a third were cross-national in format. The countries most frequently written about were the USA and the UK. Thus the attention was mainly focused on Anglo-Saxon and European rather than on the Third World, with the notable exceptions of India and China. The topics most frequently selected for study included: educational development, educational reform, methodology, colonial education, political education, educational theory, education and opportunity, higher education, educational research, teaching comparative education, educational planning, educational expansion, students, educational achievement, history of comparative education, and others. An analysis of these topics indicates that development and melioristic concerns were a feature of one third of the articles, while theory and methodology and historical topics shared another third whilst the rest of the topics took up the final third.

Further reading

Bereday, G. Z. F., 'Comparative Method in Education', Holt, Rinehart & Winston, 1964 (chapters 10–12)

Bristow, and Holmes, 'Comparative Education through the Literature', Butterworth, 1966.

Richmond, W. K., 'The Literature of Education', London, Methuen, 1972, pp. 163–82.

B. Koehl, The Comparative Study of Education: Perspectives and Practice, 'Comp. Educ. Rev.', 1977. (See Part 1, ch. 3)

Resource centre Resource centres are given a variety of names, including 'learning materials centre', 'audio-visual centre', 'learning aids laboratory', or 'instructional materials centre'. Usually these centres have collections of print and non-print materials held in a room which has study carrels containing the necessary equipment to view or listen to the material. Collections are often in a limited subject area and typically include *books*, magazines, journals, *slides*, *films*, posters, audio and video tapes, overhead projector transparencies and self-teaching units containing a variety of media.

Further reading

Davis, H. S., 'Instructional Media Centres', Indiana University Press, 1971.

Clarke, J., 'Resource Based Learning for Higher Education', Croom Helm, 1982. (See Part 1, ch. 9)

Re-training A fashionable term used to describe training for a job other than that the trainee was originally trained for. The Training Opportunities Scheme has financed a great expansion of such activities. Many firms must also carry it out as their technologies change. (See Part 1, ch. 11)

Revised Code By the late 1850s the Education Department (see *Committee of the Privy Council on Education*) had become one of the largest civil establishments of the state with only one clerk less than the Foreign Office. Its budget of nearly £1,000,000 was roughly one-fifth of the total amount needed for the civil estimates. In a period of financial retrenchment after the Crimean War it was a prime candidate for expenditure cuts. In an effort to contain, if not reduce, the education budget, *Robert Lowe* introduced a new grant, the Revised Code. At the annual inspection children had to satisfy the Inspector that they had reached a certain standard in reading, writing and arithmetic and to have made 200 attendances since the last inspection. At first the grant was confined to the 3Rs, but during the course of its existence it underwent considerable modification with the introduction of new subjects such as French, German, Latin, elementary science, and geography. After a Royal Commission chaired by Viscount Cross had criticised it in 1888 for being too rigidly applied, major changes were introduced from 1890 onwards. The practice of examining every child was modified, first by examining a sample in the 3Rs, and then stopped altogether in 1895. Examination in other subjects was gradually replaced by a system of block grants dependent on inspection of the school as a whole. Controversy still surrounds two issues: Lowe's precise motives for introducing the Revised Code, and the effect it had on educational standards. (See Part 1, ch. 10)

Further reading

Marchum, A. J., Interpretations of the Revision Code of Education, 1862, in 'History of Education', VIII no. 2, 1979, pp. 121–33, an up-to-date review of the relevant literature.

Role *Structural-functionalism* sees interactions as possessing stability because they are regulated by *normative* demands to which the participants are responsive. Those rules which pick out the specific way in which a particular individual is required to act in a certain form of interaction constitute his role in it. Structural-functionalists also claim that the internalisation of the agreed rules of conduct within the personality structure of the respective role-players is a further condition of the stability of the interactions concerned. This claim has led to the criticism that structural-functionalists portray human beings as no more than passive enactors of the various roles laid down for them by the external rules of society, rules that take complete control of them by means of the process of internalisation.

Symbolic interactionism puts forward an alternative concept of role, maintaining that the way in which an individual makes himself capable of interacting with other people is by achieving an understanding of what they are doing and what they have in mind. He does this in the first place – as Mead is said to have shown – by 'taking the attitude' of the others and coming to know the meaning of their actions from the inside. He can then frame his own actions as meaningful responses in keeping with the meaningful actions of the others. His own part or role in the interaction consequently becomes one that he is constantly creating and re-creating as his interpretation of the situation progresses and changes.

Their reaction against structural-functionalism tended to push some symbolic interactionists towards representing the two concepts of role as strictly antithetical and mutually exclusive, but on each side there are, in fact, many

intermediate positions that can be taken. For an exploration of some of the middle ground, see Peter Berger, 'Invitation to Sociology' (1963).
Further reading
Berger, P., 'Invitation to Sociology', Doubleday, 1963.
Musgrove, F. and Taylor, P., 'Society and the Teacher's Role', Routledge & Kegan Paul, 1969. (See Part 1, ch. 15)

Role-playing Participants are asked to enact a role during training, usually that which they have at work, in order to learn. Most role-plays deal with face-to-face, one-to-one problems and events. Good role-plays can reproduce real-life in a safe environment. (See Part 1, ch. 12)

Royal Society of Arts The Society for the Encouragement of Arts, Manufactures and Commerce was founded in 1754 at the suggestion of William Shipley of Northampton. It received its royal charter in 1908. As well as offering prizes to encourage inventions, it started examinations in a wide variety of subjects in the 1850s, primarily for members of mechanics institutes. With the incorporation of the *City and Guilds of London Institute* which became a major body for examining technical subjects, the RSA examinations in commercial subjects have become nationally recognised. (See Part 1, ch. 10)

Sample Because the *population* (say all 13-year-olds) being investigated is usually too large, it is normal to use a smaller number (a sample) of the population. The smaller number is chosen to be as representative of the population as possible. (See Part 1, ch. 8)

A sample is a carefully chosen group of people, objects or events such that the results from the sample can be said to represent the results we would expect from the total *population*. It is therefore necessary in choosing a sample to have a well-defined population so that the sample will not reflect a greater or lesser quantity of the attributes present in the whole population. For example, a sample of British schoolchildren would have to reflect the proportion of children in the various areas of Britain. A biased sample would result if a certain factor, such as the number of children at independent schools, was not properly represented. (See Part 1, ch. 6)

Scale A scale is defined as a system or model for grading by size, quantity, quality or degree. All measurement, therefore, results in a numerical value on some scale or other. There are three basic kinds of scale, which differ in the properties attributed to the intervals between points on the scale. The three kinds of scale are called ordinal, interval and ratio scales.

An ordinal scale is one where each category represents a point on the continuum of 'most' to 'least'. Numerical coding systems for filing cabinets do not represent points on a scale, since a random reordering of the numbers would not change the 'interpretation' for each category. Therefore ordinary grouping or classification does not involve scaling and does not constitute measurement. On the other hand, a teacher ranking the pupils in his class according to how fast they can run does constitute measurement using an ordinal scale. The number of a child's rank position would tell us whether he was faster or slower than a child with another rank number.

An ordinal scale becomes an interval scale when we can say something about the distance between numbers on the scale. This is achieved by having equal units on the scale so that, if X *scores* 10 more than Y and Y scores 10 more than Z we can say that X would score 20 more than Z. Such linearity is true only in relation to a specified judgment or operation. Thus loudness can be judged in terms of the number of amps being used by a resonator to produce sound. This produces a relation of the X, Y, Z kind where the units are amps. We could have a situation where X is '20 amps worth of sound' more than Z. However, in terms of perceived loudness this scale is certainly not linear. A person asked to judge a sound halfway between X and Z will not choose (X − 10) amps worth of sound. Different units would be required to produce an interval scale for observed loudness.

A ratio scale goes further than an interval scale in having a meaningful zero point. In considering temperature in degrees centigrade a value of 0°C to 10°C represents the same increase in heat as 10°C to 20°C. We cannot say that 10°C represents half as much heat as 20°C. Temperature can, however, be put on to an absolute scale where these kinds of statement would be true; but most educational measures cannot. The centigrade scale is analogous to the card game of bridge where six tricks is taken as an arbitrary zero and therefore a bid of 'one trick' in bridge terminology means obtaining seven tricks. We cannot then say that two tricks in bridge (i.e., eight tricks in reality) represent twice as many tricks as one trick (i.e., seven tricks in reality). A ratio scale, which enables us to make such comments as twice as much or half as much, is characterised by having a true zero and having equal units of measurement. In the strict sense, therefore, no such scales exist in educational measurement since we are not justified in saying that someone who *scores* zero on a *test* of intelligence, or mathematics, say, has no intelligence at all. On those educational tests concerned with knowledge of a *domain* a true zero point may exist but the equality of intervals is suspect. (See Part 1, ch. 6)

Scaling The units of the marks or scores obtained in a test are arbitrary and depend on the method used by the investigator. Ideally the scale units should be equal (e.g., the difference between 2 and 3 and 18 and 19 are the same). There are statistical techniques available, to give scaled scores. (See Part 1, ch. 8)

School attendance The *Elementary Education Act 1870* permitted school boards to make full-time education compulsory between the ages of 5 and 10 and on a part-time basis to the age of 13. In 1876 Lord Sandon's Act granted school attendance committees in non-school-board areas similar powers. The Elementary Education Act 1880 at last made compulsory attendance to the age of 10 universal. Further acts in 1893, 1899, and 1900 raised the age for full-time attendance to 12 and for part-time to 14. By the outbreak of the First World War in 1914 half the children in elementary schools were leaving between the ages of 12 and 14 under local by-laws that allowed them to do so on reaching a prescribed standard of education or having made 300 or 350 attendances a year for the previous five. The Education Act 1918 abolished all part-time exemption from 1921 onwards and made provision for Local Authorities to raise the leaving age to 15, an option that the inter-war depression made inoperative. A second attempt under an act of 1936 to take effect from 1 September 1939, the day Germany invaded Poland, also foundered. Success finally came in 1947. School attendance to the age of 16, a limit recommended by the Spens Committee in 1938, became compulsory in 1972. See also: *Factory children, compulsory school attendance.*

Further reading
Lowndes, G. A. N., 'The Silent Social Revolution: an account of public education in England and Wales, 1895–1965', Oxford University Press, 1969. (See Part 1, ch. 10)

School-based curriculum development Though often placed in the context of complex argument about centralised v. localised control of schools, teacher autonomy, etc., the idea underlying school-based curriculum development is simple. It is the idea that the best place for designing the curriculum is where the learner and teacher meet (Open University, 1976). Its fuller rationale is a complex blend of pragmatic and ideological considerations. It claims, for example, that the teacher is in a better position than outside 'experts' to appraise the learner's needs and interests. Individual teachers need freedom to regulate the range and tempo of curriculum tasks, to form the educative relationships with pupils which externally imposed syllabuses and examinations distort, and to use the local environment and culture as a curriculum resource. If the school has sufficient autonomy over its curriculum, then it can engage in constructive exchange of ideas and skills with its surrounding community. In fact, the case for school-based curriculum development derives much of its force from an implicit diagnosis of the tendency for the curriculum to become insulated and inert, which results from teachers' too ready acceptance of the limited instructional, control and selection function that society assigns them.

But the cogency of the idea depends equally on the analysis of the constraints to be overcome to make school-based curriculum development feasible. For example, it first requires a national curriculum framework which establishes an appropriate core curriculum; and an appropriate teacher education and support system, so that teachers may develop adequate design and evaluation skills, and can be kept in touch with criticism and research. Thus the idea needs to be seen in conjunction with that of rational-interactive planning and the problem-solving model of knowledge-utilisation. See also: *curriculum planning models*, *knowledge utilisation*, *core curriculum*.

Further reading
Dalin, P., 'Limits to Educational Change', Macmillan, ch. 6, pp. 95 – 108, 1978.
Eggleston, J., 'School-based Curriculum Development', Routledge & Kegan Paul, 1979.
Open University, 'School-based curriculum development' (W. Prescott), Unit 26 of course E 203, Open University Press, 1976. (See Part 1, ch. 4)

School examinations From the early 1840s onwards the *Committee of the Privy Council on Education* began setting examinations to test students in training colleges. Many other bodies followed this example in the 1850s. The *College of Preceptors* began in 1850, the *Royal Society of Arts* followed suit in 1853, the newly appointed Civil Service Commissioners started filling minor vacancies by a qualifying examination in 1855, and in 1857 some children in Exeter sat papers intended for 'middle-class' or secondary schools. On the basis of the Exeter experiment the University of Oxford conducted its first local schools examinations the following year, an example that Cambridge followed shortly afterwards.

These examinations had two great assets. They provided potential fee-paying parents with a yardstick by which to assess the efficiency of a particular school when teaching standards in many were low. By putting the control of the examinations in the hands of the universities links were made between them and the schools, thereby warding off any threat of state control over middle-class education. The School Certificate, introduced in 1917, gave grammar schools a similar academic boost. It was replaced by the General Certificate of Education at 'Ordinary' and 'Advanced' levels in 1951. At first a lower age limit of 16 was imposed at a time when pupils normally left secondary modern and technical schools at 15, a restriction that confined the examination effectively to the grammar-school pupil. However, the age limit was virtually abandoned two years later. Meanwhile secondary modern schools had begun to enter their pupils for a wide variety of examinations that did not always suit their needs, a development that led to an investigation by a committee chaired by Robert Beloe. Its recommendations led to the introduction of the *Certificate of Secondary Education* in 1965. See also: *public examinations*.

Further reading

Bruce, G., 'Secondary School Examinations: Facts and Commentary', Pergamon, 1969.

Roach, J., 'Public Examinations in England, 1850–1900', Cambridge University Press, 1971.

'The World Year Book of Education, 1969. Examinations', Evans, 1969. (See Part 1, ch. 10)

School health service The reorganisation of the health service in 1974 resulted in the transfer of responsibility for the school health service from LEAs to Area Health Authorities. The intention is to provide a comprehensive service for children in which the school health service is integrated with hospital, specialist and general practitioner services to cover all facets of health care for children.

The Area Health Authorities cover the same geographical area as individual LEAs (or in parts of London, a combination of LEAs). The key officers are the Specialist in Community Medicine (child health), the Area Dental Officer, and the Area Nursing Officer. They have responsibilities both to the Area Health Authority and to the LEA. The services provided include the provision of doctors, nurses, and therapists (physiotherapists and speech therapists) to all LEA schools; arrangements for medical examinations and immunisation, eyesight and hearing tests, inspections for infection and infestation, and the general oversight of health care, including dental care, in schools. Moreover, advice is given on the educational needs of handicapped children in special schools. (See Part 1, ch. 1)

School meals and the school health service The *Elementary Education Act 1870* brought the previously uneducated poor and underfed child into the classroom, thereby raising the problem of the kind of welfare services that should be provided to enable him to benefit from the education being provided. The first attempts, both to give him meals and rudimentary medical care, were made by private agencies. Following public concern about the state of the nation after the Boer War, 1899–1902, the Education (Provision of Meals) Act was passed in 1906. The following year provision was made for the medical inspection of children. In 1909 Local Authorities were permitted to provide medical treatment but, as with school meals, they had to recover costs from the parents wherever possible. During the inter-war years the school meal service made little progress despite the high rates of unemployment and the meagre payments permitted by the Unemployment Assistance Board. The most noteworthy innovation of those years was the introduction of the milk in schools scheme in 1934, under which children either had free milk or paid half the retail price, a halfpenny for a third of a pint. Despite war time progress less than half the children were having school meals in 1945. With its costs charged to the education budget, the school meal service has been a ready target for cuts. In contrast the school health service, which has been absorbed into the National Health Service since 1974, has escaped such attacks.

Further reading

Henderson, P., 'The School Health Service, 1908–74', HMSO, 1975.

Leff, S. and V., 'The School Health Service', H. K. Lewis, 1959.

Bulkley, M. E., 'The Feeding of School Children', Bell, 1914.

Hurt, J. S., 'Elementary Schooling and the Working Classes', 1860–1918', Routledge & Kegan Paul, 1979.

'Catering in Schools', HMSO, 1975.

'Nutrition in Schools', HMSO, 1975. (See Part 1, ch. 10)

School psychological service In England and Wales almost all LEAs employ educational psychologists and have a well-developed school psychological service. The present ratio of psychologists to the school population is an average of one to 11,000. The school psychological service is primarily involved in work with individual children, including assessing their needs and making recommendations for individual programmes for them within the curriculum, and providing support for schools and parents. (See Part 1, ch. 1)

Schools Council for the Curriculum and Examinations Established in 1964, this independent body is equally funded by the local authorities and the DES. It is charged with the responsibility of undertaking research in England and Wales on the development of the curriculum, teaching methods and examinations at school level. Its findings form the basis of advice to the Secretary of State on examination policy. Fundamental to its operation is the principle that each school should have the fullest possible measure of responsibility for its own curriculum and teaching methods based on the needs of its own pupils and evolved by its own staff.

The Council now has three information centres in England (London, Wakefield and Newcastle-upon-Tyne) and there is an office for the Schools Council Committee of Wales. In addition to the staff at its London head-quarters and the two other regional centres the Council operates through 15 regional field officers covering England, Wales and the Channel Islands. (See Part 1, ch. 1)

Schools of psychology Psychology as a discipline has not yet achieved the degree of organisation of its knowledge that is to be found in the natural sciences such as physics or chemistry. This is partly because psychology still lacks fundamental concepts comparable to the laws of conservation in physics, and partly because there is no firm agreement amongst psychologists on how the study of human experience and animal behaviour and their determinants should be conceptualised.

During this century there have been a number of different approaches taken, which some writers have grouped into 'schools of psychology'. R. Woodworth identified six main schools in America (where the majority of psychologists were to be found) during the first half of this century. Structuralism, functionalism and associationism have not survived as separate schools. Gestalt psychology, with its insistence that the whole is greater than the sum of its parts, was especially concerned with perception, learning and thinking. Its main findings have been absorbed into the mainstream of psy-

243

chology, but the influence of its approach continues in Gestalt therapy which is part of the contemporary interest in a more humanistic psychology. The two schools identified by Woodworth which still exert a significant independent influence on contemporary psychology are *behaviourism* and psychoanalysis. *Humanistic psychology* is comparatively new and a growing influence.

Most contemporary psychologists are eclectic in their approach, not adhering to any particular school. They recognise the breadth and complexity of the subject matter they have undertaken to study and draw their theoretical concepts and methodological approaches from whatever sources seem appropriate, including physiology, medicine, statistics, electronics, computer technology, and the other social sciences. The problems of the study of man and of behaviour are too complex to be approached from one perspective alone. See also: *theories of learning, psycho-analytic psychology.*

Further reading

Woodworth, R. S., 'Contemporary Schools of Psychology', 3rd ed., Methuen, 1965. (See Part 1, ch. 14)

Science and Art Department The Department of Practical Art, Board of Trade, began to offer grants to the Schools of Design. It was transferred to the Lord President of the Council in 1856 and became part of the new Science and Art Department which began to offer grants for the teaching of science from 1859 onwards. Except for the years 1873–4, there was no effective integration with the Education Department until the formation of the Board of Educaton in 1899. (See Part 1, ch. 10)

Score There are two main kinds of score – a raw score (RS) and a standardised score (SS). The RS is the simple sum of *items* correct. This can then be translated to a SS. The purpose of this transformation is to provide scores which have greater interpretability. (See Part 1, ch. 6)

Scottish Council for Educational Technology (SCET) Founded in the 1930s as the Scottish Film Council, the Scottish Council for Educational Technology was brought into formal existence in 1975. Over a long period of promoting the use of film in education through its 'Scottish Central Film Library', the Film Council developed a programme of promotion and development of services that took in all aspects of audio-visual media and subsequently educational technology. SCET is made up of representatives from all aspects of education and industrial/commercial training in Scotland, together with representatives of the Scottish Education Department and appointees of the Secretary of State. The Council operates an advisory and consultancy service, courses, conferences and a range of developmental projects and publications. The Information Service offers data on both software and hardware. Equipment is loaned out through the Technical Service, as are a number of cinemas.

The Council also maintains an active programme in film culture through the Scottish Film Council, a division of SCET, which in addition to promoting and supporting community and cultural interests in film and video has established as part of its programme seven regional film theatres and runs the Edinburgh Film Festival.

The recently established Scottish Film Archive, in addition to its declared archival function, creates new learning materials for education through the transfer of archival material to video tape. Direct contact with the classroom teacher is in part maintained through the Scottish Educational Media Association, a voluntary association with regional branches. (See Part 1, ch. 7)

Scottish Education Department (SED) The Scottish Education Department is a sector of the Scottish Office which, though it is regarded as a single Government department of Whitehall, reflects through its large number of internal departments the degree of difference between many of the systems in Scotland and England. The Scottish Education Department itself reflects some of these differences in that it provides not only for Scotland the functions of the DES in England and Wales but also includes other responsibilities.

The main divisions are: Primary and Secondary Education, Local Government, Special Services and International Relations, Educational Planning, Schools Examinations, Research and Educational Technology, Schools Curriculum, Statistics, Formal Further Education, Higher Education Awards to Students, Informal Further Education, Supply and Training of Teachers, Teachers Record Card System, Salaries and Income, Administration of Colleges of Education, Educational Building, Social Work Services Group, Museums, Children's Hearings, Probation Research, Social Work Staffing and Training, List D Schools, Child Care, Central Advisory Service, and as with the other Education Departments, the Inspectorate.

Whilst the SED is not in direct control of the Scottish universities, which look to the *University Grants Committee* for support, there are inevitably close ties between these two bodies because of the necessary collaboration over examinations and curriculum. Scotland has a single examination board, the Scottish Certificate of Education Examination Board (see *examining bodies*). In Scotland the function of *polytechnics*, higher education in technology, art, domestic science, music and agriculture is provided by central institutions, and the lower-level courses by the colleges of further education. (See Part 1, ch. 7)

Scottish Health Education Group (SHEG) The Council provides assistance to Health Boards and Local Authorities, through the promotion of health education, the running of courses for staff and the provision of resources. This last function is carried out through the Scottish Health Education Unit, which actively creates materials on health education, some of which reach the public through the media. Films are distributed via the Scottish Central Film Library. It assists local bodies in the creation and evaluation of materials and courses. The unit has funded a number of Senior Lecturer and Lecturer posts at Scottish universities and promotes several fellowships. Research and evaluation projects on major topics of health are funded at universities. (See Part 1, ch. 7)

Scottish Institute of Adult Education The Institute is an advisory and consultative body reflecting nationally the interests of organisations, institutions and individuals concerned with the provision of education for adults. It arranges conferences and training courses, undertakes research, acts as an information centre and maintains links with international bodies in the adult education field. The Scottish Adult Basic Education Unit and the Scottish Telephone Referral Service are agencies of the Scottish Institute. (See Part 1, ch. 7)

Screening hypothesis The 'screening' or 'filter' hypothesis suggests that employers use educational qualifications simply as a screening device which enables them to select workers who have certain natural abilities or attitudes which will make them more efficient in a job. This view denies that education has a direct role in improving workers' productivity, by giving them skills or knowledge, and implies that educated workers earn more than uneducated workers simply because of their superior natural ability. (See Part 1, ch. 5)

Secretarial courses New technology is changing the role of the secretary, from shorthand-typist (purely mechanical skill) to genuine personal assistant or administrative assistant to a boss. Secretarial courses, especially at senior level, are increasingly reflecting these changes. (See Part 1, ch. 2)

Secretary of State for Wales The provisions of the 1944 Act as amended and the 1980 Act apply equally to Wales as to England; but there was a major change in administration in 1970 when responsibility for primary and secondary education in Wales was transferred from the Secretary of State for Education and Science to the Secretary of State for Wales. Further and higher education (excluding the University) and other matters were transferred later, so that he is exercising in Wales the functions of the Secretary of State for Education and Science with the exception of the supply, training, qualifications, remuneration and superannuation of teachers; teacher misconduct cases; and appointment of H. M. Inspectorate. (See Part 1, ch. 1)

Selection for secondary education The pioneering work of Sir Francis Galton, Carl Spearman, Alfred Binet, and Victor Simon made possible the development of intelligence testing. In England Sir Cyril Burt carried this work a step further, so that by the early 1920s there were group tests, that is written tests administered and marked by laymen, and individual tests available. The earliest use of large-scale testing was to identify the mentally handicapped child (see *handicapped child*) for whom Local Authorities had to make special provision from 1914 onwards. The use of *intelligence tests*, however, is popularly associated with the problem of selecting abler children for a grammar school education. From 1870 onwards public and private funds began to provide a limited number of scholarships. In 1900 about 5,500 received help in this way, a figure that rose, thanks to the Free Place Regulations of 1907, to nearly 50,000 by 1912, and 72,386 out of a secondary school population of 246,000 by 1920. During the inter-war years competition for secondary school places intensified as the expansion of available places failed to keep pace with demand. Yet in 1936 only 34 of the 146 County and County Boroughs were using intelligence tests in their selection procedures. With the abolition of fees in all maintained secondary schools after 1944 the use of these tests became widespread. Increasing doubts about their validity in the 1950s played an important part in the move away from the *tripartite system.*

Further reading
Hearnshaw, L. S., 'Cyril Burt: Psychologist', Hodder & Stoughton, 1979.
Simon, B., 'Intelligence Testing and the Comprehensive School', Lawrence & Wishart, 1953.
Sutherland, G., 'The Magic of Measurement: Mental Testing and English Education, 1900–40', trans. Ryl Hist. Soc., fifth series vol. XXVII (1977), pp. 135–53, on which much of the above is based. (See Part 1, ch. 10)

Self-assessment/self-development These rapidly growing systems attempt to put into practice the idea that most people are aware of how they are performing, are able to diagnose areas for improvement and have a responsibility for their own development. The use of these systems places great demands on training and development departments for support and resource services; and great demands on bosses because of the need for sound *coaching* and *counselling*. (See Part 1, ch. 12)

Self-concept The self-concept has three main components: the self-image, or impression we hold of ourselves, which is constructed largely from how we think we see ourselves reflected back from others; the ideal self, which is our image of how we could or should be; and self-esteem, which has its origins in the feelings we have about the self we believe ourselves to be.
Further reading
Cooley, C. M., 'Human Nature and the Social Order', Charles Scribner's Sons, 1902.
Mead, G. H., 'Mind, Self and Society from the Standpoint of a Social Behaviourist', University of Chicago Press, 1934. (See Part 1, ch. 14)

Self-monitoring Self-monitoring is the form of action research important in curriculum development as the means to foster teachers' capacities for *evaluation* and self-criticism. Many curriculum ideas (for example, *discovery learning*) fail because the teacher is only partly aware of how his classroom practice negates his curriculum aims. Thus the teacher can get research data on his actual performance in several ways: feedback from pupils; the audio-taping of classroom transactions; or 'triangulation', where a third party observes teacher-pupil interactions. (See Part 1, ch. 4)

Self-rating A procedure used to enable a person to find out something about himself. Self-rating may be on the basis of a *questionnaire* with a scoring system (commonly used in magazines). Self-rating scales are not renowned for consistency or reliability. (See Part 1, ch. 8)

Self-teaching techniques Self-teaching techniques are those which show a realisation of the learner as central to the teaching-learning process. Such techniques reflect the change from a teacher-based process to one where the student actively takes responsibility for his own progress. This change of emphasis has expressed itself in the emergence of the discipline of educational technology. (See Part 1, ch. 9)

Semantic differential A procedure using words which are opposite. By placing a *scale* in between, say four or five points, respondents are required to select a position on the scale in relation to their reaction to the words in their context. (See Part 1, ch. 8)

Sensitivity training This, the general term, is used to describe several techniques, deriving from *T-group* (training group, originally), that use highly participative methods to improve skills in working with people by increasing abilities: to understand how others react to one's own behaviour; to gauge relationships between others; and to behave as required by the situation. Terms like sensitivity, group dynamics and group relations are used as synonyms for this kind of training. (See Part 1, ch. 12)

Sensory memory The sensory memory is a hypothetical first stage in the memory process where the effects of sensory stimulation are held in storage for a brief moment after they have been experienced. Some of this transitorially stored material will be transferred to the *short-term memory* but most is lost immediately.
Further reading
Gregg, V., 'Human Memory', Methuen, 1975. (See Part 1, ch. 14)

Setting In a school organised by *streaming* a child might be in a class of a certain 'average' level of ability for a whole range of subjects. Setting is a refinement of this system, practised especially in secondary schools, whereby children are grouped according to their ability in specific subjects. (See Part 1, ch. 1)

Seven-point plan Roger has suggested seven headings for selecting and classifying information which is relevant to determining the appropriateness of occupational choice for an individual. His seven headings are: (1) physical make-up, (2) attainments, (3) general intelligence, (4) special aptitudes, (5) interests, (6) disposition and (7) circumstances. As much relevant information as possible should be gathered under each heading for the requirements of the job and for the individual before a decision is made.

Further reading

Roger, A., 'The Seven-Point Plan', Paper no. 1, National Institute of Industrial Psychology, 1952. (See Part 1, ch. 14)

Short-term memory Short-term memory is a hypothetical second stage in the memory process, where a limited amount of information can be held briefly in storage for immediate use. Coded information can be used to increase its capacity for storage. Information in the short-term (or working) memory is rapidly lost unless it is rehearsed or goes forward to the *long-term memory* stage.

Further reading

Gregg, V., 'Human Memory', Methuen, 1975.

Baddeley, A. D., 'The Psychology of Memory', Harper & Row, 1976. (See Part 1, ch. 14)

Significance Significance is often used in the statistical sense to mean that a certain event is unlikely to have occurred by chance. It is usual to assume that two events, such as the differences in test scores only reflect chance differences (referred to as the *null hypothesis*). The significance test then defines a model of what would occur by chance. The difference between the events predicted by the model and the actual events can then be compared. The likelihood that the differences can have occurred by chance can then be estimated. (See Part 1, ch. 6)

Simulation This is a general term to describe a large number of techniques that use models, mathematical or otherwise, to represent reality. It is often a means by which very complex systems (e.g., an aeroplane) can be represented in a simpler way (e.g., by a Link-trainer) to allow the practice of skills without the severe punishment that could result from real-life errors. It can also be used for human relationships. (See Part 1, ch. 12)

Sixth form College Sixth Form Colleges attained prominence as a means of educating pupils aged over 16 at the time when various forms of *comprehensive secondary school* organisation were being discussed after 1965, though they had had their advocates before then; and where they have been established, they serve a consortium of comprehensive schools with the age range 11–16. Traditionally the Sixth Form was a stage of education which concerned itself mainly with A-level courses, and some of the Sixth Form Colleges continue this tradition by being academic institutions with a restricted entry and a preponderance of A-level courses. Most colleges, however, have 'open access' requiring no qualification on entry and providing courses for a wide range of ability. See also: *tertiary college* (See Part 1, ch. 1)

Skew A skewed *distribution* is one in which there are more high or low *scores* than medium scores. The distribution is therefore not symmetrical. Compare the normal distribution and the skewed distribution in the diagram. The skewed distribution has a positive skew. (See Part 1, ch. 6)

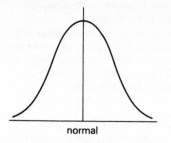
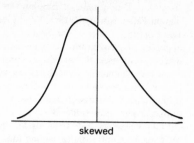

normal   skewed

Skill centre Skill centres are former Government training centres now operated by the *Division of Training Services*, the *Manpower Services Commission*. They specialise in accelerated vocational training for adults. There were 69 centres with 42 annexes; they cost £84 million to run in 1978 and 22,738 people completed courses. It has been estimated by the Civil Service Union (representing skill centre instructors) that 70 per cent of the said centres' output find jobs in their chosen skills within three months of completing their courses. (See Part 1, ch. 11)

Skills analysis In learning which involves dexterity, a means of identifying the skills required is used. There are particular procedures (skills analysis) using checklists and charts which enable a careful analysis to be carried out. (See Part 1, ch. 8)

Amongst a variety of techniques (including *job analysis* and *training within industry*) used to help to identify training needs, skills analysis is probably the most widely used, not only for manual jobs but also for many others.

The technique is derived from work-study and was developed to its present levels by Seymour. It is a detailed and systematic study, consisting of 'identifying and recording the psycho-physiological characteristics of skilled performance, and determining the cues, responses and decision-making functions involved'. ('Glossary of Training Terms', HMSO, 1971) In essence the work of skilled performers is subject to examination, and those special skills required by the task analysed in depth. A less intensive technique (like *TWI*) is used for the 'easier' parts of the task. This leads to the design of a training programme to enable people to learn the skills.

When analysing in this way, two further sets of skills can be examined. First, it is possible to collect information about faults which commonly occur and those which are costly in either time or money or both. It can be held that this is a separate technique (and it can be so used), but most trained skills analysts also carry out faults analysis at the same time. Second, many tasks require inter-personal skills (face-to-face, social or *interactive skills*). These also need a detailed analysis if they are to be taught systematically and effectively. In many jobs inter-personal skills are of critical importance but are rarely subjected to the same kind of attention received by manual tasks. The development of techniques is now relatively well advanced and no doubt they will become as much part of the trainer's repertory as manual skills analysis.

Further reading

Seymour, W. D., 'Industrial Skills', Pitman, 1967.

Seymour, W. D., 'Skills Analysis Training', Pitman, 1968.

Jones, S., Department of Employment and Productivity, 'Training Information Paper No. 1', HMSO, 1968. (See Part 1, ch. 11)

Skinner Skinner's article 'The Science of Learning and the Art of Teaching' appeared in 1954. In this he made the following comment on the reinforcement of responses: 'It has become a routine exercise to demonstrate this in classes in elementary psychology by conditioning such an organism as a pigeon.' He then went on to discuss the classroom situation and was critical of the relative infrequency and delay in reinforcement of material presented to and produced by students.

In an article entitled 'Teaching Machines' (1958) Skinner examined *Pressey's* work, maintaining that some form of teaching machine would be like having a private tutor who insisted on the material being understood before the student moved on. Skinner's ideas laid the basis for the *programmed learning* movement.

Further reading

Skinner, B. F., The Science of Learning and the Art of Teaching, in 'Harvard Educational Review', 24, pp. 86–97, 1954.

Skinner, B. F., Teaching Machines, in 'Science', 128, pp. 969–77, 1958. (See Part 1, ch. 9)

Slide The slide often used in education is 35mm film horizontal format mounted in a card or plastic mount. As slides are usually of high definition and in full colour the resulting projected image can be large and yet of very high quality. Slides thus have these advantages over *television* pictures but obviously cannot show movement, although animation can be achieved using *tape/slide* techniques. (See Part 1, ch. 9)

Social aspects of learning Almost all formal learning takes place in social settings of one kind or another. Each individual learner is involved in a system of numerous overlapping social groupings, some formal, some informal, which will influence his approach to learning through the attitudes, assumptions and predispositions to behave in certain ways that he acquires from them.

Within each group of which he has membership the individual will have a role and a status which will determine the nature of his interactions with the other members of the group and influence the contribution he will make to the formation and maintenance of the group structure. *Sociometry* is a way of examining aspects of this. Some individuals take on leadership roles; some leaders are task-oriented, concerned with the purpose for which the group came into being; others may be more concerned with the socio-emotional well-being of the members within the group. Different leadership styles can influence the effectiveness and well-being of the group. Each group develops *norms*, and these affect the way the group members perceive each other and the patterns of communication that will exist both within the group and with the outside world. Groups exercise a powerful influence upon the *attitudes* held by the group members, especially in areas of concern to the group. A member whose attitudes deviate from the norms of the group will be subjected to considerable social pressure in order to persuade him to become more conformist in his views. The organisational setting within which groups exist can have an important influence upon the learning of individuals, as work on the effects on streaming in schools has shown. See also: *language and thought*; *motivation*; *handicap*: *intellectual, social, emotional and physical*; *streaming*; *delinquency*.

Further reading
Cortis, G., 'The Social Context of Teaching', Open Books, 1977.
Johnson, D. W., 'The Social Psychology of Education', Holt, Rinehart & Winston, 1970. (See Part 1, ch. 14)

Social class Social class is a concept rooted in everyday life, where references to the upper classes, middle classes and working classes are continually being made and understood without any apparent difficulty. Yet sociologists find the concept far from easy to analyse at a theoretical level.

One mode of theoretical analysis stems from *Weberian sociology*. Weber makes a basic distinction between class and *status*. People belong to the same class when they have a similar position in the economic sphere in relation to opportunities for income and the acquisition of goods. People have the same status when they are commonly accorded a similar degree of prestige in the eyes of others. This kind of analysis makes possible the construction of a hierarchy of social classes either on the basis of Weber's concept of class, or, alternatively, on the basis of the two categories – class and status – in combination. The establishment of such a hierarchy is necessary in many studies, such as studies of *social mobility* and equality of educational opportunity.

Marxian theory puts forward a more complex concept of class. On its analysis, both the everyday and the Weberian pictures of the class structure belong equally to the level of *ideology*, and need to be re-interpreted in terms of the continuing *class struggle*. Various class divisions in society will then come to be recognised as significant because they will be clearly perceived as the effects of this fundamental struggle between an oppressing class and an oppressed class.

Further reading
Giddens, A., 'The Class Structure of the Advanced Societies', Hutchinson, 1973.
Lawton, D., 'Class, Culture and the Curriculum', Routledge & Kegan Paul, 1975. (See Part 1, ch. 15)

Social control According to *structural-functionalism*, one of the basic problems of any society or social system is to ensure that its members do not pursue their own self-interest in a manner that brings them into serious conflict with each other and leads to social disorder. *Socialisation* is the primary means of social control whereby such tendencies are curbed. The internalised sets of *norms* that are acquired through socialisation have the function of inducing conformity with the requirements of the social system as a whole.

On the other hand, deviance – or behaviour that contravenes these norms – is always possible. When deviant behaviour does occur, appropriate steps have to be taken by others to defuse the situation. A range of supportive, permissive, or restrictive responses can be enlisted in such circumstances as mechanisms of social control. The coercive power of the state, expressed through an institutionalised legal code and code of punishment, provides the most extreme restrictive form of social control; but society possesses a large number of less visible mechanisms enabling it to control deviant behaviour.

Many sociologists other than structural-functionalists agree with their general claim that there are numerous forms of social control, of varying degrees of invisibility, aimed at preventing certain forms of behaviour or keeping them in check. The concept of social control, moreover, does not preclude a critical standpoint. Ivan Illich, for example, regards the school as an agency of social control which in Western society typically fosters a new type of *alienation*, and he is therefore led to call for *deschooling*.

A wide variety of sociological perspectives has, in fact, informed the analysis of schooling as a means of social control.

Further reading

Davies, B., 'Social Control and Education', Methuen, 1976.

Sharp, R. and Green, A., 'Education and Social Control', Routledge & Kegan Paul, 1975. (See Part 1, ch. 15)

Socialisation The classical starting point here is Durkheim's conception of socialisation, and his view of education as methodical socialisation (see *Durkheimian sociology*). Parsons attempts to refine upon Durkheim's argument, and to give a detailed analysis of the socialising process, which in his opinion hinges on the employment of sanctions. He sees each actor within an interaction as sensitive to the expectations of those interacting with him and to the sanctions they use in order to achieve their expectations. The effect of such sanctions, Parsons maintains, is in the course of time to create and sustain *norms* and values that regulate any interaction and determine each actor's *role* in it. These norms and values are given stability by internalisation: that is, they are integrated within the actor's personality at the level of his basic need-disposition structure, so that they are no less imperative for him than his own needs.

An example of the kind of application that Parsons's theory of socialisation can have in the sociology of education is afforded by Robert Dreeben's 'On What is Learned in School' (1968). This is an American work, but it gives a generalised analysis relevant to schooling in Britain, discussing in detail the way pupils learn to adopt various norms.

There are many alternative perspectives on socialisation. *Symbolic interactionism* calls attention to the new meanings and values that can be created through socialisation; *phenomenological sociology* views socialisation in relation to modes of acquisition of common-sense knowledge and interactional competence; and Marxian theory tends to consider it in relation to the concept of *ideology*.

Further reading

Durkheim, E., 'Education and Sociology', Free Press, 1956.

Dreeben, R., 'On What is Learned in School', Addison-Wesley, 1968. (See Part 1, ch. 15)

Social lag A concept which identifies the source of social problems to be the differential rates of change between organisations and normative patterns known as social lag.

Further reading

Ogburn, W., 'Social Change', Allen & Unwin, 1923. (See Part 1, ch. 3)

Social mobility The reference of the term 'social mobility' is to the actual amount of movement between occupations and social positions. However, what has to be presupposed for the concept's dimensions of horizontal mobility and vertical mobility to have point is that occupations and social positions are arranged in a number of layers or strata. It then becomes meaningful to talk of movement from place to place within a layer or stratum (horizontal mobility) or of movement from one layer or stratum to another (vertical mobility).

In this way, the concept of social mobility is bound up with the concept of *social stratification*, and one major difficulty is that of identifying the strata into which society is stratified. It is here that the concepts of *class* and *status* become important as keys to the establishment of criteria for determining the composition of the various layers or strata and their hierarchical structure.

The use of the concept of social mobility in the sociology of education has typically been associated with a concern to discover how far differences in social class are linked with differential access to education. In 'Origins and Destinations' (1980), A. H. Halsey, A. F. Heath and J. M. Ridge examine this issue in a wide context that includes arguments put forward by Pierre Bourdieu in terms of the concept of *cultural capital.*

Further reading

Goldthorpe, J. (in collaboration with C. Llewellyn and C. Payne), 'Social Mobility and Class Structure in Modern Britain', Clarendon Press, 1980.

Halsey, A. H., Heath, A. F. and Ridge, J. M., 'Origins and Destinations', Clarendon Press, 1980. (See Part 1, ch. 15)

Social sciences approach This approach is typified by a more frequent use by comparativists of the methodologies of anthropologists, sociologists, economists and others.

During the 1960s a body of criticism was directed against the work of the *historical-humanistic school.* Some of these criticisms have been mentioned briefly. For example, Kandel and others were alleged to have been highly subjective, since they used indeterminate concepts such as *national character* and a level of generality which led to misinterpretation of their findings. Their main emphasis lay in the past rather than the present, while their identification of antecedent causes was not always relevant to the solution of current problems. It was generally held that there was a need to focus on more rigorous approaches to theory generalisation, on policy-making considerations and on the solution of problems in education.

Thus comparativists looked to the philosophies and techniques used by social scientists in order to achieve the academic and research rigour they sought. In attempting theory generalisation social scientists employed methods similar to those used by their colleagues in the physical sciences, in an attempt to control or predict social phenomena. They reflected on the problem, established and tested hypotheses by a rigorous, often total, analysis using appropriate social sciences. These could be used not only in identifying but also in collecting and analysing relevant data which would be employed to establish universal laws concerning school and society.

It could be argued that the indiscriminate use of the social sciences might lead to a superficial investigation, with a consequent lack of academic rigour. The predominance of one major science, in which the investigator has been trained, in the study should mitigate against this defect. Again it has been argued that social scientists differ so much in their orientations that they find it difficult to appreciate the common ground between them. Philosophers, for instance, focus on the intellectual and moral development of children; sociologists, until recently, sought to demonstrate empirically the relationship between social class background, attitudes and expectations to educational achievement and career patterns; while educators have been mainly concerned with service-oriented professional activities. Thus a knowledge of two or more social sciences by the researcher is desirable. Other criticisms have been made by radical anthropologists. Included in the social science school would be those who use the *problem approach* and the *philosophical,* the *sociological,* the scientific and the *ecological* and *cross-disciplinary approaches.*

Further reading
Kazamias, A. M. and Massiales, G. B., 'Tradition and Change in Education', ch. 1, Prentice Hall, 1965.
Fischer, J., 'The Social Sciences and Comparative Study of Educational Systems', Scranton, 1971. (See Part 1, ch. 3)

Social stratification Stratification has in many societies involved a system of castes or estates. Weber (see *Weberian sociology*) distinguishes such examples of *status* stratification from *class* stratification. People, he says, think more in terms of status stratification when economic conditions are stable, and more in terms of class stratification in periods of economic transformation. Many studies of present-day society do use indices of status mainly to support a class analysis. However, the continuing relevance of status stratification is the theme, for example, of Randall Collins's Functional and Conflict Theories of Educational Stratification (in 'American Sociological Review', 1971), where Weber's concept of status is made the basis of a *conflict* view of stratification.

Further reading
Littlejohn, J., 'Social Stratification', Allen & Unwin, 1972. (See Part 1, ch. 15)

Society for Academic Gaming and Simulation in Education and Training (SAGSET) An international association devoted to the promotion of academic gaming and simulation at all levels of education, training and business. SAGSET organises an annual conference, publishes a quarterly journal and provides an information service to members. (See Part 1, ch. 7)

Society of Education Officers This society, whose membership includes County Education Officers, Chief Education Officers, Directors of Education, Deputies and Assistants, represents those senior officers in education authorities in England and Wales responsible for the conduct of education. In addition to the nationally elected and regionally appointed members of the executive committee, England and Wales are serviced by a series of Regional Secretaries. (See Part 1, ch. 7)

Sociological approach This offers no new method but uses existing sociological methods and recommends that more acute questions should be posed, combined with the use of more dependable research techniques.

Further reading
Anderson, C. A., Methodology of Comparative Education, in 'International Review of Education', vol. 7, vii, pp. 1–10, 1961. (See Part 1, ch. 3)

Sociological relativism The issue of sociological relativism as this affects the *'new' sociology of education* bears on its interpretation of the claim that all knowledge is socially constructed. Some of its proponents argue that it is impossible for anyone attempting to judge the validity of what is taken to be 'knowledge' to disengage himself from his socio-historical circumstances and so come to a context-free decision. Therefore all knowledge is relative in the sense that no one can claim it to be valid except, at the most, for his own particular time and place.

Further reading
Young, M., Taking Sides Against the Probable: Problems of Relativism and Commitment in Teaching and the Sociology of Knowledge, in 'Educational Review', No. 25. pp. 210–22, 1973. (See Part 1, ch. 15)

Sociologist's contribution Sociologists can provide comparative studies giving valuable indications of the interdependence of major social institutions, help the development of typologies, and estimate the influence of *roles*, groups and *social stratification* on educational processes.

Further reading

Fischer, J., 'The Social Sciences and Comparative Study of Educational Systems', Scranton, 1971. (See Part 1, ch. 3)

Sociology of knowledge There are two distinct versions of the sociology of knowledge: the one might be called the traditional version, and the other the political or class version.

The traditional view was that what might be called 'the spirit of the age' affected judgments and influenced ideas about what was true or false. Descartes, for example, could be seen as a philosopher who was trying to find a method which would enable him to escape from these influences. However, it might be suggested that it is not only beliefs, but also the manner of assessing beliefs which is affected by social conditions. Thus Descartes, it might be alleged, could never hope to find a method which would free him from this kind of error. An updated version of this is that *knowledge* is a means of control, so certain types of information are awarded the accolade of 'knowledge' because this type of knowledge is useful to the dominant group, etc. However, the presupposition that the standards by which knowledge is assessed or examined are somehow either arbitrary or unwarranted, holds in both cases. There can be no knowledge because there can be no 'real' standards of assessing beliefs. Similarly there could be no means of assessing the claims of magic or modern science, because the standards of assessment are equally 'arbitrary'.

A society may reject one type of knowledge and accept another; e.g., Western Europe 'chose', for various reasons, the mathematical and scientific view of the world. But it would be difficult to maintain that the methods are themselves arbitrary or unsubstantiated. (See Part 1, ch. 13)

Earlier this century, Karl Manheim was notable both for his development of the sociology of knowledge and for his groundwork in the sociology of education. However, this connection between the two spheres is of much less contemporary significance than the connection between the sociology of knowledge and the *'new' sociology of education*. What especially needs to be understood is the way in which the very concept of the sociology of knowledge recently underwent a transformation through the influence of Berger and Luckmann's innovative study, 'The Social Construction of Reality'. Marx's thought had long been recognised as crucially relevant for the sociology of knowledge, but Berger and Luckmann caused Schutz's thought, too, to come to be viewed as equally relevant.

Marx insists that it is not people's beliefs that determine the nature of their social life, but rather the nature of their social life that determines their beliefs. More specifically, he explains the development of various forms of *ideology* in terms of the relations of material production and conditions of production arising in class societies. All such attempts to explain the beliefs people hold by reference to the circumstances of their social life belong to the sociology of knowledge.

Schutz does not himself see his *phenomenological sociology* as occupied with this kind of theoretical enterprise. Berger and Luckmann, however, incorporate his thought within the sociology of knowledge by widening the concept of the sociology of knowledge itself, arguing that Schutz's major preoccupation, the analysis of the social construction of reality, should be re-defined as one of the sociology of knowledge's essential tasks. See also: *reflexive sociology, sociological relativism.*

Further reading

Berger, P. and Luckmann, T., 'The Social Construction of Reality', Doubleday, 1966.

White, J. and Young, M., The Sociology of Knowledge: A Dialogue, in 'Education for Teaching', No. 98, pp. 4–13, 1975; No. 99, pp. 50–8, 1976. (See Part 1, ch. 15)

Sociometry Sociometry is a technique that was developed by Moreno to improve small-group morale and work. It can also be used as a research tool. Sociometry involves asking each group member to state their social preferences for companions in a range of situations. The sociometric status of each individual can be calculated by adding up the number of choices each receives. The sociometric structure of the small group can be shown diagrammatically using a sociogram.

Further reading

Morrison, A. and McIntyre, D., 'Teachers and Teaching', Penguin, 1969. (See Part 1, ch. 14)

Special education The Education Act 1944 required LEAs to establish special schools or classes to meet the needs of children needing special educational treatment. This and subsequent legislation and regulations which followed have been superseded by the Education Act 1981 which relates to children with special educational needs. This carried the obligations of the LEAs much further. The Area Health Authorities have to identify such children by the age of two or even earlier with the aim of assessing the individual educational needs of each child. Parental involvement in this process is envisaged. Such education should be provided as far as is possible and practicable in ordinary schools where handicapped children can integrate with their peers. The education of children recorded as having special needs is the responsibility of the LEA until they reach the age of nineteen.

Sports Council of Great Britain The Sports Council, together with the Sports Council for Wales and the Scottish Sports Council, has the primary aim of promoting and fostering sport and recreation. Though this is for the public at large, all three bodies have a proportion of their programme devoted to the pursuance of their aims within education. (See Part 1, ch. 7)

Standard deviation A measure of how far a score is from the mean. If simple differences from the mean are used, when added they give zero. By squaring the difference (or deviation), the minus signs are removed. The mean of the deviations is then square-rooted for the standard deviation. The simplest calculation described above is expressed mathematically:

$$\sigma = \sqrt{\frac{\Sigma x^2}{N}}$$

x = deviation from mean
N = number of scores
Σ = sum of standard deviation
σ = standard deviation
(See Part 1, ch. 8)

Standardisation This term is used in two ways in educational measurement, but both uses are interdependent. The first concerns the attempt to make the interpretation of scores as meaningful as possible by having a standard against which the *scores* can be compared. The second use concerns the attempt to make the measuring instrument as consistent as possible by administering it under standard conditions. Consistency is obviously a precondition for meaningful interpretation.

The standardisation of a *test* in terms of interpretation requires that the scores can be compared with an acceptable standard. In educational measurement this is often achieved by comparing a testee's scores with the scores obtained by a relevant 'other' group of testees. Thus, in educational measurement, the relevant 'other' group is called the standardisation sample, and the process of standardisation refers to the administering of a test to such a sample. The relevant 'other' group is often a sample of children who represent a local or national group. Scores can then be compared with the score obtained by such a group, and it can be estimated whether a person is performing better or worse than the average member of this *population*. More precise information can also be obtained. We can quantify how much better or worse than average a certain score rates.

The standardisation of a test in terms of the conditions under which it is given involves the attempt to control certain variables which could make the scores fluctuate but which are not variables which are considered necessary to be reflected in the resulting scores. These variables can be classified under three headings: testee variables, situation variables and instrument variables.

Testee variables involve, among others, fatigue, motivation, preparation and stress. Thus the testee being measured should not be too tired; he should not be unmotivated to perform as well as he can; he should be equally familiar with the task to be done as other testees and he should not have undergone any traumatic experience (such as bereavement) which would affect his internal state. It is impossible to remove the effect of all these variables, but it is necessary to ensure that their effect is minimised.

Situation variables involve basic conditions like heating and lighting, which should be adequate for testees to perform to their maximum ability.

Instrument variables involve both the way in which the instrument is administered and the quality of the instrument's materials. The first requires that a person administering a test should use the same instructions for administration, usually requiring the administrator to read out the instructions from a test manual. The second requires that a pencil and paper test, for example, has the same quality of print legibility for all testees. It can be seen that if one is interested in ability, for example, one will not wish to measure the effect of the above variables on performance.

Further reading

Angoff, W. H., Scales, Norms and Equivalent Scores in 'Educational Measurement' ed. by R. L. Thorndike, ch. 15, 2nd ed., American Council on Education, 1971. (See Part 1, ch. 6)

Standardised score Standardised scores are derived from tests where information is required about a person's performance in relation to the *population*. However, it is seldom possible to try out tests with the whole relevant population. A *sample* is used which is representative of the population (for example, 3,000 to 5,000 are samples used over the entire ability range to represent the population of, say, 11-year-olds in the United Kingdom.) Standardised scores are usually used for one age group rather than across age groups. The scores that are actually obtained when marking the test are converted mathematically to a standardised score. A standardised score could have a *mean* value of 100 and a *standard deviation* of 20, e.g. a difference of 60 from the mean represents three standard deviations. The distribution of scores can be corrected to a *normal distribution* because this enables some tentative comparisons between standardised scores based on different abilities. The deductions that can be made from the standardised scores on a test relate to a person's position in relation to the population; for example: a person being given a standardised score of 110 indicates that on that test 75.8 per cent of the population will score 110 or below. For further information on calculating standardised and normalised standard scores a book on statistics should be consulted. See also: *norm-referenced measurement*.

Further reading

Guilford, J. P. and Fruchter, B., 'Fundamental Statistics in Psychology and Education', 1978.

McCall, W. A., 'Measurement', ch 22, Macmillan, 1939. (See Part 1, ch. 8)

Standards of the Revised Code 1862

Standard I

Reading	Narrative in monosyllables.
Writing	Form on blackboard or slate, from dictation, letters, capital and small, manuscript.
Arithmetic	Form on blackboard or slate, from dictation, figures up to 20, name on sight figures up to 20; add and subtract figures up to 10; orally, from examples on the blackboard.

Standard VI

Reading	A short ordinary paragraph in a newspaper, or other modern narrative.
Writing	Another short ordinary paragraph in a newspaper, or other modern narrative, slowly dictated once by a few words at a time.
Arithmetic	A sum in practice or bills of parcels.

The requirements of each Standard were gradually raised and a Standard VII introduced during the life-span of the Revised Code. (See Part 1, ch. 10)

Standard scores All the *scales* used in *norm-referenced measurement* can be said to use standard scores in the sense that they have been converted from raw *scores* by comparing the results obtained on 'standard' groups of people. However, the term is used more specifically to mean those scores which have been converted to give a *normal distribution*. This distribution is given an arbitrary mean and standard deviation (which does not alter the shape of the distribution) which is often 100 and 15 respectively, although any values can be used. When the mean is set at 100 the standard scores must not be confused with *quotients*. (See Part 1, ch. 6)

Status Weber analyses *class* and status as two separate dimensions of social power. The status people have is determined by the degree of social honour or prestige that is seen as their due, and an index of this status is provided by their 'style of life'. Some sociologists also use the term 'status' to refer to a firmly institutionalised *role*, and this is its usage in *ethnomethodology*.

Further reading

Bendix, R. and Lipset, S. M. (eds), 'Class, Status and Power', Routledge & Kegan Paul, 2nd ed., 1967. (See Part 1, ch. 15)

Strategies of curriculum change Though 'strategy' has an inappropriate military connotation, it is a useful concept to concentrate attention upon the enmeshment of curriculum development within complex social interactions, and hence on the need to steer those interactions towards long-term aims. Without the adoption of a 'strategic approach', curriculum development tends towards two extremes: over-cautious, piecemeal evolution, which has little effect on basic practices and habits of mind; or radical changes which fail because neither the commitment nor the understanding to implement them have been developed. Thus to have a change strategy is to have decision principles for situations in which minds and practices need re-interpretation. Ideally, change strategies should mesh with broader 'developmental strategies' which draw upon models of knowledge utilisation and dissemination (Open University, 1976).

But 'change strategy' does not imply that there are specific guidelines that can be generally applied. The idea as such can be used to analyse tendencies in how curriculum workers try to bring about change; for example, by relating their approach to their 'targets of change'. Three main approaches have been conceptualised: power-coercive, to change organisation structures, etc., where the medium of change is a directive or law; normative–re-educative, to change attitudes, values, etc., where the medium is inter-personal relationship and trust; rational-empirical, to change teaching content, etc. where the medium is an evaluation report, lecture, etc. (Bennis, 1961). A comprehensive strategy will of course be adapted to a particular situation and may use all three emphases at different phases. In fact, the idea of strategy can articulate the sense in which teachers might conceive themselves as 'change-agents', emphasising that to be fully effective they need to analyse the social constraints within which they work, and to develop concerted, collaborative strategies to minimise them (Skilbeck, 1971). See also: *school-based curriculum development*, *knowledge utilisation*, *curriculum planning model*, *support system*.
Further reading
W. G. Bennis (ed.), 'The Planning of Change', Holt Rinehart & Winston, 1969.
Skilbeck, M., Strategies of Curriculum Change, in J. Walton (ed.), 'Curriculum Organisation and Design', Ward Lock, 1971.
Open University, 'Innovation: Problems and Possibilities', Unit 23 (E. Hoyle) of Course E 203, Open University Press, 1976. (See Part 1, ch. 4)

Streaming The internal organisation of a school can have a considerable effect on a child's academic performance and his social and personal development. Children, whatever their original abilities, tend to move towards the *norms* set for their stream once they have been in the stream for a sufficient length of time.
Further reading
Jackson, B., 'Streaming: An Education System in Miniature', Routledge & Kegan Paul, 1964. (See Part 1, ch. 14)

Streaming by ability The basic aim of streaming is to obtain classes which are fairly homogeneous in ability in the belief that children of about the same level of ability can be taught more effectively and easily. It is claimed that pupils who make good progress, or fail to make progress, can be moved up or down to other streams which correspond more to their abilities or levels of attainment. Streaming, however, is under attack from several quarters.

It is argued that a curriculum should be geared to a child's learning needs and that teaching should be centred on individuals or small groups and not

259

on larger classes, which in practice are not homogeneous in all curriculum subjects. But it is also criticised on its own assumptions that as a system it is flexible enough for a pupil to move from one stream to another according to level of attainment. In practice streaming has been found to be a fairly rigid system. The streams turned into glaciers. Whilst expectations from 'a' streams are high, they decrease correspondingly through 'b', 'c' and lower streams, and there is evidence to show that children perform to the level expected of them, so that levels of attainment match degrees of expectation. (See Part 1, ch. 1)

Structural-functionalism The term 'structural-functionalism' has different usages, but one of its standard references is to the sociological theory developed by Talcott Parsons in association with Robert Merton and others; and that is its specific usage here. In the 1930s Parsons laboured to construct a theory of action that would preserve Weber's concern with social action at the level of each individual actor's meanings and yet include a Durkheimian account of the moral regulation imposed upon its members by society. (See *Weberian sociology* and *Durkheimian sociology*.) His later work, however, put so much emphasis on the regulative structure of the wider society and its sub-systems that the individual appeared, from a sociological point of view, to have become little more than the sum of his internalised *roles*, and the Weberian perspective seemed virtually to have disappeared.

The term 'structural-functionalism' came to be commonly applied to Parsonian theory in this later form: and, indeed, the theory does have its explicit functional and structural orientations. It considers, first, the functional requirements of social systems, identifying these as (1) goal-attainment, (2) adaptation, (3) integration, and (4) pattern-maintenance; and it considers, too, the structural components of such systems, which are taken to consist of relatively constant *normative* patterns of culture.

Pattern-maintenance, which is concerned with the actual formation of the normative patterns of culture as well as with their maintenance when once formed, operates primarily through the process of *socialisation*. From this structural-functionalist viewpoint, one of the chief goals of the educational system is to contribute to pattern-maintenance in the wider society by way of the socialisation of its pupils.

Further reading

Adriaansen, H., 'Talcott Parsons and the Conceptual Dilemma', Routledge & Kegan Paul, 1980.

Parsons, T., The School Class as a Social System, in 'Harvard Educational Review', vol. 29, pp. 297–318, 1959. (See Part 1, ch. 15)

Structure To say that a curriculum design has a structure often means no more than that there are connections of some kind between its components. The concept of structure has much more force when it means the basic schema or sets of ideas which we use to organise and interpret our experience of the world, and which communities of scholars have refined and articulated through traditions of research and criticism into conceptual structures (Bruner, 1960). A course based on such conceptual structures should exhibit not merely a logical framework but, in effect, a recapitulation of the evolution of its knowledge-base; that is, of the interdependence of its ways of recognising problems, its methods of enquiry, its ways of assessing evidence, as well as the central concepts themselves. An example might be a curriculum design in biology based on the research problems revealed and resolved by such concepts as structure and function, homeostasis and regulation, etc.

Pupils' cross-application and sequential mastery of ideas can obviously be enhanced through learning activities guided by such structures, but it does not follow that selection of content for the curriculum should be based only on knowledge which manifests such structures. In fact, culture and human experience are structured in a variety of ways, not all of which can be derived from formalised bodies of knowledge. There are, for example, disciplined, expressive activities like writing a poem, persuading an audience, acting out a role, which are poorly represented within academic disciplines. They have a legitimate claim for inclusion in any curriculum concerned with the development of mind (see Pring, 1976, pp. 28–46), though how to discern their 'structure' remains uncertain. See also: *spiral curriculum, disciplines of knowledge.*

Further reading

Bruner, J. S., 'The Process of Education', Harvard University Press, 1960.

Pring, R., 'Knowledge and Schooling', Open Books, 1976. (See Part 1, ch. 4)

Student loans Student loans, which are extensively used in Europe, the USA and Canada, are a form of financial assistance for students, given to help students pay either their fees or their living expenses, which must be repaid after the student graduates. A number of different kinds of loan exists. In Scandinavian countries students receive financial aid in the form of a mixture of grants, which do not have to be repaid, and low-interest loans. These loans are provided, for the most part, from government funds. In Scandinavia, university students do not pay tuition fees, so their loans are used simply to help to pay students' living expenses.

In the USA students in universities can receive loans to pay tuition fees as well as living expenses, and the rate of interest which is charged varies considerably. In some cases the federal or state government provides low-interest loans, or an interest-subsidy which keeps the rate of interest charged on student loans at a very low level. In other cases the government simply guarantees that the loan will be repaid if for some good reason the graduate is unable to repay the loan.

Several economists have suggested introducing student loans in the UK instead of student grants, on the grounds that the present system is inequitable: grants transfer purchasing power, they maintain, from the average tax-payer to those who will enjoy higher than average earnings as a result of their education. A number of people suggest *income-contingent loans* or advocate *graduate tax* systems to counteract this.

Further reading

Woodhall, M., 'Student Loans: a review of experience in Scandinavia and elsewhere', Harrap, 1970.

Blaug, M. and Woodhall, M., Patterns of Subsidy to Higher Education in Europe, in 'Higher Education', 7, pp. 331–61, 1978.

Maynard, A., 'Experiment with Choice in Education', Institute of Economic Affairs, 1975. (See Part 1, ch. 5)

Study skills Students need a wide range of skills in relation to their courses of study. One of the most widely felt needs is the need to develop skills of rapid reading. However, it is better for a student to realise that mere speed is not enough. He also requires skills of selection and comprehension, the ability to pick out the main points of a passage and question its assumptions. Planning and organising time is another vital study skill, as is the development of the ability to concentrate one's attention. Other study skills include

S

the ability to use library resources, to take notes, write essays, take examinations, etc.. The development of study skills can be seen as the student developing his own *self-teaching techniques*.

Further reading

Hills, P. J., 'Study Courses and Counselling: problems and possibilities', Society for Research into Higher Education, University of Surrey, 1979.

Main, A., 'Encouraging Effective Learning: an Approach to Study Counselling', Scottish Academic Press, 1980. (See Part 1, ch. 9)

Styles of curriculum development The idea of styles of curriculum development is suggestive, although it does not work very well. It is the attempt to discern pattern in the diversity of approaches to curriculum development in different countries by applying an apparently simple hypothesis; which is that how decision-makers in partciular countries undertake curriculum development depends on their having basic and related values about schools, society and knowledge (Maclure, 1973). If this were so, curriculum development policies would embody implicit ideals about education as paintings may project aesthetic assumptions and norms. For example, countries like England and Wales seem to take a piecemeal or ad hoc approach, having heavy reliance on essentially unplanned interaction between inspectors, teachers, universities, examination boards, textbook publishers, etc. This could be interpreted as tacit acceptance of the inertia of slowly evolved balances of interest between examination boards, middle-class parents, teachers' associations, etc, and scepticism about the motives for and outcomes of large-scale reforms. Alternatively, policy may reflect a systematic or heuristic approach; that is, based on national priorities and centralised research and development projects which produce tried and tested courses of study for schools in general. This might be interpreted as an expression of a more radical, socially-conscious set of values.

These examples greatly simplify the idea of styles of development, but are sufficient to bring out a major difficulty: in many countries, such as this, there are instances of both ad hoc and systematic approaches. There certainly are different emphases between countries; for example, between the 'subject-based' and 'good practice' penchant of the Schools Council here, and the cross-curricular and 'applied science' orientation of curriculum development in Sweden. But these differences seem explicable in terms of differing loci and processes of control as much as of shared educational and social values. See also: *curriculum control, politics of the curriculum, knowledge utilisation, strategy of curriculum change, curriculum planning models.*

Further reading

Maclure, S., 'Styles of Curriculum Development', Unit 7 (author: H. McMahon) of Course E 203, Open University Press, 1973.

Centre for Educational Research and Innovation (CERI), 'Handbook on Curriculum Development', OECD, 1975. (See Part 1, ch. 4)

Substitutability There is said to be a high degree of substitutability between two factors of production, if one can be substituted for the other without causing a decline in output. Economists are interested in the extent to which it is possible for employers to substitute labour for capital, or vice versa, and the extent to which workers with different educational qualifications can be substituted for each other. The extent to which employers can substitute less qualified workers for highly educated manpower, if there is a shortage, or a change in relative salary levels, is still a controversial issue in the economics of education. Forecasts of *manpower* requirements usually assume that there is little scope for such substitution, but many other economists challenge this view. (See Part 1, ch. 5)

Summative evaluation Summative evaluation takes its meaning through its distinction from formative evaluation. Whereas the latter provides rapid and constructive feedback while a course of study is being tried out and modified, the former supplies potential adopters of the curriculum with objective information on its finished qualities. Thus summative evaluation is especially important when curriculum development takes place largely through centralised research, development and diffusion (RD & D) projects. However, the contrast between formative and summative evaluation loses some of its force in practice. It is very difficult to make fair comparisons between a new curriculum and an existing curriculum; and complex decisions have to be made about how the new course may be adapted to the existing school context. Thus a summative evaluation may have a formative function within curriculum practices. But the distinction has value in sharpening analysis of the kind of decisions that evaluation is to guide. See also: *curriculum evaluation*, *implementation*, *styles of curriculum development*.
Further reading
L. Cronbach, Course Improvement through Evaluation, in M. Golby (ed.), 'Curriculum Design', Croom Helm, 1975. (See Part 1, ch. 4)

Sunday School In December 1783 Robert Raikes inserted the following announcement in the Gloucester Journal:

> Farmers and other inhabitants of the towns and villages complain that they receive more injury to their property on the Sabbath than all the week besides: this, in a great measure, proceeds from the lawless state of the younger class, who are allowed to run wild on that day, free from every restraint.

Unlike a few pioneers who had been running Sunday Schools from the 1760s, Raikes was such a successful publicist that he is generally accepted as the effective founder of a movement credited with 200,000 pupils by 1786. Not only did working children have an opportunity of learning to read their Bibles on Sundays, but the schools also had the merit, in the eyes of their social superiors, of teaching the children to spend their leisure time profitably.

> Thanks for Thy work, and for Thy day,
> And Grant us, we implore,
> Never to waste in sinful play
> Thy holy Sabbaths more. (William Cowper, 1731–1800)

Initially the schools attracted adults as well as children by giving rudimentary teaching in the three Rs, especially in learning to read the Bible. The emphasis on secular education with additional meetings at night during the week was probably longest lasting in the Lancashire textile towns. With the rise of day schools the Sunday School curriculum became less secular and eventually concentrated on religious education.
Further reading
Laqueur, T. W., 'Religion and Respectability: Sunday Schools and Working-Class Culture, 1780–1850', Yale University Press, 1976.
Rodgers, B., 'Cloak of Charity: Studies in Eighteenth Century Philanthropy', Methuen, 1949. (See Part 1, ch. 10)

Supervisory management Supervisory management is concerned with managing a particular area of work, and has only limited involvement with the setting of *objectives*, planning and implementing roles of *management*. However, most supervisors are involved in target setting for immediate work results, resourcing their work groups, progressing work, and so on. As technology advances, the role of the supervisor in facilitating work is developing rapidly, and the traditional, discipline-based role decreasing. This means a very considerable shift in the education and training needs of men and women working in supervision.

The major institution catering for supervisors is the Institute of Supervisory Management. This body aims to raise the standards and aid the development of supervisory management in industry, trade and commerce. It has a substantial organisation through its regional, district and company membership activities. It is heavily involved in such activities as advising industrial film-makers ('The Man in the Front Line', made by Cygnet Guild Films, is probably the best contemporary film on supervisory management). The ISM has a number of membership grades, most of them requiring a satisfactory standard of academic qualification as well as experience. It approves exam-inations, including its own Certificate in Supervisory Management, the General Certificate of the *National Examinations Board in Supervisory Studies*, and its own Diploma in Supervisory Management Studies. Certain company-based education and training schemes are also approved. (See Part 1, ch. 12)

Support system Most curriculum development requires teachers to modify practices which have become well adapted to classroom and school constraints. Thus teachers need several related forms of support if they are to implement a major curriculum innovation. They may need to encounter its underlying ideas outside their immediate working environment, in a 'temporary system' which provides time to reflect; they may need both material help and advice through collaborative planning and consultancy. The most important influence on the lapsing or sustaining of an innovation may be the incentive system as mediated by key agencies such as *examining boards*. (See Part 1, ch. 4)

Sylbs and Sylfs Some students are syllabus-bound (sylbs) in their approach to study. They are almost exclusively concerned with getting good examination marks and happily accept the restrictions on their approach to study that results from a formal syllabus. Syllabus-free students (sylfs) have intellectual interests that extend far beyond the syllabus and often have difficulty in confining their study to the requirements of a formal, tightly structured course.

Further reading
Parlett, M. R., The Syllabus-Bound Student, in L. Hudson (ed.), 'The Ecology of Human Intelligence', Penguin, 1970. (See Part 1, ch. 14)

Symbolic interactionism The long-established American theory of symbolic interactionism was given a new impetus in the 1960s because of a growing reaction against *structural-functionalism*. The anti-structural-functionalist orientation it developed is neatly conveyed by Herbert Blumer's barbed comment in 'Sociological Implications of the Thought of George Herbert Mead', published in the 'American Journal of Sociology' in 1966, that social interaction is an interaction not between *roles* but between people. Blumer is led by his polarisation of the two theories to depict each in extreme terms, and to play down those aspects of symbolic interactionist thinking that shared any common ground with structural-functionalism. Not all symbolic inter-actionists followed him in this.

For symbolic interactionists generally, interaction is symbolic by virtue of the human ability which Mead calls taking the attitude of the other. This ability enables actions to have a similar meaning for each actor alike. It also involves each in interpreting his social world and in actively conducting his side of any interaction with the aid of the meanings he constructs. For this reason, it is important that the sociologist should study symbolic interaction not from the position of an outside, detached observer but from the position of an actor within it, discovering its meanings by interpreting it as an ongoing process no less than its participants do.

In the study of schooling, this approach has led especially to an investi-gation through participant observation of the way in which pupils construct their interactions in school. See, for example, David Hargreaves's study, 'Social Relations in a Secondary School' (1967). The work of Howard Becker and his associates in America has provided a model for this form of investigation.

Further reading

Rose, A. (ed.), 'Human Behaviour and Social Processes', Houghton Mifflin, 1962.

Hargreaves, D., Whatever Happened to Symbolic Interactionism? in L. Barton and R. Meighan, 'Sociological Interpretations of Schooling and Class-rooms: A Reappraisal', Nafferton Books, 1978. (See Part 1, ch. 15)

Systematic A term which has been derived from industry and commerce. It is used mainly in curriculum development and educational technology. Usually it means a checking of input and output and evaluation of objectives, meth-ods, testing all in relation to one another. (See Part 1, ch. 8)

Systematic training Many people may be surprised to learn that this has only relatively recently become a standard element in organisations. As business and industry have become more complex the need to train people to perform well has become more important, and this has led to Government enacting legislation to encourage systematic approaches. The precise format of sys-tematic training varies, but it is possible to generalise sensibly. The process consists of applying a series of logical steps to produce a planned basis for training. There are usually four principal steps.

Step 1: identify what training is needed. This is achieved by using analytical techniques (like *training within industry*) to determine the nature of the jobs to be trained for. It is most important that this is carried out with the appropriate managers and where possible experienced job holders.

Step 2: plan the necessary training. Once a *training needs analysis* is available the trainer and the manager concerned devise a programme (aims, contents and method) together with necessary costings.

Step 3: carry out the training. This implements the decisions made in Step 2, but with sufficient flexibility to allow for the individual's learning abilities.

Step 4: validation, evaluation and review. Validation is the process by which we test whether the training programme met its objectives. Evaluation is the process by which we seek to establish that learning is carried through to job performance. (For a fuller discussion, see *evaluation of management training*.) Review is the means by which the results of validation and evalu-ation are fed back to improve the actual training programme.

Some writers include development of training policy as part of the systematic training process; others argue that the training process is the means by which policy is carried out.

Further reading

The appropriate chapters of 'Manpower Training and Development', J. P. J. Kenny and E. L. Donnelly, Harrap, 1972. (See Part 1, ch. 12)

Systems approach A systems approach to education implies an analysis of the process into a series of systematic steps which lead to the achievement of the desired goals. Broadly speaking there are three steps in the process: (i) defining the objectives of a piece of instruction; (ii) selecting the appropriate methods and techniques; and (iii) evaluation to see if the objectives have been achieved. A simple example to illustrate this would be learning how to fire an arrow from a bow. By examining the process systematically, it is possible to specify the steps required to reach a specific goal and hence to handle the bow and arrow effectively. The goal could be set and hence the objectives of the instruction given as the need to hit the bullseye on a given target nine times out of ten with an arrow fired from the bow at a distance of 20 yards. In this case the method is obvious, that is, rather than just read about the process or be told about it, the student should practise with a bow and arrow with help and advice from his instructor. Evaluation and success of the instruction comes when the student can consistently achieve nine hits out of ten. (See Part 1, ch. 9)

Tape/slide These are usually a combination of a 35mm *slide* sequence projected in synchronisation with an audio tape recording. *Audio tape recorders* are often used for this purpose, linked to an automatic slide projector. One track of the tape is used to produce a pulse which activates the slide projector. Tape/slide materials can be used in a variety of ways for self-instructional methods or for group work. If some form of dual projection is used, then animation and fading from one picture to another can be achieved. (See Part 1, ch. 9)

Task analysis In order to carry out some learning tasks, it is useful to identify the skills and knowledge required. There are particular procedures (task analysis) using checklists and charts which enable a careful analysis to be carried out. (See Part 1, ch. 8)

Taxonomy of objectives The purpose of a taxonomy of educational *objectives* is to provide teachers, examiners, etc. with a classification of goals of learning that will give *curriculum planning*, assessment and discussion of them greater precision. The idea is particularly associated with Bloom's work in the 'cognitive domain' of learning. This divides into sub-divisions of knowledge, comprehension, application, analysis, synthesis and evaluation. The objectives of each class are specified procedurally as the mental processes that the student can have mastered; for example, to extrapolate from given information, or to synthesise proposals into plans. A particular use of the taxonomy is to ensure that an appropriate emphasis is placed in the curriculum on each class of objectives, especially higher-order objectives which are more difficult to teach and examine. There is a much less used taxonomy of objectives in the 'affective domain', which provides a hierarchical structure in terms of *attitudes*, values, and emotions.

Further reading

Bloom, B. S. (ed), 'Taxonomy of Educational Objectives, Handbook I: Cognitive Domain', McKray, 1956.

Krathwohl, D. R., Bloom, B. S. and Masia, B. B., 'Taxonomy of Educational Objectives Handbook, II: Affective Domain', McKay, 1956. (See Part 1, ch. 4)

Teachers' unions and professional associations A number of organisations have been formed to protect the interests of various groups of teachers and administrators within education. Of these, some are part of the Trades Union Congress, whilst others choose non-affiliation. Organisations exist to represent teachers at all levels of education, including colleges of education. (See Part 1, ch. 7)

Teacher training The British and Foreign School Society's Borough Road Training College, founded in 1809, can claim to be the oldest. The National Society's Central School in Baldwin's Gardens, off Gray's Inn Road, began three years later. Lack of funds meant that the early students received a short and rudimentary training (see *monitorial system*). By the mid-1840s the National Society, which had recently established over a dozen more training colleges, was in financial difficulties, making it possible for the *Committee of the Privy Council on Education* to introduce a series of grants to support intending teachers both at school and training college. These developments set the pattern of training for elementary and primary school teachers for over a century. They attended monotechnic institutions devoted to one form of vocational training. Conditions remained primitive and discipline paternalistically oppressive for much of the century. Not until the 1890s, when day training departments were opened in certain universities, did students have an opportunity of attending a secular institution offering wider intellectual horizons than a residential training college with a heavy emphasis on religious instruction. In contrast, grammar school teachers were university graduates who before the 1970s did not even have to follow a training course in teaching. In an attempt to remedy the disparity between the two types of teachers, the Department of Education and Science lengthened the training course in colleges from two to three years from 1960 onwards and introduced the BEd degree in 1964, the first step towards making teaching an all-graduate profession, a target expected to be met from 1984 onwards.
Further reading
Dent, H. C., 'The Training of Teachers in England and Wales, 1800–1975', Hodder & Stoughton, 1977, provides a brief outline.
Hurt, J., Education in Evolution', Rupert Hart-Davis, 1971.
Jones, L. G. E., 'The Training of Teachers in England and Wales', Oxford University Press, 1924.
Rich, R. W., 'The Training of Teachers in England and Wales During the Nineteenth Century', Cambridge University Press, 1933. (See Part 1, ch. 10)

Teaching/learning methods Teaching and learning are processes in the education of a student which require interaction between the teacher and the student. In the past teaching methods were often thought of in terms mainly of the need to impart information to the student and little was done to investigate or help the learning process. Now there is available a variety of teaching/learning methods which range from the giving of information from one teacher to a large group of students, to small group interactions and individualised methods where the student may be working in a self-teaching situation, controlling his own intake of information and testing himself. See also: *individualised instruction*, *self-teaching techniques*, *games and simulations*, *programmed learning*.

T

Further reading

Entwistle, N. and Hounsell, D. (eds), 'How Students Learn', Institute for Research and Development in Post-Compulsory Education, University of Lancaster, 1975.

MacKenzie, N., Postgate, R. and Scuphern, J., 'Teaching and Learning: an introduction to new methods and resources in higher education', 2nd ed., UNESCO, 1976. (See Part 1, ch. 9)

Team teaching This is a concept which originated in the USA. It may be defined as a form of organisation in which two or more teachers working together are given responsibility for all, or a significant part of, the education of the same group of pupils. In its pure form the basic principle is that the staff work as a co-ordinated team under the direction of a team leader who allocates the teaching load and co-ordinates the work of the staff. The teaching group will vary in size and composition according to the nature of the activity, and the special qualifications and talents of the teachers will be used to best advantage. Team teaching in this sense is a highly organised activity demanding the total co-operation of the teachers, the sharing of ideas and the evolution of common methods of working.

Team teaching as described above is often modified or adapted to different situations, when it is sometimes known as co-operative teaching. There are situations where two or more teachers jointly plan their work (usually with classes of similar age) to make wider use of their individual specialisms. This can involve the sharing to varying degrees of resources, equipment and space, without, however, abandoning the traditional concept of the class and class teacher. (See Part 1, ch. 1)

Technical and scientific instruction In 1851 Great Britain won the palm of excellence in nearly all the 100 or so departments of the Great Exhibition. Even at this moment of triumph some argued that the maintenance of Britain's manufacturing leadership depended on the provision of adequate scientific and technical education. In 1859 the newly-created *Science and Art Department* started to offer grants for the teaching of science. Britain's showing at the 1867 Paris exhibition, where she won only 10 top prizes out of 90 departments, provided such propagandists as *Henry Cole* and *Lyon Playfair* with further ammunition. Although the Taunton Commission (1864–7) took some evidence on the matter at Playfair's behest the important enquiries were those of the 1867 Select Committee, and the Royal Commissions of 1871–5 and 1882–4. In a free-trade era the idea that the Government should assist technological instruction and the teaching of trade practices was opposed by businessmen, fearing that the state might set up rival manufactories, and by skilled artisans, who feared the dilution of labour. The state's role in teaching trade practice was confined to the armed forces and the state arsenals. Thus the 1889 Technical Instruction Act allowed the county and county borough councils, formed the previous year, to levy a rate for teaching scientific principles but excluded instruction in trade and industrial practice. '*Whisky money*' was granted the following year on similar terms. The breakthrough, however, had already come to the Polytechnic, Regent Street, where trades were taught in an institution partly financed from private sources, the Parochial Charities Act 1883, and the *City and Guilds of London Institute*.

Further reading

Argles, M., 'South Kensington to Robbins', Longmans, 1964.

Bell, Q., 'The Schools of Design', Routledge & Kegan Paul, 1963.

Cotgrove, S., 'Technical Education and Social Change', Allen & Unwin, 1958.

Sanderson, M., 'The Universities and British Industry, 1850–1970', Routledge & Kegan Paul, 1972. (See Part 1, ch. 10)

Technical Education and Training Organisation for Overseas Countries (TETOC) During the past few years it has become clear that industrial education and training is a valuable invisible export for the UK, either in the form of students coming to this country to acquire skills and knowledge or in the form of educators and trainers running programmes overseas. British technical and industrial training is widely admired and imitated. An aspect of this is industrial and technical education and training as an instrument of policy. TETOC is a specialist agency of the Ministry of Overseas Development (ODM) and acts as its primary source of specialist, professional advice on overseas aid in technical education, agricultural education and training, industrial administration and management development.

TETOC is directed by a Board of Governors (all appointed by the ODM) and controlled by a Director General. It helps to diagnose overseas needs, identifies resources in the UK which can meet those needs, and matches the two. It has responsibilities for monitoring the results of this work and developing means to improve the UK contribution to those nations overseas using the services of TETOC.

TETOC works by planning, developing and monitoring programmes and projects, recruiting staff (a constant problem because of the general supply shortfall in the UK of technicians and technologists) and building links between institutions at home and overseas. TETOC is also responsible for arranging training programmes and courses both in the UK and overseas. The organisation works closely with the British Council and UK diplomats overseas.

It is perhaps unfortuante that current economic stringencies may adversely affect this work. Apart from the value of representing Britain, TETOC, the British Council and other similar organisations undoubtedly create substantial markets for British education and training. Further information can be had from H. H. Stewart, Director General, TETOC, Dacre House, 17-19 Dacre Street, London SW1. (See Part 1, ch. 11)

Technician Technicians, according to the Committee on Manpower Resources for Science and Technology, are those skilled people with an understanding of general principles in their specialisation who occupy a position between the scientist, engineer or *technologist* and the skilled craftsman. There are non-industrial technicians who, according to the Haslegrove Committee, have acquired very considerable expertise in a specialist field or less detailed knowledge and skills in several fields. Wherever they work, technicians seem to require education and training to cope with three distinct roles.

First, the technician is a decision-maker, relying to a very large extent on his discretion. This considerably influences elements of the firm, like the quality of the product, efficiency of machinery and plant and the effectiveness of production areas. He can, if he is wrong, cause a great deal of lost effort, output and money. Second, he is nearly always an adviser to managers. He supplies data, makes recommendations and can by the way he assembles and discriminates technical information influence managerial decisions. Third, he is nearly always a skilled practitioner with a range of techniques available to him in his chosen technical field.

Many entrants to technician-level careers now have A-levels and begin their education and training at 18-plus. It is still possible to enter at an earlier age. Apprenticeship schemes often give the chance of transfer to a technicians scheme.

The patterns of education and training now emerging owe a great deal to the work of bodies like the *City and Guilds of London Institute* and latterly the *Technician Education Council*. The essence of most programmes is to produce people capable of exercising technical judgment rather than relying on established practice. Diagnostic and analytical skills are of prime importance. (See Part 1, ch. 11)

Technician Education Council (TEC) and Scottish Technician Education Council (SCOTEC) This independent organisation was established in 1973 by the Secretary of State for Education and Science. It is charged with the development of policies for national technical education schemes for all levels of technicians in industry and elsewhere. It plans, administers and keeps under review the development of a unified national system of technician-level courses. It is not primarily an examining body but is responsible for the arrangements for assessing students by devising or appraising suitable courses, establishing and assessing standards of performance, and awarding certificates and diplomas. It validates courses submitted by colleges of *further* and *higher education* including the provisions of assessment schemes and external moderation. The Council's administration is handled by the *City and Guilds of London Institute*. A rational and simplified range of courses is gradually emerging from the work of TEC. It now offers four awards: Certificate, Diploma, Higher Certificate and Higher Diploma, which are progressively replacing the National and Higher National Diplomas, and the technician courses. TEC programmes use a flexible unit system of study and are offered *full-time*, part-time, *block release* or sandwich courses.

SCOTEC is the parallel institution, also established in 1973, for technicians' courses in Scotland. For further information contact: TEC, 76 Portland Place, London W1N 4AA; 01–580 3050; or SCOTEC, 38 Queen Street, Glasgow G1 30Y; 041–204 2271 (See Part 1, ch. 11)

Technologists Technologists are usually qualified engineers or applied scientists. Their work involves design, planning and management, and depends on the support of technicians and at lower levels on craftsmen and operatives.

Nearly all authorities lay great stress on the level of education needed for technologists. They are generally required to have studied the fundamental principles of a particular technology. They should be able to apply their skills, knowledge and experience to practical developments. They are expected to accept high responsibilities and sometimes to contribute genuinely new knowledge in their particular field. There are requirements of technologists other than academic and educational attainments. They are not only highly educated narrow specialists but often members of a multi-disciplinary team which places requirements on them for social and *inter-active skills*. Far too many academic courses ignore this vital element of the technologists' work and most organisations find they need to provide lengthy periods of initial in-company training.

Technologists are in short supply in the UK. It has been estimated that there are currently around 500,000, using the definition above, but that the employers need at least a quarter more. Some of the major UK engineering companies report persistent shortfalls in their technologist recruitment programmes.

Most technologists are now educated through sandwich courses, either thick or thin. Thick sandwich courses usually involve a three-year degree course with one year in industry; and the thin sandwich is a four-year course with alternating six-month periods in industry and in education. The *CNAA* (Council for National Academic Awards) is now very influential in sandwich-course development, and for all their courses the industrial experience must aggregate at least one year.

Technologists have been subjected to a great deal of attention in recent years, as Government, industry and education have tried to solve the supply problem. Unfortunately, the UK as a society does not give technologists very high status nor adequate financial rewards, so that it is unlikely in the short term that supply will match demand. (See Part 1, ch. 11)

Television Like *film*, television presents a projected representation of reality and can be used to present the past, the present and the future. It can generally be used in many of the ways in which film can, but it differs from film in certain fundamental respects. Unlike film, television pictures are usually confined to a relatively small screen and cannot achieve the quality of the film image because of the relative lack of definition of the scanning method by which the picture is formed. Simplicity and immediacy are two of the main characteristics of the television image. (See Part 1, ch. 9)

Terminal This usually consists of a keyboard like a typewriter connected to a computer. Someone wishing to use the computer types messages on the keyboard and these are transmitted to the computer. The terminal can also incorporate a video screen or printer so that output from the computer can be displayed on the screen or printed out on paper. (See Part 1, ch. 9)

Tertiary college Unlike a *sixth form college*, this is not a school but an establishment of further education which provides for all post-16 education in an area, ranging from A-level courses to full and part-time further education and vocational courses. (See Part 1, ch. 1)

Test A test is a compact task or series of tasks designed to ascertain the merit or quantity of something. The driving test is a test for which there is no graduation other than pass or fail. Other 'tests' such as an athletics event provide a very accurate ranking of people. Educational tests constitute a series of *items* for which a *score* is obtained. Depending on how they are constructed, they can serve either of the purposes above. (See Part 1, ch. 6)

T-group These highly participative methods aim to improve people's skills in working with others. Genuine T-groups are structureless, leaderless (in the formal, appointed sense) and taskless except that the study of the behaviour of the group itself is the task. The key study of the behaviour of the group itself is the task. The key study question is: what is happening in the here and now? Originally a therapeutic tool, it enjoyed a vogue in the middle and late 1960s. It is now another tool trainers use, but because of its intensive nature the role of consultant to the group is critical. A deep understanding of individual and group psychology is necessary. (See Part 1, ch. 12)

Theories of learning Psychologists have been concerned with learning since psychology became an experimental science during the closing decades of the nineteenth century. Although many of the psychologists who have investigated human *learning* have held some assumptions in common about how the learning process should be conceptualised, the variations between different *schools of psychology* have often been very great. At the present time there is no single, comprehensive, closely integrated theoretical account of how the full complexity of human learning comes about.

During the first half of the twentieth century very different ways of thinking about learning developed, in particular those of the stimulus-response associationists, the Gestalt psychologists and the *behaviourists*. The stimulus-response associationists, in particular E. L. Thorndike, were concerned to identify the successive steps in learning. Thorndike formulated the law of effect, which says that acts followed by a state of affairs which the individual does not avoid and which he often tries to preserve or attain, are selected or fixated, to account for the way in which specific responses become linked with specific stimuli. The Gestalt psychologists took the view that successful learning resulted from the learner integrating and organising in new ways what was perceived or studied. Many of their ideas have been adopted by cognitive learning theorists. Psychologists working within the behaviourist tradition regard observable behaviour as the sole permissible data from psychology and have argued that learning should be defined in operational terms. Two major areas of learning have been explored by the behaviourists: *classical conditioning* and *operant conditioning*.

Many contemporary psychologists do not adhere to one theoretical approach but are eclectic. The work of R. M. *Gagné* is an interesting example of an attempt to integrate different theoretical approaches to learning. See also: *cognitive approaches to learning*; *motivation*; *learning, retention and recall*.

Further reading

Borger, R. and Seaborne, A. E. M., 'The Psychology of Learning', Penguin, 1966.

Gagné, R. M., 'The Conditions of Learning', 3rd ed., Holt, Rinehart & Winston, 1977. (See Part 1, ch. 14)

Theory There is a considerable difference between the way in which the word 'theory' functions in common speech and the way it is applied in the physical sciences. In ordinary language it can be used as a synonym for moonshine. In the physical sciences a 'theory' is used in order to make accurate predictions, even though scientists would dispute that their theories were 'true'. The point is: should an 'educational theory' be afforded the scepticism given to the word 'theory' in ordinary language or the respect afforded a theory in science? O'Connor has suggested that in education the word 'theory' is a 'courtesy title' and should not therefore be considered in the same way as in physical theories. Hirst has criticised O'Connor for taking his standard use of the word 'theory' from the sciences. The word 'theory' has a legitimate use in education. However, despite Hirst's objection, O'Connor's point would seem to stand. It is part of the philosopher's task to point out how the same word may function differently within different contexts. The more willing educationalists become to see themselves as parasitic on the social sciences, the greater the danger of confusing educational theories with psychological theories. Scientific theories demand quantitative analysis; so that any theory which cannot be usefully employed in this way cannot be understood as a scientific theory.

Further reading

O'Connor, D. J., 'An Introduction to the Philosophy of Education', Routledge & Kegan Paul, 1957.

Hirst, P. H., Philosophy and Educational Theory, in 'British Journal of Educational Studies', vol. 12, pp. 51–64, 1963.

Smart, P. B., Education: an Art or a Science? in 'Proceedings of the Philosophy of Education Society of Great Britain', vol. 8, pp. 61–75, 1974.

Scheffler, I., Is Education a Discipline? in 'Philosophy and Education' (ed. Scheffler), Allyn and Bacon, 2nd ed., 1966. (See Part 1, ch. 13)

Thurstone scale The scale is used to determine *attitudes*. Statements in interviews from individuals relating to the topic under consideration are collected: e.g., learning is exciting; learning is sometimes interesting; learning is a waste of time. The statements are short and open to only one interpretation. The statements are classified by judges into favourable, neutral or hostile. Each group is further sub-divided. The most relevant, least ambiguous set of statements which covers the whole range of values is chosen. The student selects statements which agree with his feelings. (See Part 1, ch. 8)

Trades Union Congress The Trades Union movement policy on education is made at national level through the Congress and the Executive but is carried out at regional and local levels by TUC Regional Councils and Trades Councils (See Part 1, ch. 7)

Training There is no clear line between education and training. Some suggested differentiations can be made. *Education* deals a great deal with the acquisition of *knowledge*. Training deals more with the application of knowledge. Thus, within one learning system, we can find elements of both.

It is also possible to argue that training is primarily a modifying process, through which behaviour in particular is changed in desirable directions. There are philosophic difficulties here, raised by the word 'desirable'. Desirable to whom, the trainer or the trainee? However, in most organisations, it is held that training is a process aimed at preparing people for jobs, helping them improve their performance and developing their potentials to the fullest. Training systems usually include *off-job* and *on-job* schemes. Methodologies and techniques develop rapidly and tend to be fashion-conscious, as with *programmed learning*. What remains clear is that a good master-pupil relationship continues to be an effective means of transmitting skills: this is the basis of all apprenticeship systems. For knowledge, conventional teaching techniques have limitations but are nevertheless extensively used. For attitude change (a frequently mentioned training requirement) there are many suggested techniques, none of them wholly successful.

In summary, it may be said that training is a process using a wide range of techniques to modify attitude, knowledge or skill behaviour so as to achieve effective performance (usually defined as experienced worker standard) in a particular task or set of tasks. It tends to be results-oriented, although within this constraint much training emphasises the development of individual abilities. It is usually part of a *manpower planning* system, as its prime function must be to provide the trained people the organisation needs to achieve its purpose. (See Part 1, ch. 2)

Training and Further Education Consultative Group Advisory to the further education field and providing the link with training, this group contains representatives from education authorities, colleges of *further education*, the *Confederation of British Industry*, the *Trades Union Congress*, the *Manpower Services Commission*, *examining bodies* and *Industrial Training Boards*. (See Part 1, ch. 7)

Training needs analysis Several of the entries have dealt with various techniques of analysis that lead to the preparation of training programmes. In this entry, we will attempt to provide an overview.

Kenny and Donnelly distinguish between macro (organisation-wide) and micro (individual job-based) analyses. Macro-analysis deals broadly with the organisation, parts of the organisation (such as a department), or groups within the organisation (like all financial accountants). The macro approach is very closely related to *manpower planning*. The present and future of the organisation are examined (often nowadays through corporate forecasting and planning techniques) and estimates prepared of the necessary manpower to enable business objectives to be met. The manpower estimates are then broken down into a plan which identifies the numbers and categories of staff and, amongst them, those who will need training or *re-training*.

Certain issues arise for the trainer. If he is to perform macro-analysis properly he needs access to and involvement in the organisation's planning processes. If he does not have this he is working blind and cannot produce proper budgets, training programmes or effective results. The trainer also needs an understanding of manpower planning techniques and a close relationship with his organisation's specialists in this, if such persons exist. If they do not, the trainer will have to exercise some of these functions.

Micro-analysis is the process by which the training needed for the effective performance of a particular job is identified. It must obviously be within the constraints of the macro-analysis, but it concentrates on the skill and knowledge required by particular jobs, together with assessments of the present competence of the job holders. (See Part 1, ch. 11)

Training Services Division (TSD) The Training Services Division was set up in 1974 under the Employment and Training Act 1973. It is now one of the three operational branches of the *Manpower Services Commission*. Amongst its aims is that of increasing the efficiency and effectiveness of training. The field organisation of TSD is based on seven regions covering the UK. Because of its relevance to post-school and further education training the TSD has close working links with a great many organisations within both the formal and informal education system. The MSC is currently reorganising its structure.

The entry on the *Manpower Services Commission* states that the TSD is an operating division with wide-ranging responsibilities, such as the Training Opportunities (TOPS) scheme and the *Industry Training Boards*. In this section, that part of the TSD known as the Directorate of Training will be examined, because of its apparent importance to practising trainers and educators.

The overall aim of the Directorate of Training is to ensure that nationally important needs are met for providing training knowledge and professional advice. In fact, one of the Directorate's own publications says its aims are 'to help improve the efficiency and effectiveness of training in Great Britain'. To achieve this it carries out or supports a wide range of activities. It has, for instance, been deeply involved with the Industrial Training Research Unit at Cambridge; it works closely with the *Industriy Training Boards* (ITBs). Some of the Directorate's current concerns are of interest. As an example, it is examining the training of trainers in considerable detail. Its first report on this was interesting, perhaps even exciting, and a number of developments are taking place that will undoubtedly improve the status and professional skills of trainers. However, the initial impetus has slowed considerably and recent reports suggest an over-attention to detail rather than the broad approach. It seems sensible to proceed with the development of guiding principles from which other bodies can design the appropriate and detailed educational and training programmes.

The Directorate provides help and advice on office training, health and safety training, management development, and so on. It produces very large amounts of reports and papers. But after six years it seems reasonable to ask what all the money, all the time, all the paper and all the effort has actually produced. Further information from the MSC, Moorfoot, Sheffield S1 4PQ. (See Part 1, ch. 11)

Training within industry (TWI) 'The training within industry scheme for supervisors' (TWI) has as its aim the training of supervisors in the broad principles of good management (C. Mee, 'Training within Industry', Department of Employment, HMSO). TWI was launched in the USA in 1940 and brought to the UK in the Second World War to aid the substantial training effort needed for the improvements in productivity demanded by the national emergency. Since 1945 it has become a widely accepted method of training. The term TWI now is used to describe two principal activities.

First, TWI is a series of courses designed to develop the skills of supervision. Group discussion is used to identify general principles, which are explored through practical application in a series of exercises and case studies. The contents are firmly based on problems within the experience of course members. The courses are conducted by TWI training officers of the *Training Services Division* (TSD), or by trainers trained and qualified by the TSD. The four basic courses are: job instructions and communications (JIC); job relations (JR); job safety (JS) and job methods (JM), designed as interlocking modules. For further information, contact MSC, Moorfoot, Sheffield S1 4PQ.

Second, TWI has by extension become a term to describe a particular technique to enable job skills and knowledge to be analysed and recorded for training purposes. The technique is best applied to jobs with relatively short learning times (hours or days rather than weeks). It can be used for the simple parts of other tasks, but not where they are complex. For further details, consult *Industry Training Boards*. (See Part 1, ch. 11)

Trait A trait is a characteristic of an individual. It can be cognitive, emotional, part of the personality, or behavioural. It is therefore little used in educational measurement, which concentrates on description of attainment. However, psychological measurement, which concentrates more on underlying attributes, is more often concerned with the measurement of traits. (See Part 1, ch. 6)

Transport The LEA is obliged under the Act to arrange free transport to schools, where pupils under eight years of age have to travel over two miles and older pupils over three miles. (See Part 1, ch. 1)

Tripartite system During the inter-war years there was a largely successful attempt to replace the separate elementary and secondary school systems with an end-on one, thereby meeting the demand of R. H. Tawney's famous book, 'Secondary Education for All' (1922). The Hadow Committee's report, 'The Education of the Adolescent' (1926) recommended a break at the age of 11 between the primary or elementary school and the secondary one. There were to be two types of secondary school: the *grammar school* and the modern. Where reorganisation was difficult (for example, in sparsely populated rural areas) the upper classes of the elementary school were to be called 'senior classes'. A common criticism of later developments was that they amounted to little more than the relabelling of existing schools. The Spens Report 'Secondary Education' (1938) went a stage further by recommending a third type of secondary school, the technical high school. By this time some two-thirds of all children of secondary-school age were in reor-

275

ganised schools. The Norwood Report 'Curriculum and Examinations in Secondary Schools' (1943) classified children into three groups that fitted conveniently into the three types of school in existence. Under the post-war Labour Government the Ministry of Education in its first pamphlet 'The Nation's Schools: Their Plan and Purpose' (1945) accepted the tripartite system, declaring that the most urgent reform the Local Authorities faced was that of completing the Hadow reorganisation. (See Part 1, ch. 10)

Tyler rationale Tyler's book 'Basic Principles of Curriculum and Instruction' formulated a framework of four central questions which, he argued, demand answers for *curriculum planning* to proceed rationally: (1) what educational purposes should schools pursue? (2) what learning experiences can be provided that are likely to attain these purposes? (3) how can these experiences be organised? (4) how can we decide whether these purposes are being attained? The questions imply that planning the curriculum can be a controlled, logical process, of which the first step is the most important. The framework has been very influential in the USA, where major decisions about curriculum content are made by local boards of education. This framework makes public evaluation of the work of schools possible through comparison of *objectives* with discernible outcomes. (See Part 1, ch. 4)

Type of study The type of study used by comparativists tends to reflect the scope, the interest, and the purposes of the individual and the institutions he serves. *Area studies* are one of the most frequently used types, while cross-cultural studies provide a second format. The latter may follow one of a number of patterns. They may be global, such as UNESCO's World Surveys of Education (and such mammoth tasks are more properly carried out by international organisations which have the duty and the resources to carry though these projects). Another variation is the inter-regional type of study, which involves comparisons between a group of countries in one region and a group of countries in another. An example of this format is Thut and Adam's 'Problems in Contemporary Societies' (1964). Other cross-cultural studies are solely regional in scope.

Cross-cultural studies do not always involve total analysis, and, for reasons of economy of study, scholars focus on the more relevant *data*, factors, processes and *ideologies* in their comparisons. Yet another format is the case study. This involves investigation in depth of particular groups, institutions or problems. A good example of the case study is OECD's 'Case Studies of Innovation'. Cross-cultural studies involve comparison of education and society at one point in time with their relationship at a different point.
Further reading
Bristow, T. and Holmes, B., 'Comparative Education throughout the Literature', Butterworth, 1966. (See Part 1, ch. 3)

UNESCO United Nations Educational, Scientific and Cultural Organisation, founded in 1945, has made a considerable impact on the work of comparative educators. UNESCO has promoted conferences and meetings of experts, supported projects, stimulated research, and commissioned consultancy services and comparative publications. It has also been engaged in educational planning through one of its agencies, the *International Institute of Educational Planning*, curriculum development and *agricultural extension* projects. It has established regional offices in many countries. It has co-operated with other international agencies such as the *International Association of Universities*.

The *International Bureau of Education* acts as a documentation centre for UNESCO, the parent body. UNESCO has been responsible for publishing the monumental World Survey of Education, a four-volume work devoted to primary, secondary and higher education. Each volume contains data from all members of the United Nations Organisation and their dependent territories. Each education system is described in brief and its structure represented diagrammatically. Tabular materials are provided giving details of the number and type of institutions and the student and staffing enrolment figures at the various levels. UNESCO published an annual statistical review of educational systems as well as a wide-ranging series of publications of considerable interest to comparativists. (See Part 1, ch. 3)

Unified vocational preparation (UVP) A substantial proportion of boys enter working life through *apprenticeship*, but for the majority there are limited opportunities for such formal schemes. Vocational preparation is an attempt to meet their needs.

Basically, vocational preparation is designed to give a systematic preparation for working life. It aims to promote improved performance at work, personal adaptability and personal development. The process should begin at school, and particularly in the last year. The school system can provide only some elements; and for the full aims to be met it is necessary to have a fully structured programme of education and training based on experience of a job or, for the young unemployed, through the Manpower Services Commission's work experience programmes. Off-job learning is an integral part of such schemes.

Unified vocational preparation has at present two meanings, one general, one specific to a particular programme. One refers to schemes combining direct job training and off-job *further education* to help young people going into jobs at below craft level. They are designed to fulfil the aims outlined above, together with providing a better means of adjustment to adult working life. The other is the Government-sponsored and financed pilot schemes of unified vocation preparation, which began in 1976 for a period of five years. They have been designed to develop, implement and test a variety of designs which are acceptable to both young people and employers. One element which is already regarded as highly successful is the new course that seeks to give young people the numeracy and literacy skills required at work. For further information on the Government schemes, consult the regional offices of the MSC. (See Part 1, ch. 11)

Universities Central Council on Admissions UCCA acts as a clearing house for first-degree and first-diploma course admissions to all UK universities with the exception of the Open University and the University College at Buckingham. Additional information on entrance to Scottish universities can be provided by the Scottish Universities Council on Entrance. A similar clearing house function for entry into teacher training courses at university departments of education, colleges of education, colleges of higher education and polytechnic departments of education is provided by the Central Register and Clearing House Ltd. (See Part 1, ch. 7)

Universities of Oxford and Cambridge In the early nineteenth century dissenters were barred from the degrees, fellowships, and scholarships of both universities, whose main function was the training of clergy for the established Church. Although fellowships at Cambridge were open to competition, only those at Balliol and Oriel were awarded on a competitive basis at Oxford. The introduction of honours schools at Oxford from 1800 onwards and the

U

growing political influence of middle-class dissent and radicalism were amongst the influences that made for reform. After two Royal Commissions had reported, acts of parliament in 1854 and 1856 opened Bachelor's degrees at both universities to dissenters. In 1871 the University Tests Act opened all posts in the universities, with minor exceptions, to dissenters, thus allowing them access to Master's degrees and the government of the universities. Another Royal Commission in 1876 produced an act of the following year releasing Fellows from their obligation to remain celibate.

Despite the 1877 Act's requirement that the universities should support the teaching of science, Oxford remained until 1907 without a professor of engineering. Cambridge, with its long tradition of mathematical teaching, widened its curriculum more rapidly. In 1848 it instituted the natural sciences tripos and was donated the Cavendish Laboratories in the 1870s. Towards the end of the century the development of non-collegiate institutions lowered the cost of a degree from around £600 to half that figure or less, thus breaking down the previous social exclusiveness of the universities and permitting a few boys from an artisan background to take their degrees.

Further reading

Mallett, C. E., A History of the University of Oxford, vol. III, 'Modern Oxford', Longmans, 1927.

Roach, J. P. C., The University of Cambridge, in 'Victorian County History of Cambridgeshire', vol. III, Oxford University Press, 1959.

Winstanley, D. A., 'Early Victorian Cambridge', Cambridge University Press, 1955.

Winstanley, D. A., 'Late Victorian Cambridge', Cambridge University Press, 1947.

(See Part 1, ch. 10)

University Grants Committee (UGC) The University Grants Committee is the body which administered the allocation of the quinquennial grants to British universities. Allocations are now made annually. Though each university retains its autonomy, a large measure of overall policy emanates from the University Grants Committee. (See Part 1, ch. 7)

Utilitarianism An attempt to justify *ethical* judgments by maintaining that an action is morally right if it will increase the amount of happiness in the world. Thus, the theory centres attention on the end of the action and not on the action itself.

Criticisms of this are that: (1) such a theory could foster the notion that the end justifies the means; some acts, it may be insisted, are morally bad, irrespective of any prospective happiness; (2) an inherent problem for utilitarianism has been providing adequate criteria of 'happiness'. Mill, for example, insisted on a 'qualitative' interpretation of happiness: that some kinds of happiness were more worthwhile than others; e.g., that poetry is more worthwhile than pushpin. However, once this is admitted, utilitarianism has been altered to allow for *'intrinsic* goods', or a hierarchy of goods which it would be different to maintain on utilitarianism alone.

Further reading

Bentham, J., 'An Introduction to the Principles of Morals and Legislation: vol. X, Collected Works', Routledge & Kegan Paul, 1969.

Hudson, W. D., 'Modern Moral Philosophy', Macmillan, 1970. (See Part 1, ch. 13)

Valid The philosopher uses the term 'valid' to assess the logical form of an argument and not its truth, so that in logic an argument might be valid but false. In ordinary language, the term is used simply to refer to a 'good' or 'telling' argument or piece of reasoning. (See Part 1, ch. 13)

Validity The most crucial concept in educational measurement is validity. No matter how reliable our *test* or how sophisticated our *scale*, the value of any test rests on the extent to which it measures what it purports to measure. The process of validating any measurement instrument is one of building up a fund of information about how our instrument performs in practice. To understand how this is done consider the following two examples.

We can presume that the first thermometers were constructed after it had been observed that a subjective judgment about increase in temperature coincided with certain objects and liquids increasing in size. Test construction follows from equivalent observations about how certain kinds of behaviour relate to certain outcomes. Writing *items*, however, often relies on simplifying the behaviours from those observed in real life. No one would argue that the real behaviour relating to the ability to reason verbally is far more complex than the process involved in answering verbal reasoning items. In such cases, therefore, the need to obtain validity information is all the greater. The principles involved can be understood by considering a simple validation for the thermometer.

A person can be asked to place his finger in ten bowls of water in order to rank them from hottest to coldest. By marking the mercury level for each bowl a second ranking from highest to lowest can be obtained. If the two rankings coincide we have evidence supporting the hypothesis that our thermometer measures temperature. By obtaining lots of evidence of how our thermometer relates to other independent measures of temperature we are building up evidence for the validity of our instrument. In the same way we see how test *scores* relate to independent measures of the attribute the test was designed to measure.

There is, therefore, no stage at which we can say that an instrument has been fully validated. We can only say that the evidence from particular situations supports its claim to be valid and this evidence can, as in the case of the thermometer, become overwhelming. It is still theoretically always possible that negative evidence will make us adjust our view. (See Part 1, ch. 6)

Validity and reliability To be of use any psychological test must have a high degree of validity and reliability. Validity is a measure of the extent to which the test measures what it is intended to measure. The test's reliability depends upon the extent to which it measures accurately each time it is used.
Further reading
Cronbach, L. J., 'Essentials of Psychological Testing', 3rd ed., Harper & Row, 1970. (See Part 1, ch. 14)

Variance Variance is a measure of variation or dispersion. As such it can be derived from a number of methods. The one which has proved most fruitful so far is

$$\text{Variance} = \frac{\Sigma x^2}{N}$$

where x^2 = the deviation from the mean squared
N   = no. of measurements

The *standard deviation* is obtained by finding the square root of the variance. See also: *measures of dispersion*. (See Part 1, ch. 6)

Verification The principle of providing *empirical* evidence in support of a statement. A scientific statement is held to be verifiable in principle. But no empirical general statement could be conclusively verified, so philosophers prefer to speak not of 'verification' of a hypothesis but of 'confirmation' or 'corroboration'.

Further reading

Ayer, A. J., 'Language, Truth and Logic', Gollancz, 1946.

Popper, K. R., 'Conjectures and Refutations', Routledge & Kegan Paul, 4th ed., 1972. (See Part 1, ch. 13)

Vertical (or family) grouping This is a form of class organisation found in primary schools, more especially among the infants. A class is formed of children in a two- or three-year age range (say ages 5 to 7), so that a teacher is responsible for a 'family' of different ages and different abilities and attainments. This form of organisation may be deliberately chosen for the reasons given below, but it may be forced on a headteacher because the numbers on roll leave no alternative, as in a small village school.

One advantage is that class sizes in a school can be equalised, large year intakes being divided between all the teachers. It was developed in response to the practice of admitting children to school at the beginning of each term in order that the youngest children would be in small groups in each class, and able to be given more attention on starting school. They are more easily assimilated in a class which has already existed for some two years. Other advantages are that younger children imitate and are stimulated by the work of older children, who in turn consolidate their own learning by demonstrating to the younger children what they can do. In these classes there is a variety of materials and learning situations to meet a whole range of development, and not confined to what may be expected of a single age group. Vertical grouping does, however, place a greater responsibility on the teacher, who will have to organise the group activities within the class to ensure that children are occupied and extended at all levels. (See Part 1, ch. 1)

Videotape recorder Television pictures can be recorded by means of a videotape recorder or a video cassette recorder. These can be used to record from broadcast television programmes, subject to the observance of the relevant copyright laws. When a video recorder is linked to a television camera they can together be used to record material of the teacher's choice for later playback. The use of the video cassette recorder and television camera is part of the technique of *microteaching* used in the training of teachers. (See Part 1, ch. 9)

Vocational development and guidance Many factors, both psychological and sociological, influence the career choices that individuals make. It is undeniable that the education system plays an important role in vocational choice, and yet the processes through which individuals come to develop their choice of vocation is still only poorly understood. Many people still drift into jobs for inconsequential reasons without any advice or guidance. Talent is often wasted.

Ginzberg identified a sequence of developmental stages that the maturing individual goes through in establishing his occupational choice. The first stage, which covers the period from 6 to 11 years, involves fantasy choices; this is a period when nothing seems impossible or unrealistic to the child.

During the period of adolescence there follows a time of tentative choices. This stage begins with the individual taking an interest in a number of possible jobs. He considers the capacities these jobs require and matches them against his own capacities. His system of values begins to influence his decisions. There follows a transition phase as the individual's increasing self-knowledge in relation to possible jobs leads into the stage of realistic choices. The final stage, which leads to the selection of a job, begins with a phase of exploration leading to a crystallising of ideas and a commitment to a specific occupation.

Factors which influence vocational choice include socio-economic background, job opportunities and personal factors such as *personality*, intellectual ability and *aptitude*, as well as the processes of selection over which the individual has little or no control. Vocational guidance is concerned with attempting to fit the individual to a suitable job. Roger's *seven-point plan* offers a realistic tool for making a systematic appraisal of the individual's vocational potential. See also: *intelligence, educational assessment, mental testing*.

Further reading

Hopson, B. and Hayes, J., 'The Theory and Practice of Vocational Guidance', Pergamon, 1969.

Ginzberg, E., Ginsberg, S. W., Axelrad, S. and Herma, J. L., 'Occupational Choice: An Approach to a General Theory', Columbia University Press, 1951. (See Part 1, ch. 14)

Voluntary schools Voluntary schools are schools maintained by the LEA but not established by them as opposed to county schools which are built and wholly maintained by the LEA. Their present status is a result of the compromises made in the 1944 Act in order to create a more uniform system. There are three categories: aided, controlled and special agreement schools. The main points of difference centre on the financing, the religious education provided, the constitution and powers of the governing body, and control over the use of school premises.

(i) Aided schools

The Governors are responsible for the external repair and alterations to the school buildings, but 85 per cent of the cost is recouped from central Government. Similarly, when a new school is built 85 per cent of the capital cost is funded from central Government. Internal repairs and running costs fall upon the LEA. The Governing body has a majority of foundation members. They appoint the head and teaching staff, subject to an establishment fixed by the LEA, which pays the salaries. The appointments have to be confirmed by the LEA but may be rejected only if the qualifications of staff giving secular instruction do not satisfy the criteria laid down by the LEA. The Managers or Governors control both religious and secular education. They also determine to what use the school building may be put after school hours.

(ii) Controlled schools

The Governors have no financial responsibility for the school, which is maintained wholly by the LEA. Religious education is in accordance with the agreed syllabus, but denominational instruction may be given for up to two periods a week where parents request it. In this regard foundation Governors have the right to be satisfied that there are 'reserved' teachers appointed; i.e., a defined proportion of the staff suitable to give denominational instruction. The foundation Governors may determine the use of

V

the school building on Saturdays and Sundays. The Governors have the right to be consulted on the appointment of the headteacher.

(iii) Special agreement schools

This category relates to schools established under the Education Act 1936, under which LEAs could, by special agreement, pay between 50 and 75 per cent of the capital cost of building a voluntary secondary school. The Governors control religious instruction and have to be consulted over appointment of the appropriate teachers, but other teachers are appointed by the LEA. The provisions of the 1936 Act have been overtaken by the Education Act 1944, but the agreements made are kept. There are some 150 schools in this category. (See Part 1, ch. 1)

Weberian sociology Max Weber insists that a necessary feature of the social scientist's work is the interpretation of the meaning given by people to their social actions, a feature which does not – and indeed cannot – figure in the physical scientist's study of natural objects. In this way, critics of *positivistic sociology* see Weber as basically supporting their position. Weber specifies that it is only when human behaviour has a purpose or intention that it qualifies as action, and only when an individual's action takes into consideration the action of others that it becomes social action. The meaningfulness of social action has therefore to be understood in terms of the purposes or intentions of the individuals engaged in it.

Weber's emphasis upon the meaningfulness of social action has influenced the sociology of education in its search for an alternative to *structural-functionalism*, but this influence has been limited for reasons that can be explained by reference to Alan Dawe's paper 'The Two Sociologies', first published in the 'British Journal of Sociology' in 1970. Dawe's claim here is that there are two sociologies irreconcilably in conflict with each other: a sociology of social system, in which society is taken as defining the meaning of its members' actions for them; and a sociology of social action, which, based on subjective meaning, views man as an autonomous being. Weber is seen by Dawe as having finally moved to a sociology of social system centred on *bureaucracy*, even though he started with a sociology of social action; and this latter is seen as having been revived by *phenomenological sociology*.

The *'new' sociology of education* began by aligning itself with a sociology of social action very much as Dawe delineates it, and with Weberian sociology only within these limits.

Further reading

Freund, J., 'The Sociology of Max Weber', Allen Lane, The Penguin Press, 1968.

Wrong, D. (ed.), 'Max Weber', Prentice Hall, 1970. (See Part 1, ch. 15)

Welsh Education Office As part of the Welsh Office, many of the educational functions of administration and policy are undertaken by the DES, but the Welsh Education Office runs a separate Inspectorate. (See Part 1, ch. 7)

Welsh Joint Education Committee In addition to representation on the *Council of Local Education Authorities*, the Welsh Joint Education Committee acts as a central office for the Welsh Authorities. It was established in 1948. Its membership consists mainly of representatives of Welsh LEAs, together with Chief Education Officers, teachers' representatives and university representation. It is, de facto, an association of Education Authorities in Wales, with an advisory and coordinating role which ensures that Welsh views on education are expressed. It is an examining board for GCE and CSE examinations and is the regional advisory council for further education. It has established the National Language Unit, which is concerned with developing the teaching of modern languages, especially Welsh both as a first and second language. (See Part 1, ch. 1)

Whisky money The 1890 budget increased the duty on whisky to provide funds to compensate licence-holders of redundant public houses. The plan to reduce the number of licensed premises met with such strong opposition that the Local Taxation (Customs and Excise) Act reallocated the money, already voted by Parliament, to the County Councils. Within five years 93 of 129 county borough councils were spending the whole of this money on technical education. (See Part 1, ch. 10)

Whole curriculum The term 'whole curriculum' is not synonymous with 'the curriculum', and tends to be used to distinguish concern with the overall balance and coherence of the school's programme from concern with separate courses of study. Thus decisions about the whole curriculum depend on questions about longer-term processes of schooling, and what constitutes an appropriate 'selection from culture', and hence a particular pattern of study for all or particular groups of pupils. For example, the establishment of *comprehensive secondary schools* in the UK has underlined the need to merge two distinct approaches to the whole curriculum; that of the *grammar school* tradition and that of the elementary/secondary modern schools tradition. (See Part 1, ch. 4)

Workers Educational Association The Workers Educational Association, organised across the whole of the United Kingdom through a series of district secretaries, has for a long time provided a valuable opportunity for informal further education through the provision of a wide range of evening and week-end courses. (See Part 1, ch. 7)

Works manager In any economy it can be held the single most important group of managers are those in charge of making things, as in the long run this is the basis of wealth creation. The Institute of Works Managers (IWM) is a qualifying body for managers in all types of productive industry. The aims of the IWM are to increase industrial productivity by developing and raising the standards of management. It also aims to promote management education through its training courses and examinations. Members are drawn from a wide range of industrial management in many industries, and cover all levels from junior to director.

It has four grades of membership, of which the main three (Fellow, Member, Associate) require both academic qualifications and experience. Age influences the former, because of the development of education over the recent past. The examinations offered are wide-ranging, as are the courses (now available at some 170 technical colleges). The Certificate in Industrial Management is designed to be essentially practical and human, and is based on active student participation through solving management problems by applying the most modern techniques. The Diploma in Industrial Management is run by higher educational institutes (usually *polytechnics* or equivalent) and is aimed at developing the individual to acquire skill, experience and subsequent increase in managerial capacity. These courses qualify for credits with the *Open University*. The Certificate in Industrial Relations is aimed to provide manager with a full, practicable understanding of the complexities of the subject. Further information can be had from:

IWM, 45 Cardiff Road, Luton, Beds, LU1 1RD; 0582 37071. (See Part 1, ch. 12)

Youth service The 1944 Act placed upon LEAs the responsibility of providing for the leisure-time occupation of young people. The youth service was therefore developed with the aim of providing opportunities for young people to acquire new skills and interests and grow up as responsible citizens. The network of LEA–sponsored youth clubs dates from this Act. Many youth organisations are voluntary bodies; but LEAs are empowered to help such bodies with financial and other assistance. The pattern of provision is therefore a mixed one, with LEA clubs existing side by side with voluntary clubs, many of which are assisted to varying extents by the LEA. (See Part 1, ch. 1).